Your Friend

N. B. Wolfe

STARTLING FACTS

IN

MODERN SPIRITUALISM.

BY

N. B. WOLFE, M. D.

"SUPPRESSIO VERI, SUGGESTIO FALSI."

SECOND EDITION.

CHICAGO:
RELIGIO-PHILOSOPHICAL PUBLISHING HOUSE.
FOR SALE BY
COLBY & RICH, Boston; A. J. DAVIS & CO., New York; ROBERT CLARKE, Cincinnati; H. SNOW, San Francisco. *Foreign Agencies*: J. BURNS, London; VICTOR ALEXI, Paris; W. H. TERRY, Melbourne, Australia.
1875.

INTRODUCTORY.

THIS book contains a record of mental and physical phenomena witnessed by the author, for which is claimed a supernatural origin. It may properly be called a Journal of his personal experience for twenty-five years, while investigating the various phases of modern Spiritualism.

When making his researches in this department of human science, he neglected no fair opportunity for obtaining the most reliable information appertaining to the facts presented to his senses and appealing to his judgment for indorsement.

His object has been to ascertain by indubitable testimony whether "if a man die he can live again," and if so, is it possible for him to make the fact of his existence known to those who dwell on the earth?

When he began to pursue these inquiries he had no reliable evidence that there was any life, after death had fixed its seal upon the human form. To his mind, all animal existence depended upon the presence of the "animating breath," and in its absence the heart stopped, consciousness was lost, and the sun of life set, in an atheistic sky—a rayless and eternal night.

He was not ignorant of the Biblical and ecclesiastical assurances of the existence of an after-life; but these were so vague, contradictory, or fantastically stated, and the inheritance of their Utopia subject to so many contingencies of "vicarious atonements" and "plans of salvation," that they, instead of removing his doubts, confirmed his unbelief. Writers and speakers there were in abundance, each advocating some individual "scheme" or "plan" for securing the *comforts* of the after-life; yet in their zeal to gain the "flesh pots" they neglected to present the "proof palpable" that an after-life really did exist. By this omission they leave a stumbling-block in the pathway of millions. In sensible accord with a German atheist it may be asked, "What 's the use of talking about 'plans' and 'schemes' to gain the after-life, when there ain't no after-life?" You can not catch whales in a mill-pond, because there are none there to be caught. There is an old adage which says, "You must never cook a lobster till you catch him."

No manly mind *can* believe without evidence. Immaterial *faith* will not create material *facts*. The fact must first exist, then you can have faith in it. It is useless to try to terrify a free mind with the priestly penalty of unbelief—"damnation to the soul." It will not be frightened into the admission of a monstrous lie. In their frenzy priests may curse the man who unflinchingly stands by the rectitude of his own heart until their throats crack with profanity; but they can not scorch one hair of his head, and *the maniacs know it.*

The foregoing will show the *dark* condition of the author's mind when he began to study the alphabet of spiritual literature, consisting of "table-tipping" and "spirit-rapping." Such manifestations were of profound interest to him until the Buffalo doctors and Rochester priests discovered that the "tips and taps" were *produced by the double-jointed toes of the Fox girls.* This learned exposure of the impostors it was thought would be fatal to Spiritualism, and so, after laying out its form and sprinkling holy water in its face, they "consigned it to the tomb of the Capulets," never again to be resurrected.

In this exhibition of high farce and low comedy we see in what manner science and religion greeted spiritual manifestations twenty-five years ago in the cities of Buffalo and Rochester, New York.

If these fellows had been competent to rightly

interpret "the tips and taps" of the invisibles, instead of indulging in such silly clap-trap to please idiots and allay the ghosts, they would have addressed their fellow-men with candor and told them frankly, for the sake of truth, to investigate these mysterious manifestations of power and intelligence carefully and patiently, because if they originate with spirits, as claimed, and declare the verity of the after-life, nothing can prevent their final recognition and universal acceptance. Truth is a positive principle, that pervades and sustains all the phenomena of nature, and it is at once both the endowment and the glory of the human soul. The *mind*, in the pursuit of truth, will rise to lofty pinnacles of thought, and find no resting-place but in the bosom of eternal verities. It scales empyrean heights to count the stars, and will not be satisfied until a knowledge of the laws regulating their movements is obtained; when left untrammeled by fear, and not degraded by ignorance and superstition, it will create forces which cause the human soul to develop in beauty and grace, and grow in intellectual strength and moral grandeur, until qualified to take its position in that celestial Valhalla where is held the senate of the gods.

As already intimated, this book contains an account of startling and significant phenomena which have occurred in the presence of the author. To his mind, these manifestations of the spirit-world proclaim the *dawn of a new era in the history of the human race,* the importance of which to the best interests of men he does not pretend to estimate.

While making this record he has not paused to consider the influence it may exert upon the minds of men. Truth has a good character for taking care of itself. It was enough for him to know that he was dealing with *facts,* and his business was simply to arrange these facts for the critical inspection of the mind's eye. If he has failed to perform this service well, no one will more sincerely deplore the dereliction than himself; for the tribulation of the world's great heart finds its source in perverted views of life, and every successful effort to supplant ignorance with knowledge saves mankind from physical pain and mental anguish.

It will be seen throughout the book that the author has not hesitated to express freely his personal opinions whenever occasion seemed to require. He has done this with no view of begging favor for the facts presented; neither does he care whether the reader likes them or not. He has written them because they are crystallized convictions of his mind, and he makes no effort to disguise them in wordy superfluity.

He asks the ingenuous reader to discriminate between the author's *opinions* of a fact and the *fact itself*. The first are of but little value, because they are personal, and may be swayed from the plumb-line of rectitude by the common infirmities of man's nature; but the latter are of paramount interest to all men, because they co-exist with all time, seeking neither place nor applause, nor bowing at any human shrine. They should be espoused with love and served with reverence.

146 SMITH STREET,
CINCINNATI, O., July, 1875.

CONTENTS.

CHAPTER I.

CHAPTER II.

CHAPTER III.

CHAPTER IV.

CHAPTER V.

CHAPTER VI.

CHAPTER VII.

CHAPTER VIII.

CHAPTER IX.

CHAPTER X.

CHAPTER XI.

CHAPTER XII.

CHAPTER XIII.

CHAPTER XIV.

CHAPTER XV.

CHAPTER XVI.

CHAPTER XVII.

CHAPTER XVIII.

CHAPTER XIX.

CHAPTER XX.

CHAPTER XXI.

CHAPTER XXII.

CHAPTER XXIII.

CHAPTER XXIV.

CHAPTER XXV.

CHAPTER XXVI.

CHAPTER XXVII.

CHAPTER XXVIII.

CHAPTER XXIX.

CHAPTER XXX.

CHAPTER XXXI.

STARTLING FACTS

IN

MODERN SPIRITUALISM.

CHAPTER I.

PERSONAL RECOLLECTIONS OF WIZARDS, WITCHES, AND WITCHCRAFT.

A BELIEF in the supernatural thrives best in an atmosphere of ignorance. It is peculiar to the childish instincts of our nature, and never attains sturdy growth and development when the lungs of our manhood are fully expanded. Indeed, there is no power in such a belief; for all falsities tend to degrade and enervate the soul.

My personal recollections of witches and witchcraft must therefore be associated with my childhood, or childish instincts, and not with the maturer years of life, when the thoughtful mind is sustained by its judgments and held firmly by its convictions.

I remember, when a child, of having my curiosity excited by seeing horse-shoes nailed over the doors of several houses in my native town, and the perplexity of my mind when trying to discover the purpose for which they were nailed there. Curiosity in a child can only be sustained during the period of mental adolescence; when the mind begins to quicken with its new powers, it demands knowledge, as the unfolding flower demands light and heat. So I began to ask questions of old people in regard to the horse-shoes: what they were put up for; and who nailed them there? It was not long before I obtained the desired information; for almost every body I spoke to in regard to this matter, told me they were put there to "keep out the witches!"

"To keep out the witches?" I said; "what are witches? what do they want to keep them out for? what do the witches want to get in for? what will they do if they get in? can't they get in other houses that have no horse-shoes over the doors? how do the horse-shoes keep them out?"—and a hundred other questions to which my childish fancy gave birth.

Witches, I was informed, could put spells on people; could make folks sick or well, as they felt inclined; that they could assume any shape they pleased (sometimes they went into a black cat, or a black dog); that they traveled through the air, riding a broomstick; and if any body offended them, such offender they would certainly destroy.*

* Could a more graceless exhibition of ignorance and prejudice be given than is found in the oft-quoted discourse of Bishop Jewel, delivered in the presence of Queen Elizabeth, over three hundred years ago (1558): "It may please your grace to understand that witches and sorcerers, within these four last years, are marvelously increased within your grace's realm. Your grace's subjects pine away, even unto the death; their colour fadeth; their flesh rotteth; their speech is benumbed; their senses are bereft. I pray God they may never practice further than upon the subject."

"But who are the witches?" I would ask, resolving not to expose myself to their resentments, if I could possibly avoid doing so.

"Witches!" said old Sam Wade to me, as we sat together on a log behind Sam Heise's barn, while he was tying the brail of a flail with an eel-skin; "why, old Bets Parks is a witch! Don't you know old Bets Parks?"

"Why, no!" I said; "where does she live, Mr. Wade?"

"Live? why, she lives in that old slab-cabin, over on the commons, near Malson's."*

"Is that Jake Pugh's mother?" I said.

"Yes, that's her; she's the witch. Didn't you never see that hole in her cheek?"

"Yes!" I said, with trepidation; for I already began to fear she might be about, listening to our conversation.

"Well, that's where she was shot with a silver bullet! You see, you can't kill witches with leaden bullets. You put a gun right up against their head, and shoot it off, and you can't faze 'em. They'll only laugh at you through the smoke. They can't be

* Witches always live in cabins, or tumble-down, out-of-the-way places. An abode of a Pythoness is thus admirably described by Spenser, in the "Faerie Queen:"

"There, in a gloomy hollow glen, she found
A little cottage built of sticks and reeds,
In homely wise, and wald with sods around;
In which a witch did dwell, in loathly weedes
And wilful want, all careless of her needes.
So chooseing solitairè to abide
Far from all neighbours, that her develish deeds
And hellish arts from people she might hide,
And hurt far off unknowne whom ever she envide."

killed only with silver bullets; and you must git the silver to make the bullets with from the witch herself; then you kin shoot 'em."

"Who shot old Mrs. Parks?" I inquired.

"Why, Uncle Joe Hinkle done it; but he did n't kill her—only shot her through the face. That hole in her cheek is where the silver bullet went in; and it never came out!"

"It never came out! Why, what became of it?"

"O, she swallowed it. You see, old Bets bewitched one of Uncle Joe's horses, and it fell down on the road and died. You see, the day afore the horse died, old Bets went out to Uncle Joe's to buy a chicken; but she only wanted to witch something. Uncle Joe was afeerd ov her; so he sold her an old black hen for a levy and a fip. So, you see, when the horse died, then he knowed at once that old Bets had witched that horse; and what did Uncle Joe do, but pounded the levy and fip into a bullet, and loaded his big duck-gun with the bullet? He went down to the barn and chalked a picture of old Bets on the barn-door. Then he said, 'Old Bets Parks, I 'm going to shoot you, you old witch!' He then fired, and struck her on the cheek. The next morning, old Bets had a big hole in her cheek; and it is there to this day. That 's how she got the hole in her cheek."*

This marvelous story had a wonderful effect, and made a lasting impression on my mind. However skeptical I may have grown by subsequent mental development, I never doubted the sincerity of old Sam's belief in what he said, though the statements

*The "hole" in the old negress's cheek was the deep scar of an old abscess.

were as logically loose in the joints as a supple-jack. Still, for a long time, my faith in the existence of witches was not entirely destroyed. Early impressions are hard to outgrow; they seem to stick to the very bone, and penetrate the marrow of our mind. Thus, when I first read Cotton Mather's "History of the New England Witchcraft," my sympathies were enlisted for the victims who had fallen under the ban of the "black art," not for the "witches." In full sympathy with Sir Matthew Hale, I thought the man who did not believe in witchcraft "an obdurate Sadducee, and should be made happy in his disbelief by a little roasting." Though not much of a Biblical student, still the story of the woman who had a familiar spirit, and who was employed by Saul to consult the deceased Samuel concerning the issue of his contest with the Philistines, was sufficient authority to rest my belief upon, at that early day.

What wonder, then, if in after life, when the subject of witches or witchcraft came under my notice, I pricked up my ears to hear every thing that was said. And this brings me to my first experience with a veritable witch, the particulars of which I will state as briefly as possible, as they came under my personal observation:

In 1844, I was a student of medicine in Ebensburg, Cambria County, Pennsylvania. This town is located on the summit of one of the swelling knolls so common on the western slope of the Alleghanies, about eight miles north-west of *Cresson,* the famed mountain retreat for Summer excursionists, and hypochondriacal moribunds.

One morning, before the sleepy-heads of the town had opened their eyes, a well-known sturdy old Welshman by the name of Lloyd, who lived some three or four miles west of the village, made the board-walks rattle with his heavy brogans, as he wended his way along the principal street in quest of a magistrate. Being an early riser, I met the brave old farmer, and gave him a cheery "good-morning," before any other pedestrian had yet appeared in sight. He inquired for 'Squire Roberts's house, which I pointed out to him.

"But what 's the matter, Mr. Lloyd, that you should be looking for 'Squire Roberts so early in the morning?" I asked.

Hereupon he wiped the perspiration from his forehead, and seemed a little confused as to how he should reply.

I said, "The 'squire won 't be up for an hour yet; so you 'll have to wait awhile."

He then sat down on a store-box, and, looking me steadily in the face, he said:

"Do you believe in witches?"

"Certainly," I said, "though I have never seen but one."

His eye lightened, as I told him about the old negress, Betsy Parks; but he derived very little comfort from my statement that they possessed an ubiquitous character, and could be killed only by being shot with a silver bullet in the manner already described.

He did n't want to kill Tom Evans, he said; but he wanted the 'squire to put him in jail!

"What has Tom Evans done, that you want to put him in jail?" I asked.

"He has bewitched my child, and I am afraid he will kill her," said the old man, with a sigh of despair.

"In what way, Mr. Lloyd, has Tom Evans bewitched your child?" I asked, partly through curiosity, I admit, and partly with the wish of disabusing his mind of the absurd fear under which he labored.

"O, in many ways," he said. "She talks and sings all night; and when she lays down to sleep, he drags the clothes off her bed, and tears her dress, and ties them in knots. He throws the dishes at her at the table, and breaks them on the floor."

This, and much more, did the old man state, without manifesting any symptom of insanity in his look, manner, or speech. He was a hard-working, plain, sensible, but illiterate man. He had gone into the woods with a stout arm, a courageous heart, and a heavy ax. He had opened up a highway for the sun to shine upon the earth and fructify its bosom. He had built his home of logs, and was now rearing a family of children, to be his comfort in age. He had neither ability nor time to joke, but was in dead earnest when he preferred the charge of witchcraft against his neighbor, Tom Evans.

Tom Evans was also a farmer, with habits more like Rip Van Winkle's than Lloyd's. Unlike Rip, however, he was quite a student, and was the owner of an old illustrated volume on Astrology, wherein an incantation scene was represented, showing the incantee and incanted to be in the possession of horns tails, and cloven hoofs. There was a striking likeness in their general appearance. On one occasion, when Lloyd was making a friendly call upon his neighbor, he found him pondering over this book, when Evans, in his waggery, exclaimed: "This book teaches a man how to raise the devil. It is the science of the 'black art.' I can turn any man into a horse, if I choose, and ride him all night through swamps and mill-dams, like a wild beast." That was enough for Lloyd. The direful picture was but too vividly imprinted on the tablets of his lack-luster imagination. Henceforth, he feared Evans, and avoided him. This presentation of the two "wad" neighbors must suffice. The knowledge here imparted will assist the intelligent reader to form more rational conclusions than he otherwise could do.

'Squire Roberts heard the story of Lloyd, and was puzzled. There was no statute under which he was authorized to arrest a wizard, that had not been repealed. He could not even claim authority from English law; for the act of Henry VIII, adjudging "all witchcraft and sorcery to be felony, without the benefit of clergy," had long since been removed from the statute-books of the Kingdom. But, law or no law, Lloyd had made up his mind that Evans was a wizard, and had, as he alleged—unfortunately for himself and family—only too much proof that he was practising his detestable "black art" on one of his children; and therefore demanded a warrant for his arrest.

Ebensburg is not a large town, and it did not require a long time for the story of Lloyd to be known to every man, woman, and child in the place. It was curious to see how soon the people were divided into partisans on this subject of witchcraft; and there was no lack of zeal manifested on either side of the question. To satisfy Lloyd, and relieve 'Squire Roberts from an unpleasant dilemma, a party of ten men volunteered to go home with Lloyd, promising, if they found the evidence of witchcraft, as represented, and Tom Evans's complicity with the same clearly established, to arrest him, and put him in jail.

This proposition found favor at once; so Sheriff Murray, George Zahm, Charles Litzinger, Alexander Cummings, John Blair, George Harncame, James M'Guire, Andrew Lewis, Edward Mills, and myself, were the self-constituted *posse comitatus* who volunteered in the service. Lloyd went home at once, and we followed him a few hours later in the day.

When we arrived at his house, we found him in a condition of mind almost helpless with fear. He met us at the door, and, judging from his manner, he seemed to deprecate the notoriety he had given himself and family. He, nevertheless, maintained stoutly that the statements he had made were true, and expressed his approbation at our coming, as we could now "see for ourselves." That was the sentiment of all present—to see for ourselves.

The house was built of logs, unplastered—two rooms on the first floor, and an attic floor, reached by a ladder. In this loft the older children slept. One of the rooms on the first floor was used for general family purposes, embracing kitchen, dining, and drawing-room. It was furnished with a large, stiff table, two or three chairs, two benches, a shelf for dishes, and a corner next the outside jamb of the chimney was filled with barrels and trumpery. The other room contained a plain chest of drawers, a table, two bedsteads—one a trundle-bed—and a number of Sunday suits of clothing hanging on pegs fastened in the logs of the wall. A saddle and bridle also decorated one of the pegs.

The inventory was soon taken; and as we entered the kitchen-parlor, "ten men strong," the juveniles opened their eyes, with big wonder in their faces. A little social chat soon put all hands at ease, when we were prepared to witness and bear impartial testimony to whatever might be presented. Of course our interest centered on the bewitched child, who was the oldest and largest of the group of six tow-headed children before us. She was a stout, healthy-looking girl, twelve years old, and large for her age. Her hair, a shade darker than her younger sisters' and brothers', hung loosely about her neck, tangled and uncared for. There was a thoughtful expression in her face and large dark eyes, into which you could look as into a well of clear water, and fancy any thing. This child was much loved by her parents; her disposition, they said, was sweet, as her manners were gentle. She stood in the center of the group, timidly shrinking from our prying gaze, quite conscious that she was the object of supreme interest to us all.

After our scrutiny had been satisfied, the other children were called away from her, and she was left alone. She was barefooted, and her dress--a homespun linsey-woolsey—hung barely to her stoutish ankles. She had outgrown several tucks, that had left bright flounce-marks about the bottom of the skirt. We had barely time to make these observations, when the first symptom of witchcraft made its appearance. About six feet from the child, on a wooden bench, sat a patent-pail filled with water. This began to show symptoms of unrest, the pail rocking on its square bottom. After making two or three efforts to slide along the bench, it careened and fell to the floor, sending its tiny deluge to our feet.

This was the beginning of the trouble. Of course we examined the wooden bench and pail, but discovered nothing to arouse the least suspicion of trickery. How the "Old Scratch" the pail was propelled to the performance of such a feat, puzzled our wits. We could see nothing by which the gravity of the pail could be disturbed—no inequality of the legs of the bench, nor depression in the floor; and yet there lay the pail, and the water still standing in pools at our feet! The feat was quite interesting to several half-scared gentlemen; and their surprise was not lessened a bit as one of the chairs in the room made first a conge and then a start from where it stood, toward the child, who stood about six feet from it. When half the distance had been passed, the chair stopped, as if to consider the propriety of its strange demeanor, toppled a few times on its back legs, then fell to the floor. I bear a cheerful testimony to the fact that the chair projected this movement of its own will and accord, without any aid, advice, or encouragement from any visible being in the room; and should be held alone responsible for any fractures, bruises, or contusions of legs, back, or pediment, it may have sustained.

The general verdict of the jurors assembled was, that the devil was in the chair; but whether in the bottom, back, or legs, or all together, we could not decide.

This diabolical manifestation put us all more or less in an "eerie swither," and we began to look at the little girl with something like fear and trembling. The poor child then leaned up against the chimney-jamb, over which was a board serving as a mantel. It was a shelf upon which all kinds of traps had been placed. A few old Welsh books, one of which was a Holy Bible, took a notion to "raise Cain," and made a perceptible movement toward the middle of the floor. They succeeded admirably in their intentions, if I have correctly anticipated them—the Bible a trifle ahead, as it was the most sprightly. Then came several pairs of undarned stockings, without fleshly legs in them; and they were quickly followed by an old witch-lamp, as a light to their feet. The value of that shelf for house-keeping purposes will never be accurately estimated. There was no end, seemingly, to the traps that flew from that perch. A japanned candlestick started, as if suddenly kicked on end, and lighted unpleasantly near our feet. Then some tin pans, pie-platters, started on a skimming expedition, and there was no telling just where they would hit; so we began to juke and duck, and dodge and bow, as if paying a most respectful obeisance to "Old Nick" himself. The occasion was full of interest, and we were having a happy time of it. An old spinning-wheel, of the large, trotting kind—that turns as you run backward, and spins a hank of yarn in a minute or more—now began to cut up didos by rotating on its center with a velocity that was "stunning" to see; and if the periphery had snapped by the momentum, would have been "stunning" to feel, by some of us who stood in the line of its motion. After littering the floor with the fragments of a few dinner-dishes, the performance intermitted, and the spectators adjourned to the outside of the house for consultation.

"Don't it beat the devil?" said one.

"It *is* the devil," said another; "and he can't beat himself, can he?"

"Exactly; but what of old Tom? Do you think he is flying around here on a broomstick, a prince of the power of the air? If it's Tom, it an't the devil! If it's the devil, it an't Tom!" quoth logic.

"That's a fact," said the sheriff. "I guess we had better not disturb old Tom, if we want to keep out of trouble."

Just here our short conference was interrupted by the appearance of Lloyd at the door, beckoning us to come in, as the row had commenced again. So in we went, and found this time that the manifestations had been transferred from the kitchen drawing-room to the room containing the beds. As we entered, the first thing to arrest my attention was the old saddle and bridle hanging on the peg. The bridle came rattling to the floor first, with a clattering noise; then, soon after, the old saddle-stirrups began to shake; the flaps extended themselves like the spread wings of an eagle, and the saddle, literally raising itself like a huge bird, swept, with its leather wings outstretched, from its peg-top aerie to the middle of the floor, quite near to where the child was standing. If the devil was seated on that saddle, he certainly received some bruises in the fall.

Next, the trundle-bed began to exhibit symptoms of tribulation, or a fancy to show its agility to our astonished eyes. It first made a dart into the room, entirely clear of the mother-bed overspreading it, in a most lively manner; but as it had nothing to say, and offered no explanation for its obtrusion, and no apology for its rudeness, it was forcibly pushed under the large bed again, *half-way*. At this juncture, it seemed to take on the sulks—or perhaps it is better to say, the disposition of the mule—and would go no farther on compulsion. This put two of our party on their mettle, who pushed hard enough at that bedstead to have shoved it through adamantine gates, though guarded by cherubim or seraphim; but the trundle-bed seemed immovable. For several minutes the issue was uncertain; it was a kind of "pull-Dick, pull-devil" contest, when, while the boys were a-blowing and getting their "second wind," without aid or abetment, the little bed went right under the big one, itself, as naturally as a kitten goes under the mother cat! Having performed this feat voluntarily, this power demonstrated its satisfaction by pounding on the floor under the bed, as if with a muffled mallet.

This ended the witch-show on the day of my visit, and to all present the occasion had been of strange and absorbing interest. The evidence of a power existing, though invisible to our natural eyes, quite capable of doing mischief, was apparent to all. The question was now seriously discussed, What could it be? what object could be attained by annoying this family of poor people, and frightening them out of their wits? Some thought the child was a witch! Others sympathized with the belief of Lloyd, that his child was simply the victim of Evans's "black art!" But then it was urged that no ill was done the child, save only a little fright; and that the things we had witnessed seemed to act by a volition of their own. Of course, no intelligent conclusion could be attained. The more the matter was discussed, the more opaque the whole subject seemed, There was enough of superstition, however, in the party to ascribe the things we had witnessed flatly to witchcraft; though when called upon for the *rationale* of this belief, none could be given. The ascription was a mere substitution of terms for *devil.* But had we not better give this power no name, until the mantle of ignorance shall be lifted from our minds, and we can see with clearer view the hidden cause? A belief in the supernatural ceased to be a part of my mental code when I ceased to be a child. "ALL THINGS ARE GOVERNED BY LAW!" has been the axiom upon which my mind has rested, with a sense of entire security, for many years. Outside of law, there can be neither order nor justice—in heaven, or on earth, or in hell. Chaos would come again, when law ceased to govern matter.

Our senses were manifestly at fault in discovering the law which overcame the inertia of these bodies. But let us with humility ask ourselves, How much or how little of the great system of laws governing matter do we comprehend? Ignorance is always arrogant. I speak for myself only—I did not pretend to understand the law as it manifested itself on this occasion. Still, I could not surrender my faith in the eternal principles of nature to any slavish fear or degrading superstition.

Competent men bore concurrent testimony to the reality of the manifestations we had witnessed. In them the law of inertia seemed to be superseded; but there was power behind the manifestation, and power can not exist without law; and law is but the reflection of perfect intelligence. Is there still hidden in the arcana of nature, forces yet unrevealed to mortal sense? Is there a power we do not understand? Is there a God we do not perfectly comprehend?

CHAPTER II.

MANIFESTATIONS IN COLUMBIA, HARRISBURG, AND THE QUEEN'S BUSH, CANADA.

THE incidents recorded in the preceding pages had almost become a forgotten circumstance, when they were again revived in my memory by some singular manifestations of an occult character, which transpired six years later in my native town, Columbia, Lancaster County, Pennsylvania. These I will briefly relate as they came under my personal observation. By way of preface, it may be said that, though a man may have no honor in his own country, it rarely happens that he is not "well known" in the neighborhood of his birth-place. Sometimes this is a pleasant thought, and sometimes it is not. Very much depends upon the light in which he is seen, and the character of those who estimate his worth.

It was some time during the early part of the Winter of 1850 that I read the first intelligent account of the "Rochester Knockings." The letter was written by a correspondent of the *New York Tribune,* who was upon the ground, and gave what seemed to be a fair statement of what he saw and heard in Hydesville, at the residence of the Widow Fox and her daughters. I had read other statements of these wonderful "knockings," but they seemed to be disingenuous, and failed to impress me as being truthful. But this letter in the *Tribune* gave a most graphically minute and circumstantial account of the origin, progress, and character of the knockings, which at once captivated my mind and enlisted my sympathies. I clipped the article from the paper, and carried it with me several weeks. It so happened that, one evening, in company with several ladies and gentlemen, at my Aunt Odell's, the conversation turned upon the Rochester knockings, when I remembered the printed letter of the *Tribune*, which I then had in my pocket. I produced it, and read it aloud ; and as I did so, I, somehow or other, was thinking of the witchcraft scenes narrated in the first chapter more than those I was reading about. There seemed to be a family resemblance between some of the witchcraft scenes and some parts of the Hydesville manifestations, though I said nothing about my discovery to any person at the time.

After I had concluded my reading, one of the young ladies present, an accomplished daughter of Governor Wolfe, who had but recently returned home from a visit she had been making to her friends in Little York, gave a very interesting account of a table-tipping *seance* she had witnessed while absent. The table, she said, *really moved over the floor, without any person touching it.* This statement at once brought my witchcraft experience so vividly to mind, that I ascribed both manifestations to a common cause, whatever that might be. So, when the proposition was made to form a circle, then and there, around a table, to see if we could n't have some fun with it,

I at once gave my consent to join hands, and assisted to bring a heavy, old-time, solid mahogany table to the center of the room. It was not on casters, and the heft was not less than fifty pounds. Around this table seven or eight chairs were placed, and occupied by as many persons. We first joined hands, and, after fifteen or twenty minutes, laid them disconnected on the table, the palms downward. Very soon an unpleasant feeling in the arms was complained of by several; but all felt like sticking to it until the table would move. In this way, we had sat almost an hour, chatting and talking on various subjects, having almost forgotten the object of our being there, when, of a sudden, the table gave a quick movement to the left, describing about a quarter of a circle; and so rapid and unexpected was the evolution, that it slid from under our hands.

It is needless to say how much excitement this movement created, and how much interest it awakened. After a few minutes, we all sat at the table again; and it soon became apparent, if we desired to keep our hands on the "mahogany," we would be compelled to "locomote" quite lively to keep pace with its voluntary movement. It began again by repeating the "spasmodic jerks" which had so surprised us at first; but at each succeeding paroxysm the movement seemed to increase in power, until a full circle had been described; then, as if gaining momentum by the motion, and gathering new force, it would rotate two or three times in the most rapid manner, causing all hands to break from a "lively trot" to a "double-quick." The exercise was rather too much for the ladies. Some of the less pulmonary robust gave it up for want of breath ; but two or three remained, with myself, to brave it through to the end.

The table now began to make lateral as well as circular movements, and to slide over the carpets almost as smoothly as if it had been on ice. Here the ladies gave out, leaving Mr. Craven and myself alone to accompany its peregrinations from one parlor to the other, perhaps a distance of forty feet. Mr. Craven soon became "a straggler," when, solitary and alone, I kept my pace alongside of the pesky runaway, my hands all the while resting on the top. The speed of the table seemed to be increasing, or perhaps it may have been I had less power to keep up with it, when, of a sudden, it darted across the room toward my dear old aunt, who sat folding her hands over her breast, amazed at what she saw. Becoming alarmed, she stepped upon a sofa, and beseeched me to put an end to this play. Before her the table stopped, and began tipping, and tilted back and forth several times, while my finger tips rested upon it. I now withdrew them, and the table stopped all movement.

The evidence was conclusive that I had "played the trick ;" and that it was cleverly done, all acceded. I now attempted to push the table over to its place, about ten feet distant, but I could not budge it. I put my whole strength to it, but with no better success. I seized hold of the top, determined to carry it over to its place, but could not lift the one end of it. It yielded gracefully to the united efforts of two young ladies, who lifted it to its proper position in the room.

Various were the speculations about the evening

entertainment. There was a little too much of it, to give me all the credit, so opinions were divided. All conceded it to be a splendid parlor amusement, and there were ever so many people who heard of it, who expressed the wish that they had been there. It became the talk of the town; and quite a new interest was taken in me as the "magician" on the occasion. I never was just so much talked of as during the discussion about the table-turning. I received many "invitations" to hold circles at places I had never visited, and with people I hardly knew. Still I maintained my equilibrium of mind and deportment, and declined. They honored me overmuch! I was interested, but was not willing to make sport of this thing for any body. One of our town clergymen, who had much wealth and respectability in his congregation, came to see me. He became interested, and I consented to spend an evening with him and a few friends at the table. They met; but I was detained by professional engagements, and could not be with them. However, the play went on without Hamlet. They sat down to the table; and, observing the rules I gave, it was not more than an hour, so I was informed, before it began to grow "frisky," and "kicked up behind and before, like old Joe." The table rotated, so I was told, making it quite lively for all hands round. While evoluting in this way, Rev. Mr. E. concluded the exercise was rather laborious, so he thought to take a comfortable seat on the table, and have a nice ride. But there was no comfort in it. It was a most unfortunate conceit; for no sooner had his clerical cloth been spread on the table, than it made a bound that sent him flying through the air like a trap-ball. He alighted with his head on the fire-rug, about ten feet distant, his heels describing the segment of an arc in his flight. Several minutes elapsed before the tangle could be got out of his reverence's hair, so that he could be made to understand the exact situation he was in, and how he happened to be there. It was only for a moment that he was discomfited. "This was the *devil's* work, for nothing less irreverent would deal so roughly with the cloth." That was his conclusion, and so he declared it; and "one blast upon his bugle horn was worth a thousand men." What he said, his congregation echoed.

It was an unexpected turn in affairs. Personally, I felt aggrieved; for I was in the zenith of popularity, and enjoyed the joke hugely—that is, if it can be called a joke to be not only suspected, but openly accused, of being the author of all this pow-wow. Alas! my honors faded in a day. The devil had superseded me, as I had superseded the Welsh wizard, in the authorship of this eccentric power. I had tasted the sweets of public appreciation, and now the savory fruit turned to ashes on my tongue. It is a curious thing to watch the mental evolutions of the human mind. They are by no means uniform in different people; they vary widely. Your poor stupid Welsh farmer, when he sees his household traps flying about his humble dwelling, as if suddenly endowed with wings, thinks of his neighbor whom he has feared for his intelligence, and secretly invests him with a power to do mischief, which could only be obtained from the "roaring lion" that he has heard so often in his sleep. But there is your preacher—a good, sweet-hearted man! He dresses so nicely, that he is the admiration of his whole congregation! His walk is so demure, his conversation so pious and elevating, that, next to the great Spirit of the universe, he is held in popular esteem. To touch him is as much a sacrilege as to spit on a Hindoo's wooden-headed idol!

All that is false affects our manhood. A lie hurts. It may not produce physical pain, but always a spiritual deformity. The declaimer and acceptor of the falsehood are alike injured. Justice is assailed, the heart insulted, and the intellect assassinated. The devil is no more to be lied about than the Welsh wizard or myself. A lie shows the depravity of both the head and heart that concocted or uttered it, no matter against whom it may be aimed.

One step had been taken, however, in the direction leading to a right solution of this subject. Table-tipping was no longer thought to be the work of man, but the devil. This carried the spirit of investigation among the imponderable forces, and divested the phenomena of all human agency. That was something gained—an important step; for science was now authorized to step in, and apply her crucial tests in determining what power it was that could project a heavy man kiteing through the air like a paper balloon. Scientists rarely take any stock in the devil. It is a poor investment, say they. So, regardless of what the pulpit might say, in its own way, investigation went forward. Nothing could be evoked that gave much light upon the subject. The tables continued to tip; and science, weighed in the balance, was found wanting. No proper solution could be given for the manifestation of this odd force. Many theories were advanced; but, on close analysis, none were found tenable. Speculation was rife. The press came in to aid the pulpit; and while it was truculently engaged in disseminating false theories and devilish ideas, a new manifestation was given at the table. Heretofore, when the desire was expressed that the table should move, it obeyed. Now it stood still, and *spoke.* Language is the utterance of *sound;* simply, successive waves of air that strike the sensorium as the billows of the ocean break upon the shore. The interpretation of sound—its investment with sense—is purely conventional. We may build up a system of laws to enable us to give a proper and uniform expression to it, but we make sound to signify just what is most convenient for us. When it is conceived in the brain of man, and uttered by the mandates of his will through the lingual structure, we call it speech. Sense is thus vocalized, and conventional forms of great truths are expressed and understood. Taking this view of the subject, the assumption that sound means speech is not an unwarranted license by any means.

In this sense, the table began to speak. Sounds were distinctly heard, as if reflected upon our sense, from the under surface of its top. What can they mean, was the question I asked myself, again and again. Somebody had told me that *one rap* or sound signified *no*, and *three raps, yes; two* indicated a *doubt.*

This was the triple key to unlock the mystery that had been called *witch, devil, and doctor.*

> The joyous news throughout the land was rung,
> That every table now had found a tongue.

I began to question the raps, and found them apt in their responses. In company with others, and when alone, the raps showed a willingness to answer questions at all times, when asked to do so. To be sure, their communications were limited to signify, "aye, aye, or nay, nay;" but even these simple monosyllables can be made to express a great deal. I said to them, "Can you rap sixteen times?" and they answered, "Yes." "Please rap sixteen times." And so they did, and then stopped. I did not bid them stop; but of their own accord they stopped at sixteen. "Can you rap one hundred times?" I asked; to which "Yes" was replied. "Please rap one hundred times." It was done with accuracy, and I made the count inaudibly. I asked, "Are you a witch?" The answer was, "*No.*" "Are you a devil?" The same answer was given. "Are you Doctor Faustus?" Again, "*No*" was responded. "Well, once more, please answer me. Are you a *preacher?*" "*Yes,*" was emphatically pronounced, by unusually loud raps. "Then I'll watch you closely," I said. "Have you any odor of brimstone about you?" "Not an odor," was signified. I was a little puzzled; but let that pass.

I was soon made to understand that, by using the alphabet, certain letters would be indicated by raps, which would spell names, words, and sentences. So I began to call the letters; and when I had called "C," a rap arrested my progress for the time. I put down "C," and commenced calling the alphabet again. When I reached the letter "h," another rap was heard. "Ch" I put together; and continued to repeat this system, until CHARLES ODELL was spelled out. This was the name of an uncle, who had been dead several years; and it was at the house of his widow where the table performed the antics I have already described. To my inquiry, he said that he had operated with the table, and was glad to be able to let his friends know that he still lived.

Up to this time, though I had sought diligently for the knowledge of the fact here announced—namely, the existence of an after life—I had no evidence that I could rely upon, that after death I should live again. Hearing the many conflicting theories of men—springing from systems of religion, plans of salvation, involving vicarious atonements, murder, and devilish passion—I had become hardened in the belief that no affirmation could be given to the question, "If a man die, shall he live again?" I doubted not the existence of a supreme intelligence, occupying all space and pervading all matter—governing all things by immutable laws; but that man had an individual life after death, and that he could be recognized by his fellow-mortals in the sphere of the great unknown, were problems of such distracting doubt in my mind, that I had long settled into the conviction that no satisfactory solution could be given them while we dwelt upon the earth.

These tiny raps, and this brief-worded communication, unsettled the foundations of my belief. They had spoken to my mind two great truths upon which the soul could rest; and, with the power of a talisman, had opened up a fountain of sweet waters in my being. They demonstrated two new problems at the same instant: the verity of the after-life; and the power of our friends who had passed, as we thought forever, from our sight, to visit again the "pale glimpses of the moon"—in such a form, at least, that we could recognize their actual presence.

The importance of this discovery will be variously estimated by different persons, according to their spiritual temperaments and needs. There are those who place so low an estimate upon their value that, to them, "a mess of pottage" or a glass of beer would send them to chancery in eclipse. There are others, however, who hail their advent as the dawn of a new era, and in them see and hear the heralds of the good time coming, proclaiming, "Peace on earth, and good to willing men." But here we leave off speculation for the present.

During the Winter of 1851, I had private business that called me to Harrisburg, the capital of Pennsylvania. At the time of my visit, the Legislature was in session; and to meet conveniently several members of that body with whom I had business, and who were boarding at the "Coverly House," I made that my stopping-place. This house was the place of *rendezvous* for a number of the members, who, every night, came there to caucus, "lay pipe," or have "a good time" generally, as our public servants best know how. Simon Cameron had an ax to grind that Winter; and many of the honorable gentlemen were flush of means and full of wine, until his ax was ground.

There were those, however, who were upright in heart, and who enjoyed a joke for the love of fun. One evening, a small party of this character, perhaps a dozen—among whom was Mr. Wells Coverly, the proprietor of the house—retired to a private parlor to hear the "spirit-raps." General Bartram Shaeffer, a senator from Lancaster County, being one of the party, invited me to join them, which I did. It was near midnight when we entered the parlor, and fastened the doors to keep out intruders; for many gentlemen (?) were then in their cups, and scarcely in condition to interview the living or the dead.

Mr. Coverly took a position in the middle of the floor, standing; while around him, at a distance of six or eight feet, sat the party who had just entered, all curious to hear the raps. Mr. Coverly said: "Are any spirits here that wish to rap? If so, please signal your presence." Before he had pronounced the last word, a rapid succession of bumps under the floor was loudly given. That was the beginning; and I thought there would be no ending to this strange interview. It was kept up for two hours, during which time all kinds of questions were asked and answered, by all kinds of spirits, who claimed to be present. It is not expected, I know, that I should enter into details in this matter, further than to state that Mr. Coverly again and again stated he had no confederate in this; and also, if it were not spirit-rapping, then he could not tell what it was; that the noise was heard about him, no matter where he would go; neither did it make any difference in regard to time—day or night—still they were heard: in his bed, on the head-board, at his table, on the floor, in the office, he could hear them, though sometimes more distinctly than others. The sounds were loud by times, but always as if muffled—as if a cushion intervened between the rapping substance and the floor, or wherever the concussion was heard.

Whatever others might think of it, Mr. Coverly believed—else there is no dependence to be placed in any man's word—that the sounds we heard were produced by spirits. This is all it is necessary to say about that night's *seance*. I never expected to record it in the manner it now appears to the reader; and hence it has only been preserved in memory as an experience of which the mind could not divest itself.

My chain of testimony would be incomplete were I to omit a link that belongs to it, in chronological order, in this place.

I was engaged in the practice of medicine in the Winter of 1853, and was located in the village of St. Jacobs, Waterloo County, Canada West. My ride extended to the north and west of this point as much as thirty miles. The country was sparsely settled, by Irish and Scotch emigrants from the Old Country, and was known as the "Queen's Bush," much of it being unsurveyed, and large tracts of it yet unreclaimed from the proprietorship of the wild animals that still fed and flourished upon it. Surveys were made as fast as the country filled up. To one of the new townships I was called to see a sick child, belonging to Mr. Charles Burrows, who was the pioneer merchant of the township of Mornington. It was a full day's ride to get to his residence, and no less to get home again. This was my first visit to Mornington; and, notwithstanding the generous hospitality and genial companionship of Mr. Burrows and his estimable wife, I sincerely hoped it might be my last.

But, to the point. After the comfort of the sick child was assured, and we had taken supper, Mr. Burrows, while at the table, asked me if I had had any experience in spiritism; to which I replied by asking him if he had had—remembering Robbie's advice to his young friend, to

> "Still keep something to yoursel'
> Ye scarcely tell to ony."

He was free to tell me of a shoe-maker, who lived only four miles distant, following the blaze on the trees, who was a writing medium.

"A writing *what?*" I inquired, not understanding exactly his meaning, and for the first time hearing the word in that connection, and with a somewhat dubious sense.

"A writing medium," he said. "The spirits take possession of his arm and hand, and write whole pages of the most wonderful things."

I looked incredulous; if I did not, my feelings were not reflected in my face.

"Are you jesting?" I said.

"By no means! I was thinking of sending for him to come over, to let you see him write. How would you like it? We can have him here in two hours. Or are you too tired to be curious?"

"O no; send for him. Let us have a time of it," I said. "I have never heard of such a thing, and am curious to see the operation. Did you say the spirits write by controlling his arm and hand against his own will?"

"Exactly; that 's what they do. He has a barrel full of manuscript; and keeps paper and pencil on his shoe-bench beside him, to be prepared for them at a moment's warning. He may be engaged pegging a shoe-bottom, when he is suddenly seized, and takes up the pencil and paper. His lapboard serves as a desk or writing-table. He will then write a page or two, or more, rapidly, when the power leaves him, and he resumes his work. He pays no attention to the manuscripts, but chucks them into an old trunk. He is now on his second barrel. I have seen some of these manuscripts, and they exhibit a grasp of intellect very far beyond any I have as yet discovered in the shoe-maker. I 'll tell you something in confidence; but 'dinna ye be speakin' o' 't.' You have heard, no doubt, that my mill was destroyed by fire, last Fall. Well, I know I have enemies; and the way the fire originated led me to suspect that some one who did not 'love me o'ermuch' might possibly have accidentally dropped some lucifer-matches in a dangerous place. Well, the shoe-maker was over here last week, and I got him to write for me; and I was amazed to receive a letter from an old friend who had been dead several years, informing me of all the particulars of the burning of my mill. He referred to the circumstance that made a certain man my enemy, who had no other way to express his resentment than by destroying my property." After giving me still further particulars in regard to this transaction, Mr. Burrows asked me what I thought of it.

Of course, I had no opinion to offer until I had met my cordwainer; so, until eight o'clock, we passed the time in interchanging views on this strange subject. Mr. Burrows was a man of education, young, energetic, and enterprising, having no time to fool away upon abstract questions of any kind. He meant business. I listened to him, therefore, with more consideration than I do when addressed by a *speculating* philosopher.

A little after eight o'clock, the shoe-maker came in—a dark-haired, sallow-complexioned, medium-sized man, about thirty years old—spare and angular, as shoe-makers generally are. His eyes were dull, and indicated a lack of that intelligent fire which an education would have lit up in a flame. His speech was an index to the character of the man—slow, drawling, commonplace, with no magnetic life in it. He was not above the average intelligence of the Old Country poor people, and even lacked the proverbial native wit of the Irish peasant. He had only been out from the Old Country nine months, had landed at Quebec, and made his way straight up the lakes to the Queen's Bush, where I now for the first time met him.

Skipping all preliminary details, Mr. Burrows, his wife, Crispin, and myself, became seated at the table, and the writing soon commenced. It was only a name at first; but that was sufficient. The hand was strangely moved or controlled; and, by a close analysis of the movement, it could be seen that the action was involuntary. The name written was

CHARLES ODELL.

Startling as an apparition, the characters stood out upon the paper. I affected ignorance, and asked Mr. Burrows if he recognized the name as belonging to any of his friends. Of course he did not; neither did the shoe-maker medium. I said:

"The surname might be Irish. Did you know any body by the name of Odell in Ireland?"

The medium said he did not. Just then his hand was controlled again to write.

"Do you doubt me? It was I that moved the table that frightened your aunt. CHARLES ODELL."

The identification was complete; but, while the opportunity presented, I desired to make a crooked matter straight. I said:

"Uncle Charles, this is the third time you have manifested to me: first, in your parlor, with the table; the next time, by rapping the letters of the alphabet in my office; and now you announce yourself in writing. Do you remember you told me, the second time, by rapping, that you were a *preacher?* How shall I understand you? Have you changed your profession?"

The answer came quickly: "Have I not taught you great truths?"

"Certainly," I said; "but—

"The man or spirit who teaches a truth, *preaches* it. Am I not a preacher?"

"O yes; I comprehend you now, and will remember your definition of preaching."

Our sitting at the table lasted two hours, during which time as much as six pages of ordinary-sized foolscap paper were closely written over. Most of this writing purported to be done by Charles Odell; and if it were not, the indicting intelligence certainly knew very much of his private business and family relations; for these were the topics written upon. It was impossible for me to think that there was any collusion between Mr. Burrows and the Celt; for I was personally but little known to the first, and, to the latter, was an utter stranger. The subject-matter of the communications could only have been given by one most intimately informed of the private affairs of my uncle's family.

The next morning, I started for home, revolving in my mind the strange circumstances that had transpired on the preceding evening; and resolving, if an opportunity should ever offer, to investigate this subject further.

CHAPTER III.

INVESTIGATION CONTINUED IN BOSTON, MASS.—MANSFIELD, THE SPIRIT POSTMASTER, ETC.

FOR several years after my experience with the writing medium in the Queen's Bush, I had no opportunity for investigating the subject of "spirit manifestations" in a satisfactory manner. Mediums were not "as plenty as blackberries in August;" and those that were known as "public mediums," both the pulpit and the press began to stigmatize as frauds, cheats, charlatans, and by other opprobrious epithets, which somewhat cooled my zeal, and even lessened my confidence in the genuineness of the manifestations I had already witnessed. Again and again, I recalled to mind all the circumstances under which they had transpired, to ascertain, if possible, some weak point in the testimony upon which to hang a suspicion or doubt; for I had no motive to deceive myself, and I certainly had no desire to deceive others. Unfortunately, too, for me, in the pursuit of knowledge on this subject, the mediums accessible to the public lived in remote parts of the country, which I could not reach without incurring much loss of time, and what I then considered an inadequate expenditure of money. Thus circumstanced, my interest in the whole subject began to flag, and I felt more like lapsing into the infidelity of unbelief, than going forward to secure a demonstration of the verity of an after-life.

Just here the literature of spiritualism began to engage my attention; and I read with amazement and most absorbing interest the great work of Mr. Davis, "Nature's Divine Revelations, and a Voice to Mankind." In this historical compendium of the origin of the universe, I found so much that was sublime in thought, grand in sentiment, and noble in expression, that it gave a complete diversion to my mind, and engaged all the grasp of its powers. His other volumes, "The Physician," "The Teacher," "The Seer," "The Reformer," "The Thinker," "The Magic Staff," followed in the order of my reading, sandwiched with Ambler's "Birth of the Universe," Linton's "Healing of the Nations," Tuttle's "Arcana of Nature," and "Scenes in the Spirit World;" Harris's "Lyric of the Golden Age," and "Epic of the Starry Heavens," and many other productions that were claimed to have a spiritual origin.

It is not necessary to indicate more minutely the course of my reading, further than to say that I read most of the books, as they appeared from the press, that have since become standard works in the literature of spiritualism.

This mass of reading, instead of satisfying my mind, only whetted my appetite for personal knowledge of such facts as were spoken of by others. I could not build my faith upon the experience of others, but wanted facts for myself—broad, solid facts, such as I had started out with—whereon to rest my hopes of an after-life. Different men read and reason from different stand-points; their conclusions are dissimilar. But when a fact is presented, as if struck with a bullet, they stand dumb, and meditate upon the producing law.

My desire to see for myself the manifestations others had witnessed and recorded, grew upon me day by day, until I finally resolved to have my curiosity gratified, at whatever expense it might be of time, labor, or money. It was a felt importance to know something of the destiny awaiting me. In the pursuit of such information, men had, in all ages, made sacrifices of every thing they held dear, even life itself, that the "great riddle" might be expounded. Nations had poured out their treasures of money upon the altar of investigation; wars had been waged in the same spirit; and the earth had been reddened with the blood of martyrs in the same cause.

I could not, therefore, be indifferent to the only promised practical solution of this great problem of life. A knowledge of the after-life seemed, to my mind, to be a necessary complement to all we know of this; as it would enable us to understand the relations men should sustain to each other, and discharge their duties with clearer judgment and forethought. Some spiritual organizations can be sustained by faith; but such natures are of a sickly sentimental growth, lacking the development of power and force. They take to pious water-gruel as a child to milk. To build up the gristle and bone of manhood, you must have the substantial aliment of facts. To build a dwelling-place for all time, the foundation of your house must be laid on granite ledges—solid facts! Here the man can build securely until the dome of his thought is lifted to the heavens.

I had read enough, and the time had arrived for a new departure in the track of investigation.

Boston seemed to be the center of interest in the spiritual movement. Here were located several public mediums, whose names began to be familiar to those interested in the subject living in remote sections of the country. The secular press spoke of spiritualism as a "Yankee trick," a Boston notion, and a dollar speculation. But time has shown how untruthful the press was in its stigmatic epithets. To the everlasting credit of the Yankees, be it said that they were the first to recognize this divine babe in the manger, and had the manhood to declare the manifestations to be genuine.

Among the Yankees I went, to obtain more light upon the subject. Distrustful of trickery, I visited many mediums, and discovered already, under the livery of spiritualism, much given out as genuine manifestation that was unreliable. There was a class of people anxious to monopolize the privileges of media, who pretended to be entranced by spirits, who would, in this condition, give utterance to the most silly and ungrammatical drivel that ever assailed the ear of credulity. All they had to do was to shut their eyes, squirm a trifle, and then begin a dribble of shilly-shally stuff that the poorest devil in the spirit-world would be ashamed to own. If these people were not self-deceived, they were harmless, for surely they did not deceive any man who had capacity to distinguish the difference between a hen and a hand-saw. They were the baser sort of Yankees.

But among all this swash, there were a few genuine mediums, whom it was a pleasure to meet—ladies and gentlemen of good education, culture, social position, and honorable. From among this class I selected one to assist me in my investigations. My attention was directed to him by the following Card, which I saw published in the *Banner of Light*, at that time, I believe, the only Spiritual newspaper published in the United States:

"MR. J. V. MANSFIELD.

"This distinguished 'Writing Test Medium' for answering sealed letters, may be addressed at Chelsea, Massachusetts, Box 60. *His fee is three dollars* and four postage-stamps. Persons wishing his services will please not write any superscription on the letter they desire the spirits to answer, but seal it so it can not be disturbed or tampered with, without detection. The answer and the sealed letter will be both promptly forwarded to the writer."*

Being upon the ground, I did not write to Mr. Mansfield, but called upon him at his residence, when he was not engaged as a medium, to make arrangements for a systematic examination of his peculiar phase of mediumship.

It was finally arranged that I should become an inmate of his house, and, for the time being, a member of his family. This was an important step to me, as it gave me facilities to study the character of Mr. Mansfield, when he was most open to criticism. I did this for myself, and with no view to betray any weakness I might discover in his character, unless I held my duty to society at large more binding upon me

* Mr. Mansfield is now (1875), and has been for several years, located at No. 361 Sixth Avenue, New York, where he may be addressed.

than the law of hospitality, which admitted me to confidence, and provided me with food and shelter. If Mr. Mansfield had been a private citizen, I should not have gone to his house; but as he was not, it was my bounden duty to know all I could of his private and public character, that I might form the clearer judgment of the reliability of his mediumistic pretensions. It was of much importance to know what manner of man I had to deal with—something of his personal habits, his reputation for speaking truthfully. These discoveries in a man's character can be best made in his own house. Here it is, if anywhere, a man shows his real self; and, though it is humiliating to confess, yet it is nevertheless true, that "a man is rarely a hero to his own valet." The lesson is, that when you know men intimately, they cease to command your respect. But there are exceptions, and these challenge the closest scrutiny, and loom up in importance as the inspection is intensified. Among these I place Mr. Mansfield. An inmate of his house, I have met him in his hours of social relaxation—in his gown and slippers; no studied word or categorical look to disguise the real man, or mar the harmony of his action. With him I have broken bread and "tasted salt," and, for months at a time, have been to him almost as a shadow to the substance. From this intimacy, I claim to speak of this man's character with more judgment and honesty than those who know nothing of him personally, but who seek to disparage his excellence, and destroy his good name. With him in every test condition, watching him closely day by day for months,—if all this will not enable me to speak of this gentleman understandingly, then there can be no reliance on the judgment of man.

And now what testimony am I expected to offer in regard to this man? I will speak of him as I know him. You who know him better, may criticise my opinion; but you who do not know him at all, for God's sake, put your hand upon your mouth, and be silent. You had better be a dumb beast than a chattering rascal.

I will anticipate the desires of the candid reader, and state fairly what I know about this singularly endowed man and medium. It is not expected, of course, that I should speak of his private character further than to say, if I had detected any thing upon which I could have rested a suspicion that his mediumship was a human contrivance, and in any sense unworthy the great cause to which it is devoted, I should have relentlessly exposed the fraud, and abated no jot or tittle of my zeal in condemnation of the man.

I believe Mr. Mansfield to be an honest man; and that he is a genuine medium for the spirit-world to communicate with this, I have ample proof. It will be my business to lay this, in part, before the reader. To present it all, would fill a volume. And just here is a proper place to put investigators on their guard, when they begin to examine this subject of spirit manifestations.

Do not make up your mind too soon, nor bring to the investigation of the subject antagonizing prejudices. When you have discovered a fraud, keep quiet until you know it to be *really* a fraud; then expose it. If you speak of it too soon, you may expose yourself. I do not wish to be understood as deprecating a full and fair criticism, but only enjoin upon the hypercritic the additional quality of *prudence.* It may save you blushes and remorse, when you become older and wiser. Guard sedulously against that carping criticism that doubts without reason, and condemns without proof. Defer judgment until you have all the testimony before you; then sift it closely, that you may find the grain of truth in the chaff of error. If your mind is poisoned with malice or prejudice, you are not fit for a judge. It will be difficult for you to understand this. Exercise your severest judgments upon your own ability to examine this great subject. A drunken tinker, with tobacco-slavers dribbling from his mouth, and hiccoughs in his diaphragm, wanted to explain the whole matter to me, while he leaned against a lamp-post, in Cincinnati; said he could do it in five minutes. Thus "fools rush in where angels fear to tread."

It is hard to get men to understand how little they know of this matter.

It will be seen, from Mr. Mansfield's Card, that his specialty is to answer sealed letters. Hence, he is known far and wide as the spirit-postmaster. His correspondence is very extensive, reaching to all parts of the United States and British Provinces. Letters come to him, indeed, from every quarter of the globe, and in every language that has a grammatical structure.

It is a curious thing to look at the outside of the letters Mr. Mansfield receives. On the supposition that he is a trickster, the writers frequently seal their letters with Spalding's glue, cover them with paint or varnish, smear them with wax, and I have seen them stitched by a sewing-machine, until the decimal of every square inch of the envelope was secured by thread. Some were sweet-scented, and some were not.

Mr. Mansfield and myself would take "turn and turn about" in fetching the mail from the post-office, he bringing my letters, and I his. I have, by this arrangement, been the first to handle the letters sent to the "spirit-postmaster." The answering of these letters was a matter of more interest to me than to Mansfield. With him it was an old song; it meant work, thankless work in most cases, and complete physical exhaustion. But not so with me. This unknown power to answer a letter, without knowing a word contained in the letter, was a novelty that interested me much. The letters I would bring to Mr. Mansfield very rarely got out of my sight before they were answered, and returned with the answer to their authors. The people for whom Mr. Mansfield performed this service exhibited, by their method of sealing their letters, a suspicion of fraud, or that their letters were opened or tampered with. I failed to make any discovery that would tend in the least to confirm such impressions, and I certainly did not lack opportunity to detect such practice, if any had been attempted. It may be of general interest to know exactly how the "spirit-postmaster" answered sealed letters.

Being seated at his writing-table, I lay before him a half-dozen letters, bearing post-marks, perhaps, from as many different states in the Union. The outside envelopes are now removed, and thrown in the waste-basket. He has now before him a half-dozen securely sealed letters, without a mark or superscription to afford the slightest clue to the authors, or to the name of the spirit addressed. Over these he now passes, very lightly, the tips of his fingers, mostly of the left-hand. He touches them so delicately that you could fancy him picking up gold dust, a grain at a time. He passes from one to the other until all have been touched. If no response is elicited, he puts them in a drawer and locks them up. In a half an hour or more, he renews the effort to obtain an answer to the letters. They are again before him, and, like a bee passing from flower to flower, his finger-tips pass from one to the other of the letters. He turns them over, and senses every part of the envelope. The glue, paint, or wax, has almost destroyed the magnetic condition of the letter; but he finally gathers it up, when his left-hand closes with a spasm. That is the signal of success. The spirit addressed in the letter, that exerted this strange influence on his hand, is present, and is prepared to answer it. The other letters are now pushed aside, and this particular one remains before the medium, with the fore-finger of his left hand touching it. He has in a convenient place long strips of white paper, and a pencil, to be ready for the emergency. All is now ready for writing—the pencil at rest in his right-hand. The point of interest is now in the finger of the left-hand touching the letter. It begins to tap on the letter like the motion of a telegraph key, making like irregular sounds. Simultaneous with this tapping, the writing begins with his right-hand, and, without intermission, continues until the communication is finished. There is no rest, after the influence begins, until the completion of the work. I have seen as many as twelve strips of paper closely written upon at one sitting, though three or four, perhaps, would be a fair average of the length of the communication received. The writing is very rapidly executed; and varies in style as much as is common to men.

When the writing is completed, the left-hand, which has been closed all the time with a spasm, now opens, and the influence is gone. It is only for a few seconds; for it returns again to write the address of the person to whom the letter is to be sent, on the envelope. This being done, the letter and answer are immediately inclosed in the directed envelope, and promptly mailed. The whole thing is business-like, orderly, and straight.

I have watched this operation closely, and have seen it repeated a thousand times. If there are many letters to answer, Mr. Mansfield very rarely spares the time to read what he has written; but if he has a little leisure, he reads the communications carefully, and seems to study them with the interest of a student. I have seen him for an hour at a time trying to understand the exact sense of one of these strange missives, using an "unabridged Webster" to assist him to comprehend the definition of words, strange and unknown to him. When names were given in the communication, the fact was always of more than usual interest to him. These were what he called his *tests*. While reading a letter, I have seen his eyes filled with tears, as the pathetic story of a spirit would be read, in which perhaps the first announcement of its translation would be communicated to friends in the form. I remember the letter of a young man who, in the early excitement, went to California to obtain gold. He was an only son, and the stay and support of a widowed mother. He had been successful in his object, and had transmitted the evidence of his success in handsome amounts to his far-away home in the East. His preparations for leaving were completed, and the last letter written to his anxiously awaiting parent. Day by day he was expected home. The little cottage was kept in order, to give him a pleasant welcome; whilst a doting mother's heart was warm with love to greet his return. He did not come. The distance was long, very long; he must have been detained; perhaps had changed his mind, and gone into the mountains again. Weary months passed away, and still that mother awaited the return of her manly son. But he came not.

One day she received a letter. It was not in familiar writing, but the language was couched in the same affectionate terms with which her son was wont to address her. It was the story of his death, by fever, on the isthmus, with all the particulars attending it. He had hoped to comfort her old age, and be with her in the closing hours of life; but it was not so ordained; and wanted his mother to be comforted, and reconciled to the will of his Heavenly Father, who doeth all things well. He was happy, and would meet her first when she entered the spirit-world, and would take her to a beautiful home he was preparing for her.

A recital like the above would affect him to tears. He would say, "Wolfe, I'd give any thing to be assured that the story in this communication is true!"

"Do you doubt it, Mr. Mansfield?" I would ask.

"O no; I have no reason to doubt it. I have never known a statement to be false that came in this way; and yet this thing is so marvelous that I can not comprehend it at all. I sometimes feel that my life is a dream, and my existence a myth, and that there is nothing real or substantial in all we see. Yesterday, that little boy wrote to his mother trying to comfort her in his absence. To complete his identity, he recalled the particulars of his death by drowning; how he had gone into the creek to bathe, and by accident got into deep water; how he struggled to save himself, but felt no pain as he quietly yielded up his life. He spoke of the discovery of his body; named the person who found it; how the news of his death caused his mother to swoon, in which condition she again beheld him, and of her loud lamenting over his lifeless body; how she kissed his cold lips and forehead again and again, crying 'O, my son, my son!' Then again, he spoke of her placing her picture on his pulseless heart, and filling the coffin in which his body lay with flowers. It was a pitiful letter, and has made me feel sad ever since I mailed it."

"Perhaps it will be a comfort to the mother to learn that her child still lives, and is able to return and watch over her," I said.

"That is very true," he replied; "perhaps it is all right, as friend Childs puts it; and we ought not to feel so."

I have known Mr. M. to be suddenly influenced to write; and, without a break in the conversation, he has seated himself at the table, when a long letter has been written. I say influenced to write. This is known by a slight muscular spasm of the arm, which will generally show itself when he folds his arms across his breast, or clasps his hands, or rests them on his knees. These positions form what the spirits term an electro-magnetic circuit, enabling them to approach and influence the nerve-center of his motor system. He seems, at such times, to be inadequate to the exercise of his will-power over the motor nerves; but his thinking faculties are as lucid as when not under any influence at all. Blind Tom I have seen, with his right-hand playing, in a very clever manner, a piece of difficult music, while, at the same time, he performed with his left-hand another intricate composition, and set in different time. While thus engaged differently on his right and left, he sings a song, different in time, the sentiment of which he must memorize. In like manner, I have seen Mr. Mansfield writing two communications at the same instant, one with the right-hand, the other with the left, and both in language of which he had no knowledge. While thus engaged, he has conversed with me on matters of business, or continued conversation begun before this dual writing commenced. It may thus be seen that while Mr. M. himself talked in a very sensible manner, as men ordinarily talk, both his right and left arms and hands were engaged *talking, too.* On one occasion, I remember distinctly, while Mr. M. was writing with both hands, in two languages, he said to me, "Wolfe, did you know a man in Columbia by the name of Jacobs?" I replied affirmatively; when he continued, "He is here; and wants to let you know that he passed from his body this morning." This announcement proved to be true. But what we are most interested in, is the triple manifestation presented on this occasion: Both hands engaged, not on the same subject, but each differently writing, one in a back-hand, the other straight as we ordinarily do; the matter written differing in character; the language different: and yet, while our very senses ache to think of it, a third man speaks, and announces a startling fact which had occurred, since we were seated in that room, several hundred miles distant. What solution can be offered to this triple manifestation of intelligence, power, and organization?

The communications thus received, while they seemed to be intended to show that no ordinary man was equal to their spontaneous production, had really a different purpose. The letters were frequently for persons by whom they would be esteemed "godsends," and upon subjects of the deepest interest. It looked to me as if the spirits were making the best use of time, with the limited means at their command—really utilizing the mediums, as the telegraph is kept at its fullest working capacity when business is brisk.

Such occasions were rare, to be sure; for the

medium could not stand under such a drain upon his nervo-vital organization without suffering from complete exhaustion;* but that a manifestation of this character can be made, affords the mind a center from which to reason that is of first importance to the proper appreciation of this entire subject.

One morning, Mr. M. and I were seated in his office, engaged in conversation having no bearing whatever upon the circumstance I am now about to record, when very abruptly he said: "I feel Father Pierpont! He is now entering the city. He will be here soon to see me."

"Do you mean the Reverend John Pierpont, the poet, and Unitarian minister?" I said.

"Yes. He is one of God's make of noble men. You will love him very much."

We talked about Mr. Pierpont quite a while, when our conversation was interrupted by the entrance of a gentleman who desired to have a letter answered which he had in his possession. Both retired to the writing-room, and left me alone in the reception-room. Very soon the servant opened the door, and, without announcement, a spare-made, tall gentleman, with the most courtly manner, entered. His hair was white as silk floss, and his face was a blazon of intelligence and benevolence. His voice was as musical as the child's first utterance to its idolizing mother.

* Mr. Mansfield, I regret to learn through the press, has become a victim of paralysis. What influence his mediumship has had in producing this distressing condition, can only be conjectured, of course; yet I incline to the belief that such nervous exhaustion as he is subject to, when overtaxed with writing, favors the development of paralysis.

Extending his hand, with a slight forward inclination of his body, he said:

"Good-morning, sir. My name is John Pierpont. Whom have I the pleasure of addressing?"

"My name is Wolfe. I am interested in the subject of spiritualism, and am stopping with Mr. Mansfield to examine the manifestations through his mediumship," I replied.

"You are highly favored, sir. Mr. Mansfield's mediumship is very remarkable, and presents to my mind incontrovertible evidence of spirit-power. Is Mr. Mansfield engaged at present?"

"Yes, sir; but will be free to see you very soon. He was apprised of your coming an hour ago. He then said, 'I feel Father Pierpont; he is now entering the city; he will be here soon to see me.' Have you just come from Medford?" I asked, seeking to confirm the statement of Mr. Mansfield, or to refute it, as the facts might be.

"No, not from Medford; but from New York. An hour since, I arrived at the Old Colony Depot, and from there came straight here, to obtain information respecting the whereabouts of a lady medium whom I have been directed to find, but of whom I have never heard a word."

"Perhaps I know the person you seek; and can give you the necessary information."

"Perhaps, so," he continued. "I have been visiting New York; and last night attended one of Mrs. French's circles. She was controlled, imperfectly, by the spirit of my wife, who said, 'There is a lady medium in Boston, by the name of Hyde, whom I can manifest through much better than I can through this organization. Call upon her when you return home, and I will meet you, my dear, and talk to you of our children and beautiful home.'"

"I know Mrs. Hyde very well," I said. "She lives on Portland Street, near Causeway, and, I think, is a very fine personating medium."

Here our conversation was interrupted by the entrance of Mr. Mansfield, who greeted the venerable poet, prophet, and philosopher, with the warmth of a loving son. After chatting awhile about New York, spirit-mediums, and the premonition of his appearing in the city, Mr. Pierpont left, to call upon Mrs. Hyde.

He visited our rooms several days afterward, and gave a most pleasant and highly artistic description of his interview with his cherished wife, as she manifested through this lady medium. Speaking of his dear one, as of his son, he said, "I can not think her dead!"

My object, however, in this conversation, is to call attention to this phase of mediumship.

Mr. Pierpont visited Boston, on this occasion, at the instigation of his spirit-wife, and started on the very night he received the suggestion. His visit was, therefore, unexpected to himself, and unlooked for by others; and was undertaken by the awakened enthusiasm of his own soul. Neither Mr. Mansfield nor any of his friends knew of the coming of the "sweet singer," only in the manner already described.

It is pertinent here to ask whether Mr. Mansfield can manifest this power of conscious discernment to all people. I learned from himself that he could not.

It was only toward those with whom he was on the most intimate and fraternal terms. He could, however, in this way, *sense* the approach of a person who was repugnant to his subtile feeling, squares away; and would shrink from their presence as the sensitive-plant from the touch of rudeness.

CHAPTER IV.

PERSONAL TESTS—PICTURE-WRITING—STRANGE VISITORS—THE MEDIUM'S SENSIBILITY.

IT was not long before I made the discovery that spirits out of the body do not differ very much in their dispositions from those in the body. Let us illustrate this proposition. Mr. A., while in life, was a truth-loving and benevolent man, had a scrupulous regard for his word, and in every relation of life sustained a comeliness of character *sans* reproach. He passes to the spirit-world; and, from his new sphere of being, is invited to return to tell us the experience he has had in passing through the great transition. In doing this, he is not likely to depart from his pre-spiritual habit of speaking the truth. He may be relied upon as telling exactly what he believes to be true. In the spirit-world he has much to learn that is new and valuable, and also much to unlearn that is old and worthless. He must outgrow the errors of his earth-life, and learn the truths of his new existence, before he becomes a competent teacher to those who call him to return. He will come, however, and do his best to advise, instruct, and inform you; but he is as liable to err in judgment as are those he seeks to gratify. He is therefore to be reasoned with—to be met with the amenities of controversy such as distinguish civil and enlightened debate; and it is by no means arrogant to assume that a mortal frequently exhibits profounder thought, and a more thorough appreciation of the real realities of spirit-life, than those who have actual experience to offset the argument. Thus an uninformed person may travel from a rural district to a large city, and find himself lost in the crowd of pedestrians with which he meets and mingles upon its thoroughfares. He repeats the motive of his walk, and makes the same optical observations, day after day, month after month, until years have passed. He finally returns to his country home, and with him brings the personal experience he has had; only this, and nothing more. He begins to speak of things he has seen, and feels that he is competent to instruct those who hear him. He describes with rustic power things which most attracted his attention. Mr. B., who has never traveled beyond the boundary of the cloud-skirted hill which he sees from the open door of the house in which he was born, asks Mr. A. a question about something of which he has read pertaining to the city. A. is blank. "He did n't see it. He does n't believe the thing in question is in the city, else he would have seen it." How preposterous! If it be understood that information is limited to what we see, then really but little can be known of the great realm of truth which lies beyond the scrutiny of sense. It is the brain that thinks, that possesses knowledge. He who absorbs what he sees, feels, and hears, and gives the *esse* a healthy digestion—one who grasps the whole can speak of parts the best.

Thus, when we commence our investigations of the spirit-life, we should think that but little is understood of its actual condition, and by no means make that little knowledge the boundary limit of our thought. We have capacity to know all; and the more our faculties for acquiring knowledge are exercised, the larger will grow the area of truth to our apprehension.

When I began my correspondence with inhabitants of the spirit-world, I yielded an implicit belief to all I received from them, until I found myself the dupe of an overcredulous mind. Then I quickly turned to the austere extreme of skepticism, and maintained a chilling distrust toward all I saw and heard. Both conditions of mind were incompatible with a just appreciation of facts when presented; and so I settled down from the extremes of credulity and skepticism to that common-sense mean through which we sift and filter the communications we receive from our fellow-men, and applied this rule to the intercourse I held with those who had "passed to the land o' the leal." Let us not essay to supersede human nature in thought, word, or deed, and then we shall be as near right as it is profitable to be.

In this *animus*, I opened my correspondence with the spirits, through Mr. Mansfield. I wrote my letters plainly, and with as little ambiguity of sense as I was capable of doing. I wrote to those who, I felt confident, would have honored my correspondence in the form and with the same familiarity with which I would have addressed an old and intimate friend. I reserved as little to myself as possible, acting in this as well upon the impulses of my nature as upon the advice of the Ayrshire bard:

> "Ay free aff-hand your story tell,
> When wi' a bosom crony."

It was not always convenient for Mr. M. to give my letters immediate attention; but this did not deter me from writing. Living in an atmosphere of harmony, in a place where spirits held convocation night and day around their favored medium, I almost felt the presence of my friends in spirit-life, as Mansfield had sensed the presence of Mr. Pierpont. At such times, I would sit down and write a free, frank, familiar letter, put it in an envelope, and await a favorable opportunity to have it answered. Before this could be done, however, I would write other letters; and, in this way, have had at one time as many as *twenty-five letters*, all ready, as opportunity favored, for Mr. Mansfield's delicate manipulation. These I would carry with me, each inclosed in an unsuperscribed buff envelope. As the envelopes were uniform in size, shape, and color, I had no marks upon them to distinguish one from the other. As an opportunity occurred—that is, when the medium was not too much exhausted by work, and not otherwise engaged—I would lay before him my whole batch of letters, to ascertain whether any one of the twenty-five spirits addressed in the letters were present, and could control to write. Under such conditions, it was very rare that the effort failed to obtain a response from some one or two. He would pass his hand over this epistolary display, and pick up a letter at random, as already described, and proceed to answer it. It is worthy of remark, that I have never known him to fail to be accurate in obtaining the name of the party addressed, and either a message from the said party, or a reason given why they did not write. The response always evinced a perfect familiarity with the subject, circumstances, dates, or persons alluded to, in my letter, when the indicting spirit was the one addressed.

Their replies were often of the most astonishing character. They were not simply pert and pointed, but in them were often embodied the new thought, the new fact, new names, new circumstances, new dates; and, when I say *new*, I mean that by no forced construction of the language of my letter could such information be obtained as was frequently imparted, even had my letter been openly submitted to the inspection of any number of doubting, caviling, or critical readers. I will take, without any special reasons for doing so, the following letter, from among a hundred I received, to illustrate this curious proposition. The letter was inclosed in a sealed envelope, among twenty-five others, and was undistinguishable from the rest. But to enable the reader to try his powers to give a satisfactory reply to it, consider the letter open and under your eye, and then speculate upon it as much as you like. Here it is:

ROBERT SPEER, *late of Cassville, Huntingdon County, Pennsylvania, now in the Spirit-world:*

DEAR FRIEND,—Can you, by any means you may employ, satisfy my mind of your personal presence, and establish your individual identity beyond a reasonable doubt? Any communication you may give of such a character will, I need not tell you, be gratifying to, and gratefully appreciated by, your friend for aye,

N. B. WOLFE.

Now, let the reader consider this was a concealed letter, and occupied a promiscuous place among more than a score of other equally ambiguous letters now lying before Mr. Mansfield. I need not again explain the manner of his selection: how he delicately touches the letters with the tips of his fingers, turns them over, and again solicits the end of attenuated thread that will unwrap the mystery of death and the after-life.

At last he finds the influence. Robert Speer has heard the call, and responds to my request. He comes to establish his personal identity—through what difficulties I can not tell, at what sacrifices I have no means of knowing. How shall he begin? The situation is awkward. He may revive some story that is laid away in the storehouse of my own memory; but that won't do. I must have proof, outside of my own mind, of my friend's presence.

The medium's hand begins to move over the white paper. The pencil-marks were irregularly drawn, and by no conjecture could I guess the meaning of all this scribbling. But patiently I sat, and noticed this strange device; for I had no doubt it was intended as a reply to my request: A horse began to shape up; another followed, though in the lead. What could it mean? It now began to seem

"A mighty maze, but not without a plan."

The pencil glided more swiftly than ever, and, at each stroke, some line of development was unfolded. I need not continue to mark the curious tracery to the end. The picture—for such it was—was completed in thirty minutes. Now let us examine the details of this uniquely-produced composition.

Above the "Jack's Narrows," in the Valley of the Juniata—a point formerly known as "Van Devender's Lock"—you have as beautiful a river, valley, and mountain view as can be found anywhere on the continent. The scenery is composite; the pastoral and the wild form a most enchanting picture to the rapt senses. From this point, you see Sideling Hill, stretching to the west as far as the eye can reach, or until the horizon abruptly closes the view. This was the general outline of the picture. Now for the details. Along the hill-side, a much-traveled road is plainly discerned from the river valley. The farmers from Trough-creek Valley, of which Sideling Hill forms the southern boundary, haul their produce over this road to the Pennsylvania Canal, at Van Devender's, whence it is shipped to Philadelphia in common freight-carrying boats. In the picture we have the mountain, with a loaded four-horse wagon descending—the road, the valley, the river, and the canal, fairly presented; a canal-boat, with two horses tandem attached; and a little mischievous driver flourishing a whip by way of stirring up the leader. On the boat is painted the name "*Thomas Jefferson.*" On the bags in the wagon is printed "*R. Speer.*"

"Now what of all this description?" says the impatient reader. But that is my question. I ask, "What of all this?" I have shown you the letter to which this is a reply, and now I wish you to decide upon its pertinency. Cassville is in Huntingdon County; that is true. And this scenery is in the Valley of the Juniata, and can be appreciated from Van Devender's Lock. But remember, I have told you all this. You could learn nothing of this from the letter. Now, what else do you see in the picture that is an apt reply to the letter? Nothing, absolutely nothing! But I forget; you are not expected to see it. Robert Speer was called upon to give me *a test of his personal presence, and his individual identity!* Has he done so? The only writing discernible was this brief sentence:

"Mother is here, and will communicate."

Still no clew to the proper interpretation of the picture; rather, the whole subject is more ambiguous than before.

Now for my interpretation of this picture-writing; the reader may then understand it more clearly than at present.

In my early life, I was in the service of Robert Speer. He lived beyond the mountain described, in the Valley of Trough Creek. He was the merchant of the valley, and bought the grain, and other produce of the farm and dairy, from the farmers. Those who could deliver their produce at the canal, the boat, *Thomas Jefferson,* was there to receive it, until laden for her trip. Daily trips of wagons from Cassville to the canal and back, were made. Bags of grain marked "R. Speer" generally stood upright in the wagons, a sketch of which we have in the picture. I was, as already stated, in Mr. Speer's employ, and served in the capacity of cow-boy, store-boy, and boat-driver. I suspect the chappie on that hind horse, who is now making the leader, "Old Mike," frisky, by tickling his rump with a new silk cracker, is about thirteen years old, with a shocking head of hair the color of tan-bark, his face freckled; and if he answers you civilly when addressed, will likely tell you his name is *Nep*.

But, again the impatient reader exclaims: "What of all this? We can see nothing in your story that has any bearing upon the letter addressed to Robert Speer."

Well, then, God pity you! Why did n't you answer my letter, with your eyes upon it, before this answer was given? This illustrated reply to my letter, I submit, is as apt and germane as any reply could be. There was no equivocal sense conveyed in this rejoinder. It was all true to life; and if the personal identity and individual presence of Robert Speer was not clearly manifest, then I am graceless enough to ask, "What character of testimony can establish a fact?"

The reader's own good sense will discern the strong points in this test of spirit presence and identity. There has been no theory advanced that will explain all this so satisfactorily as that which admits the presence or agency of Robert Speer as an individualized spirit.

My mind upon this latter point was clear and decided, and there did not seem to be any necessity for more testimony to confirm my convictions. Nevertheless, the medium's hand was again put in motion, in reply to some conjectural remarks in reference to the announcement made in the picture that "mother would communicate." It will be remembered that I made no allusion to "mother." My mother was still in the form; and Mr. Speer's mother was but little known to me, and there was no reason why she should have any desire to write me a letter. Still, she was announced as being present, and would write. That was my understanding of the message.

As already stated, the medium's hand began to be agitated again; and while the picture was still undergoing a critical examination, moved with the pencil over the paper. The result of this control was simply a chest of drawers, or bureau. There was no evidence of skill displayed that the veriest tyro in drawing might not successfully compete with; still, there were four drawers in the set, upon which the following names were inscribed:

GEORGE.
WALTER.
NAPPY.
JOHN.

Underneath this was written:

"You were all children to me, and required a mother's care. Did you not call me 'mother?' MOTHER SPEER."

If I had had any doubts in my mind as to the veritable presence and individuality of Robert Speer, this unlooked, uncalled for, manifestation completely dispelled them. It is necessary to offer some explanation of the above volunteer test, that its value as such may be the better appreciated.

I have intimated that, at the age of thirteen years, I was, by the stress of "iron fortune," thrown upon my own resources in the world. It is not necessary to enumerate what these resources were. I was a mere child, and small for my age. I had "straggled" from home, and engaged to "drive boat" for Robert Speer. The first boat I ventured my fortune with was the old *Stephen Girard;* but she was not a "dainty skipper," and was found to be "unseaworthy" for the "raging canawl." Captain Querry and the *Girard* were soon superseded by Captain Miller and the *Thomas Jefferson.* In the transfer, I was left out, and was taken from the boat by Mr. Speer, and admitted into his family. Here I received the same training and attention bestowed upon his own children. Mother Speer was mother to all of us; and if she discriminated in her love among us, I was too young to notice it, and too well satisfied to prefer a complaint.

That there was no partiality shown in her great motherly heart, was sufficiently evinced by the care she displayed for all our childish wants. None of us had yet outgrown the reckless period in life, when accidents to *trowsers* were both frequent and common—sometimes, I may add, fatal to their comeliness *a posteriori.* But, no matter how terrible the accident might be, a patch or a stitch could mostly repair it, if "taken in time." That was always done. If there were but two buttons left, after a hard contest with a more skilled "pitcher and tosser" than myself, in due course of time the despoiled garment would find its way into "drawer number three"—marked on the diagram "Nappy"—with all the buttons intact for use on Sunday morning. Need I apologize for calling this great good woman "mother?"

George was her eldest son—about my own age. He had by the right of seniority the first drawer. Walter was the second son, to whom was given the second drawer. John was the third son; but here arose the question, whether he ought to have precedence over my age? He was very much younger than I. It was finally settled that my drawer should be the third, and John's the fourth. This, it was alleged, would make me feel more satisfied, and like one of the family. It was a fine display of delicate thought and feeling, which I recall with pleasure after sleeping over it almost forty years. Goodness, when it touches the heart, is "a thing of beauty and a joy forever."

The reader will now see the bearing of the test given in the picture of the bureau. Let him couple this and the picture of the boat and driver together, and then candidly say whether it is not more difficult to disbelieve the assumed presence of Robert Speer and Mother Speer, than to admit their presence and their authorship of the pictorial communications I had received.

If these were isolated cases, unsupported by other concurrent testimony in favor of the spiritual theory, then we might abandon the ground assumed, and say a deception had been practiced; but, on the contrary, every letter I submitted to the touch of Mr. Mansfield elicited facts and responses no less striking and conclusive than those I have cited. He has answered for me more than one hundred letters in this manner; and it has happened but very rarely that the spirits communicating failed to give the most indubitable evidence of their complete identity.

I have seen Mr. Mansfield answer more than one thousand sealed letters, and under such circumstances that to suspect him of tampering with seals, or having personal knowledge of what was written through his hand, is simply a sad reflection upon one's sanity.

The office of a spirit-postmaster (as Mr. Mansfield has been called) is a very interesting place to outside observers. People come there or send for letters, who are little suspected for having any correspondence with the "dead." Many are manly, outspoken, and openly avowed believers in spirit-intercourse; "but others are *afraid*, you know, that something might be said, you know; and they would n't, for the world, let it be known, you know, that they really believed in this thing, you know!" This kind of twaddle you hear every day from people who go spooking through life, unknowing and unknown. They drop out of existence, and their memory rarely survives the discharge of the undertaker's bill, which is always grumbled at for being too high—too much expense for burying such a carcass. One day, *two people* entered Mr. Mansfield's office, muffled and hooded like two thieves on a professional visit. Thick black veils covered the face of the woman; and the man had his hat drawn over his forehead to his eyebrows, and a huge muffler about his face. He squeaked out, in a disguised voice:

"Are you the spirit-postmaster?"

"No!" I said, with a voice like a cutting knife: "what is your business with the spirit-postmaster?"

"We want to get a letter from the spirits," said the simpering woman.

"O! I beg your pardon! I thought you were thieves, and wanted to steal something. Mr. Mansfield is engaged just now."

I left them free to choose whether to remain or go. They preferred to stay. It was but a little while before the medium entered the room, when he at once penetrated the disguises of these poor foolish people, and said:

"Mr. P., your daughter Minnie is beside you. She is weeping because you and her mother are in disguise. She says, if you loved her as much as you pretend to do, you would not be ashamed to seek her presence with an open face. She is so much agitated that she can not write to you to-day."

These people threw off their disguises, and the man was found to be a well-known clergyman in Boston, and the woman was his wife. They turned out to be very genial people, but lived in mortal dread of public opinion. The next day, they entered the reception-room with the assurance of well-bred people, and were treated with the respect due their honesty, intelligence, and position, and received satisfactory communications from their daughter and other members of their family in the spirit-world.

In speaking of Mr. Mansfield as "penetrating their disguises," I wish not to be understood as intimating that he saw through the obstructing material as people ordinarily see by the use of their natural eyes;

but, on the contrary, it is the clearly perceiving senses of the spirit that take cognizance of facts on such occasions and lay them bare to the bone. In the instance before us, the medium was instantly endowed with clear hearing and clear seeing; hence, he heard Minnie speak, as well as beheld her beautiful form bowed with grief and shame in the presence of her insane parents.

It is needless to further extend my observations on this wonderful endowment of Mr. Mansfield. I studied the manifestations of his power for several months, and under the best of circumstances arrived at safe and satisfactory conclusions. The final result was in the thorough conviction of my mind that the spirit-world was as real as the natural; that life was as much individualized there as here; and that death, like its twin-sister sleep, was a beautiful ordinance of nature, into whose loving embrace we could yield our spirit as confidingly as the weary child sinks to repose upon the mother's bosom.

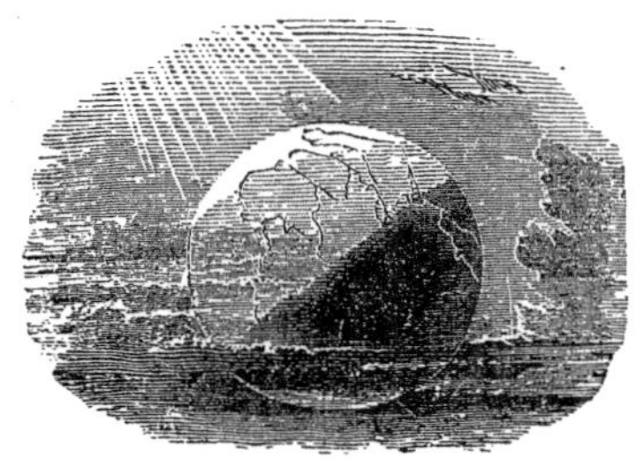

CHAPTER V.

GUARD AGAINST IMPOSTURES—UNRELIABLE MEDIUMS IN THE FIELD.

THERE is no subject to which the investigating mind can be invited where it may be so egregiously deceived and so grossly imposed upon as that which appertains to the phenomena of spiritualism. He who undertakes to examine it critically, must sharpen his wits, and not be overcredulous to believe, or ready to indorse as gospel, all that he sees and hears. Without intending any reproach upon the cause, it can not be denied that a majority of so-called spiritual media are either rank impostors, or so little trustworthy in their pretensions, that it is best always to be on your guard when brought in contact with them. My experience with this class of people has been varied and extensive; and it may be doing a good service to the reader, though the task is as unpleasant as it is thankless, to sample the mediums who, in my judgment, have given the cause of spiritualism more discredit than all its open foes have done. In doing this work, I hope I am animated by a truer charity than that which excuses private vice at the expense of public good.

I have now in my mind's eye a large number of men and women who properly deserve animadversion.

From these I can only select a few, as my space is limited, to illustrate the character of this pernicious mediumship. They, however, as already stated, will sample the whole.

To all well-informed spiritualists, the name of L. Judd Pardee is quite familiar. He was what is called a trance-speaker, and an accredited minister of the new gospel of spiritualism. I met this gentleman in the early period of my investigations of spiritualism, and formed for him a warm personal attachment, and had a high esteem for his mediumistic powers. By birth and education, he was a North Carolinian, though I never met him outside of Cincinnati, where he was well known to the spiritualists, among whom he had many friends. Here I engaged him to lecture for a month, and procured for him, first, Melodeon Hall, and afterward the Mechanics' Institute. I was at the time serving as president of the spiritual platform.

Pardee, at that time, was about thirty-five years old, personally about medium height, with a delicate, almost feminine, physical structure and voice. In ordinary conversation, he spoke like a girl just entering her "teens," not a romping girl either, but one of the timid sort that are still led by mamma's apron-strings. This man possessed a fine, subtle, analytical mind, and, when on the rostrum, a voice of almost Websterian compass, with which he could make echoes ring and electrify the hearer in every part of the largest hall.

A natural metaphysician, he seemed sometimes to want ballast to prevent him voyaging in midair, where he was not in heaven, and yet he had cut loose from earth. He was a good reasoner, and could thrill the hearts of as many as heard him with delight. He had the most ready command of language I ever knew a man to possess. Words and phrases were marshaled as playthings, and, in their gorgeous display, you almost forgot their mission. He chose them more for their musical rhythm than their signification; and yet they were always appropriately chosen and strongly expressive of the sense intended. Pardee was a most interesting conversationalist, and had a very retentive and compliant memory.

When he appeared on the platform, his general mien of face and form was demure. His dark-blue eyes could scarcely be seen under the long pale lashes. He covered his face with his right-hand, as he sat for a few minutes before speaking, as preachers do when they enter the pulpit. Look at the man closely, and you will see his shoulders shrugging a kind of a twitch, as if a wheat-head had got down his back; and then he sits upright, and passes his hand over his forehead, first to the right, then to the left. His eyes are now tightly closed, and, after oscillating, as it were, upon the extremity of his spinal column for a moment or two, he takes a deep inspiration, when he is said to be entranced. In other words, Pardee has vacated his body; and the implication is, that the spirit of Saul, Socrates, Demosthenes, or the Nazarene, has taken possession of it. Gudgeons are supposed to believe this.

The medium being entranced, all is hushed into a death-like stillness, that the first faint sound from his inspired lips may be heard. His words are soft and low, like the ripple of waters along a meadow-bank, and musical as the first carol of a Spring bird. Gradually they increase in power and force, until that frail, delicate form seems to dilate with strength, and become invested with a mantle of grandeur or a kingly robe. He rides, as it were, in a chariot of flame, leading captive the hinds who listen to his majestic eloquence. He stretches forth his hand, as a king his scepter, and all hearts acknowledge the mastery of the man.

No word-painting can do justice to Pardee's style, and delivery of his impassioned thought. He must be seen and heard to affix his image forever in your memory. But here commences our humiliation. After the storm has passed, this man feigns to be unconscious of the power he has displayed. After swaying a multitude for two hours, at the caprice of his will, he pretends to know not any thing of what he has done. Out upon this hypocrisy! Unconscious, indeed! Why, see how "a plain, unvarnished" statement of facts will put to blush this glaring falsehood!

In the Summer of 1864, Pardee was recuperating his wasted energies in the vicinity of Patriot, Indiana. While there, he prepared a half-dozen or more lectures, which he designed delivering during the Fall and Winter campaign. These he submitted to my inspection from time to time, while in course of preparation, and solicited for them a free and impartial criticism. Some of my suggestions were accepted, and incorporated into the body of the lectures. After their completion, he asked my assistance in the procurement of a suitable place for their delivery in this city, during the hot season, as his finances were low. This I did, and advertised Greenwood Hall as the place, and invited the attention of the public to the intellectual feast in store for them; for I knew precisely what I was promising.

A few days previous to the lecturing time, Pardee came to my house as my guest. He and I again looked over the manuscript of his lectures, as critically as I was capable of doing. I do not claim any merit for the suggestions I made; but I simply wish to show that the lectures were carefully prepared and maturely considered before they were delivered. Now, see what follows.

On the occasion of the delivery of the first lecture, being a Sunday morning, I accompanied Pardee to the hall, and acted as chairman of the meeting. At the proper time, I made some introductory remarks, and presented the lecturer to his audience.

I, of course, expected Pardee to read his lecture, or speak with his manuscript before him. Such was not the case. Having advanced to the speaker's position, he sat down on a chair, and then went through the flummery of entrancement, as already described. He then spoke an hour; and I followed the lecture with the closest attention, *as I was familiar with every part of it.* My object was to see how close to the text he adhered. He was scrupulously exact in every word, so far as my memory bore its attestation. I have a friend who, when she desires to express her admiration for any thing, exclaims, "Is n't it lovely? is n't it perfectly splendid?" Some such adjectives I found myself repeating at the conclusion of Pardee's masterly speech. I was the first to take his hand and congratulate him on his fine effort; the audience thronged around him for the same purpose, animated by a similar feeling of respect and admiration for the man.

Among those who took his hand was an old spiritualist, who claimed to be a seer, or clairvoyant. He said to the speaker: "Pardee, do you know who it was that spoke through you? I could see his form, but could not distinguish his face."

"I think it was the Nazarene," said Pardee, "or John the Baptist; both have been with me a great deal of late. Their influences are very similar, and I can't tell which of them spoke."

I thought he was joking at first; but, after looking him directly in the eyes, I could detect no lambent evidence of humor in them. He was in square earnest. I felt like asking him, "Do you know who you are talking to?" But I was powerless for speech or action. The fellow's impudence was as sublime as his eloquence; and for both, to this day, I have a profound admiration. He was as cool in his utterance of this falsehood as a "polar wave," and his face was as imperturbable as a lying horse-jockey's. He deserved to be blowed; but I could n't do it. I was too weak for the effort.

But why expose Pardee, and let the other thirty thousand privileged rascals go scot-free, who practice their impositions, every day in the week, upon a credulous world? "No," I said; "Pardee is no worse than the rest of them, and all I blame him for is, that he is not better." An entranced speaker should be better than an orthodox preacher; but, alas! I fear he is not. I wish those gentlemen all would speak the truth, when it is even more fitting than a falsehood. We owe something, surely, to the dignity of human nature, even should we lose sight of self-respect entirely.

It is hardly necessary to say that I have but little confidence in the pretensions of trance-speakers. As a class, in this respect, they are not reliable. I have heard the best of them, and rarely have I listened to their utterances under the so-called divine afflatus, that excelled in thought the mental births of their normal conditions.

Among this class, few have attained more distinction for their eloquence than Miss Emma Hardinge. This woman has great power on the rostrum; all who have heard her will admit this. But she is a woman of fine education and superior culture. As an elocutionist, she had distinction before she became a speaker on the spiritual platform. In her social relations, her conversational powers are quite equal to any of her forensic efforts. Then, why does she speak with that repulsive, staring entrancement? It is a sham, and ought to be abated.

And there, too, is Mr. Thomas Gales Forster, who will persist in shutting his eyes, and shaking himself out of his "seven-league boots," that Dr. Dayton may step into them and make a speech in his absence. Now, this is all nonsense; and it's high time that this silly custom should be honored in the breach. Mr. Forster is not only a man of fine education, but he is "well-read" in the legitimate sense of the term; that is, gives a thoughtful digestion to every thing he reads. His memory is wonderful, and never fails to supply data, when required to elucidate a point or fortify an argument. He is not a ready debater, owing to the detestable habit of speaking with his eyes closed; but he is always massive in argument, and solid in fact. As a speaker, he is more logical than Clay, and but little less ponderous and weighty than Webster. His blows are heavy and slow, but they tell every time on his subject. Rather sluggish in his intellectual habit, he requires an occasion to develop his strength. He is familiar with the classics, and has read Scripture to some purpose, as he exhibits upon suitable occasions an intimate knowledge of the Sacred Writings, even such as the most learned commentators might aspire to emulate. In discourse, he is as prolific of Scripture texts as a jockey is of horse-stable slang; but why he will *shut his eyes and chew tobacco* when he quotes from the Bible, is to me as much a mystery as the profligate assumption of the departed Pardee. But, "*suus cuique mos.*"

Another of the able speakers on the harmonial platform, who has fallen into the silly habit of entrancement, before she will consent to utter her own brave thoughts in her own brave words, is Miss Lizzie Doten, one of New England's most accomplished women. This lady is a fine intuitionalist, and grasps the subtler truths of the Great Harmonia with the power of a master's mind, and weaves them into a fadeless wreath of song. The fiber of this woman's brain is akin to that of Emerson and Holmes. She crystallizes her thoughts, and utters them with an energy that makes them cut their way into the understanding of men. In her poetry she embodies her highest truths. Then, if ever, she "cuts loose from the mooring of reason," to float at random along the glowing stream of her inspiration. Then, like a musical swan, she sings as she floats adown the river of harmony, and celebrates the real and ideal in her wedded verse. But why mar this picture, Lizzie Doten, by playing "bo-peep" with your staring auditors? You can *write* as good sentiment as you can *speak*, and your own style and composition are not inferior in fervor or eloquence to those which are falsely ascribed to the lamented Poe. Remember that the suppression of a truth is the suggestion of a falsehood.

It is not necessary, I hope, to extend the list of trance-speakers, to show my reprobation of the "shut-eye" habit. I want to look my educator in the eye; then I can tell whether he is honest and in earnest. It is the organ of a language that is always truthful.

I have now to deal with three or four derelicts of a less dignified character than those I have already introduced to the reader. They command attention simply because they assume to be shepherds over spiritual flocks, and cling to spiritualism as barnacles to a ship or fungi to a rock.

The first of these is a man well known, far and wide, as the leader of a movement that has its foundation in selfishness and dishonesty. *Mr. John M. Speer* will be at once recognized as the one of whom I intend to speak. He is a professed spiritualist, and a trance-medium for a specific work. This man has the craft and cunning of an Indian in his nature, and I would as soon trust a Modoc or Kickapoo with my reputation, my fortune, or my life, as this gypsy leader. When this man makes overtures, reject them as a rule. He does not mean well by you.

John M. Speer is an enigma to most people. If he were not a trance-medium, he would be an enigma to none. Under this garb, he concocts and conceals his real purposes. He has dubbed himself a missionary for the upbuilding of a new government; and for the attainment of this object, he wanders over the country, in Europe and America, to consecrate (?) men and women to this new work. He is generally accompanied by his "second wife," who acts as his amanuensis, and two or three of the "faithful," who have deserted their homes to share their fortunes with this infatuated old man.

I had heard much of this infatuated party, of their Unitary Home movement at Kyantone, and their wandering o'er a foreign strand, but never met them until they floated to the levee at Cincinnati, in a flat-boat; I think, in 1859. That was a sight worth seeing, as it taught me a lesson I shall never forget—this huddle of world-reformers (?), living in a sensual sty of filth and degrading familiarity, houseless and homeless. What a commentary upon their movement! But let us look at the work they propose to accomplish.

The form of government Speer seeks to establish, differs from any known to exist on the earth, excepting it be in Utah, though it is claimed to have its counterpart in the spirit-world. Its executive is to be a theocrat, in whom is centered all social, civil, and ecclesiastical power. John M. Speer is, of course, to be, *par excellence, the Theocrat.* This is not all there is of it; but is n't it enough? The smell of Limburg cheese ought to satisfy a dainty stomach. You can best detect its quality by sample.

The method of winning converts to this movement of Speer is worthy of notice. Some of his party "spot" their man, or woman, generally from among the crazy sort of spiritualists. An interview is managed, and brought about, between the victim for "consecration" and the theocrat. The object is not stated or hinted to the candidate. Such persons generally have means, or something else that can be made useful in the new work—all of which belongs to the theocrat, of course, as soon as you admit his authority. It is arranged to meet at the boat or some private house to spend the evening. A free, glib talk about matters and things in general is indulged in, when you are surprised by a sudden reticence of the Speer party. They all reverently look at the theocrat, who has shut up his eyes, *a la* Pardee, and vermiculates his long spinal column, like a boa-constrictor preparing to strike a calf. Of course, his victim sits quiet, though an interested spectator of all this flummery. The moment for something to "turn up" arrives, when Speer begins to mumble something which can only be understood by "Carrie," his second wife. You now begin to wonder what the "Old Scratch" is driving at. Carrie is saving every word that falls from his oracular lips, and rapidly puts them in phonetic characters. The light of the room is *en sombre*, and the voice of the old man sepulchral. The solemnity of the occasion becomes oppressive, and you feel that the tomb of the Capulets would be a frisky place beside the presence of this old mortality. The great high-priest now steps forward, and, without as much as saying, "By your leave, sir," places his hand on your head. It is a harsh, bony hand, that rattles o'er your bumps like the digits of an Egyptian mummy. Then you have something like this, spoken in mobbled accents:

"To this great work do I consecrate thee, and thy title shall be recorded as '*the projector*.' Your business will be to provide a home for the wandering members of the New Covenant, to furnish it comfortably, and to stock it well with 'good wittles.' You will find a house on Arch Street, No. 16, that will answer the purpose 'werry well' for the present, until you can provide more comfortable quarters. Write out the projector's commission, Carrie; write it down my dear, devoted second wife, and mother of my child, the embryo of 'the coming man;' write it, and give it to the doctor, and he will pay you two dollars and sixty-five cents for the commission, on delivery of the goods. Amen."

At the conclusion of this knavish ceremony, "the theocrat" opened his eyes, when I was congratulated by the several members of the government on my admission to their emasculated phalanx. I have given the substance of Speer's charge, though not in his exact words.

Up to this time I, of course, treated the whole

thing as a joke; but when poor Sheldon came the next day to see me in regard to making provision for the party, I began to understand the true character of John M. Speer. Sheldon was broken in health—in the last stage of pulmonary disease—and when I began to realize how his confiding nature had been abused, I became indignant at the outrage. The man was tired—spitting his life away—and only needed a place of comfort to rest and die. As I looked into his large lustrous eyes, sunken deep in their orbits, I said:

"Sheldon, when the spirits controlling John M. Speer shall 'project' the means necessary to provide a home for the new government, I may then think of becoming their agent in this matter; but neither you nor I will live, I hope, to see this vagary of Speer's assume any greater proportions than it at present presents. This is a cruel joke on you. This man has separated your family, destroyed your home, and squandered your means. He will soon desert you, as you have nothing left to excite his cupidity, and leave you broken in health, mortified in spirit, a friendless man, the toy of poverty, and a victim of want. Why not see this man's true character? In holy phrases he transacts his villainies, and steals the livery of the court of heaven to serve his evil ends.*

* A somewhat similar character to this man Speer is found in another professing trance-speaking spiritualist by the name of Chauncey *****. This fellow perambulates the country like a vagabond, billeting himself wherever he can find people foolish enough to entertain him. He attends all conventions and meetings of the spiritualists of America wherever there is a chance for a free feast or a free blow, and always manages to make himself heard. At one of these irresponsible meetings, recently held in Cincinnati, to which he was a self-

Do you see what a tool he would make of me? He would squander my means, as he has yours, and then seek other dupes to rob. It is time you should quit the presence of this old, bad man!"

My admonition came too late for any retraction of error into which the dying man had fallen. His strength of body and brain had departed, and he was as helpless in the power of John M. Speer as a child in the grasp of a giant.

For myself, I took a soap-bath, and washed my head free from the vile contact of this old man. But, alas! poor human nature!—there are those who are weak enough to think his hands possess the virtue of consecration. Thousands and tens of thousands, if I have been correctly informed, have submitted to the imposition of these hands, as if they were immaculately pure, and not as sordid as Iscariot's. I have seen his commissions copied on parchment, and beautifully framed, suspended upon the walls of

accredited member, he visited my house to "bum." To get clear of the nuisance, I gave him money to pay his hotel-bill for two days. Nevertheless, he managed to visit me most regularly about dinner and tea time. Being seated at my table when he last called, he was permitted to sit in the parlor until dinner was over. Receiving no invitation to dine, he retired from the house while we were sitting at dinner, and left as rascally a looking old weather-worn and sweat-bleached plug-hat on my piano as ever graced the graceless head of a loafer. A new seven-dollar silk hat, one of David Baker's best, with all the luster of newness, and free from taint or smell, was taken in its stead. This fellow has since written me a characteristic letter, in which he justifies his larceny by the following plea: "It was the spirits that tuck your hat, and they would not alow it to be tuck back. I am the chosen one of the Lord, and all things belong to Me and him." How very like the argument of the tithing priest is this—only more lawyer-like!

comfortably furnished parlors, in the New England States. How long will men make monkeys of themselves?

I am not in sympathy with shams, tricksters, or sycophants. Time-servers will find no friendly office at my hands. Spiritualism presents itself to my mind as the grandest revelation of truth vouchsafed to modern times. Its advent constitutes a new hope and a new era for the world. It embodies a religious thought that will ultimately pervade the minds of all men, and redeem the world from the error and wrong under which it has long suffered. Millions will defend it, when its teachings and its authority are better understood. Impostors may retard its advent and tarnish its fair name; but it will at last triumph over all opposing conditions, and stand before mankind as the embodied voice of God to the human race.

Among the notable expounders of the new gospel in the United States, Mr. E. V. Wilson occupies a prominent public position. Without scholastic attainments, he is, nevertheless, hard-sensed, and, like Warren Chase, an able debater of the harmonial philosophy. He is, physically, an athlete, and possesses that courage which is found peculiar to high muscular development. So far, so good. I believe he does not classify himself among the entranced speakers, but claims to be a seer and clairaudient. In the exercise of these latter functions, I take my exceptions to the man as a reliable medium.

It is his custom, after or during the delivery of a lecture, to make some startling announcement of what he sees and hears that is not appreciable to ordinary senses. In this way he has singled me out, on several occasions, as being accompanied by a spirit, who says: "My name is ——— ; I was your companion and friend when you were secretary to Mr. Buchanan, in the White House, at Washington. We had many 'good times' together." Mr. Wilson has repeated this story twice before public audiences, and I can only say it *is false.* At one time I did writing for Mr. Buchanan, at Wheatland, but only as an assisting friend, not as a hireling, or paid secretary. In an easy conversation, I told Wilson this, some time prior to his first public announcement of the fact; but the fellow got it crosswise in his head, and so he continues to blunder over it. But a still more glaring testimony of the unreliability of his seership was elicited by his announcement, before a public audience, of the spirit of a man who was supposed to be dead, but had not, as yet, shuffled off his mortal coil. He said, "I see before me the spirit of a man who says his body is near Madison, Indiana, in the Ohio River, and he gives me the name of Professor Wm. Holt."

"Just as I thought!" exclaimed a number of persons who knew the professor. "Poor fellow! he did n't seem to get along well, and so he drowned himself."

To understand the value of this test of Wilson's seership and clairaudient powers, it is necessary to make some explanation. Just before the startling announcement was made, Professor Holt left Cincinnati in a manner peculiar to himself, without advising any of his friends of his purpose. For several weeks no word or clew to his whereabouts could be obtained, and the apprehension of his friends was, that he had become tired of existence and had thrown his life away in the river. This was talked freely in the presence of Wilson, and hence this manifestation of his seership, etc. Now for the sequel to all this. About six weeks after the public mind had settled into the conviction that the body of Holt would never again be seen, only in its revised condition as catfish or buffalo, upon our breakfast-table, lo and behold! Micawber-like, he turns up in St. Louis, sprightly as a cricket, with not a scale or smell of a fish about him. But what of all this? Why, simply, that Wilson's seership is a fraud, and his clear-hearing is no better. As to whether he is self-deceived, or is unscrupulously deceiving others, the candid reader must decide for himself. It is obvious to every intelligent mind, however, that spiritualism is brought into undeserved reproach by the conduct of such charlatans.

A milder and less pernicious form of imposture is practiced by your impressible mediums, which may, as well as not, be ventilated in this place. The following case will serve as an example:

When an inmate of Mr. Mansfield's house, one of the genus impressible shared his hospitality, like myself. She had come from a distance—even from Buffalo, New York—and was a lady of education, means, and good social position, enjoying the personal esteem of President Fillmore and his family. All this, one would suppose, should have protected the lady from the folly of impressible mediumship, but it did not; so she declared, without reserve, her possession of wonderful powers in that line of business, and came on partly to make Mr. Mansfield's family a social visit, and partly to illustrate to him and others her extraordinary endowment. Her infatuation was complete.

As I had no confidence in the thing, but not doubting the woman's integrity, I took no interest in the matter. I studiously avoided speaking on the subject, and evaded all remarks that would lead to its discussion. But all the precautions I could use would not suffice. I was cornered, and compelled to make a trial of her powers. The manner was some like that of testing Mr. Mansfield. I was requested to write my thought, and await the reply as it came written through the medium's hand by impression. My first effort was as follows:

"MR. SAMUEL PATCH,—Putty is rising. If you want any for skylight purposes, remit your order through the medium at your earliest leisure, and oblige, Yours, etc."

This plain business note I inclosed in a buff envelope, and laid it before the impressible medium. It was not long before the wanted impression arrived, as it was announced in straggling pencil scrawls over a page of foolscap, and somewhat thusly it read:

"DEAR BROTHER,—You are exactly right. The same causes will produce uniform results. Do not let your heart fail you, for you must surely succeed. Persevere to the end. Nature is boundless in her resources, and she never fails to supply every reasonable demand. You must work for the grand result. Nothing is attained that is worth the possessing, without labor. Do not become discouraged. All great enterprises are difficult to accomplish. Achievement and push are twin-brothers. I am with you to the end."

There was a "goody" in this communication which commanded my respect; but I confess I could not see its pertinency to my plain, matter-of-fact business note. There was no allusion to putty, excepting where it is said, "Nature is boundless in her resources, and she never fails to supply any reasonable demand." Putty may have been alluded to in her "boundless resources," but the construction was not satisfactory. I was a trifle confused, and I suppose the medium was impressed to ask me, "How do you like it?"

This question was a relief to my mind; for I confess to a great perplexity as to what I should say to the woman. It gave direction to my thought. I said, "Madam, this is marvelous; there is a trifling ambiguity I should like to have cleared up. Will you try again, if I write another note?"

"Certainly," she said, with a simper of satisfaction; "it always is a pleasure to write for my friends. We should assist each other to the extent of our ability."

"You are very kind. I will be brief, that neither your time nor strength shall be unduly taxed. Such efforts must be very exhausting upon your vital resources."

I hastily wrote:

"SAMUEL,—Am I to understand that you will get your supply of putty for skylight purposes from the boundless resources of nature, and not from me? My heart does fail me, if I read you aright. In vain you tell me, 'Achievement and push are twin-brothers.' What has that to do with putty? I know very well that nothing is attained without labor; but, my dear sir, have n't I labored? You discourage me. Can you not give me a word of encouragement by ordering a few pounds of prime No. 1 skylight putty through this medium?

"Yours, etc."

This note was inclosed, as the first, in a buff envelope, and laid before the "medium." The pencil was soon seized, and the hand was nervously influenced by a tea-drunken brain to twitch, dash, skip, and scrawl in a most bewildering manner. After some painstaking effort, the hieroglyphs were deciphered to convey the following:

"DEAR BROTHER,—Go ahead! You are on the right track! Before you lies the royal road to knowledge! Knowledge is power! Truth is the Archimedean lever that raises the world! Stand firm, and be steady to your purpose! Do not doubt success! Trifles may intervene, but the will is omnipotent! Faith in it will move mountains! That which is most valuable is most difficult to attain."

In neither case did Samuel attach his name to the reply given my notes; but that did not seem to be of much consequence, as he assured me I was "on the right track." He was not. He studiously avoided making any allusion to putty, however; and it was that which mystified me. "Business before pleasure," is a popular maxim among men with "level heads;" but Samuel did not seem to subscribe to the dogma in this instance. I thanked the medium for her attention, and expressed myself as quite well satisfied with her mediumship and the tests I had received. I pocketed the notes and replies, and said nothing more at the time to any one.

After a few days, it came to my ears that the "medium" was exulting over the fine tests she had given me, and the satisfaction I evinced with her mediumship. Still I said nothing. At last Mr. Mansfield spoke to me of the tests Mrs. C. had given me. It was now time to correct the errors into which these reports had led several well-meaning people. This I did by simply showing Mr. Mansfield my two notes, and the replies she wrote. I thought that would be sufficient; but how sadly I was mistaken! Mansfield told the joke to his wife, who, with a womanly sympathy for the impressional medium, informed her of the facts of the case. The medium became exasperated, and no longer called me "dear brother"—not much of any thing in that line. I walked straight for several days, but it was of no use; the conflict was inevitable, and it burst forth at the breakfast-table. I had been reading the *Herald of Progress*, and Mr. Mansfield said, "Any thing new in the *Herald?*"

"Mr. Davis disclaims having said, at any time," I replied, "that there were three hundred people in Buffalo who have no souls. A correspondent asks him whether he ever made such a declaration, and he says he never did."

"Mr. Davis did say it, and he need not deny it. *I heard him,*" said our putty medium, in a tone that was as purely personal to me as if she held my nose between her thumb and finger.

I could not escape; her beautiful eyes grew brilliant, not with love-light. Still, as Sam had told me to "stand firm and be steady to my purpose," I replied, "But Mr. Davis disclaims having said any thing of the kind that could either be constructively or otherwise made to imply such a declaration."

"Mr. Davis need not deny that which can be proved," said "putty," with an acerbity of manner I had not before witnessed. "Either he tells a falsehood, or I do!"

I could not resist the opportunity, and I beg my reader to believe that it was with no feeling of exultation that I triumphed over my fallen foe. It was her own unruly "nag" that placed her at my mercy. I waited a moment, but she was too proud to ask it. I looked pityingly at the fallen medium, but met only defiance in her eye. So, as a *coup de grace*, I said sternly and deliberately, "*I believe Mr. Davis.*"

That settled the business of the impressional medium. Before noon she got an impression to go home; and I really think, if spirits ever engaged in such pastimes, that they came to Mrs. C.'s relief upon this occasion.

Before taking leave of Boston and this part of my subject, I must pay my respects to Mrs. Nelly, a trance-personating medium, who had some local celebrity at the time I was seeking for "more light" on the subject of spiritualism.

She lived in a fashionable part of the city, in good style, and her house was frequented by many persons, who, like myself, were interested in every thing pertaining to the new religion. I found Nelly a beautiful young widow of several years' standing, a blonde, with sparkling blue eyes, and a mouth full of delicately-formed teeth, as pearl-like as could be. She was about medium height, and no longer a slender-waist girl. Chatty she was, and full of delicious small-talk.

Nelly's controlling spirit was represented as being an Indian girl, whose christened name was Shanandoah. She was the daughter of Powhatan, and sister-in-law of Captain Smith, who so far forgot the dignity of his Saxon blood, and the odiousness of miscegenation as to marry her eldest sister, Pocahontas. This spirit they called Shanny, for short.

Her habit was to eject Nelly from her corporal dwelling, and take possession of the nest herself. Then she would cut up dido in high Injun style. She would squeal and dance and jabber Injun magnificently. When a real good-looking, manly man of a marriageable fellow was present, Shanny would make love to him straight, in the most unaboriginal fashion. Nelly being absent, she could take many liberties with her tenement, to which Nelly, I think, would have objected, had she been present and mistress of the situation. But, then, it was only Shanny, you know; and she was only a pure, simple-hearted child of nature, and did n't mean any thing. I sometimes thought I could see a "lurking devil" in Shanny's eye, which looked so much like Nelly's, that the coincidence became an interesting study. The upshot of all this was, that Shanny fell desperately in love with a gentleman of our party, and he with her. They plighted their vows of constancy, and, of course, were married. But how, you will ask, can a spirit marry a mortal?

Certainly! You see, Shanny took possession of Nelly's body, after serving upon her an act of ejectment; and possession being "nine points in law," Nelly was left out in the cold. Having a beautiful form at her disposal, in which she could entertain her friends as she felt inclined, she stopped playing Injun, and became Mrs. Nelly—but I forgot myself—Mrs. Shanny Jones, quite as aristocratic a patronymic as Mrs. Captain John Smith. Shanny is pleasantly married, and what more do you want to know? She fulfilled her mission as a trance-medium, and then dropped out of sight.

What we most need to know is often what we most dislike to hear; but those who are hurt by the truth, should remember the proverb which says, "Faithful are the wounds of a friend."

CHAPTER VI.

CLASSIFICATION OF PHENOMENA—SPIRITUAL PRIEST-CRAFT—DEATH—THE BODY—MRS. MARY J. HOLLIS.

SPIRITUAL phenomena addresses itself to my mind under two characteristic heads; namely, *physical* and *mental.*

In these two general divisions of the subject, the whole range of spiritual manifestations may properly be classed. Under the first head we put table-tipping, spirit-rapping, spirit-writing, picture-drawing, the movement of inert bodies, spirit-voices, and the materialization of heads, faces, bodies, arms, hands, clothing, jewelry, flowers, fruits, paintings, the transformation of water, the dissipation of matter, and all other phenomena which we recognize by the legitimate exercise of our five senses.

Mental phenomena embrace that class of manifestations which can only be exhibited through the mental structure of man. In this division we place psychometry,* psychology, clairlativeness,† trance, somnambulism, magnetic exaltation, phantasms, sympathy, mental impressibility, catalepsy, hysteria, and religious ecstasy.

* See Denton's work, "The Soul of Things."

† This is the new word employed by Mr. Davis as a substitute for *clairvoyance.* He defines it in his autobiography—"The Magic Staff"—as "the clear production of clairvoyance."

It is not our intention, at this time, to speak more particularly of these varied phases of spirit manifestations, or to offer any special plea for the recognition of the genuineness of their character. Such service must be performed by the student of mental phenomena when he is brought face to face with the facts. When these occur, he must engage his own logic and furnish his own rhetoric in forming his own conclusion.

The object of my writing is to present the facts as they occurred to me with as much fidelity as I am capable of doing, leaving them to the judgment of the reader on their own distinctive merits. Let the testimony be scrutinized, analyzed, and sifted, until the truth be ascertained. A witness, to be valuable, should have knowledge to impart, and competence to testify. All dross must be purged from the pure metal before its intrinsic worth can be ascertained.

In the physical department of the spiritual phenomena, the course of investigation is beset with less difficulty than in the mental. Herein your *senses* witness the facts, after which, if you doubt their testimony, you may exercise your reasoning faculties to assist you to arrive at other conclusions. But when a mental manifestation is given, you have no power to examine its claim to spirit-origin but through the medium of the mind, which rarely acts without bias or decides without prejudice. It is not worth while to higgle at the truth, that, in these days of political depravity, religious bigotry, and loss of public virtue, children are born with perverted judgments; or, if not, "their column of true majesty" is warped by educational vices. Pure reason is seldom exercised by man, as it can only be developed when harmonious conditions surround him, in both his antenatal and natural life. But deficient as man is in his mental capacity to reason purely on this occult subject, he may, nevertheless, discover surface indications of truth underlying it that will encourage him to "dig deeper for the hidden treasure."

The mental organization of man is too imperfectly understood for us to sit in sober judgment and pronounce upon its capabilities. Few men have any just conception of the sublime possibilities of human nature. When we reflect that every man has wrapped up in himself the capacity to reproduce all that has ever been achieved by the human family, we should pause before deciding upon the extent of his power. Hence, are we not liable to err in our judgments when we ascribe mental phenomena to a supersensuous origin, which may be shown, *a priori*, to be the legitimate product of an overstimulated or excited brain? Under such influences the mind may be startled by the grandeur of its power, the boldness of its conceptions, and the prolification of its thoughts; but we must be careful how we accept this bewildering display of latent capacity of the normal mind, and ascribe its action to the quickened impulse of the spirit's touch.

"A little learning is a dangerous thing;
Drink deep, or taste not the Pierian spring.
A shallow draft intoxicates the brain;
But drinking largely sobers it again."

It is evident to the careful observer that media for mental phenomena frequently represent what may be called mixed influences. That is, a spirit may get a partial control or power to manifest itself through the organization of the medium, while the will-power is but partially abeyant. When such conditions exist, the spirit and the medium will jumble their ideas, and the communications will be limp and unsatisfactory. This is an undeveloped phase of mediumship, and never to be relied upon. Indeed, the more thought I give this class of mental manifestations, and the more I see of them, the less confidence do I have in their trustworthiness. Still I by no means denounce them as entirely unreliable. I can not forget that to this class of media originally belonged Mr. Davis, when his great work, to which I have already called attention, was given to the world. I also remember that, while in profound trance, the grandest poem of the nineteenth century, "The Lyric of the Golden Age," was given to mankind through the organization of Mr. T. L. Harris. Others of almost equal distinction and value to the world could be cited, to show my appreciation of mental phenomena; but when I reflect on the many miserable shams I have seen, simulating spiritual control, I am almost led to exclaim against them all. If we had nothing better than mental phenomena to demonstrate the fact that the spirit-world was in communication with this, we might be satisfied with the testimony it furnishes; but as we have more direct, positive, and less equivocal evidence of this grand truth furnished by physical phenomena, it would be no great loss even were mental phenomena dropped entirely from sight.

When we see a chair move without a visible power to change its position, we must seek to discover the cause of its motion by every means we can employ. If we fail to find the source from which motion is obtained through the channels of sense, or the ordinary methods of reasoning, then we must employ new agencies in the investigation of the phenomenon. It does not enlighten us any to say that "the devil has a hand in the business;" neither does it improve our understanding to allege that "the chair is bewitched," or that a "wizard has woven a spell about it." Such shifts only show the poverty of your mind and the extremity of your resources. If you want to establish a reputation for ability and fair dealing, you must meet the case with clear ideas. These alone will secure confidence and favor. Do not dodge the *fact*, for it will outlive all your sophistries, and triumph in the end. The chair moves! Explain the law of motion as you may. Facts are the foundation of all philosophy. What philosophy can you offer to explain this simple fact?

While both phases of spiritual manifestations present claims for the recognition of their genuine character, I am free to declare I have more confidence in the physical than in mental phenomena. The first crystallizes itself in facts, the second diffuses itself in fancies. A fact is a central truth already established. The philosophy of a fact may be corrupted in the whirligig speculations of an erratic idealist.

Men do their own thinking; thought is the true standard of manhood. The royal stamp of individuality is affixed to the thinker only. When he speaks, he wields a power over the human mind. His thoughts are organized forces, compelling homage. Nature stamps him with nobility. Emerson lives a thousand years in advance of the pious multitude who mumble over a rosary or gabble responses before a perfumed altar. To him, how pitiful must seem the thoughtless throng who are harnessed by priests to pull the ponderous car of sect!

The mental phenomenalists are already clamoring for organization. A new worshiping sect is proposed, and chartered rights are invoked for their protection. Let sturdy men be alert, and slow to encourage the organization of a spiritualistic Church. This proposition comes from the "Greeks," those who would be high-priests in the new synagogue, or, from pitiful incompetents. What does organization mean but the surrender of your manhood into the hands of your officers? *Men* do n't think alike. Why should they act alike? Bigots and dogmatists form societies, and build Churches, and curse the world. Truthful, honorable, noble men and women are not clannish. Truth is as free as the air, as pervading as the sunshine.

Spiritualism is not a religion in a partisan sense. It is greater than this: *it is a science.* With no Church but the universe, with no creed but truth, with no formulated prayer to sustain it, it constructs itself a power to rescue mankind from the sin of ignorance, from the crime of false worship. In its selfhood it will stand the admiration of the world—hale and hearty, when the systems of religion now building churches shall have been forgotten, and their proudest edifices crumbled to decay. To surrender this science into the hands of a wily priestcraft, is to betray the dearest interests of humanity to its worst enemy. The fact is not changed, the guilt no less, or the enormity of the act mitigated in the least, because a multitude of crazy imbeciles or zealots do this degrading thing. The *vox populi* is not the *vox dei.*

Spiritual priests are no more to be trusted than others who claim in an orthodox way to be spiritual teachers. They shut their eyes, and then, with a "thus saith the Lord" authority, harangue their disciples. Whether they say wise or foolish things is not to the purpose; the objection is to the special privilege they have to speak without contradiction. No right to reply to a pulpit falsehood is granted, no matter how grossly your judgment may be insulted. The priest, it is asserted, is simply a medium through whose organization a returned spirit speaks. His assumption may be true, or it may be false. How are we to determine? We can not even "try the spirit," as the privileges of the order debar your questionings. That is the point of danger. A hook is put into your jaw that it may not open. "Believe, or be damned," is the language of our moral pirate. Beware of organization! As well tie your neck to a mill-stone, and plunge it in the sea, hoping to swim, as to freight your manhood with a creed and expect it to live. Consecration to the Church is death to the soul's development. Accept the benison of the priest, and you become a slave for life. The spiritual priest, while under the influence of Jesus, Swedenborg, or Socrates, demands the surrender of your judgment and the homage of your heart. He will soon make a similar demand when no such influence is claimed. This mischief will follow closely upon the heels of the first absurdity.

I once heard the spirits of Thomas Starr King and Colonel Baker speak through the organization of a Dutch woman; at least so it was claimed, and accorded by a houseful of half-fledged mental phenomenalists. Colonel Baker was perorating about the time I entered the audience-room, and, as soon as he had spoken his piece with a decided Teutonic accent, Thomas Starr King took possession of the wardrobe of this remarkable medium. O, but he was happy in his new inclosure! How he rattled around in that organization—did Thomas Starr King! Did I say he was happy? No: I meant it not! Like the caged starling, I fancied I heard him exclaim, "I want to get out! I want to get out!" It was a vile imprisonment for such a spirit as Thomas Starr King's. He essayed to speak—to tell us something of the after-life; but his voice was reedy, his language low, coarse, and ungrammatical; and to call it commonplace would be simply to compliment it. So unlike Thomas Starr King was this dialectical phonograph, that his nearest friend would have been the last to recognize his presence. How others felt while listening to this mental phenomenalist, I know not; but I left the place in disgust, and with a sense of compassion for the credulous man or woman who could for a moment believe that the disjointed and pointless utterances we had listened to were the axiomatic sentences of the classical King or the polished diction of the eloquent Baker. Before I had lost all faith in mental phenomena and human nature, I put a safe distance between myself and Dayton Street, where I had listened to the contemptible drivel.

It is sad to think how much of this kind of stuff spiritualism is made to father. It is growing less, I know; and for this we are sincerely thankful. But let us hasten the "good time coming" by every means that the end will justify, to abate the nuisance speedily and altogether; for, at the very best, "while it makes the groundlings laugh, the judicious grieve." The surprise is, that the great truth of spirit-communion can, under such absurd exhibitions, secure the thoughtful respect of men at all.

Spiritualism has too many sincere friends to permit either the buffoon or charlatan to bring upon it unmerited reproach, without rebuke. Its mission is too important to mankind to allow it to become the toy of the ignorant or the agent of the rascal. Its truths will bring all races of men together, and unite all peoples of the earth in a fraternal bond of fellowship. It proposes to abolish expensive and tawdry "plans of salvation," and in lieu establish a free intercourse between the natural and spirit world. Under its benign influence, ignorance, bigotry, slavery, and crime will gradually disappear. "Free thought and unrestricted inquiry" is the armorial motto of its power. Creeds that corrode with death the souls of men, will dissolve in its benignant light, as hoar-frost before the morning sun. Such a cause, let us hope, may never want defenders.

While I was investigating spiritual phenomena in Boston, the Southern Rebellion began, and monopolized so much of public attention that I was compelled to abandon the further prosecution of my object. Up to this time, however, the information I had acquired on the subject of spirit-intercourse, was of such a character as to give me new views of life and death, and to relieve the mind of a painful uncertainty respecting the destiny of the human spirit. It is not becoming in this place to enter more minutely into my mental experiences, than to say that I had studied the subject in every practical aspect, and was well assured in my mind that communication with the spirit-world was fairly established, and that but comparatively a short time would elapse before the truth would be universally admitted. With this conviction in my mind, I settled down to business, and for several years scarcely made any allusion to the subject of spiritualism, unless it was introduced by others in casual conversation. Even then, I said but little about it, as I found but few who could listen complacently to a candid statement of the facts, such as I had gathered in my researches after truth, and of which they had no corresponding knowledge or experience. "It can not be," said the Oriental prince, "that water gets hard, as you say. None of my people or myself have ever seen such a thing." Had the prince visited Boston, as I had, he would have discovered his logic to be faulty.

An event transpired in our family, on the 9th of January, 1869, which brought the practical lesson of spiritualism again prominently before my mind. It was the passage of my mother to the spirit-world. "She passed away quietly in the night." That was the short but expressive story that was told me when I reached home, the day after it had occurred.

She had lived in the form almost seventy-six years, an active and useful life. That was sufficient time to have matured her spirit and developed its faculties for the beginning of a higher life. Her transit to the spirit-world was to be expected at that age. Therefore the event was a natural one, and should have created no surprise nor excited any regret. She had fulfilled the measure of life, and the law of change had enfolded her in its loving arms.

Her old casket was well worn, but even when the "bright inhabitant" had left, it was still beautiful to the eye and tender to the heart; for it reminded us so much of mother. The loving associations of our whole life clustered around that inanimate form, and, as if in recognition of our thoughts, it wore the imprint of a smile upon the face.

My mother did not live in any fear of death. She had a desire to live to see her children settled in life; but was at all times prepared for the event, and cheerful in its contemplation. She and I had talked over the subject often, calmly, and without reserve. It was not a morbid theme with her. She surrounded herself with too many active duties; but she had thought maturely on the inevitable change, and had found peace in her soul. She said to me the last time I visited home before her death: "Napoleon, I will not be here long; death will soon stop my work; my age and bodily infirmity both tell me this; my life has been a busy and I hope a useful one to all about me. It will not be hard to die when my time comes. I think a great deal on this subject, more than I did in former years." . . .

"Your intellect gives no expressive evidence of decrepitude, as yet, mother; what makes you think you will soon pass to the higher life?"

"As I grow old," she replied, "I have new sensations, which, I think, are peculiar to age. When my slumbers are light, I have visions of beautiful landscapes and pleasant abodes, which no language I can employ will adequately describe. But what is most strange of all, these places are peopled by those I formerly knew when living on the earth, but who have passed long since to the spirit-world. At other times, when I am alone and most calm, I hear voices speak my name, and I recognize them as belonging to those who have long since died. It was only last week, while I was working among the flowers in the garden, I heard Aunt Hannah [her sister in the spirit-world] call distinctly, 'Polly! Polly!' and so real was it, that I answered aloud, 'What do you wish, Hannah?' At the instant I had forgotten your aunt was dead. *It must have been her spirit that called my name.*"

"Quite likely," I said; "and it was your interior sense of hearing that heard the sound. This is what is called clairaudience, or clear-hearing. The same change takes place in the sight. When impressions grow dim to the external organ, through age, it frequently occurs that the interior sight is developed, and takes cognizance of things which the natural eye can not see. You know old black Timothy that comes to prepare kindling-wood for us: he is ninety-five years old, and is a most remarkable man for his years. When he was here last, I asked him some questions touching this same subject of "second sight" and "second hearing," and he made answer almost exactly as you do. Being psychologized with religious ideas, he said he saw Jesus and Paul and John the Baptist (Timothy believes in water), and many other of the blessed saints, in his cabin every night, and heard them pray and shout, and have a good time generally.

"With your interior faculties not stimulated with religious ecstasy, you see John, Hannah, Peggy, Charles, Sam, and Thomas, the whole family of brothers and sisters, dwellers in the spirit-world, who await your coming to complete the circle so long since broken. That to which I wish to call your attention is the phenomenal fact that, as you grow old, and the natural senses grow dim, the spiritual faculties unfold, and sweep, with their powerful reaches, boundaries beyond the scrutiny of common ken."

On another occasion, when talking with my mother, she said:

"While we can, let us help one another to do right. Always do what you think is best for all. Selfishness will destroy your happiness. Think of others, and forget yourself. That is the best religion you can have. God is our common Father. Surely he wants all his children to be happy. He loves them all alike; the serpent and the dove belong to him. He has no favorites, nor acts by partial but by general laws. The unjust are never happy. Do your duty to all men; then only are you true to yourself."

These fragments of talk with my mother will serve to show the quality of her spirit, whose casket we were now assembled to look upon for the last time, ere it was buried forever from sight.

The preparations were complete, kindred and friends filled the house, and a settled sadness seemed to pervade the very atmosphere on the occasion. My sisters were stricken with grief, and lamentation was loud. Death had overtaken the best of us, and there seemed no comfort.

Something said in my ear, "Napoleon, speak!" I heard it distinctly, and it sounded like the voice of my mother. Believing it to be her wish, I rose to my feet and said:

"It is not my intention to speak a eulogy on the well-spent life of my mother. That you have already in your hearts, you who knew her best. We will improve the occasion by uttering a few reflections on the subject of death:

"It is customary to invest death with a frightful sense of dread or terror. Let us to-day honor this custom in the breach. Here, in the presence of its latest victim, whose mortal remains my eyes now rest upon, and the dearest object of my heart, I can say truthfully that no such feeling darkens my understanding or affrights my soul. But, on the contrary, this hour, death seems beautiful to me, and beneficent in its mission. We have no fear of that which is natural; and *it is as natural to die as to be born, and the one event is no more a mark of displeasure of the Almighty than the other.* Properly considered, death is really the complement of life, *a second birth*, through whose divine agency the spirit passes from a rudimental body to a more ethereal one, and from the earth-plane of life to one more beautiful, developed, and refined.

"We celebrate such an event by our presence to-day. The occasion should not be a sad one, and, if we understood it correctly, it would not be. Were it not for sundering the social ties, the rude separation of* love's strong ligaments, the occasion would

*Mr. Davis, in his first volume of the "Great Harmonia," pages 163–172, gives this lucid description of the process by which the spirit, at death, separates itself from the material body. It is somewhat lengthy for an extract in a work of this kind, but the universal interest felt in the subject of death, will be sufficient apology for giving it so much prominence in these pages.

"DEATH is but a DOOR which opens into new and more perfect existence. It is a triumphal arch through which man's immortal spirit passes at the moment of leaving the outer world to depart for a higher, a sublimer, and a more magnificent country. And there is really nothing more painful or repulsive in the *natural* process of dying (that which is not induced by disease or accident) than there is in passing into a quiet, pleasant, and dreamless slumber. The truthfulness of this proposition is remarkably illustrated and confirmed by the following observations and investigation into the physiological and psychological phenomena of death, which my spirit was qualified to make upon the person of a diseased individual at the moment of physical dissolution:

"The patient was a female of about sixty years of age. Nearly eight months previous to her death, she visited me for the purpose of receiving a medical examination of her physical system. Although there were no sensations experienced by her, excepting a mere weakness or feebleness located in the duodenum, and a falling of the palate, be one of felicitation and gratitude, rather than of grief and despair.

"The separation of the spirit from the body is a natural and beautiful process of law. There is noth-

yet I discovered, and distinctly perceived, that she would die with a cancerous disease of the stomach. This examination was made about eight months previous to her death. Having ascertained the certainty of her speedy removal from our earth, without perceiving the precise period of her departure (for I can not spiritually measure time or space), I internally resolved to be present and watch the progressive development of that interesting but much-dreaded phenomenon. Moved by this resolution, I, at a later period, engaged board in her house, and officiated as her physician. When the hour of her death arrived, I was fortunately in a proper state of mind to induce the superior condition; but, previous to throwing my spirit into that condition, I sought the most convenient and favorable position, that I might be allowed to make the observations entirely unnoticed and undisturbed. (For an explanation of what is meant by the superior condition, and of the nature and character of my spiritual perceptions, I refer the reader to the department of this work which is particularly devoted to the philosophy of psychology.) Thus situated and conditioned, I proceeded to observe and investigate the mysterious processes of dying, and to learn what it is for an individual human spirit to undergo the changes consequent upon physical death or external dissolution. They were these:

"I saw that the physical organization could no longer subserve the diversified purposes or requirements of the spiritual principle. But the various internal organs of the body appeared to *resist* the withdrawal of the animating soul. The muscular system struggled to retain the element of motion; the vascular system strove to retain the element of life; the nervous system put forth all its powers to retain the element of sensation; and the cerebral system labored to retain the principle of intelligence. The body and the soul, like two friends, strongly resisted the various circumstances which rendered their eternal separation imperative and absolute. These internal conflicts gave rise to manifestations of what seemed to be, to the material senses, the most thrilling and painful sensations, but I was unspeakably thankful and delighted when I perceived and realized the fact that those physical manifestations were indications, *not of pain or unhappiness*, but simply that the spirit was eternally dissolving its copartnership with the material organism. Now the head of the body became suddenly enveloped in a fine, soft, mellow, luminous atmosphere, and as instantly I saw the cerebrum and the cerebellum expand their most interior portions. I ing in the act to jar our sensibilities or excite our fear. Let us be calm now, while we examine the body of a human being, and ascertain how fearfully and wonderfully it is made.

saw them discontinue their appropriate galvanic functions, and then I saw that they became highly charged with the vital electricity and vital magnetism which permeate subordinate systems and structures. That is to say, the brain, as a whole, suddenly declared itself to be tenfold more positive, over the lesser portions of the body, than it ever was during the period of health. This phenomenon invariably precedes physical dissolution.

"Now the process of dying, or of the spirit's departure from the body, was fully commenced. The brain began to attract the elements of electricity, of magnetism, of motion, of life, and of sensation into its various and numerous departments. The head became intensely brilliant, and I particularly remarked that just in the same proportion as the extremities of the organism grew dark and cold, the brain appeared light and glowing. Now I saw, in the mellow, spiritual atmosphere which emanated from and encircled her head, the indistinct outlines of the *formation* of another head. The reader should remember that *these super-sensuous processes are not visible to any one except the spiritual perceptions be unfolded; for material eyes can only behold material things, and spiritual eyes can only behold spiritual things.* This is a law of nature. This new head unfolded more and more distinctly, and so indescribably compact and intensely brilliant did it become that I could neither see through it nor gaze upon it as steadily as I desired.

"While this spiritual head was being eliminated and organized from out of, and above, the material head, I saw that the surrounding aromal atmosphere, which had emanated from the material head, was in great commotion; but, as the new head became more distinct and perfect, this brilliant atmosphere gradually disappeared. This taught me that those aromal elements which were, in the beginning of the metamorphosis, attracted from the system into the brain, and thence eliminated in the form of an atmosphere, were indissolubly united in accordance with the divine principle of affinity in the universe which pervades and destinates every particle of matter, and developed the spiritual head which I beheld. With inexpressible wonder, and with a heavenly and utterable reverence, I gazed upon the holy and harmonious processes that were going on before me. In the identical manner in which the spiritual head was eliminated and unchangeably organized, I saw, unfolding in their natural, progressive order, the harmonious development of the neck, the shoulders, the breast, and the entire spiritual organization. It appeared from this, even to an unequivocal

"Scientifically and critically speaking, the human body may be said to be an aggregation of elements, or chemical vapors. Its purposes we have already stated. We now pass it to the analytical chemist,

demonstration, that the innumerable particles of what might be termed unparticled matter, which constitute the man's spiritual principle, are constitutionally endowed with certain elective affinities, analogous to an immortal friendship. The innate tendencies which the elements and essences of her soul manifested by uniting and organizing themselves, were the efficient and eminent causes which unfolded and perfected her spiritual organization. The defects and deformities of her physical body were, in the spiritual body which I saw thus developed, almost completely removed. In other words, it seemed that those hereditary obstructions and influences were now removed, which originally arrested the full and proper development of her physical constitution, and therefore that her spiritual constitution, being elevated above those obstructions, was enabled to unfold and perfect itself, in accordance with the universal tendencies of all created things. While this spiritual formation was going on, which was perfectly visible to my spiritual perceptions, the material body manifested, to the outer vision of observing individuals in the room, many symptoms of uneasiness and pain; but these indications were totally deceptive; they were wholly caused by the departure of the vital or spiritual forces from the extremities and viscera into the brain, and thence into the ascending organism. The spirit arose at right angle over the head or brain of the deserted body. But immediately previous to the final dissolution of the relationship which had so many years subsisted between the two spiritual and material bodies, I saw, playing energetically between the feet of the elevated spiritual body and the head of the prostrate physical body, a bright stream or current of vital electricity. This taught me that, what is customarily termed *death*, is but a *birth* of the spirit from a lower into a higher state; that an inferior body and mode of existence are exchanged for a superior body and corresponding endowments and capabilities of happiness. I learned that the correspondence between the birth of a child into this world and the birth of the spirit from the material body into a higher world, is absolute and complete, even to the *umbilical cord*, which was represented by the thread of vital electricity, which, for a few minutes, subsisted between and connected the two organisms together. And here I perceived what I never before obtained any knowledge of, that a small portion of this vital electrical element returned to the deserted body, immediately subsequent to the separation of the umbilical thread; and that that portion of this element which passed back into the earthly and he must tell us of what it is composed. He finds in it more primary elements than is found in any other mass of matter of equal avoirdupois. Indeed, all other forms of matter seem but to furnish

organism, instantly diffused itself through the entire structure, and thus prevented immediate decomposition.

"It is not proper that a body should be deposited into the earth until after decomposition has positively commenced; for, should there be no positive evidences of such structural change, even though it seems surely to have departed, it is not right to consign the body to the grave. The umbilical life-cord, of which I speak, is sometimes not severed, but is drawn out into the finest possible medium of sympathetic connection between the body and the spirit. This is invariably the case when individuals apparently die, and, after being absent for a few days or hours, return, as from a peaceful journey, to relate their spiritual experiences. Such phenomena are modernly termed trances, catalepsy, somnambulism, and spirit ecstasies. There are many different stages, or divisions and subdivisions, of these states. But when the spirit is *arrested* in its flight from the body, and when it is held in a transitional or mediatorial state for only a few hours or minutes, then the mind seldom retains a recollection of its experience. This state of forgetfulness seems, to a superficial observer, like annihilation, and this occasional suspension of consciousness, or memory, is frequently made the foundation of many an argument against the soul's immortal existence. It is when the spirit entirely leaves the body—only retaining proprietorship over it through the medium of the unsevered umbilical thread or electric wire, as it might be called—that the soul is enabled to abandon its earthly tenement and interests, for many hours or days, and afterward to return to the earth, ladened with bright and happy memories. As soon as the spirit, whose departing hour I thus watched, was wholly disengaged from the tenacious physical body, I directed my attention to the movements and emotions of the former; and I saw her begin to breathe the most interior or spiritual portions of the surrounding terrestrial atmosphere. At first it seemed with difficulty that she could breathe the new medium; but, in a few seconds, she inhaled and exhaled the spiritual elements of nature with ease and delight. And now I saw she was in the possession of exterior and physical proportions, which were identical in every possible particular—improved and beautiful—with those proportions which characterized her earthly organization. That is to say, she possessed a heart, a stomach, a liver, lungs, etc., just as her natural body did previous to (not her, but) *its* death.

"This is a wonderful and consoling truth. But I saw that the supplies of elements for this. They are held together, temporarily, by agents whose power may be neutralized by the genius of the laboratory. Why should we not look at this subject as the chemist does?

improvements which were wrought upon and in her spiritual organization were not so particular and thorough as to destroy or transcend her personality; nor did they materially alter her natural appearance or earthly characteristics. So much like her former self was she that, had her friends beheld her (as I did), they certainly would have exclaimed—as we often do upon the sudden return of a long absent friend, who leaves us in illness and returns in health—"Why, how well you look! how improved you are!" Such was the nature—most beautifying in their extent—of the improvements that were wrought upon her.

"I saw her continue to conform and accustom herself to the new elements and elevating sensation which belong to the inner life. I did not particularly notice the workings and emotions of her newly awakening and fast-unfolding spirit, except that I was careful to remark her philosophic tranquillity throughout the entire process, and her non-participation with the different members of her family in their unrestrained bewailing of her departure from the earth, to unfold in love and wisdom throughout eternal spheres. She understood, at a glance, that they could only gaze upon the cold and lifeless form which she had but just deserted; and she readily comprehended the fact, that it was owing to a want of true knowledge upon their parts that they thus vehemently regretted her merely physical death.

"The excessive weeping and lamentation of friends and relatives over the external form of one departed, are mainly caused by the sensuous and superficial mode by which the majority of mankind view the phenomenon of death. For, with but few exceptions, the race is so conditioned and educated on the earth; not yet having grown into spiritual perceptions; not yet progressed to where "whatsoever is hid shall be revealed;" realizing, only through the medium of the natural senses, the nearness of the beloved; watching and comprehending only the external signs and processes of physical dissolution, supposing *this* contortion to indicate pain, and *that* expression to indicate anguish,—I say, the race is so situated and educated that *death* of the body (to the majority of the earth's inhabitants) is equivalent to an annihilation of the personality of the individual. But I would comfort the superficial observer, and I can solemnly assure the inquirer after truth, that, when an individual dies naturally, the spirit experiences no pain; nor, should the material body be dissolved with disease or crushed by the fearful avalanche, is the individuality of the spirit deformed, or in the least degree obscured. Could you but turn your

Is there no truth in his science? Who will question eternal principles but the knave or fool? Ignorance may deplore the utterance of a fundamental truth, and grief may cry aloud its senseless wail over a

natural gaze from the lifeless body which can no longer answer to your look of love, and could your spiritual eyes be opened, you would behold, standing in your midst, a form, the same, but more beautiful and living. Hence, there is great cause to rejoice at the *birth* of the spirit from this world into the inner sphere of life; yea, it is far more reasonable and appropriate to weep at the majority of marriages which occur in this world than to lament when man's immortal spirit escapes from its earthly form to live and unfold in a higher and better country. You may clothe yourselves with the dark habiliments of woe when you consign at the altar a heart to a living grave, or when you chain the soul to breathe in an uncongenial atmosphere; but robe yourselves with garments of light to honor the spirit's birth into a higher life.

"The period required to accomplish the entire *change* which I saw, was not far from two hours and a half; but this furnishes no rule as to the time required for *every* spirit to elevate and reorganize itself above the head of the outer form. Without changing my position or spiritual perceptions, I continue to observe the movements of her new-born spirit. As soon as she became accustomed to the new elements which surround her, she descended from her elevated position, which was immediately over the body, by an effort of the will-power, and directly passed out of the door of the bed-room, in which she had lain (in the material form) prostrated with disease for several weeks. It being in a Summer month, the doors were all open, and her egress from the house was attended with no obstructions. I saw her pass through the adjoining room out of the door, and step from the house into the atmosphere. I was overwhelmed with delight and astonishment when, for the first time, I realized the universal truth that the spiritual organization can tread the atmosphere, which, while in the coarser, earthly form, we breathe—so much more refined is man's spiritual constitution. She walked in the atmosphere as easily, and in the same manner, as we tread the earth and ascend an eminence.

"Immediately upon emergement from the house, *she was joined by two friendly spirits from the spiritual country;* and, after tenderly recognizing and communing with each other, the three, in the most graceful manner, began ascending obliquely through the ethereal envelopment of our globe. They walked so naturally and fraternally together, that I could scarcely realize the fact that they trod the air. They seemed to be walking upon the side of a glorious but familiar mountain. I continued to gaze upon them until the distance shut them from beautiful manifestation of a natural law, but both are impotent to change the eternal order of things. For this we are grateful.

"The distinguished German scholar, Liebig, the chemist [since passed to the spirit-world], invited his class of students to his laboratory to witness the *chemical analysis, or decomposition, of a human body.* Pausing at the door, he turned to his 'three hundred' and said: 'This temple is devoted to science. We here seek to discover the great truths that are enveloped in matter. If any of you hesitate in the pursuit of knowledge, such as the crucible and retort unfold, do not enter here. God wants no wavering service from those who seek him. His laws are not past finding out, if we seek them diligently.'

"Before him on the table lay a human body. This he prepared to dissolve by chemicals, and with test conditions to secure the recognition of the elements composing its organization. The process was slow, the interest intense, but the fact was accomplished. He reduced one hundred and forty-five pounds of matter to an impalpable, elementary condition. The gases floating on the viewless air were inhaled into the lungs, such as were needed, by those present, and the remainder settled in the house, or escaped to the fields or woods, where they

my view, whereupon I returned to my external and ordinary condition.

"O, what a contrast! Instead of beholding that beautiful and youthful and unfolded spirit, I now saw, in common with those about me, the lifeless, cold, and shrouded organism of the caterpillar, which the joyous butterfly had so recently abandoned!"

were taken up by the respiration of flowers, vegetables, or the leaf-lungs of the forest-trees.

"His work being completed, he said: 'Gentlemen, the matter you have seen dissolved, has not been lost in any other sense than to the natural eye. It still exists in an elementary condition, and will enter millions of new organizations. Some of you have inhaled the oxygen, the flowers will take in the hydrogen and carbon, and the grain you see waving in yonder field will feed upon its liberated gases. The body which you saw can never be reorganized; it has passed away, and so will all our bodies, by the chemistry of the grave.'

"There is no appeal from the decisions of science. The destructibility of the human body for all time has been fairly demonstrated. It is senseless gabble to talk of its resurrection. Physical dissolution is proved—a *fait accompli.* It avails nothing what men may say, do, or believe to the contrary, the fact remains undisturbed. A million of undeveloped people can neither falsify a truth nor dignify a lie. We owe it to the world, that this fact shall be made known. There has been too much evasion, too much plastic rhetoric, displayed on such occasions. Let the truth be for once spoken, that, though the body is consigned to eternal oblivion, the spirit lives forever.

"Why, then, do we honor these ashes? Because it was in this temple her spirit dwelt. Here it gave out the only expression of itself, with which we were familiar. In this tenement her spirit unfolded in wisdom as it grew in stature and loveliness. To lay this casket aside with becoming respect, is the tender dictate of affection, and the only means we have left of expressing our feelings and appreciation of her worth. As we look on this familiar face, we think of the excellent qualities that adorned it in life. It is hard to disassociate them. But the light has gone out, the color has faded from the cheek, and the accents of love have died forever on these motionless lips. Still all that was essentially *mother* lives. Love never dies. The spirit is immortal."

These remarks reminded some people that I entertained opinions of my own; but, excepting this occasion, and the one to which I have alluded before, when I presided at Pardee's meeting, I had given no public testimony for ten years of my convictions and adherence to the teachings of the Harmonial Philosophy. Indeed, I had attained that maturity of age when men cease to parade before the world, uncalled for, the convictions of their mind, which quietly mold and regulate the actions of their life. Lapsing again into the pleasant retirement of my own home, after the death of my mother, the curtain dropped, as I supposed, upon the final act of life's busy drama, and I had only to live quietly, growing old as gracefully as circumstances would permit.

I was mistaken. Perhaps the wish was father to the thought. But on the 5th of February I received a letter from Mrs. Annie Wood, a resident of Louisville, Kentucky, in which she stated that herself and Mrs. Mary J. Hollis intended making a visit to Cincinnati for a day or two, on a "shopping" expedition, and that they would give me the pleasure of their company as guests during their short stay. Lady-like, there was a postscript to the letter, which read as follows:

> "P. S.—Mrs. Hollis is a trumpet-medium. I presume you have heard of her through the spiritual papers, as her manifestations have been reported quite frequently in the *Banner of Light* and *Religio-Philosophical Journal*."

My correspondent had presumed too much. I had never heard of Mrs. Hollis up to that time. Her name was now first announced to me, and if she had been an embassadress from Kamschatka she could not have been a more utter stranger.

CHAPTER VII.

DARK CIRCLES—MRS. HOLLIS IN TERROR—EXTRAORDINARY SIGHTS—A NEW THEORY OF SICKNESS—A "WHAT IS IT?"

THE ladies arranged a programme to suit themselves. I was to meet them at the wharf on Friday, A. M., on the arrival of the steamer *General Lytle*, and convey them to my house. They would do their shopping on the same day—have Saturday for matinée and promenade, and attend church for the fashions on Sunday. Monday was the day fixed for returning to Louisville.

Accordingly, I was on the levee at day-dawn with my carriage, Friday, waiting for the *Lytle*. She was an hour late, in consequence of floating ice. At last the steamer came in, and the ladies were—not on board. That was very pleasant.

They had changed their minds, and had taken another boat. By this new arrangement, they arrived in the evening. As we were sitting to tea, the hack drove up with our guests.

"It is too bad," said Mrs. Wood; "but I'll just tell you how it was."

She did, to my entire satisfaction. She is immense in straightening a crooked programme. She has "a gift" in that way; most ladies have.

"You have forgotten to introduce ——."

MRS. MARY J. HOLLIS.

"O, I beg pardon. Mary, this is the doctor."

"All right, so far as it goes; but who is Mary Annie?"

"Why, Mrs. Hollis, to be sure. Did n't I write to you she was coming?"

"So you did. Mrs. Hollis, I am glad to see you, and hope you may have a pleasant visit. Take off your wrappings, and sit up to the table. Tea was announced just as you rang the bell."

In a few minutes the ladies were sociable, lively as crickets, and talkative as children.

"Is it your first visit to Cincinnati?" I said, addressing myself to Mrs. Hollis.

"No, sir. I once lived in this city, and consider it almost my native place."

"O, then, you are not a stranger here?"

"Well, I suppose the city has changed a great deal in fifteen years, so that it has outgrown my acquaintance to some extent; yet I am not wholly a stranger in Cincinnati."

"The old land-marks remain; still you will find many changes have taken place in that time. Are you a native of Kentucky?"

"No, sir. I was born in Indiana, and by accident became a Hoosier."

"By *accident?* That is a curious way to speak of a natural event."

"Why, at the best, it is but an accident where one is born. In 1837, it so happened that mother was temporarily residing in Jeffersonville, and so I became a Hoosier. If my mother had been in Cincinnati instead, would n't I have been a Buckeye?"

"Certainly."

This short introductory colloquy will show that Mrs. Hollis is not a simpering sentimentalist. It must be remembered that she is the mother of four children, none of whom were born where she at present resides. As she will be a conspicuous character in the remaining part of this book, this seems to be a proper and fitting place to give her a more general introduction to the reader. She was born, as I afterward learned, on the 24th of April, 1837, in Jeffersonville, Indiana, of wealthy and educated parents. She was the first-born of her mother's family, and was married, I believe, in her seventeenth year. In her early childhood she was slow to receive a school education; and was an exemplary member of the Episcopal Church, until she began to see spirits and talk with them. When this occurred, she gradually lost faith in the gown and surplice, and ceased to be a fashionable worshiper. With a spotless reputation, she has taken the vows of dedicating her life to the service of the spirit-world. That means a great deal more that we can find room to record in this place. Of her personal appearance I will adduce a few pen-sketches, delineating her "face and form," by acknowledged masters in the graphic art.

Colonel Don Piatt, the widely-known and able editor of *The Capital*, presents this picture of the lady in question:

"I was introduced to Mrs. Hollis—quite a handsome, dark-eyed brunette, weighing about a hundred and forty, and about thirty-five years of age. She is personally attractive, unassuming, and rather diffident. After her personal attractions, the chief characteristic that impressed me was the exceedingly frank and honest expression of her face. A judge of human nature would dismiss all suspicion of fraud, after taking one good look at her kind, gentle countenance."

Another distinguished journalist, F. B. Plimpton, Esq., a leading editor on the *Cincinnati Commercial*, who investigated spiritual phenomena in Mrs. Hollis's *seances*, and of which he makes able reports in letters published in the *Commercial* and *Capital*, writes personally of the "medium:"

"Mrs. Hollis is of middle age, but looks younger than she is; of good form, rather stoutish; has lustrous black eyes and hair, and regular and pleasant features. Her manner is rather retiring, always modest, as that of a cultivated, sensitive woman, who has, however, been enough in society to acquire an easy and graceful self-possession. On this occasion she was dressed in a light morning-wrapper, tastefully but plainly trimmed."

Mr. Reed, the chief editor of the *Cincinnati Gazette*, saw in Mrs. Hollis only "a demure face and soft figure."

Another writer in the *Commercial* said of her: "She is a woman of fine appearance, a brunette, with a fine head of dark hair, dark eyes, and beautiful face."

Similar sketches could be multiplied to almost any extent, but enough has been given to furnish the reader with a general idea of her style. The fine steel engraving will do the rest.

As I saw Mrs. Hollis for the first time at my tea-table, and in my parlor during the evening, I discovered her to be a woman of more than average intelligence, *not* diffident of speech, apt in her remarks, and quick in repartee.

The evening was passed pleasantly, and in conversation no allusion whatever was made to spiritualism or any reference to her mediumship. Had I not been previously informed that she was a spiritualist and medium, no clew would have been furnished on this occasion by which to discover either fact.

On the following day (Saturday), I accompanied the ladies while they made their purchases among the fashionable shops on Fourth Street. It was not until after dinner that Mrs. Wood spoke of holding "a dark circle" in the evening. I had a prejudice against "dark circles," and had almost vowed never to enter another. I had attended two, in which the Davenport brothers were the mediums, and they had failed to strengthen my belief in spirit communication. To be sure, I had heard "Johnny King" talk very plainly. The guitar was carried through the air, thrumming as it floated all about the room. My knee had been touched by a spirit-hand, and my handkerchief had been tied high up on the chandelier, requiring the use of a step-ladder to get it again; still I thought "some things could be done as well as others," and I doubted. To some extent I shared Mr. Davis's opinions of dark circles,* and concluded

* "Except for scientific investigation—that is, to test the delicacy and wondrous power of spirits over natural things—it will be found that 'dark circles' are valueless and injurious. As means of carrying conviction to the skeptical mind, the lightless sessions amount simply to this: persons by such evidences usually require periodical repetitions of 'facts' to keep their night-encompassed faith from languishing."

if Mrs. Hollis's spirit manifestations can only be produced in a dark room, that at the best her mediumship is no better than that of the charlatans noticed in a preceding chapter. To be frank on this matter, I had been the witness of so many worthless "manifestations" claiming to be produced either by the spirits direct, or through their agency, that it was as much as I could do to retain faith in the real facts I had gathered up after years of tireless painstaking. The proposition to hold a "dark circle" was not, therefore, entirely congenial to my way of thinking, and I only gave consent to join it that I might fulfill the perfect law of hospitality by pleasing my guests.

"Certainly," I said, "we will have a dark circle, if Mrs. Hollis feels like it."

A simple inclination of the head was the only assent she gave.

It was an ingenuous reply to my doubt, and placed the whole responsibility of holding the circle or not upon my own election.

I was in hopes by evening time the medium would be found with a "distressing headache," or "so much fatigued that we would please excuse her," or that "she was too nervous to go into the dark room." I was quite willing to excuse her on either of those pleas, or any other that, in the goodness of her heart, she might think of making; but to my utter discomfiture, not to put it in any stronger terms, she offered no such paltry plea, nor claimed exoneration for any reason. I was on the point of excusing myself from being present by pleading a prior engagement, but was in trouble how to shape one that would not betray my duplicity. I was not a member of any "lodge," "league," "club," or "society," choir, or prayer-meeting; and could not even claim to be a sympathetic member of the Young Men's Christian Association for the prevention of cruelty to animals; and so, in utter despair, I said, "Certainly, we will have a dark circle, if Mrs. Hollis feels like it!"

Justice requires that I should state that I had no special reason for this disinclination to enter a dark circle. It was on the general principle that I had no confidence in any thing claiming to be spirit manifestations, enacted in the dark. The dark circle enveloped the mind in doubt and mystery. It could offer no convincing proof to my understanding like the information of the eye. The ear is a good reporter of facts, but the eye is better. "What communion hath light with darkness," that we should ignore the use of the most important one of the five senses?

I had ceased to take any interest in spirit manifestations after, as I supposed, I had witnessed the whole range of spirit phenomena, ten, fifteen, twenty years before. It was not congenial to my tastes to go over the old trodden ground again, excepting to revive old associations; and these had not been pleasant in the dark circle. This was the churlish view I took of Mrs. Wood's proposition.

I might have omitted all this confession of qualms with entire propriety. I know this; but it comes within the line of my duty to journalize all the facts that have any bearing on the extraordinary manifestations it is my province to record in this volume. It gives me no concern how I may personally appear to the reader: I am here as a witness to testify to the truth. That is all.

It was only intimated that the spirits might speak in the dark circle. Nothing was said about the length of time they would speak, how loud they would talk, nor were any particulars given that might have added interest to the occasion. The trumpet, too, had been spoken of. What part was it to play in the dark? I could not tell, and it was hazardous to guess. I decided to await developments, and, meanwhile, to scrutinize closely all "manifestations" which came under such suspicious circumstances.

After tea, the ladies felt rested and refreshed, and did not complain a bit of "headache" or "fatigue." So, under instruction, I proceeded to darken the room by draping the windows. The room selected by me was about sixteen feet square, on the second floor of the back building, immediately over the dining-room.

Five adult persons, including my two guests, entered this room about eight o'clock in the evening, four of whom took seats in front of Mrs. Hollis's chair, which was placed in the middle of the floor, arranged in the form of a semi-ellipse. The horn was placed on end, about midway between the medium and the circle, and could, by a mischievous prompting of the mind, and an inclination of the body, be reached by any one of us. "I liked not that." The light was now extinguished, and surely ancient Night never presided with more "rayless majesty" over Chaos than it now did in our presence. No "pitying ray" penetrated crevice, crack, or corner, to "lighten or to cheer." There was an "awful pause" of silence, until Mrs. Wood began to sing "The Ever-green Hills," and I heartily wished myself on them. Any place but here, I thought; when, as if catching the impression of my mind, Mrs. Hollis asked:

"Doctor, what kind of a place is this?"

"Very oppressive and dark, Mrs. Hollis."

"I need not be told that; but what kind of a room is this?"

"A square room, as you saw; but why do you ask?"

"Because it is full of sick spirits."

"Do spirits get sick?" I asked.

"I suppose so, for the room is full of them."

"What do they complain of, and how do they look?"

"They seem to be only skin and bone. They cough and spit in the most sickening manner. I never saw any thing like this before."

"Can you ascertain, Mrs. Hollis, why these spirits come here?"

"No! There is a physician among them, who is prescribing for their relief. I am impressed to say he is a Frenchman. He has approached you several times, and placed his hands over your head and along your back, and then on corresponding parts of the sick person. When he does this, it seems to revive them, and they look more cheerful and encouraged."

"Do you not feel his hands touch you, Doctor?"*

"No. I can't say that I do."

"O, heavens! he is going to lay a sick person on my lap. I'll not allow it. Open the door, quick; let me out! I won't remain here another minute. I must get out of this place;" and, with a spring, the affrighted medium caught the latch, and opened wide the door.

When we returned to the parlor, her face wore the expression of fear, with the pallor of death. She seemed to be almost terror-stricken, and for a few minutes unable to utter a word. When sufficiently collected, she apologized for her "nervousness," and then asked: "What kind of a room is that? It is full of sick people, and they seem to use it as a hospital."

"O, that's my consulting-room. It is in that room I examine sick people. You are aware, Mrs. Hollis, that I am a medical specialist, and devote my

* "In all ages of the world," says a great writer, "these truths [the laying on of hands and magnetic manifestations] have been recognized and applied to the sick and the suffering, There have lived many individuals whose physical and spiritual constitutions pre-eminently qualified them to exert a powerful influence on the body and mind of others, even to the working of miracles and curing the lame and palsied. But while the ancients employed the indwelling virtue (or magnetism) in the curing of diseases, they unfortunately believed that human diseases were caused by wicked spirits or devils, and though Swedenborg regarded this superstition as a truth, of which the world in those days had manifold evidences, yet I am impressed to regard it as a great obstacle to the manifestation of pure and important principles. And I think that even yet the inhabitants of the earth are too much under the control of ignorance and superstition to understand the higher truths of psychological science. It is ignorance and false education that cause the human mind to manufacture a personal devil, and to build for him a fiery abode of vast dimensions."

attention exclusively to the treatment of thoracic diseases? Did you not know this? Has Annie not told you all about it?" I asked, inquiringly, to try to get a clew to the real source of her startling sight-seeing in the dark.

Mrs. Hollis answered: "I never heard of your special practice until this minute. Annie has told me you were a physician, but never, I believe, has she intimated that your practice was special in its character."

I was incredulous; and yet there was so much frankness in her statement, and so little apparent motive for deception or fraud in the matter, that I was mystified; and so I made a diversion in the line of thought by asking: "What of the horn? We have overlooked it in the scare. What did you intend to do with the horn, Mrs. Hollis?"

"The spirits talk through the trumpet."

"Do they entrance you when *you* speak through the horn?"

"O no! they use the trumpet themselves."

"But you mean that you speak for the spirits through the trumpet, when entranced?"

"I mean no such thing, sir. It is just as I say: the spirit puts the trumpet to its mouth, and speaks through it, just as you would."

"Why, I never heard of such a thing!"

"And because you have not, you seem to doubt its possibility."

"No: I hope I have too much modesty to say what is possible and what is not. Can you hear them speak distinctly?"

"As you hear me now."

"And can you talk back to them? Can you hold a free conversation with them?"

"Certainly. Why not?"

"Nay, I know not why; but will they answer me?"

"If you give them a chance, and they have the power and inclination to do so."

"Ay: that's the rub. How will I know whether they have the power and inclination?"

"In the same way you would make a similar discovery when talking to spirits in the form."

"Do they stand upon ceremony—*punctilio?*"

"Do you not?"

"But a spirit?"

"Is only the real man or woman out of the flesh?"

"Yes: that is true; but why do they speak through a horn, Mrs. Hollis? Why not, if they possess organs of speech, speak without the horn?"

"The spirits say the horn enables them to concentrate their power, to focalize the waves of sound. You know how that is."

"Do they ever try to speak without using the trumpet?"

"Yes: and some spirits succeed; but the sound is always very feeble, in comparison to what it is when spoken through the trumpet. There is an Indian spirit that can be heard, when he speaks, in any part of the house, without using the horn."

"How does it happen that he can speak so loud and not use the horn?"

"He is an Indian, and they are found, as a general rule, to have more power to manifest than other spirits. Then, again, he has been in the spirit-world so long that he has completely outlived most of the infirmities of his natural life; besides, he is almost a giant in stature, and possesses more strength than we find ordinarily among men."

"I was not aware that such distinctions existed in the spirit-world."

"Have you given the subject any thought?"

"I have not, and that is the cause of my ignorance. Have you seen this Indian, Mrs. Hollis?"

"A thousand times; he is now beside you, taking notice of every thing you say."

"I should like to know what he thinks."

"Perhaps not."

"Well, I mean I would like to hear a spirit talk on a subject that I was personally interested in. Do you ever hold any controversy with them? or simply listen to what they say?"

"They talk just as you would, observing all the proprieties of speech and general amenities belonging to polite conversation. If you can instruct them in any way, they will allow you ample time to present your information. As a general thing, however, you will find more pleasure in listening to them than in hearing yourself speak. The Indian is very interesting to most people."

"Does he speak often?"

"Yes: he belongs to the band that claim me as their medium. He can speak when others can not. He assists others to speak."

"Does he still wear Indian toggery?"

"Yes: his head decorated with feathers, and a mixed costume of blankets, skins, and ornaments."

"To what tribe or nation did he belong?"

"He was a chief of the Cherokees, whose hunting-grounds, in his time, embraced the states of Florida, Alabama, Georgia, and Mississippi."

"Does his name appear in history?"

"I do not know. He gives it as *Skiwaukee*."

"I'm sorry, Mrs. Hollis, I did not select some other room for the dark circle. Would it be too late to try another room to-night?"

"As you please," she replied.

"Yes, we will," said Mrs. Wood. "We'll try again in another room."

Accordingly, we all went into a spare room, and re-formed the circle just as it had been in the consulting-room. The trumpet was in its place, as in the first circle.

The lights had been extinguished but a few minutes, when Mrs. Hollis said: "That French doctor has followed us with the sick spirit! If he attempts to come near me, I will leave the room. I don't know what he means. He talks, but I can not understand what he says."

This declaration of the spirited lady seemed to have the desired effect. The presence of the physician and patient was no more complained of.

I subsequently learned in regard to this matter, that persons who die with exhausting diseases continue to be feeble for some time after they enter the spirit-world, and that they are frequently brought into the presence of healthy persons, from whom they inhale or absorb elements of health and strength, by which their wasted energies are restored. This operation would seem to exhibit the value of human magnetism to spirits as well as mortals, as a remedial agent.*

The philosophy of this treatment is to equalize magnetic conditions. Disease is superinduced by an excess or deficiency of this nervo-vital emanation from our bodies. Old persons rob the young of it, when they sleep together. The sick rob the healthy, when sustaining similar relations. The principle under consideration is, the ground-work of temperamental physiology, which determines compatibilities in all social relations. One person's touch and power will "sustain and soothe" you as a blessing. Another's will feel like a vampire and a curse.

It is a new thought to my mind, this furnishing a supply of elemental health for the use of sick spirits. May not the spirit-doctor sometimes take too much, and leave us in that exhausted state peculiar to typhoid and low-conditioned fevers? May not that large class of diseases, which are said to arise—*de novo*—in the human system, and for the origin of which our ablest etiologists are unable to account,

* "Every human soul," says Mr. Davis in Vol. I, page 286, of the "Great Harmonia," "is surrounded with an atmosphere more or less pure and influential. This atmosphere is an emanation from the individual, just as flowers exhale their fragrance. In consequence of this pure and inestimable endowment, or rather the result of the organization, the soul can and will exert a favorable or unfavorable influence upon contiguous individuals, but always in proportion to their approximation to the reciprocal state of positive and negative relations."

be traced to this cause? Don't answer hastily, I beg of you, but think over the proposition seriously. There may be more in it than at first seems.

But to return to the circle-room. After a short pause in the conversation, Mrs. Wood again sang a verse of a familiar song, and at the conclusion I heard distinctly a succession of sounds, such as could be made with the lips by blowing in the horn. They were crisp and explosive, like blowing in water through a straw. Mrs. Hollis and Mrs. Wood said they were spirit-voices, but I could not recognize any articulate words as they seemed to do. It might have been all right, and it might have been all wrong. I thought it best to hold my opinion in abeyance, for a short time at least. After several attempts of this kind, I did hear a voice say in a half-smothered whisper, "*We can not talk to-night; the conditions are very bad.*"

"Did you hear that, Doctor?" said Mrs. Wood.

"O yes: I heard *that!* What was it?"

"Why, a spirit, you goose! Did n't you hear it say, 'The conditions are very bad; we can not talk to night?'"

"I heard it; but why does it say so when it was talking all the time?"

"O, but you're smart! You do n't believe it was a spirit spoke at all. You'll soon get out of that conceit, my chappy," said Mrs. Wood, with animation.

"I hope so; but I guess we had better light the gas, if they can't talk any more. Blessed be light! What a relief after an hour in darkness—utter darkness!"

The horn had been slightly moved out of its place, nearer the medium; but, with that exception, no change had taken place in any of the appointments of the room.

Well, what do you think of it? I asked myself, as soon as I had time to gather my thoughts. The best conclusion to which I could come was, that Mrs. Hollis might be a mental phenomenalist, and, being in the dark, I could not tell whether she spoke through the horn with her eyes open or shut, nor did it make much difference to me which. As a spirit *seance*, I was less perplexed in my opinions; it had been a signal *failure*. Even as a source of entertainment and merry-making, it could by no means be construed into a success. I could see nothing in it, not even the point of a joke. It was too dark. The situation afforded a splendid opportunity, however for indulging in any amount of quiet mirth. That was the advantage of the dark circle; only this, and nothing more.

But what about the spirits?

O, bother the spirits! They could n't talk that evening. Did n't you hear them say the conditions were too bad? That's all I know about them. Those who know more, let them speak. We'll adjourn.

CHAPTER VIII.

SLATE-WRITING—STARTLING COMMUNICATIONS—MOTHER ANNOUNCES HERSELF IN A DARK CIRCLE—JAMES NOLAN SPEAKS FOR HER—A REMARKABLE TEST BY SKIWAUKEE—HOW I WAS NAMED.

AT the breakfast-table next morning, Mrs. Wood said: "Isn't it funny, Doctor, that you should have visitors all the way from kingdom-come, to be doctored?"

"It is rather a strange conceit."

"Conceit?"

"At the best, what else is it?"

"See here, my old chappy, you used to take a great deal of interest in spiritualism. Now, I want to know if you have gone back on it?"

"What kind, Annie?"

"Did you ever! What a question to ask a lady! 'What kind?'"

"You have it exactly!"

"Well, now, Master Nep, just tell me how many kinds of spiritualism you know of."

"Two!"

"Please state them, like a good boy."

"Yes, ma'am; the true and the false."

"What do you mean by that? Explain yourself squarely."

"By *that*, I mean that spiritual manifestations in the *light* are more to be relied on than those which take place in the *dark*."

"Did n't you hear the spirits talk last night?"

"I suspect I did!"

"You *suspect you did!* Well, that is cool! O, I see how it is! You suspect either Mrs. Hollis or myself as representing the spirits!"

"Annie!"

"Yes, you do; do n't deny it."

"Why will you embarrass me?"

"Fiddlesticks! I just want to tell you one thing, that you were never more mistaken in your life."

"Mistaken?"

"Yes, when you suspect that we have been trying to impose on your good-nature."

"How you talk!"

"You do n't believe the manifestations last night were genuine, and I know it."

"Did I say so?"

"Not in words, but in tones, looks, shoulder-shrugs, and pantomimes."

"You read closely."

"Accurately."

"Well, well, now that you have unriddled me, let us change the subject. Will we go to the St. Paul's to-day? You will see the most lovely church and the latest styles at the same time."

"As we are going home to-morrow, Mrs. Hollis will give you some slate-writing to-day, instead of going to church."

"Some what?"

"Slate-writing!"

"I beg pardon; but I do not understand you."

"Why, don't you know that Mrs. Hollis is a writing-medium?"

"I was not aware of it. Are you a writing-medium, Mrs. Hollis?"

"It seems so!"

"Only *seems?*"

"Of that you must be the judge. Have you a slate?"

"Won't paper do as well?"

"A slate will do better!"

I scanned her face closely to find the faintest trace of the "putty" medium's infatuation; but I could not discern it, if she had any. Her features were in entire repose, and made no revelation of such a weakness. It was an affliction I would have cheerfully escaped, had there been any way of retreat without grossly violating the proprieties of hospitality. I thought over the suggestion for a minute or two, and mentally complained that my mission was so unpleasant. "Here," I said to myself, "is another hallucination, and if it had been presented in some other than my own house, I would explode it with pleasure. But it makes a difference when those who are under your own roof are to be rebuked. They have a claim upon your protection so long as they are your guests. No matter what personal infirmities may afflict them, the law of hospitality requires them to be treated with tenderness and forbearance. Still, there is another view to be taken of the subject, which is quite as legitimate as the one presented. The guest is the recipient of favor, and it is not only an infraction of the law of hospitality, but unjust to repay kindness with ingratitude and injury. Why should this attempt be made to deceive me? "Well, I'll humor your inclination," I thought; "but it will bring trouble on your head. If your writing is as much a fizzle as your dark circle, I will speak of it as it merits; no more forbearance. Won't she hate me for it? Her suppressed rage will give a flaming brilliancy to those 'lovely eyes,' and how pitilessly she will sacrifice my 'good name' to her resentments. If you will expose yourself to criticism, 'Barkis is willin',' go ahead."

"Do you write by impression, Mrs. Hollis, or are you controlled by the spirit to write?" I asked, with a view of "drawing fire," that I might learn her position exactly.

"Neither," she replied.

"I am not acquainted with any other methods by which spirits write through media."

"No! you have a slight misapprehension of my mediumship."

"In what particular, Mrs. Hollis?"

"In supposing the spirits use my organization in any perceptible manner when they write or speak."

"When *they* write or—"

"Yes: I have nothing to do with it; and yet my presence seems to be necessary."

"I do not understand you, Mrs. Hollis. What you say—"

"Is a truth for those who can comprehend it, and an extravagance for those who can not."

"Well, but don't you do the writing with your own hand?"

"Bless you, no; the spirits do the writing."

"But you hold the pencil, do you not?"

"I do not touch the pencil."

"Who does?"

"If it be not the spirits, I can not tell."

"But spirits have no hands?"

"Perhaps they write with their wings."

"O, that's an absurdity."

"Which?"

"Your suggestion of *wings*."

"O, I thought it was your suggestion of *armless* spirits. To be serious, how can they hold a pencil and write, without the possession and use of hands?"

"But do they hold the pencil and write without your assistance?"

"I have told you I do not touch the pencil. All I do is to hold the slate under the table while the writing takes place."

"Under the table? Why under the table? Why not lay the slate on the top of the table, where we can see it?"

"I fear I can not answer you in a satisfactory manner, as I do not really understand why it can not be done. Those who witness the writing have different theories as to the way it is produced, but all agree in ascribing its execution to an intelligence independent of myself."

"But what is your theory?"

"I have a habit to first exhibit the manifestation; and afterward to offer no theory, but the fact."

"You are *level*, Mrs. Hollis. That is a safe rule. 'The smartest woman in America' could not do better than that. Observe that rule, and you will never get into trouble. Your prudence is worthy of commendation. People like to make their own discoveries. First give the fact, then the theory. Now, let me see! You want a slate and pencil; and what else?"

"A small table, with a plain top, and a shawl to throw over it."

"And a dark room?" I suggested.

"Not a bit of it!"

"In a light room?"

"Certainly."

"I'm glad of that. I like to see things. Will that little work-stand answer for the table?"

"It's the very thing. And bring that shawl that lies on the piano. Now give me the slate and pencil. All right. Here they go, under the table. Look how I hold the slate. It rests upon the four fingers of my right-hand, the thumb making the steady pressure on the top. You discover there is no place to rest the slate upon, and that it is impossible for me to handle the slate and pencil both so as to execute any writing on the former. You see, I sit apart from the table, with no part of my person in contact with it or under it, excepting the hand holding the slate. Now the arrangements will be complete as soon as you spread that worsted shawl over the table. Let it hang down all round, as far as it will reach. My hand is under the table, holding the slate. You perceive my wrist and arm are exposed. Now, if you can see the faintest motion of either, to give you the slightest suspicion that I do the writing, speak of it. Now, what do you expect?"

"To sit here until doomsday, if I am to wait until the spirits write on that slate."

"I hope not," was the only reply made to my faithless remark.

It was only a few minutes until I heard something, a tiny noise, like the faint "nibble of a mousie." It proceeded from under the table, and I called Mrs. Hollis's attention to it.

"They are writing!" she said, with as much composure as if it were not the most extraordinary thing I had ever heard of.

"Who are writing?"

"The spirits," she said.

There was a full light in the room. I watched the wrist and arm belonging to the hand under the table, and there was not the slightest twitch of a muscle or tendon, to indicate any movement of the fingers. This friction continued several minutes, when a succession of raps, as if with the end of the pencil on the slate, signified the conclusion of the writing.

The slate was now withdrawn from under the table, and, without examining it particularly, Mrs. Hollis handed it to me, saying: "I guess the writing is for you!"

The upper half of the slate was covered with writing. The letters were well formed, the words accurately spelled, and the sentences grammatically constructed. The reader will have an opportunity to judge of the merits of the composition.

The writing was executed in parallel lines across the slate, about the same distance apart as ordinary ruled lines on common letter-paper. The part of the slate upon which the writing appeared was most remote from Mrs. Hollis's hand. The fingers could not reach the writing by several inches, and had the slate been shifted, the writing would have been made upside down, or she must have possessed power to write under very disabling circumstances in this most difficult manner. A careful scrutiny of the situation enables me to say that it was physically impossible for Mrs. Hollis to do the writing.

Much as I was perplexed with the writing, when I came to read the communication apart from its mysterious origin, I was not a little surprised to find the name of a sister, long since dead, attached to it. As the note is of general interest, no apology is offered for presenting it to the reader. It was as follows:

> "MY DEAR BROTHER,—Every day furnishes some new testimony to establish the great truth that individual life does not terminate when death takes place. Life is a progressive lesson which all must learn; and death is but an event which passes the individual into a higher 'grade' of being, whether he be matured and qualified for preferment or not. This is universally known in the spirit-world, and many in the natural world already comprehend the same truth. A band of progressed spirits have surrounded this medium, to teach this glorious lesson to the world. They are mostly French. It is intended that you shall render assistance in this great work. Mother and I are often with you, and impress you when we can. EMMA FRANCIS."

"Has the doctor got a flea in his ear?" said Mrs. Wood, in her quizzical way. "What is it that has taken the talk out of him so suddenly?"

"What is it?" was my involuntary echo, as the only reply I could make. "This is certainly the strangest phenomenon I have met in all my spiritualistic experience. That name—"

"Is your sister's."

"How do you know?"

I don't know; I only *guess*. Else why call you brother?"

"But how came it there?"

"What?"

"The name!"

"Just as the writing came!"

"But how came the writing? It is that which perplexes me."

"Can't you tell?"

"I would not ask, if I could."

"Can you explain how the speaking was done last night?"

"Is that a banter?"

"Do you want a fight? ha, ha, ha! Here's more than a wind-mill for my gallant Don. The 'what is it.' Do you see it?"

"What has the speaking to do with the writing, Annie?"

"Do they not both belong to the same mysterious family?"

"Hardly. When a spirit says, 'I can't speak,' it sounds very much like a man saying, 'Now I'm dead!' We are at liberty to doubt the veracity of both."

"Bah! Did n't they tell you the conditions were too bad—that they could n't talk much?"

"*Much?*"

"That's what they meant?"

"Why did n't they say so?"

"Why do n't you tell how the writing is done?"

"Yankee!"

"Dutchee!"

"I can't speak!"

"Do tell!"

"Come, Annie, let us be serious."

"Agreed! How came the writing? Come, cudgel your brains! Let's know all about it!"

"'Pon honor, I do not know! Will they write again?"

"Who?"

"The thing—"

"Do n't you dare call your sister by such an opprobrious name! Ain't you ashamed to employ such an epithet against ——?"

"Well, the spirit, then, if you insist!"

"It's an ill-mannered concession; but it's better than *thing* or *no thing*. Mrs. Hollis, please hold the slate again for 'Uncle Nep.' I think he is on the anxious-bench. He has been an arrant backslider, and another conversion will do him no harm."

"Certainly," said Mrs. Hollis; "but please wash the slate first with clean water."

I did so, and wiped it quite dry with my hand. There was a dun spot on the slate, caused by iron pyrites, which served as a private mark to identify it, if need be. The slate was one I had used on my desk for several years. I gave it to Mrs. Hollis, who received it with her right-hand. I then placed the bit of pencil on it, when she put both under the table. After scanning the situation closely, and satisfying myself that there was no hocus-pocus attempted, I again spread the shawl over the top of the table, leaving the wrist and arm of the medium fully exposed to view in a good light. The slate was held about five inches from the top of the table, grasped in the manner I have stated, with the thumb on top, the fingers underneath.

It was only two or three minutes after I had completed my inspection, when the mysterious scratching on the slate began again. I could hear it distinctly, and it continued several minutes. The sound was irregular, just such as would be made by a person writing with a pencil. Again the shower of tiny raps was given at the conclusion.

"Before withdrawing your hand, Mrs. Hollis, permit me to look at the position of the slate."

"Certainly," she said.

I lifted the shawl from the little stand, and discovered the slate to be held in the same position, precisely as when I put the shawl over the table. No perceptible change had taken place, excepting that the slate was almost covered with writing. Mrs. Hollis, without reading the communication, handed it to me. The writing was in a large, free, bold hand, contrasting strongly with the lady-like hand of Emma Francis' note. It read nearly as follows:

"DOCTOR,—Our medium is not in good condition for giving manifestations. Last night we almost failed, and to-day her condition is such that we are almost afraid to tax her strength. This evening we will give you better manifestations in the dark circle. Your mother will try to speak, but may not succeed, as she has never uttered a human word since she passed to the spirit-world. Your uncle, Charles Odell, will also try to speak. Thomas Eller and Jacob Tyler desire me to announce their presence. JAMES NOLAN."

How mysterious all this is! Not only the writing, but the facts announced. I do not know what to think of it. My mother will try to speak, but may not succeed! Uncle Charles Odell will also try to speak! And, too, there are the names of my two brothers-in-law announced! How came all these names on that slate? If by Mrs. Hollis, how, first, did she hear of sister Emma Francis' name? She passed to the spirit-world nearly forty years ago—before Mrs. Hollis was born—and was but an infant when her little heart ceased to throb. I only remember her name. It is too much to believe, even could Mrs. Hollis have done the writing, that she could have known Emma Francis, Charles Odell, Thomas Eller, and Jacob Tyler. And who is James Nolan, who makes these startling announcements? The name is not familiar, and he may be a man of straw, or a "make-up," to play a part set down in the programme.

And yet my own senses condemn the supposition before I dare announce it. It would incriminate Mrs. Hollis and Mrs. Wood both. Turn which way I would, I met a dilemma. My judgment pronounced against fraud, and to admit the manifestation for what it purported to be, would unsettle foundations upon which society and governments rested. Personally, I was anxious to fathom the mystery to its "deepest depths." But how to proceed?

It now occurred to me that James Nolan said, "Your mother will try to speak to you in the dark circle."

This gave me new hope; for a man never forgets his mother's voice any more than she forgets her child. If my mother speaks, it will be in no uncertain sense. No matter; make the room pitch-dark, I will recognize her voice.

"Is n't it funny, Doctor, to get such letters without paying postage on them?" said Mrs. Wood, as she finished reading the letter on the slate.

"Rather funny, if it were not so serious!"

"Serious?"

"Yes: or will you let me into the joke, and tell me how the *thing* is done?"

"There you are calling your sister a *thing* again. I 'd rather run the risk of being called *a lady*, than to be considered in the more equivocal sense of a *thing*. Now, do stop that!"

"Then explain this matter to me. *What is it?*"

"That's as good as any other name, if you are afraid to call it spiritual phenomena. Call it a 'what is it,' and send for Barnum. Why, look here, Mr. Soberside, if your sister is writing you letters from the spirit-world, can't you be as jolly over the truth she writes as if she wrote from Paris? It is not necessary to cry about it, that I can see."

"That is true, Annie; but when we speak of the dead we should not indulge in levity."

"Why not, as much as when speaking of the living?"

"Because—"

"What?"

"Well, because—"

"Exactly. I know what you intend saying. You have not outgrown your nursery superstitions of death; and, you are afraid of *ghosts*."

"No!"

"Then why not always be truthful, whether you speak of the living or the dead?"

"Why not?"

"Yes: why not?"

"I speak the truth of both!"

"Then you know but little, or you would have been hanged long ago!"

"What do you say?"

"Disguise it as you may, you are too cowardly to admit the truth of what you have just witnessed."

"Cowardly? What of?"

"Public sentiment! You may call that *a thing*, if you please; for it is a detestable tyrant, and has no virtue in it."

"But, Annie, is it not unpardonable arrogance to set up your individual opinion against the majesty of the multitude?"

"Yes, if you know you are right and are too craven to say so!"

"Your courage is bravado."

"Your prudence is fear."

"What do you mean?"

"To drive this conviction home to you, that, say what you will, you are afraid to admit the truth, not so much because it unsettles your own belief, as the fear you have of Mrs. Grundy's gutter-snipes."

"I do not care to be unsettled. Is there any harm in that?"

"That is, if you have wedded a lie, you want to abide with it forever."

"Why, Annie!"

"Neppy!"

"You will make yourself obnoxious!"

"To whom?"

"Fashion!"

"Exactly. She is the ogress that startles your poor soul with flubdub, night-mares, and hideous dreams. She prescribes for her sickly brood what they shall eat, drink, and wear; and, as if her slavery were not sufficiently degrading, she emasculates your mind, and dictates what you shall think."

"There is some truth in what you say, Annie, I admit; but why break your lance at such a time?"

"Because there is a necessity for doing it. Here is a phenomenon which, in its importance to the world, no man can as yet properly comprehend. It contemplates a radical change in the vast empire of mind. Its mission is subversive of the present order of things. It will first destroy, then reconstruct, the social condition of the world; and yet you dare not look these facts squarely in the face."

"Admitting the spiritual origin of the phenomena to be true, still I can not anticipate such stupenduous results as you predict."

"You have not thought of it."

"That is true. And yet you must admit I have had some experience in spiritual matters.

"I know; but never in any like this. Here the

spirit, reclad with the elements of flesh, takes on the conditions of mortal life, and thinks and acts again as it did before it shuffled off its cumbrous coil of clay. Why, sir, do you see that death has lost its sting? the grave its victory?"

I never could argue well with a female. They have a perverse element about them that unsettles the steady poise of a man's mind. So I said:

"Mrs. Hollis, who is James Nolan?"

"He is one of the band of spirits that forms about me to give manifestations."

"You have a band of spirits about you! I remember, sister Emma said you had a band of progressed spirits, principally French. How is that? You are not French, nor of French extraction. Is James Nolan a Frenchman?"

"I believe not. He speaks of his personal history to those who desire it, with entire freedom, and will, no doubt, give you any information in regard to himself that he may have, if you solicit it."

The writing *seance* and conversation closed here.

When the time for holding the second dark circle arrived, we again assembled in the room to hear the talking. I should rather say, whispering. I still held my prejudice against the darkness; but, as I entered the room, I had a vague suspicion that I had been uncharitable in my judgments, if not absolutely unjust, in treating the former dark circle as I had. I proposed to atone for this by giving a more candid and respectful attention to any thing that might occur on the present occasion. This was not only due the ladies, but in no other way could a reliable judgment be formed or the truth be discovered. Prejudice and bigotry are so nearly allied in character and infamy, that we can not be too careful how we entertain either, if we would escape their noxious odor. Let us be discriminating and just.

After being again seated, as in the first circle, the lights were extinguished, and Mrs. Wood was called upon to furnish the music, and with a charming voice gave "The Old Folks at Home," and followed it with "Home Again."

This matter of singing or preluding the manifestations with music, is rather mysterious. I believe that almost every form of either Pagan or Christian worship is attended with music. It is thought to be more acceptable to Deity to address him in aspirated notes than in commonplace vocal sounds. But in the dark circle I thought the exception should be made, as it was not a place for either Pagan or Christian worship. Here the æsthetic was ignored, and all the faculties of the mind were to be kept wide awake.

The effect of music on the human system varies in its expression. If the sounds are harmonious, and the chant is an old familiar lay, we soon find ourselves in accord, and helping to hum along. Even the animal, the faithful dog, when the key-note of his sympanthium is struck, as with a reed-horn it may be, gives us the charming howl which so delights our ears. But that our spirit friends consider music an essential condition before they will either orate or jubilate, is, as I said, a mystery to me. The connection of wind and worship is a subject that may some day be more fully ventilated.

While the singing was going on, I heard *something* passing over the floor. It was like the delicate foot-fall of a cat, at first; but it was soon discovered to be the horn. The sounds grew louder and louder, passing from one side of the room to the other with increasing celerity, and seemingly coinstantial, until the horn banged and jarred every-where within six feet of the medium, and about two feet from the circle, making almost a continuous dinning racket for a minute or two. It was not worth while to dodge, as you might hit a post in the dark; so, after wiping the sweat from my forehead, I sat upright, asking myself, "What next?"

I was not long in suspense. A child's voice repeated rapidly the name "Fanny, Fanny, Fanny," not less than twenty times. It then in like manner repeated the word "mother." The voice was an agitated whisper, which Mrs. Wood instantly recognized as her little son, several years in the spirit-world. She explained that "Fanny" was the name of a pet spaniel, to which her child was very much attached, and an almost inseparable companion. Mrs. Wood had frequently met her spirit-child in the "dark circle," and he never failed to announce his presence in this singular manner, first calling his pet's name, and then his mother's. After his excitement subsided, he talked in a childish manner of the things he remembered in his brief earth-life.

The voice clearly belonged to a child. I sat next to Mrs. Wood while she conducted the conversation, and there was no affectation in the maternal interest she displayed. I managed to engage Mrs. Hollis in conversation several times, while Mrs. Wood and her child were talking; and there was no other in the room that could affect such a rôle of deception if their life depended on it.

Of a sudden, at least when not expected, the voice said "Good-bye, dear mamma, good-bye!" That was the last we heard from little "Lewie" during the evening.

There was no ventriloquism in this interview. I heard the impatient mother frequently ask her child questions before his prattle was ended. Then, again, before she finished speaking, the child began talking on something that had occurred to his fancy of more interest to him than what the mother was saying. In this way their conversations frequently *overlapped* each other, so that it was impossible for one person to practice a deception in this matter, no matter how dark the room might be.

While Mrs. Hollis, Mrs. Wood, and myself were talking about the child, we all heard, in a distinct whisper, the words, "Napoleon, Napoleon, my son!" repeated quite near me, and immediately in front of my chair. The accent was unsteady, but the words were clearly articulated, though low and slowly delivered.

I could not recognize the voice of my mother in that faltering whisper. Still I said, "Is that you, mother?"

"God bless you, my dear son! I am here!" was the instant response, though, like the first spoken words, they were delivered with an embarrassing deliberation, each requiring an aspirated effort to pronounce.

"Can I be of service to you in any way, mother?" I said.

A long interval elapsed without any response being given to my question. When it came, it was in a strange voice, louder, stronger, the words more distinctly articulated and pronounced. It said:

"Your mother has not yet learned to talk. She was assisted to announce to you her presence, but can not speak any herself to-night. She is very anxious to talk to you, but has not the power. I will speak for her, and deliver her messages."

"Who are you?"

"James Nolan! Don't waste your time on me; speak to your mother."

"Very well. Has mother any thing to say to me?"

"Tell my son I am happy, and glad he takes an interest in this great work."

"What work does she allude to?"

"These new facts in spirit manifestations!"

"If all this is really what it pretends to be, I shall indeed take a new interest in spirit phenomena. But how shall I know, Mr. Nolan, that you really represent my mother on this occasion?"

"TRY THE SPIRIT!"

"Very well; that is exactly what I desire to do!" And I will also try Mr. Nolan in the difficult part he has consented to play in this.

"Are you quite sure it is my mother you are speaking for, Mr. Nolan?"

"No, sir! This spirit says she is your mother, and gives her name as Mary Lockard Wolfe Jordan."

"The *name* is correct. But I wish her to give me

a better identification than simply announcing her name. Will she please state her age at the time of her death?"

"If she had lived until May, 1873, her age would have been eighty years. Had she lived until May in the year she died, her age would have been seventy-six years; but as her death occurred in January, her age was seventy-five years and eight months when she left the form." *

"I believe the information you give is correct; and, as she is so exact in her statement, will my mother please tell whether she has any brothers or sisters living or dead?"

"She says none are dead; all are living."

"Where do they live?"

"In the spirit-world!"

"O yes, I see!"

"She says we are all here, and the family circle is again complete. I was the last to come. John, Peggy, Hannah, Sam, Thomas, and Charles, all preceded me. You did not know Sam, Thomas, or Charles. You was too young when they passed away."

"Are any of your children with you?"

"Isabella and Emma Francis are here. They passed from earth in infancy."

"Can you name your children that are still in the form, and in the order of their birth?"

"O yes! Why not? You still doubt my presence?"

* I do not recognize any characteristics of my mother in this indirect method of answering my question. She always used plainness of speech, and never failed to speak directly to the point. However, the information, so curiously stated, is in every particular true.

"I can not help it! I am in the dark! If I could see you for an instant, no more questions would be asked. I hope you will be patient with me. This is a marvelous proclamation you are making to the world, and we can not be too critical in our examination of the testimony upon which it rests."

"You are right, my son; investigation can not injure the truth. Say to Mary and Henry and Charles (as I say to you) and John and Caroline, that death can not destroy a mother's love."

"You have done it accurately. You have mentioned the names of your brothers and sisters and children, living and dead, in the order of their births. That is a remarkable testimony favoring my mother's individual presence. But I have elicited the information by the direct question. Can you, of your own choice, tell me something by which I may be more positively convinced that my mother is present, and is really talking to me?"

There was no response to my question for several minutes, and Mrs. Hollis expressed her doubt as to whether there was sufficient power for them to talk much longer. At this juncture a wild and prolonged howl or hoo-o-o! startled all in the circle. It was the "big Indian," SKIWAUKEE. His presence was instantly recognized by Mrs. Hollis and Mrs. Wood, and it was soon apparent that they were on the most familiar terms with him. I think his voice might be heard in all parts of my house. It was not harsh, but preternaturally loud and long. It is this that startles you, and makes you think of red paint and the tomahawk.

After talking to the "mejum" and "singin' squaw" a few minutes, I was formally introduced to him, and at once was distinguished as "em old chief." He takes this liberty with every one, to give them such a name as pleases himself best. He is called "*Ski*" by those familiar with him, and in his conversation speaks quite loud enough to be heard distinctly. He has not yet mastered English grammar, and occasionally makes some very funny remarks in his quaint mixture of Cherokee and Lindley Murray. Addressing me, he said:

"Em old chief; want em test?"

"Yes," I said. "I wished my mother to give me a voluntary test—to state something unthought of and unsolicited."

"Em old squaw em here!"

"Well, will you ask her to give me a voluntary test, something by which I may be positively assured of her presence?"

"Do em old chief know how em got em name *Nopol'on?*"

"No! Can't say that I do! I think my mother had an admiration for Bonaparte, as mothers have for Washington, and so gave me his name.

"I tell em! Old squaw got em papoose. In em morning old Catholic squaw, Sanna Faul [Rosanna M'Fall] come see em old squaw and papoose. Em say what em call em papoose. Old squaw say *Nopol'on.* Old Catholic squaw get em much big mad, em go home and call em dog Bonaparte."*

* I do not think this anecdote has been mentioned in our family for forty years, and it is doubtful whether my brothers or sisters knew

"Skiwaukee, you have given me a startling proof of the presence of an intelligence which, if it is not my mother, it is certainly one connected with the history of our family."

Taking it all in all, this was the most remarkable *seance* I had ever attended. To be sure, the testimony came in the dark, addressing the understanding through the ears. But examine the whole drift of the conversation, and what could strengthen the presumption of my mother's presence but the added sense of sight?

I do not think it possible that any person in the room could have given such a coherent and unbroken chain of evidence favoring the actual pres-

any thing of the circumstances detailed by the Indian. I was only a child when I last heard the story. The main facts are given with sufficient fidelity, but a trifling explanation may be added. Mrs. Rosanna M'Fall was a devout Catholic, and, next to Beelzebub, she hated the name of Napoleon, who had robbed the Church and compelled its head to dance attendance upon him. For this he was hated.

On *particular* occasions, as in "harvest," it is said all jokes are free. So the morning after my mother's tribulation being Christmas, the neighboring women came in to say a good word and have their "crack"—Rosanna among them. She teased mother to permit her to name the boy, promising a present, etc., but it was no go. That prerogative she maintained as personal, and, to get even with the Napoleon hater, said she was thinking seriously of naming the boy Napoleon Bonaparte. This was as a spark of fire to a magazine of powder. Rosanna exploded her wrath against the Little Corporal, mother, and myself, until it became a question of metal. The whole affair started in a joke, but the big name clings to me still.

To show her disrespect for the name, and to annoy my mother, Rosanna got a mangy cur, and called him "Bony." This dog she would berate on account of his name with the vilest epithets every day in her back-yard, within ear-shot of mother. Her resentment against the name continued for several years; but at last she began to give me candy, and said she hoped I would not make as big a rascal as my namesake. *Skiwaukee's* allusion to this dog is very remarkable.

ence of my mother. When I review the *seance*, I am amazed.

We had, without intending it, prolonged the sitting to an untimely hour. Mrs. Hollis complained of feeling very much exhausted ; and, had it not been for the interest awakened by the astonishing tests exhibited, we should have all been in full sympathy with her feelings, or asleep.

CHAPTER IX.

A VISIT TO MRS. HOLLIS—HER FAMILY—A PREMONITION AND PROPHECY—HOW SHE BECAME A SPIRITUALIST—DARK CIRCLE IN WHICH A SPIRIT SINGS A GERMAN SONG—MANY TALK, AND ONE SHOWS ITS FACE.

THE morning following, Mrs. Hollis and Mrs. Wood started for Louisville on the boat. I now had leisure to calmly consider the merits of the manifestations which had occurred in the "dark circle," and to determine, in my own mind, what amount of credibility should be attached to them.

In the conversation I had had with James Nolan, it was affirmed that my mother was actually present, and dictated to him the information he communicated to me. This was a bold assumption, and it became necessary to examine it critically, to find whether it was true or false.

I was inclined to think that a judicious investigation would disclose the fact that the so-called spirit phenomena could all be traced to a mundane origin. In this belief I was strengthened by the circumstance that nothing had been communicated but what I already knew. I assumed if the spirits could talk, they would say something to entertain or instruct us—tell us something of their spirit-life, the spirit-world, rather than be rummaging through the "old storehouse of memory," picking out unimportant scraps of half-forgotten information from its waste-basket. How the "old storehouse" had been entered and explored, was to my mind the most interesting part of the problem presented for solution. The answer to this should be in no uncertain sense. It was claimed that the talking was done by the spirits of those who knew the facts communicated, and that it was from *their* own personal knowledge, not mine, that the information was derived.

There may be some truth in this statement. Besides, Emma Francis' note made an announcement that was not only unknown to me, but was unpleasant in its character, and which I rejected at the time as impertinently officious. Nevertheless, the talking was done in the dark—that invested it with a doubtful character. It is true that the ear reports as faithfully the things that are heard as the eye informs of the things which are seen; but does not the eye attest more *truthfully* than the ear? This proposition we will not stop to discuss farther than to record the trite axiom: "You can believe what you hear, but what you see is truth itself."

I demurred against admitting the claim that disembodied spirits communicated the facts presented in the dark circle, for the double reason that the information communicated was not only not new, but that it could have been obtained from personal friends, or those intimately acquainted with the history of my family. I did not make these charges, but these were the mental reserves upon which I rested; and until they were successfully proved to be untenable, I could not see why I should surrender my judgment by admitting the claim to be true. I know very well that this seems like a suspicion upon the integrity of my guests, but no more so than the situation placed them in. My study is the situation. I have nothing to do with personal feeling in this matter. *Per contra,* I am free to admit that I could not discover any purpose to be subserved in the interest of the ladies by the admission or rejection of these manifestations; so they stand without any direct charge against their "good repute." I go farther, and say that, so far as I could judge, it was impossible for the ladies to have done the talking under the existing circumstances. If either had attempted to do it, I would have detected the imposition at once. Nor could they have employed a confederate to do it without my discovery of the fact. "Blind though I am, I am not dumb!" In my own household I could not be deceived, and no other was present that the eye could see, even in the light. Still an intelligent conversation was maintained for an hour, not on important matters, I admit, but on topics of great personal interest to me. During all this time there was no effort made to introduce new, abstruse, or complicated subjects, or to mislead by sophistry, or disguise truths in glittering generalities. Such subjects only were discussed with which I was most familiar. There was no hesitancy in the speech, and the words were articulated so near my ear that I seemed to *feel the breath* with which they were uttered. Still they sounded natural. That again perplexed me.

While struggling, I admit, to find a natural solution to this talking problem, I was met with the still greater difficulty of explaining the phenomena of the slate-writing. This was performed, not in the dark, but in a sunlighted room, wherein good eyes could read the smallest print or thread the finest needle.

It is not my habit to retire from every difficulty that obstructs my passage in the rugged road to knowledge; so when I found that I could not get any light to my understanding while remaining in the shadow of the phenomena, I decided to carry forward my line of investigation in a different direction. The experience I had had with Mr. Mansfield taught me this lesson, that, to value spiritual phenomena properly, you must have some knowledge of the private character of the medium through whom it occurs. Tricksters do not make good mediums. Good character, like good blood, will show itself. It has more value in this business than in preaching, or in editing a paper. Whitewash may conceal the prostitutions of the pulpit and the press; nay, I sometimes believe it does; but the character of a good spirit-medium, one selected to represent the higher truths of the spirit-world, must be *sans* reproach.

With this purpose in view, I visited Louisville in the following August, to make arrangements with Mrs. Hollis to return to Cincinnati again at an early day, that I might examine this subject more leisurely at my own house. It was my own private enterprise, for which I was quite willing to pay.

I found her at home, in the midst of her family and friends. In Louisville, she is well known and highly esteemed as a lady of refined taste and irreproachable character. To the different members of her family I was introduced, and found them intelligent, interesting, and communicative.

Mrs. Kerns, the mother of Mrs. Hollis, is a venerable lady of quick, benevolent instincts and surpassing intelligence. With her I talked very freely, and studied the character of her child from her motherly stand-point.

I was invited to spend the day and evening with them, which enabled me to make the very observations I wished. I was made quite welcome, and the place felt home-like.

During the day many persons called for manifestations, principally for slate-writing, which I was permitted to see. These were given in the open parlor, in view of persons passing along the pavement or riding on the street-cars. There was no attempt to conceal any thing connected with this business. It was a fair, open transaction. The persons receiving the communications were strangers to Mrs. Hollis, had never before visited Louisville, and yet they bore ample testimony to the genuineness of the facts that were communicated on that wonderful slate when held under the table. I watched these people staring at each other, surprised when names were given of old friends who had long since been dead; and when some almost forgotten circumstance was again recalled by which their actual presence could reasonably be inferred. Tears would frequently dim their eyes as these startling revelations would appear upon the slate. Surely, I said, this can not all be affected.

People are bad, I know; but can all this be hypocrisy? These people look too honest to shed their tears for theatrical display.

Throughout the day I watched the play of excited feeling, passion, strong and weak, upon the faces of those who sat beside that little table. It was a fit study for the facile pencil of a Hogarth. Here human nature threw off her disguises, and, to those who could comprehend her sublime mysteries, laid bare her heart for inspection.

Toward evening, visitors began to grow scarce; and when the sun had just touched the horizon with his blazing periphery, glaring, as it seemed, like the unlashed eye of God, the last infatuated investigator stepped through the yard-gate, and followed the shadow of his head eastward along Portland Avenue.

"You have had a busy day, Mrs. Hollis," I said, as we sat on the porch, in the twilight of the evening. "The gentleman and lady last here seemed to be people of quality."

"A preacher and his wife in disguise!"

"In disguise?"

"Yes: preachers are not honest in their profession; so they suspect me for being dishonest in mine!"

"Not all, I hope?"

"No: but what I say of them is true, as a class. They bring with them bad magnetism, and, by law of association, attract undeveloped spirits about them. These will frequently communicate unsavory things, for which I am held responsible. I don't admire these people for that."

"But you should not lose your patience with the preachers. They are, you know, so influential in molding public sentiment; if you can convert one of them to a belief in spiritualism, you may impress a multitude."

"I do not lose patience with any one. I think, however, your estimate of the preachers' influence in molding public sentiment is in excess of the truth. I have yet to find the first one who has had the moral courage to make a fair exhibit to the public of such tests as have been given them at the writing-table or in the dark circle. As a class, they are too cowardly to speak of the interest they feel in the subject, and, Peter-like, they will deny having visited a medium before they have wiped the tears from their eyes which their spirit-friends have evoked. They mold public sentiment! No, sir: you are mistaken. They are miserable shams, and they know it. The multitude lead them by the nose, as it does the *editors*. They may play their pranks before high heaven, as painted and patched harlequins do before men, but that they either lead or mold public sentiment is a concession made purely through ignorance or charity."

"I am sorry to hear this report of the preachers. I thought them very much better than you represent."

"They are only actors, playing a part in the drama of life, affecting virtues which they do not feel. They are not what they seem, any more than is the donkey in the lion's skin."

"I hope private citizens are better than preachers and editors."

"There is not much difference.

'Mankind are unco' weak,
And little to be trusted;
If self the wavering balance shake,
It's rarely right adjusted.'

They simply lack the opportunity or the courage to be mean. Place them in the way of temptation, and the sturdiest of them fall from grace. 'Is thy servant a dog, that he should do this thing?' asked Hazael, of old. Had he been acquainted with preachers, printers, and politicians of modern times, it were needless to ask this question."

"You estimate human nature very poorly, Mrs. Hollis, and, least of all, the preacher, the printer, and the politician."

"Not more so than they deserve. I have more than common opportunities for knowing these people; and I tell you, if they should get their deserts, they would suffer badly!"

"What have they done to you?"

"Slandered me! They make false statements, and are shameless in their tergiversation. Speaking of these men as a class, they riot in falsehood. The preacher and printer have given currency to lies that are little less than infamous; while the poltroon of a politician plays 'puppy,' and barks while they bite."

"But, Mrs. Hollis, you ought not to complain of these people. I suppose they pay you pretty well for your time?"

"That is the general supposition; and herein is great injustice done me. I am represented as a mercenary person, and as plying my vocation for its emoluments. Never was there a grosser falsehood. This slander obtained such general circulation and credibility, that the municipal government of Louisville made it a punishable offense, both by a heavy fine and imprisonment, for any spirit-medium to practice their profession, without first having taken out what all considered a proscriptive city license. This was the joint work of pulpit-preachers, pothouse politicians, and boss-printers. O, they are a pretty set of mountebanks to stand in the way of God's eternal providence! Too craven to feel the galling fetters upon their necks, too stupid to read the signs of the times, as they are written on the forehead of modern science, they will be consumed as brambles in the billowy blaze of the New Era."

"But do you make no charge for your services?"

"I do not; and dare not, if I would. My parlors, as you see, are filled from morning till night. The spirit of curiosity and inquiry brings to my house all kinds of people from all parts of the country. My doors are open, and my time is placed at the disposal of the multitude. In this way my family are deprived of my services, and my expenses are augmented by the employment of additional help. Yet the crowd come and go without being reminded of the facts I have just stated. *I make no charge* for this new gospel of life; but the time is coming when *I will.* Ministers are petted and pampered with exorbitant salaries for preaching a *free* (?) gospel to purple-robed, shoddy pew-holders. Shall I be starved to death because the angels of God announce themselves in my presence? Formerly it was the rack, the wheel, the stake, the fagot, and the halter. Now it is *starvation.* Let us pray that God's will be done on earth as it is in heaven."

"But do none pay you, Mrs. Hollis?"

"O, occasionally a pittance, ranging in value from a dime to a dollar, is left as a charity upon my table; but in the aggregate such contributions would not pay for house-cleaning and the wear of my carpets."*

"You have not as 'soft a thing' of it as I fancied, Mrs. Hollis."

"About as 'soft' as Tom Hood's shirt-maker."

"Sitting at the table so constantly must exhaust you very much?"

"Yes: I get tired. I can only rest myself by stirring around, or doing something."

"Your mediumship is a very great mystery, Mrs. Hollis. I do not wish to tax either your strength or your good-nature; still, when you feel like talking, and are inclined to gratify my curiosity, nothing would give me more satisfaction than to know exactly how you became a spiritualist and a spirit-medium."

"O, I can tell you that in a few minutes, and may as well do it now as at any other time."

"Do, please!"

*I was informed, by friends, that it was not unfrequent for persons who were quite able to pay, to visit Mrs. Hollis for manifestations, who, after monopolizing her time for several hours, would leave without even returning her the poor acknowledgment of their thanks for the sacrifices she had made. I therefore urged her to correct this injustice by absolutely refusing to give her time as a gratuity to such *cattle;* and if the spirit-world was dissatisfied with this arrangement, let them select some other medium to do their work. There is not a preacher in the land who would, in her circumstances, give his time to the *rich* (or poor) for nothing. It is literally "casting pearls before swine." Why should she do it?

"When a very little girl, I was considered 'a sleepy-headed child,' and I was so slow to comprehend the value of the alphabet, that it was feared by ma and others that I would never surmount the difficulty."

"That's true," said Mother Kerns, who had taken a seat with us on the porch, to listen to the narrative. "That's true. I thought at one time Mary had softening of the brain."

"Indeed! Well, you have dismissed all such apprehensions now, Mother Kerns?"

"O yes: long since!"

"But we interrupted you, Mrs. Hollis. Please go on with the narrative."

"Whenever I would attempt to study, I would either go to sleep or see a spectral man beside me."

"A ghost?"

"I did not know. I was very much afraid of him, though he always spoke kindly to me. When I became reconciled to his presence, I began to talk to him, until mother would frequently say, 'Child, who are you talking to?' When I would tell her who it was, both ma and pa would say that it was only a 'trick of the imagination.' It was all a mistake. The man was only a figment of the mind, and I must'nt be dribbling talk to myself in that stupid way."

"Of course, I tried hard to obey my parents; but when I would retire to my chamber at night, and after undressing for bed, then I would see my room filled with people. These kept up a general conversation; and I became so excited and nervous that I would cry, and call ma and pa to come to me from the next room. This they always did; and, after hushing me to sleep, as they would suppose, I could hear them say, 'That child has worms; she must take some pink-root and senna tea.' As my experience was somewhat singular, I gradually settled into the belief that I was very visionary, and ought not to talk about these nightly visitants.

"Still, though I ceased to speak much about them for several years, these visions were as real to my apprehension as the most tangible thing to my sight or touch. Very rarely did I go to bed that they did not occur, and continue until sleep and forgetfulness surprised my excited brain.

"My father met with a calamity, which suddenly deprived our home of its head. It was a severe shock to us all—so unexpected and terrible.*

"One day I was visiting my grandfather, and, upon the occasion, he had invited the bishop of our Church (Episcopalian) to dine with him. During the conversation at the table, the bishop said:

"'I have been visiting the Fox sisters, near Rochester, New York, to hear the spirit-raps.'

"'And found them to be arrant humbugs, no doubt?' was my grandfather's reply.

"'O no,' said the bishop; 'there is something mysterious in these raps. I believe they are made by bad spirits, or perhaps by the evil one who ensnareth the soul."

"The conversation was prolonged to the end of

* Murdered for a large sum of money he had on his person, near Seymour, Indiana.

the feast, and I remember how strangely interested I became in what was said. My conclusion was, that I wanted nothing to do with spirit-raps, as they were produced by the evil one who ensnareth the soul.

"Two years after the above conversation, I was making a visit to the house of an uncle. One evening, several of my cousins gathered around a table in the sitting-room, and began their fun by asking the spirits to rap for them. I did not take any part in this, and gave but little attention to the entertainment, until one of my cousins said, 'Mollie, come here; your father has spelled out his name.'

"I was so shocked by this irreverent use of my father's name, that I felt a cold chill run over me as if I had the real Cromwellian ague. It was only for a moment, however; for I soon timidly, through curiosity, joined the circle around the table. My father's name was again spelled, letter by letter, until it stood in completeness before my astonished gaze. I thought of this for several days, and so intensely that, turn which way I would, I could see his face plainly before me. Sometimes it was clear and distinct, as when I had seen it in life; then again it was shadowy and obscure.

"Seeing my father as I did, and speaking of the fact to our minister, with the hope of obtaining some information on the subject of his present condition, I was astounded to hear that he had died in his sins, without the benefit of clergy, and that he was now placed at the mercy of God whether he would be saved or lost."

"O, how wretched I became in thinking over the

impending fate of my good father, for weal or woe, through all eternity. God held the decision in his capricious power whether my father should be saved or lost. It was mockery to talk of mercy with such ruin impending, such wretchedness ever present. 'I will not believe it,' I said. Come weal or come woe to my father, I will share his fate.

"There were times when I earnestly prayed for a change of heart, and there were moments when I felt I was a great sinner; but that my good father should be lost, was to me a thought of agony.

"While sitting with my children, one evening, musing of times past, my eldest child asked, 'Ma, do you believe every thing our minister says?'

"The question took me by surprise, and before I could guard my reply, I said, 'No, my son; he tells falsehoods as well as other men!'

"The child was astonished—not at what I said, but at the vehemence of my manner, and the emphasis of my words. As I met the gaze of his love-lighted eye, I almost began to reproach myself for this infidelity. And yet I felt I had only spoken the truth.

"At this time my husband was in the army, and my condition was such as to prey sensibly on my health. I wasted into a pulmonary decline, and my early death was not the most improbable event that might occur at any time.

"One night, while lying in bed, unable to sleep, I put a light on the table, and began reading, as was my habit, from our Book of Prayer. I had but barely commenced, when I heard distinctly a deep-toned voice reciting, in the most impressive manner, the

Episcopal burial-service. This it repeated again and again, from nine o'clock in the evening until four o'clock in the morning.

"I could not be mistaken in what I heard; and the repetitions were made so frequently, that I called my mother to ask whether she did not hear them too. I could not rest satisfied until we had searched the house in quest of the person who had, in this mysterious way, disturbed our peace.

"On the fourth day after first hearing this, my youngest sister was suddenly taken sick, and, after only two hours' illness, died. The same funeral service I had so mysteriously heard was now repeated over her lifeless body.

"Was this a judgment of God for my infidelity—the light of our household extinguished in an hour? And in the funeral service I had heard, was I to find the discontented murmurs of an impatient and angry Deity? Perish the thought forever! I will not believe the lie!

"Broken in health, and sick in soul, our family physician was called in to prescribe for my relief. His quick eye soon discovered that mine was a sickness of the mind, and not of the body. He said:

"'Don't give yourself any anxiety about your father or sister, Mrs. Hollis. I wish you were as happy as they are. And there is no good reason why you should not be.'

"'I hope so. But it will never be in this world; and I fear it will not be so in the next.'

"'Your despondency arises from perverted views of life and death. A little knowledge on this subject, outside of your Church dogmas, would do much to relieve your mind of its painful apprehensions. I have a letter at home, on my desk, that was written by Dr. Franklin more than a hundred years ago, which I will send you to read. It was written to a young lady in Philadelphia, who had lost a dear relative, as you have, and which, no doubt, was a source of great comfort to her.' *

"'I will be very glad to read it, Doctor. But don't you belong to any Church?'

"'No: I think for myself on the subject of religion, and incline more to a belief in the Harmonial Philosophy than in the creeds or dogmas of any Church, however *infallible* they may be pronounced.'

"'What do you mean by the Harmonial Philosophy?'

"'The philosophy that establishes the truth of

* "This letter," says the HON. HORACE DRESSER, breathes the sentiments of spiritualism, and is an exponent of those religious views which ranked that great philosopher and statesman, in the estimation of the clergy and the Churches, as an infidel."

"We are indebted," says the Chicago *Evening Journal*, of January, 1872, "to C. B. Nelson, Esq., of this city, for the privilege of presenting the following beautiful and characteristic memorial of Dr. Franklin to our readers. It has never before been published:

"FROM DR. FRANKLIN TO MISS E. HUBBARD.

"'PHILADELPHIA, *February* 12, 1756.

"'DEAR CHILD,—I condole with you. We have lost a most dear and valuable relative; but it is the will of God and Nature that these mortal bodies be laid aside when the soul is to enter into real life. Existence here on earth is hardly to be called life. 'T is rather an embryo state—a preparation to living; and man is not completely born until he is dead. Why, then, should we grieve that a new child is born among the immortals—a new member added to their society?

"'We are spirits. That bodies should be lent to us while they can afford us pleasure, assist us in acquiring knowledge, or in doing good spirit-intercourse, and which enables us to communicate with the dead.'

"'O, Doctor! can you believe in any thing so absurd?'

"'Absurd? Why, Mrs. Hollis, some of the most thoughtful, learned, and scientific men living are firm believers in this same Harmonial Philosophy; and there are a large number of persons who look at the subject in so serious a light, that they consider its treatment with ridicule or jest as personally offensive.'

"'But I never heard that spiritualism was of use to any body. Our bishop said that the spirit-raps were produced by the evil one who ensnareth the soul.'

"'Your bishop talks more like a zany than a man. To me, spiritualism is not only a reality, but one of the grandest truths that has ever been made known

to our fellow-creatures, is a kind and benevolent act of God. When they become unfit for their purposes, and afford us pain instead of pleasure, instead of an aid become an incumbrance, and answer none of the intentions for which they were given, it is equally kind and benevolent that a way is provided by which we may get rid of them. That way is death.

"'We ourselves, prudently in some cases, choose a partial death. A mangled, painful limb, which can not be restored, we willingly cut off. He that plucks out a tooth, parts with it freely, since the pain goes with it; and he that quits the whole body, parts with all the pains and possibility of pains and diseases it was liable to, or capable of making him suffer.

"'Our friend and we are invited abroad on a party of pleasure that is to last forever. His chair* was first ready, and he has gone before us. We could not conveniently all start together; and why should you and I be grieved at this, since we are soon to follow, and we know where to find him?

"'Adieu, my dear, good child, and believe that I shall be, in every state, your affectionate papa. BENJAMIN FRANKLIN.'"

* Alluding to sedan chairs, then in fashionable use.

to mankind. It has brought peace and consolation to many a suffering heart, and cheered many a dying pillow. It has opened the portals of the future world, and placed us face to face with the denizens of the great hereafter, and taught us that there is an omnipresent, impersonal God, who is the Father of all spirits, and that to love and worship him is man's highest duty on earth.'

"'Is spiritualism a religion, Doctor?'

"'Yes: but not a creed. It is the religion of science, which is above reproach and can not be reviled. It stands on the recognized phenomena of natural laws.'

"'Have you any preachers?'

"'Certainly! The earth, the mountains, the rocks, the sea, the stars, and the brave o'erarching firmament, all excite the wonder, admiration, and reverence of man. They *preach* to him in his hours of solitude, and they are ever present with him in his walks. These do not bear the impress of human art, but bespeak a power infinitely higher and nobler than man. The air we breathe whispers of an all-pervading God, and these are his works. Why should a grand religion hesitate to explain these works of the great Creator from the pulpit, or call willing science to her aid? Would it not be wiser to disseminate tracts embodying the simple truths of nature, rather than the effeminate fictions of the Young Men's Christian Associations? The sermons which the Creator has written on stones, and the hymns which he sings in the running brooks, are more potent for good than all the cant flummery of pulpit maw-worms, or all the dignified mummery of scarlet-robed cardinals or pontiffs. If religion be a serious reality, it must be exemplified in the works of God. In no other way can we comprehend or approach him. All the wisdom of mortals is but the veriest nonsense, if not derived from the teachings of Nature.'

"'But I do n't see what all this has to do with "spirit-raps," Doctor. I should think no respectable person would have any thing to do with them.'

"After looking me steadily in the face for half a minute, he said: 'Mrs. Hollis, do you know what you are talking about? What has *respectability* to do with this matter?'

"'O, I beg pardon, Doctor. I did n't mean you.'

"'Of course you did n't, and it would be very difficult to know exactly who or what you did mean. Now, I will forgive your offense on one condition; that is, that you will go with me to-morrow evening to a spirit-medium, to see and hear for yourself what the spirits do and say.'

"To this proposal I consented, as I did not wish to have the ill-will of the doctor; but no sooner had he left the house, than I began to repent my rash promise.

"While in this indecision of mind, and still reproaching myself for my indiscretion, the door-bell rang, to which I gave immediate attention. I found a gray-haired old man standing on the porch, who half-apologetically said:

"'Madam, I have a son in the army who serves in the regiment in which your husband commands. I have not heard from him for several weeks. I suppose the mails have been interrupted by the enemy. I come to learn whether you have received any information of the movements of the regiment of late, or any special news of the boys that would interest us home-folks?'

"After making suitable reply, and scanning the anxious face of the old man, he was about turning to leave, when he looked me in the face, and said:

"'I see you have a sister in the spirit-world, and she desires to talk to you. She bids me tell you, that in less than three months you will see her face; and in less than five years, you will be a public spirit-medium, giving the most remarkable evidence through your mediumship that the world has yet had of the truth of spirit-intercourse.'

"Good heavens! I exclaimed, what does all this mean? Have the spiritualists conspired against me? and have I no protection from the insults of these people? I sat down to my table in anger, and wrote a note to the doctor, in which I positively declined to go out of my house on the evening appointed to meet the medium. I called my brother, and gave him the note with instructions where to carry it. As I did this, a complete revulsion in my feelings took place; and, though not much addicted to this weakness, I broke down in tears.

"I did not send the note. So, on the evening in question, the doctor, my brother, and myself started to visit the medium. It was soon after nightfall. Still I had taken the precaution to conceal my face behind two veils, fearing I might see somebody who would recognize me going into a spiritualist's house. But we arrived safely at the door, which was promptly opened to our call, admitting us into an elegantly furnished and well-lighted parlor. Here we met an elderly German gentleman, to whom brother and I were introduced. With the most courtly politeness, he said, 'My wife will soon be here.'

"I was no longer embarrassed, but felt perfectly at ease, and never more happy in my life until the gentleman's wife entered the room, when I thought of her as a spirit-medium, and became again fearful of her extraordinary power. She was a tall, beautiful woman, with the most elegant manners, and a gentle, winning voice. She had a boy in the army of blue; so we soon made up to each other, and seated ourselves at the table.

"Here she became entranced. It was the first person I had ever seen in this condition. With her eyes closed, and a pleasant smile playing over her face, she said:

"'Sis, my darling, the old man told you the truth. You will see Sallie's face in less than three months, and in less than five years you will become a remarkable spirit-medium for giving tests to the public. You are a selected instrument for doing great work, and will be gradually prepared for the mission. Do not, my darling, defeat the purposes of the spirit-world, but keep your heart from guile and your head from prejudice. Sit by a table with your mother for an hour, every other night, with your hands resting upon the top, and in less than three months you will be well convinced of our presence. Good-bye! precious one, good-bye!'

"This communication was said to be from my father; but as part of it was an exact copy of that which I had received from the old man, and to whom allusion was made, I received it with 'a grain of salt.' Still, I determined to comply with the request, as I could see no harm in doing so.

"After my return home, I informed mother of what had taken place, and, contrary to my expectations, she approved sitting at the table, as requested. We attended to this regularly, and almost from the first we received, as signals of the spirits' presence, 'showers of raps' almost every time we sat. After two or three weeks' experience in the light circle, we were requested, through the alphabet, to darken the room, and sit in the dark. This we did, and it was so early as the second sitting in the dark that I saw a light about as large as a medium-sized hand, of an oval shape, as when the palm-surfaces of two hands are put together, with the fingers extended. This floated about the room several minutes, and passed over my head three times, growing lighter and larger as it did so, until it suddenly stopped a few inches in front of my face. It now gradually began to open, as a flower unfolds its leaves, when in the center of it my sister Sallie's face was perfectly revealed, more brilliant and beautiful than it had ever appeared to me in life. 'Thank Heaven!' I exclaimed; 'Sallie and father still live.' The vision soon passed away."

"How did it pass away, Mrs. Hollis?" I asked.

"It seemed to recede and grow dim, like a bird flying in the night, until it was lost to view.

"The predictions made by the old man and German lady have been singularly verified. In less than three months, I saw my sister's face; and, against my every thought and wish, I became a public spirit-medium in less than five years."

"It has become a source of great pleasure to you?"

"Yes: it has taken away from me the fear of death; but it has invited the reproach of friends and the slander of foes."

"But you need not care for these."

"It is not pleasant to be called bad names; to be held up in print as a knave or fool; to be deserted by your friends, and shunned as if afflicted with a leprosy; to be told that you will bring ruin on yourself and disgrace on your family. I would be less than woman not to feel this injustice keenly. And what have I done to deserve all this? Simply that I have discovered at my feet a jewel of rare worth, that has been trodden in the mire for centuries, and which I have picked up. For this I must suffer all this indignity, though its possession enriches the world. O yes! I do care; but I have made my vows to the spirit-world—and will keep them too—that, come what may come, I will steadfastly maintain the truth as I discern it."

This was about the gist of the conversation I had with Mrs. Hollis in reference to her mediumship. She certainly displayed some of the material of which moral heroes are made; and I have no doubt but, under test conditions, her courage and resolution to "suffer and be strong" would challenge the respect and admiration of all persons who were not themselves cowards by instinct, and base-born rascals by nature.

Having satisfied myself of the integrity of the medium's character, I entered the dark circle that evening with less suspicion in my mind than on any previous occasion. The circle was made up of neighbors, and one or two members of Mrs. Hollis's family. Among the former was Dr. Hugh Preissler, his wife, and their son Julius. Mrs. Hollis's mother was also present.

The circle was held in the front parlor, and, to fit it for the occasion, no other preparation was necessary than simply to close the window-blinds and the doors communicating with the hall. The light was then extinguished, and but a very brief time elapsed before a spirit-voice, addressing Dr. Preissler in good German, said:

"Wie gehts, Hugo, mein lieber Sohn?"

"Mutter, wie geht es dir? Ich freue mich sehr dich zu sehen," replied the doctor.

"Willst du mit mir singen?" again said the voice.

"Ja, Mutter, was wollen wir singen?" answered Dr. Preissler.

"Der Kukuk," said the spirit.

Hereupon the doctor, who had brought his guitar, and is an excellent performer, began to thrum in low tones a simple but very beautiful ballad tune.

After a symphony had been played, a voice, said to be Dr. Preissler's mother, sang most touchingly the following German song, in an audible and strangely sweet, clear voice:

"KUKUK."

Voice.
Guitar.
Ein Schäfermädchen wei - dete zwei Lämmchen an der
Hand, Auf ei - ner Flur, wo fet - ter Klee und Gänseblümchen
stand. Da hör - te sie denn oft im Hain den Vo - gel Kukuk
lustig schrein: Kukuk, Kukuk, Kukuk, Kukuk, Ku - kuk!

Once or twice the voice faltered a little, when the doctor assisted by sounding a note or two, which seemed to give it renewed assurance of its power. After this spirit-solo was sung, Mrs. Preissler sang several German songs, in which two or three spirits engaged, carrying the different parts of the music with judgment and precision. Dr. Preissler informs me that the "Kukuk" was a nursery ballad, which his mother sang to him when a child, and that she passed to the spirit-world in 1832.

As soon as the singing had concluded, Jimmy Nolan saluted every person in the circle, and called them by name. To me he said:

"Good evening, Doctor! I'm glad to see you! You have come a long way to satisfy yourself, and I hope you will not stop until you are quite convinced. Can I be of any service to you?"

"You can. Is my mother present?"

"She is; but she can not talk."

"Will you talk for her?"

"Yes: for a short time. There are a great many spirits here who want to talk; so your time is brief."

"I have nothing to ask. Has she any thing to say?"

"She says you have been very kind to ——, and she blesses you for it. She says, don't sell the house. He will have no home if you do."

"But is it not better to sell the house than to encourage the continuance of his infirmity?"

"O no: don't sell the house."

"But I will, unless you convince me that it is not best to do so."

"What will the poor boy do?"

"He must reform, and drink less."

"But you ought to be charitable, my son."

"Is it a charity, mother, to encourage —— in his degradation? Do you not see that the more means he has, the more he will indulge in his unfortunate habit? I deplore his condition as much as you; but is it not more wise to apply the remedy than to cuddle the disease?"

"Your mother says you are right; but it is very hard."

"On the transgressor it is; but is it not best?"

This was the substance of the conversation I had with my mother. It was short, and on an unpleasant subject, in which was introduced the name of one who is an object of deepest pity to his family and friends.

This familiarity with family matters is one of the most striking characteristics of the communicative Nolan. He seems to know all about your personal affairs. He next said:

"Marshal Ney and the Empress Josephine are here! They belong to your band."

"I was not aware of having a band."

"You are quite excusable for not knowing."

"I hope so. Ignorance ought not to be an offense!"

"It is not; but a crime!"

"A crime! In what particular?"

"In every thing that entails suffering on you. Ignorance is the devil which destroys your happiness, and unfits you for the higher enjoyments of life."

"But do you think we ought to be punished for not knowing a thing?"

"What I think has no important bearing on the question. That which *is*, is all that should interest us."

"Well, but there ought to be pardon for mistakes that are committed through ignorance."

"That would be asking, as a premium to ignorance, the suspension of natural laws."

"How?"

"Why, by not understanding the law of gravitation, you would suspend its action, lest it hurt somebody who walked over a precipice. Disease is the penalty of violated laws of health, as the hurt of the fall is a consequence and penalty for disregarding the law of gravitation."

"But, James Nolan, do n't God at any time afflict us with disease as a mark of his displeasure?"

"Always! Physical law is the tribunal before which he tries wicked saints and pious sinners."

"And does he make no distinction in his awards of punishments and grace?"

"Certainly! But, in his chancery, the verdicts of men are often reversed, and final decisions of justice made."

"Always in favor of the saint?"

"Rather always against the sinner, who is sometimes a conventional saint."

"The saint becomes a sinner, if he disobeys?"

"Certainly! Why not?"

"But, James Nolan, we have a great many saints here who are afflicted with bodily infirmity, who are 'patient and long-suffering,' as the man of Uz."

"Job had scrofula, and inherited the disease from his ill-mated parents. His father was not a saint. Job's condition is sufficient testimony to show that fact."

"Your opinions are a trifle irreverent."

"Bosh! Are they true?"

"But, James—"

"Don't be shocked, Doctor; you can stand it."

"But others, you know, may—"

"Take care of themselves. It won't do them any harm. I'm pretty well acquainted in this house, and, by frequently speaking the truth, protect them against the penalties of error."

"O, very well; if it is a free concert, we can all sing."

"Sing out!"

"You don't seem to have much reverence for good people, James!"

"I have great reverence for *good* people!"

"But you speak irreverently of Job's sores. Was he not a man of God?"

"You know what a sore is, Doctor! It comes either from depravity or poverty of blood."

"But you speak of Job as if he was only a common man."

"No: he was uncommonly sore!"

"But Job lamented much?"

"He had much cause!"

"He was true to God?"

"But not his laws!"

"How know you that?"

"His sores!"

"Do they make him a sinner?"

"They only proclaim the sin."

"Good health and purity of blood is your standard of saintship. Your religion is a physical one."

"Yes, and no. Good health is something to value. It is the reward of perfect obedience to natural laws. A man in good health is much nearer the standard of perfection than a man in bad health. Saintship is a figment of the mind, as air-drawn and subtile as the lovely phantoms, sylphs, and gnomes of the mystical Rosicrucians."

"But good health is only a physical condition, which the animal enjoys as well as man."

"And is that any reason why man should not enjoy it? Do you think it too good for God's creatures? Be careful how you strike St. Hog, or you'll hear a squeal on 'change. For shame, Doctor, on your puerile conception of the goodness of God. Let me tell you something, which you may already know.

"The purpose of human life is to mature a spiritual being. To this end a perfect physical organization is necessary. If such can not be had, the perfect spirit can not unfold itself. The perfect man must have had a perfect father and mother, inheriting wisdom as well as physical perfection."

Here James Nolan left me to my thoughts, while he spoke to different members of the circle, with the same freedom with which he had addressed me. He is certainly a wonder to every man who hears him. He speaks quickly and pointedly on every subject presented, and makes no mistakes, retractions, or modifications in his remarks.

After he had concluded, and other spirits had spoken, a brief interval of silence transpired, when suddenly there arose, like tiny rockets or fire-flies, from the vicinity of Mrs. Hollis's head, a number of spirit-lights. These floated in beautiful curvilinear lines around the room, passing sometimes very near our faces, and with rapid motion. They gradually lessened their speed, until one of these lights, rather larger than the rest, stopped for a few seconds in front of my face. While my attention was fixed upon the luminous body, I discovered it to be held by tiny fingers; and, almost coinstantial, the full face of a child appeared behind the light. The object could be distinctly seen, though only for a few seconds.

Several others in the circle were similarly favored.

The light emitted no radiance, and exhibited more the properties of phosphorus or "fox-fire" than it did of heat and combustion—a pale, bluish light.

The *seance* lasted about two hours, and furnished me much food for reflection.

CHAPTER X.

MRS. HOLLIS'S ENGAGEMENTS—TABLE-WRITING—A FRENCH COMMUNICATION TO THE AUTHOR—OUT-DOOR WRITING—SPRING GROVE—SPIRIT-HANDS HANDLING MONEY—THREE HANDS UNDER THE TABLE.

THE mind becomes peculiarly interested when it begins to inquire after the hidden truths of spirit phenomena. The desire for more information on the subject is unappeasable, the appetite becomes whetted and keen, the relish more exquisite, and the craving more intolerant. "I must know more of this," is the uttered or unexpressed resolution of every intelligent man that seeks to explore the mysteries of spirit manifestations.

Stimulated by feelings of this kind, I made arrangements with Mrs. Hollis for so much of her time as would enable me to examine carefully, and under the most favorable circumstances, the extraordinary phenomena occurring in her presence. For this privilege I agreed to pay her more than she was receiving from the public for the amount of time consumed. In making this arrangement, I was governed by the maxim, that "whatever is worth doing at all, is worth doing well." I reasoned, if these phenomena are true, a knowledge of the facts will be an ample compensation for all the time and money I devote to their investigation. If they are false, the sooner I am assured of that, the better for myself.

To afford me greater facilities to carry out my purpose, Mrs. Hollis consented to visit my house during the time, where the manifestations could be more critically scrutinized than in the house of a stranger. Her stipulation was simply a quiet room, with as little intrusion from the public as possible, and also that she might not be kept too constantly engaged, as her health had become somewhat enfeebled by too close confinement to the circle-rooms. Of course, in all things I acceded to her wishes.

My *first* engagement was for two weeks. This she began on the 15th of September, 1871, terminating it on the 1st of October following, when she returned to Louisville. She remained at home until the 1st of November, when her *second* engagement for six weeks commenced, extending to the 12th December. After this, she made a visit to New Orleans, where she spent the Winter, and on her return commenced her *third* engagement, for five weeks, on the 25th of April, 1872, and terminated it on the 1st of June following. The *fourth* engagement was for seven weeks, commencing on the 20th of August, and extending to the latter part of September. A month later, she began an engagement of four weeks, being the *fifth* in the series, and, after filling it, went south, spending the Winter months in Memphis and New Orleans. She returned home in the Spring, when I made my *sixth* and final engagement with her for six weeks, beginning on the 15th of March, 1873, and terminating on the 1st of May. It will be seen that I had of her time:

In the	first engagement, ...	two weeks.
"	second engagement, . . .	six weeks.
"	third engagement, ...	five weeks.
"	fourth engagement, ...	seven weeks.
"	fifth engagement, ...	four weeks.
"	sixth engagement, ...	six weeks.

Aggregating, during the two years, *thirty weeks*, or more than twenty-five per centum of her entire time, in which to examine or witness the phenomena recorded in the following pages. It is only fair to state that the testimony I offer was obtained under most favorable circumstances, and after patient, plodding, and persevering investigation. I left no reasonable means untried to discover the truth at the bottom of this great wonder. And it is but just to say, if I have not succeeded in my purpose, it was not to the lack of industry or good-will on my part that the failure is to be ascribed. There may be those who would have theorized more about the phenomena than I; but an apple is an apple! The fool and philosopher can attest alike, and with equal credibility, to that "fact."

But, now that I am about to begin a record of marvelous incidents, which, because they antagonize popular errors, will excite a great amount of unfriendly criticism, I am somewhat confused to know just exactly how to arrange them, that they may be the more compactly and clearly presented to the mind of the reader. My desire is to make a full and fair statement of what I saw, heard, and felt, with as little ambiguity as possible. In doing this, it is already apparent to my mind, after a careful survey of my notes and memoranda, that I will be unable to present more than a tithe of the matter in hand, without transcending the prescribed limits of my writing. I must, therefore, confine myself to representative phenomena, wherein

"But a part is seen, and not the whole."

Let that be borne in mind.

When Mrs. Hollis first came to my house, she was in feeble health, caused, as she said, by sitting too constantly in the circle-rooms. I thought it best, therefore, to delay holding *seances* for a few days, until by rest she had recovered her strength. It was not my intention to examine this matter hastily—to carry my investigations forward on a swell of excitement, that would leave me floundering on the beach of speculation, when the tide-wave of facts had ebbed from under me. I desired to make haste slowly, to familiarize myself with the conditions, and to become better acquainted with the tendency of the medium's mind. For I still adhere to the unfashionable conviction, that, if the mental character of a medium is unreliable, the manifestations occurring in the presence of such medium will, in some measure, be tinctured with the same characteristic. I, therefore, never entirely disassociate personal character with spirit-phenomena. Both are worth studying—the "Scylla and Charybdis," between which lies the golden mean of truth. A perfect instrument will make perfect harmony.

In a few days it was evident that the carriage-drives, morning and evening, over Walnut Hills, through the charming retreats of Avondale, and along the imperial highways of matchless Clifton, had a most salutary effect upon the medium's health. It was to her wasted strength the "*vis medicatrix naturæ*," and she soon announced herself well enough to begin work.

In reply to my inquiry, Mrs. Hollis informed me that, after sitting at the table for two or three hours, holding the slate, or in the dark for a similar length of time, she became so feeble from loss of strength that frequently she could scarcely get to her room before entire prostration would overtake her. I have since then seen her so much exhausted by sitting, as to fall unconscious from her chair; and that, too, while the spirits were giving the most astounding manifestations.

Allusion has frequently been made to this condition of Mrs. Hollis; and, by those who are most ignorant of the whole subject of mediumship, it seems to furnish a fertile theme for personal suspicion, stupid satire, and abortive wit. Addle-pated fellows may sneer and snivel at a truth they can not comprehend. So may a moth flap its painted wings against a rock; but what then?

The explanation is, that when the spirits write on the slate, or speak in the dark circle, or materialize their presence in the cabinet, they must always put the medium under contribution for a full supply of vitalized magnetism, which they make use of in giving the manifestation. By this is meant the element of strength — the life-principle which the medium possesses. It is possible for spirits to make a fatal demand upon the vital resources of the medium, and, from the observations I have made on the brevity of mediumistic life, my mind is not clear that this is not frequently done.

I speak of this circumstance more particularly now, because I must refer to it often in my descriptions of seances hereafter; and also that the ingenuous reader may understand what is meant when I say: "The medium became exhausted;" "Her strength failed;" "She complained of feeling sick;" "Her power gave out;" or, "She grew so weak that the manifestation stopped."

Pusillanimous people have, in their sickly conceits, sneered at these phrases, and commented on them as if they were admissions of half-concealed guilt. Of course, the drivel of such idiots only shows how much they "hanker after crow." Their moral nature is poisoned with dishonesty, and their mental condition can scarcely be distinguished from animal ignorance. Indeed, their capacity for enlightened criticism may be measured by the smallest decimal part of an intellectual cube. Well-informed men and women will seek to discover and explain the law; but chattering charlatans of the pulpit and the press defame those who espouse and wed eternal principles.

The mysterious manifestations I have witnessed in the presence of Mrs. Hollis may be arranged under three forms of expression; and it is my purpose to speak of them under these several heads, that they may be more clearly comprehended by the reader. The first is the mysterious writing in the light; the second is the mysterious talking in the dark; and the third is the mysterious materialization of faces, forms, hands, flowers, etc., in the dark, but which are exhibited in the light.

I have witnessed all these forms of expression in one and the same hour; but I have also seen so much diversity of manifestation, that, if I attempted to write of them in the order of their occurrence, it would be an endless task, and less instructive than if the phenomena were classified under proper heads. I propose, therefore, to record the marvels of the mysterious writing first; then, such as occurred in the dark circle; after which I will make a faithful report of the materializations.

When Mrs. Hollis began her writing, or table-manifestations in my parlors, I requested her to use different slates and pencils, such as I would furnish her from time to time. I have already described the method of holding the slate, and the caution with which I examined the table, to satisfy myself that it was physically impossible for her to do the writing. In all announced experiments in the future, it must be taken for granted that all these precautions were observed before the manifestations were given.

The writing-table has a peculiar and fascinating interest about it. You sit beside it, or in front of Mrs. Hollis, and while you engage her in conversation, you hear the friction of the pencil on the slate. It moves rapidly or slowly, making long strokes loud, and short strokes low. That is a curious thing to think about; but can you guess who it is that is writing? Try, for the fun of it! See how near you can come to the truth. You may mention the names of a score of friends who have passed to the spirit-world, those who would be likely to write to you if they could. Now, make your guess! It is none of those you have mentioned; and you can not think of any other person that would be likely to write to you, even if they had the opportunity of doing so. Be patient! The writing will soon cease, then we can see who has thought of us. There are the "raps" that indicate the completeness of the message. "Ah, who is this?" "Isaac! Isaac Pusey:" so it is! My old friend Isaac! Well, what does he say? Let us see:

"FRIEND WOLFE,—This is the second time I have written to thee since I passed from the form. How does thee do?
ISAAC PUSEY."

Well, is'nt that 'cute! Who would have thought of him writing?

"Who is Isaac Pusey?" asked Mrs. Hollis, as she read the brief note on the slate.

"He's an old friend of mine. He says he has written to me once before. I guess that is a mistake!"

As I said this, a hard rap sounded under the table, which indicated a negative reply to my remarks. I asked Mrs. Hollis if she remembered the name; but she could not recall it. I said:

"Friend Isaac, when did you write to me before? Please answer on the slate!"

The slate was held under the table, when the following was quickly indited:

"Through Mansfield, in 1860. Thee reported it in Davis's paper."

I referred to the *Herald of Progress*, and found his statement to be correct, my conjecture false, and so announced the fact. He immediately wrote:

"My memory is better than thine. Thee finds it hard to remember; we find it hard to forget."

I recognized this name. It belonged to a "friend," an old companion, with whom many pleasant hours of my early manhood had been passed. He was "native and to the manor born," in Chester County, Pennsylvania. That will account for his plain speech. But I do n't know whether this writing was executed by Isaac Pusey. Well, that is a matter of indifference to me. I take more interest in knowing *how* the writing was done. That is the curious point around which my speculations revolve. It may or may not have been Isaac Pusey that did the writing; but if he did not, who did? That is a leading question. It could not do itself.

I will try Isaac again. "Will you please tell me something about Columbia, by which I may know more positively it is you writing?"

The slate was held as before; and, while expecting a direct reply to my question, when the slate was withdrawn, the following line was all that was found written upon it:

"How do you do, uncle?"

The writer was evidently a different person; so I said, "Who is this?"

"George M. Booth," was quickly written.

"I'm glad you are here, George. Have you any thing to say?"

"Tell mother I have been here!"

"I will! Any thing else?"

"And Mary!"

"All right. What more?"

"I'm happy!"

"What next?"

"Father is here, and the rest!"

"What do you mean by 'the rest?'"

"I never thought it was this way! Grandmother, Jacob Tyler, Aunt Betsy, Uncle John Lockard, Charles Odell, Aunt Hannah, Nathaniel, Elizabeth, and Amanda."

"Give them my love. Can any of them write?"

"Good-bye, uncle; that's all!"

The preceding colloquy took place, one evening about sunset. Mrs. Hollis had been out riding, and had just returned. Before taking off her wrappings, I requested her to hold the slate, to see if any writing would come. The foregoing was the result.

It was, of course, a surprise. The facts in the case are these: I have a nephew in the spirit-world by the name of George M. Booth. His mother is my sister. Mary is the name of his wife. The names written on the slate belonged to kinsfolks, who are all in the spirit-world. Now, as to whether *George M. Booth*, my nephew, wrote the communication I transcribed from the slate, and have faithfully reported above, I can not, of course, tell. It may have been some other *George M. Booth* or somebody else representing him. I only know it was not Mrs. Hollis who did the writing, and that fact is sufficient for my purpose. If the reader will insist on knowing *how it was done, and who did it,* he must furnish his own explanations.

There is very little in either of the communications that is worthy of a second thought. The importance of both is pivoted on the fact that they afford testimony to prove that the channels of communication have been opened between the natural and the spirit-world. That is the point of interest with me.

The bare fact that a spirit can communicate at all in this manner is of importance to the world. It implies that a million of spirits may do the same thing, through the same general law.

To secure the better tests when I sat at the table, I very rarely expressed or entertained any desire that a particular spirit should communicate. I had reason to believe, "when my mind was made up" to hear from a particular spirit, whether they had the power to communicate or not, that I was more frequently disappointed than obliged. To be in the best condition is to be passive; let come what will, receive it quietly, and as gratefully as possible. If you disturb the passivity of the medium, you will certainly mar the excellence of your communication. Like a calm lakelet, mirroring every object with entire fidelity, must be the condition of her mind. The slightest agitation of the placid water will destroy the image, or reflect it in grotesque forms.

"Pshaw! I don't want to hear from you! I want to hear from dear Charley!"

This cool reception of a spirit, who, perhaps, was preparing the conditions for "Charley" to write, spoiled the whole arrangement, and the petulant idiot was disappointed. My habit was to remain neutral, and to permit any spirit to write that possessed the power. Give them welcome, encouragement, and, if need be, advice.

In pursuing this policy, I always obtained reliable manifestations. The conditions became so harmonized, that at times it was not *necessary for Mrs. Hollis to hold the slate at all, but simply to place her hands on the top of the table, while I held the slate beneath. The writing at such times would come the same as if she herself had held the slate.* That was the triumph of harmony over discord, and the key that unlocked the outer door to the mystery of mediumship. If I had entertained any unfair suspicion, up to this time, that Mrs. Hollis had been, in any culpable sense, the author of the writing on the slate, the reception of the following communication in French, while I held the slate myself under the table, entirely removed every shadow of such doubt from my mind.

I said, "Mrs. Hollis, as an experiment, allow me to hold the slate under the table, while you simply place your hands on the top, in full view."

"I don't think they will be able to write," she replied; "but I'll do it."

After cleaning the slate well, sitting opposite to Mrs. Hollis at the table, her two hands lying on the top, my left-hand resting on them, and with my right-hand holding the slate under the table, in a few seconds I felt it touched, then stroked or caressed; and finally I felt a pressure on the slate, and heard the friction of the pencil gliding over its surface. I spoke of it, I fear, with some excitement; for it was a new sensation, and a new experience to me. On withdrawing the slate, I was amazed to find the following upon it, written in good, legible characters:

"*Je veux trouver homme que est honnete voudrez-vous concerez vous bien ce que je vous dis.* NEY."

What did it mean? Neither Mrs. Hollis nor myself were qualified to translate the writing. So I copied it hurriedly, and may have made some mistakes in doing so. The writing was a little strange, and it may have been written incorrectly. I now regret that a *fac-simile* of the communication could not have been obtained. It would have been so much more accurate and satisfactory to the reader than the transcription I made of it. It might have saved such a useless criticism as the following from being made—useless, as it does not meet the object intended in presenting it to the public. The critic says:

"Why should the spirit of Ney write imperfect or ungrammatical French when disembodied, unless when embodied he could write no other? There is no such verb in French as *concerer.* The verb *considerer* is probably meant. And if writing, "I wish to find a man," certainly no Frenchman would omit the article—indefinite articles in French being the precedent of all nouns; nor would a Frenchman fail to repeat the *je* in the second sentence, for I take it what is meant to be said is this: '*Je veux un homme a trouver qu'est honnete. Je voudrez-vous a considerez-vous bien ce que je a vous dis.*'"

From these grammatical errors in the communication, the critic proclaims the whole an imposture

Are we, then, left to infer that it would not have been imposture had the grammar been perfect in the construction of the sentence? He tells us "what is meant to be said," but signally fails to tell us *who meant it.* I care little about the grammar or the French; for both are insignificant when you consider the greater fact, as to how the writing came on the slate. The admission that the writing is French is enough for my purpose; for I do not pretend to say it was Marshal Ney that did it, nor do I say he did not. The reader has permission to form his own opinions about the matter. It might have been some other Ney. Had friend Isaac Pusey communicated in French, I should have pronounced the writer an impostor; but the writing would have remained the same mysterious fact to be accounted for. Ney or no Ney, account for the writing. What is Hecuba to you, or you to Hecuba? Do n't slash at a phantom, when a fact is before you.

I soon began to apprehend that more marvelous things were in reserve than had as yet been exhibited. The writing on the slate was not to be confined to the table; but the power accompanied Mrs. Hollis wherever she might be, and could be employed under what seemed to be the most unfavorable circumstances. Thus, in our evening drives, I would often take with me a slate and pencil, and as a test, one evening, while crossing the Ohio River, on the Ludlow ferry-boat, Mrs. Hollis laid the slate on her lap, and covered it with the linen duster belonging to the carriage. She then took hold of it with one hand on the outside of the duster, and with the other held up the cloth, so as to form a canopy beneath. Amid the crowd and confusion and noise and clatter on the boat, Skiwaukee wrote several communications, commenting upon his "big canoe ride." Below Bromley, on the Kentucky shore of the Ohio River, is a cluster of locust-trees. Here, beneath the linen duster, for an hour at a time, the spirits have written many communications, while Mrs. Hollis held the slate. All that was necessary was simply to throw the duster over a thistle-bush or an upright stick, so as to form a small air-chamber beneath it, and place therein the slate and pencil. If the medium sat near the place, with her hand resting on the outside of the drapery, it was sufficient; the writing would take place.

One Sunday afternoon, with Mrs. Hollis and members of my household, I drove to Spring Grove. While the ladies were loitering over the lawns, and reading monumental inscriptions, I hitched the horses, and threw the carriage-robe over a small head-stone of a grave. Under this I placed a slate and pencil, and then called Mrs. Hollis to come and sit near. She did so, when almost instantly could be heard a scratching on the slate. When it was announced as finished, the slate was withdrawn, and found to be covered with written characters. It was "old Ski" again displaying his peculiar chirographic art. He has a terrible fist for writing; still we could make out clearly the following edifying message:

"Much big fun! Write em in big bone-yard! Much plenty bones; no spirums here! Spirums no care for bones! Spirums no come here; do n't care for em big fuss-fuss over em bones! So!"

Here is another opportunity for our carping critic to display his talent in detecting the faulty language of the Indian. Of course, the intelligent reader will understand that the object I have in view for introducing this communication, is to show that an intelligence independent of Mrs. Hollis did the writing. Before leaving the place, upward of twenty short communications were received in this manner, from what purported to be six different spirits; one of whom, a child named "Grace," reminded me that I had bought her a little airing carriage when she was yet but a "toddlin' wee thing," less than twenty years ago.

On another occasion, while driving through the country with Mrs. Hollis, I stopped before a gentleman's house, and called him to the side of my carriage. While engaged in conversation with him on business matters, the slate lying on Mrs. Hollis's lap, covered with the linen duster, attracted the attention of the gentleman by the usual sounds of writing. Of course, I had to explain, which only drew from the astonished man a smile of incredulity. He intimated that I was playing a prank upon him, until the slate was produced, when, to his utter amazement, he read an affectionate message, signed by a daughter's full name, who had been in the spirit-world over twenty years. "How wonderful!" exclaimed the surprised parent, with his voice almost stifled with emotion, and his eyes liquid with tears.

One evening I drove my carriage to the top of the large hill just east of the "Brighton," to give Mrs. Hollis a fine view of Mill Creek Valley, the city, and a most gorgeous sunset. While on this mount, "old Ski," with a pebble, wrote on a flat rock, beside which Mrs. Hollis sat, the following message: "Em go home! Mejum hungry!"

This "new commandment" was so peremptory, and the reason for obeying it so urgent, that we stood not "upon the ceremony of going," but went at once.

All of which tends to show that we are never alone, though our company may not be visible to mortal sense. It was this thought that inspired Mrs. Sigourney to write, "I never turn a beggar unrelieved from my door, for fear of offending the beautiful angel that guided his footsteps to it."

Generally, after returning from a ride, in the dusk of the evening, Mrs. Hollis would sit for writing at the little table. The power to write seemed to be greater then than at any other time in the day. I thought it might be owing to the invigorated condition of the medium after a ride; but have since been told that when the solar rays have been withdrawn from the earth, spirit-power is increased. Hence the necessity of absolute darkness as a condition to enable spirits to talk. Whether this is true or not, is not my purpose to discuss; but I only wish to notice the fact, and, in connection therewith, certain phenomena that I deem worth while to record.

"Ney" was a frequent visitor at the table, and wrote many short notes, to which I attached no particular importance. On one occasion, it occurred to me to ask him somewhat of the political outlook of European governments, and tell me what he thought of affairs as he saw them from his stand-point. This was in 1871, at which time the following were substantially his views:

"It is written in the destiny of all nations, that all men and women shall be equal before the law. . . . These principles will ultimately be established in the fundamental laws of all governments.

"Spain will cease to exist as a monarchy. Her end is nigh.

"Italy will struggle and triumph over the intrigues of the Pope and the Jesuits.

"Francis Joseph will receive another chastisement. The House of the Hapsburgs will cease to govern Austria.

"It will require an *avalanche* to crush the hosts of tyrannical priests that now govern France. *Napoleon will never return, nor yet will the Republic stand.*

Church rule is swallowing all kinds of liberal sentiment in the United States. Tyranny comes from bigotry. . . . An ecclesiastical war is imminent. Already its dark wing is spread over your land. It is so close that you can almost feel the hot breath of its cannon, and hear the drum calling for recruits."

One morning it was written by Ney, that, in the twilight of the evening, *spirit-hands would be projected from under the table.* This was a startling announcement, and excited much interest. Evening was impatiently awaited. When the designated time arrived, Mrs. Hollis sat, as usual, near the table. The different members of my family then selected positions on the floor favorable for seeing the hands. It was only about twenty minutes after we began to watch, when the selvage of the cloth began to shake at the end of the table. Very soon the points of four fingers were indistinctly seen, just below the tassels on the shawl. They quickly retired, and, after several minutes, returned, with more of the hand exposed to view. Indeed, all the fingers were fairly exposed to sight this time, about fifteen inches from the floor. These came again and again, until a full hand was fairly seen. This exhibition was repeated several times, when two hands were distinctly visible at the same instant. This was marvelous, and excited great surprise among the members of my household. We all saw the same thing at the same time, and sufficiently long to be assured of what we saw.

I now folded a new ten-dollar bill, lengthways, and held it just beneath the edge of the cloth, until the hands appeared and seized it. It was carried up to the slate held by Mrs. Hollis, where it was rumpled crisply, and creaked quite loud in the handling. It was then dropped to the floor. I next held my *porte-monnaie* near the edge of the cloth, when it was instantly seized and carried to the slate. My knife was also taken up; and very soon followed my comb and bunch of keys. These were rattled around on the slate for several minutes, and were then all thrown into the room, one by one, upon the floor, excepting the pocket-book. This was retained, and opened. The roll of bank-bills was taken from it, and, with as much dexterity and skill as a bank-teller could display, the notes were sent flying over the floor in every direction from under the edge of the table-cover. I gathered them up, and, holding them in my hand, requested the spirits to take the notes again and replace them in the *porte-monnaie.* This they quickly did, throwing it afterward to the floor, with the money all nicely folded and put in the proper pocket, not forgetting to fasten it with the clasp.

There was no money missing; and, "by that same token," in these degenerate times, I call them honest spirits.

After these experiments had been concluded, the writing was again resumed, and the spirits seemed to be in high glee over their success. I confess, my curiosity was aroused, and I determined to see more of this thing. I accordingly placed myself in such a position on the floor that I could command a view of the position of the slate, as it was held by Mrs. Hollis under the table. By slightly elevating the cover, I was enabled to do this. I waited until the writing commenced, and, as soon as it was fairly under way, I took a fair view of the situation. It was an inhibited look, a flank movement on the domain of the spirits, for which I was subsequently reproved. My object, however, was accomplished. *I saw Mrs. Hollis's hand holding the slate, and a well-formed hand moving over the top of it, as if writing. There were two others, not so distinctly formed, under the slate, but accurate in all the anatomical outlines of the human hand. The hands were not alike in size or shape. The one which I thought to be employed in writing was noticeably a large, masculine hand, with thick, heavy fingers. The two under the slate were slender, more delicately organized, and of different size. All these hands were seen to terminate at the wrist-joint, where they seemed to be lost in a hazy, cloudy aura.*

The desire to look had been gratified, but now came the perplexing problem to find out to whom these hands belonged. They were not attached to Mrs. Hollis by any visible connection, and, so far as

I could judge, floated about and acted without her volition or control.

I have spoken of this strange or singular experience to several sober-minded people, who never, until then, exhibited any doubts about the integrity of any statement they have known me to make. Neither did they doubt my integrity in this; but, to get out of a difficulty in an easy way, they allege that I was deceived; the hands were an illusion. I was quite willing to accept this statement in good part; but what of the hands that took my pocket-book, knife, etc., as already described? Four persons besides myself attest to this fact. All witnessed the same thing. Admitting their power in the one instance, why doubt them in the other? I am not so old that any of my faculties are impaired, nor yet so young that I would form a judgment on any other than upon the most accredited testimony. I may be fretted by doubts, but I will not allow my judgment to be swayed by passion. I am only bearing testimony to a fact which I do know.

There were three hands visible under the table in the positions I have described, besides the hand belonging to Mrs. Hollis, with which she held the slate. These were all in view at the same time. They differed in size and shape. I had sufficient time to make that observation, although they faded from my view while I was gazing at them. Had they been hands composed of flesh and blood, they could not have *faded* in this manner from my sight. The testimony of my eyes has never been brought in question. The same sense that recognized the natural hand of Mrs. Hollis testified to the presence of the three ephemeral hands. If it were capable of attesting the truth in the one instance, why not also in the other? Say, if you please, that I was optically deluded; but, then, I must insist that you are not a competent judge.

> "What differs more, you say, than crown and cowl?
> I'll tell you, friend—a wise man and a fool!"

But a valiant doubter said to me: "What of all this? Suppose I admit you have seen what you say you have—three hands under the table belonging to no visible arms—what does it amount to? Are you any wiser or better for it?"

These are impertinent questions. They do not relate to the matter in issue. My object is simply to testify to the truth. A *fact* is an organized truth, and as indestructible as time. Every fact we discover is a treasure to the world. Facts are the basis of all philosophy, and the great teachers of the human race.

It may be urged that I have been quite particular in speaking of these hands. That is true. I aimed to be critically exact. When we discover a fact, we must be right sure it is a "*fact!*"

CHAPTER XI.

SPIRITS WRITING ON PAPER—FRENCH AND SPANISH WRITING—LETTERS FROM JIM NOLAN AND NEY—NAPOLEON'S REINCARNATION PREDICTED—SIX LETTERS FROM JOSEPHINE—A SLANDERER UNMASKED BY SKIWAUKEE.

MANY communications were written upon the slate which were not at all intelligible, because of being written in languages I did not understand. Those that were written in English, I, of course, had a sincere desire to retain, because of the general interest they seemed to possess. Many of these I transcribed, and to some of them I have referred in the preceding pages. To most of them, however, I simply gave a casual reading, and then rubbed them off. I did this, however, always with some qualms. It occurred to me at last that there was no reason why spirits should not write as readily on paper as on a slate. If I could succeed in retaining their own writing, a double interest would be attached to what they might say. Copying a communication, and reading it in your own familiar writing, destroys its freshness, its novelty; the fragrance of originality is gone. Then, too, how much more the curious would be interested in reading a letter that had never been written by mortal hands! The very thought of holding a letter in your hand that had been traced by spirit-fingers, looked upon by spirit-eyes, and conceived by a spirit-brain, was more than interesting; it was fascinating.

I fastened a sheet of paper on the slate, and placed upon it a small lead-pencil. In a few minutes after Mrs. Hollis put it under the table, the writing began. The experiment was a success, though I was slightly "obfuscated" in my faculties by the first communication, of which the following is a *fac simile:*

Αγαμαι ο ετης ανσορειας

Ελευς

So much was assured. For the better conservation of this idea, I had constructed from a sheet of heavy tin, a rack or frame, which would retain, in a stationary position, a number of sheets of paper. This frame was made simply by turning a half-inch edge on one end and two sides of the tin-plate, which formed a groove or rabbit. In these grooves I fitted the paper, sometimes as many as twenty half-sheets of large commercial note.

With these additional facilities for doing business, the spirits worked with a will. They seemed pleased with their success in writing literal letters to their friends in the form. In this manner they wrote a number of quite lengthy ones to their friends living in different places, with the request that I would deliver them in person or send them by mail. I did this for some time, but soon discovered it was a thankless task I had undertaken to perform, and accordingly shut down on the "dead-head" business. There is nothing like making people pay for what they get. It quickens their appreciation marvelously.

It was admitted that many of these letters bore a close chirographic resemblance to those written by the putative authors while in the form. Others, however, did not exhibit the slightest trace of similarity. This was especially true of those who communicated for the first time. They seemed not to possess the knack of writing well at the beginning; but, by practice, gradually improved, until they not only attained their former skill, but even surpassed in style the penmanship of their earth-life. When investigating this subject through Mr. Mansfield, I noticed the great variety of styles in his writing, which satisfied my mind that different spirits controlled it at different times. Still, a large number of his communications were given in one strongly-marked and individualized form of penmanship. I spoke to Mr. Mansfield one day about this, when I was quickly informed by his control (General Seth Cushman, an uncle, I believe, to Charlotte, the distinguished tragedienne,) that but few spirits had the ability to write; and, in all cases when they could not, he acted as their amanuensis. I have reason to believe this statement entirely accurate, as it is confirmed by an example which came within the range of my personal knowledge. I have in the spirit-world an old "Auntie," who received her education at a time when schools were not so common as now. Being informed that the line of communication was open, she took a strong notion to drop me a letter from the spirit-land. As her head and hand were not in good reciprocal relations with each other, her head dictated the letter, to which her hand simply subscribed her X mark. Her amanuensis expostulated, but she said, in good Jack Bunsby style: "Never you mind; gis you write my name. 'Apoleon will know it *werry* well." And I did, bless her good heart!

Independent of the interest attached to these letters, as emanating from those we have been taught to esteem as dead, many of them are entitled to consideration for the intrinsic merit they display in thought and expression. It is my purpose to transcribe a few of these for the edification of the reader. I will select those only which possess a public interest.

One of the first letters I received on the paper *slate* purported to be written by *Marshal Ney.* It evidently was meant as a reply to a remark made by a gentleman, who said he could take no stock in spiritualism, unless it could be shown that it had done some good for the world. It was the next day, while I was sitting with Mrs. Hollis, that the following communication was received:

"MY FRIEND,—Time writes its mark on all things. We change by a wise and beautiful ordination. Earth would cloy us were it eternal. The Spring-time of our existence is a gladsome time, but who would not enjoy the Summer glory of life? It has been asked, 'What good can spiritualism do?' You need no information on this subject; but for those who do, I answer, It takes away the dark veil that has been so long over your earth. To know yourselves immortal is more than all else. It gives the assurance that your friends still live.

"Why should people reject a doctrine that tells you your friends still take an interest in you, that they love with the same love? It takes away all dread of death. It has carried all the thorns and thistles out of the dark valley your preachers so often tell you of. It has brought all your friends near you; in fact, it has brought all good, and no evil. The lessons it has taught you, have been of the purest moral character. To me it seems strange that even a *pagan* should reject it.

"I am, your friend,

Michael Ney
Marshal of France May 19—1819
Duke of Elchingen
Prince of The Moskowa

If any doubt has existed heretofore about the identity of the particular "Ney" who writes so frequently at the table, and speaks in the dark circle, the foregoing signature, which is a *fac simile* of the one attached to the letter, will settle the question effectually as to whom is meant, at least. The criticism of Ney's French may be all right, but this English composition will represent a more exact knowledge of the rules of grammar.

With some writing of a personal character intervening, the following verses were received, which are said to be written in the old Castilian language. As I have no knowledge of Spanish, I will furnish the original writing as copy to the printer, from which he will "set" it in type. If there are any inaccuracies in the composition, the printer must be held responsible for them, unless he has followed copy. I can not even attempt to punctuate this composition; and, without a knowledge of the language, it is difficult to know whether the letters forming words are accurately given or not, as both consonants and vowels are almost undistinguishable. Thus, *i, e, o, a, n, u,* look as much alike as the sheep in Elisio's "flock."

"JUEVES, *Diciembre.*

"Tras su manada Elisio lamentando
Mil reces este verso repetia
Ay quien se viera cual se vio algun dia
Vime yo tan señor de mi fortuna
Tan libre de dolor tan prosperado
Que no temi jamas mudanza alguna
De aquel primero y venturoso estado
Yo todo mi ventura se ha trocado
No soy ni yo sere quien ser solia
Ay quien se viera coral se vio algun dia
Ragu cuenta sobre mi
"MARTINEZ DE IRUJO."

Of course, I was very curious to know what all this was about, and, after a great deal of painstaking, I succeeded in finding, among my most valued friends, one who could give me a literal translation of the stanza. Here it is:

"THURSDAY, *December.*

"After his flock Elisio lamented,
Thousand times this verse he repeated:—
Will one see again what he has once been?
I have seen myself master of my fortune,
Free from grief and so prosperous
That I never feared any change
From that first and happy state.
But now all my fate is changed;
I am not now, or never will be, what I have once been.
Alas! who will see himself what he has once been?
Count upon me.
"MARTINEZ DE IRUJO."

Now, what does it amount to? Well, not very much; especially to those who take no interest in the misfortunes of Elisio. It seems to have been written by one who, in his life-time, stood upon the dizzy height of wealth, surrounded by all the luxuries that a capricious taste could crave; and, by some means or other, the wheel of fortune turned (and the old, creaky thing is always turning), when Elisio went under. He might have commenced speculating on 'change, or become a debauchee or stock-gambler, or a dealer in gilt-edged paper, or engaged in the oil business,—who knows? It is no matter what. He failed, and, like a paltroon (if he was not an old sinner), he whines and desponds as if the possession of wealth did not, ninety times in a hundred, make knaves, dolts, or impotents of its cowardly slaves. In this exhibit of himself, it is quite apparent that all he lacks is the mean capacity of a city thief or boss contractor, to enable him to "see himself as he once had been." And what had he been but a contemptible, shallow-pated, daisy-decked daffo-down-dilly of a whining, wealthy blatherskite? To be sure, he might have been an opulent pew-holder, whose gilded presence gave inspiration to the priest, while, in slumber, he dreamed his pleasant time away,—

> "Free from grief, and so prosperous
> That he never feared any change
> From that first and happy state."

Death seems to have shaken him up, and he fancies he has *fallen*, whereas he has only found his level. He has, to be sure, lost his paint, as a peacock may his tail. That only puts an end to his strutting; for,

> "Pigmies are pigmies still, though perched on Alps,
> And pyramids are pyramids in vales."

But my object in calling attention to this writing is simply to show that neither Mrs. Hollis nor myself should be held responsible for its appearing on the paper. The hypercritic, I know, will ascribe its evolvement to the *circuitous action of the spinozial gland, influencing the unconscious cerebrum of his own pig-head;* but such opinions never amount to very much, only with unconscious idiots.

On a subsequent occasion the following line was given, without any apparent motive, unless it was to demonstrate that they had selected the most incapable man upon whom to play their pranks.

Beligionum animos nodis eysolvere pergo

Baldwin

In this manner spirits would communicate in Greek, Hebrew, Italian, Swede, Celt, and Arabic, until a perfect maze of roots and derivations filled the paper. Of course, I discouraged all this contemptible nonsense, and threatened a *muss* if the tomfoolery was not promptly discontinued. I had no idea of squandering time on such useless scribble.

Very soon my opposition to the language tests—for that is what they were intended for—began to show its fruits. A number of good, readable communications were given in fair English upon interesting subjects. The following was addressed to Mrs. Hollis:

"DEAR MEDIUM,—The Spring-time of spiritualism has just dawned upon the world. Its primroses and daises are just peeping through the cold soil of a fast-vanishing orthodox

Winter. The fragrant flowers of Summer, in all their beauty, will soon be here to complete the transformation. Stand firm, medium; we will protect you with our might. You are surrounded by a host of mighty spirits. We have selected you for a grand purpose—a mission that a queen would be proud to fill. You shall be honored above woman. Stand firm, and believe in your friend, JAMES NOLAN."

If Jim Nolan is insincere in this note, it is the first time I have discovered him to be so. And yet the announcement of "a mission that a queen would be proud to fill," borders somewhat on the extravagant, I admit. But see what this woman has achieved already, and then say, if you can, where her "mission" will end.

It has been announced that Josephine Bonaparte belonged to my band of spirits. For this information I am primarily indebted to Jim Nolan. Since his announcement of the fact, I have received many letters which purport to be written by her. Some of these were written at my suggestion for public use; others were given voluntarily. I did not affix dates to these letters; so I will not present them in chronological order. This, however, is of no consequence, as there is no connection in the separate subjects discussed. Notwithstanding, there is some literary excellence displayed in their compositions—it is for no such purpose I present them. It is simply to furnish cumulative proof of spirit intercourse being established between the two worlds, with the added interest of learning what the views of such a woman as Josephine Bonaparte are since her translation to the Summer-land.

I will preface these English letters by presenting

a *fac simile* autograph note, which will be read with intense interest, by such of her countrymen, at least, who are hoping and believing in the second advent, or reincarnation, of Napoleon Bonaparte:

La nation Francias recevra une person à 1902 pour delivrer le pays de l'obscenité et bigoterie son nome sera Napolean Bonaparte Alors la gloire de la France retournera ave double brillant

Josephine Bonaparte

The following translation of this remarkable note has been made by one quite well qualified for the service:

(TRANSLATION.)

"The French nation will receive a person in 1902, who will deliver the country from obscenity and bigotry. His name will be *Napoleon Bonaparte*. Then the glory of France will return with double brilliancy.

"JOSEPHINE BONAPARTE."

It is of no public consequence what I believe about this prediction. It is unquestionably an important one to the French nation, if it turns out to be true. That's the point of interest to a Frenchman. The interest I attach to it consists simply in the phenomenal fact which it presents.

There was one extraordinary circumstance connected with the reception of this note, which struck me at the time with amazement. While Mrs. Hollis was holding the paper *slate* for the communication, there was a *feu de joie* of spirit-raps in several parts of the chamber. This was extraordinary; and while I was speculating as to the object of this grand display of power, Mrs. Hollis called my attention to the action of a chair, which sat in a remote part of the room. This was seen to balance itself on its two hind-legs, rocking to and fro for as much as a minute, describing with the back of the chair one-fourth of an aerial circle. It then began to move toward the table at which we sat, one leg pushed forward at a time, until half the distance had been overcome. It then put all legs to the floor, and slid over the carpet to the table, where it again resumed the balanced, oscillating condition on the two hind-legs, which it maintained for as much as two minutes, when it fell backward heavily. As it did this, the raps were loud, and so rapid that you can describe them only by saying they came *in showers.* At the same instant the self-propelled chair made its demonstration, the prophetic note of Josephine was being written under the table. It was subsequently stated by *Ney* that the demonstration was made by a band of French spirits, to express their gratification at the success of announcing to France and the world the reincarnation of their beloved *chief.*

The reader may take this statement for what it is worth. I only record the fact.

There was another curious fact in connection with this morning *seance,* which I offer no apology for recording. It was this: When Mrs. Hollis arose from the table to repair to the breakfast-room, downstairs, the chair that had excited so much attention volunteered a peripatetic movement to accompany her. It started from the center of the room, and slid by jerks to the door communicating with the stair-hall. Here the toes of its legs became entangled with the carpet-strip, and brought it to a stop. In a few seconds it was lifted by an unseen power over the strip into the hall, where it fell to the floor, when Mrs. Hollis fled in consternation downstairs at this unusual display.

In presenting the following letters, as already stated, I have no other motive than to increase the presumption in favor of their spirit-authenticity. Still, it would be sheer affectation to say they were devoid of interest to the intelligent reader:

(JOSEPHINE'S LETTERS, No. I.)

"MY DEAR FRIEND,—The memory of the past comes over me this morning, and almost overwhelms me with its power. My husband's voice I hear echoing through the nation, and the earth trembles beneath the heavy roll of artillery and the tread of his soldiers. I see his manly form, and feel all the pride and joy of being the wife of Napoleon. Like some distant strain of music are the shoutings of my people—*Vive la France!*

"But now, alas! comes that anguish of the heart, when we see the sacrifices that must be made for the good of the land. My beloved must be torn away, and the soil receive the baptism of the best blood of the people. All this passes before me. A few more dark, weary days, when the angel of death gave me a release, and kindly took me home to the quiet Summer-land. Here, with my beloved, my worshiped one, I rested awhile. . . .

"Napoleon startled me by saying: '*My darling, I can not rest! The people of France are calling me! Come, go with me!*'

"At first I felt that I wanted to stay in the spirit-land, but now all the fires of ambition that fills my dear Napoleon's soul, sweeps over mine. I join him in this great work, and only know the feeling,—Onward, Onward! No rest till France is FREE! JOSEPHINE."

The following letter presents a picture of "home-life" in the spirit-land, which requires but little exercise of the imagination to realize. The presence of birds, fruit, flowers, paintings, and books, surrounds the place with an atmosphere of home comforts, quite pleasant to contemplate. Napoleon's reincarnation and mission is distinctly pronounced. "But is it only a dream?"

(JOSEPHINE'S LETTERS, No. II.)

"MY DEAR FRIEND,—This morning, when I left my spirit-home, it was filled with music and beautiful flowers. O, what a contrast does earth present! I often wish I could take the material veil from your eyes, and let you look into my home as it is. And now remember, to you it shall be a resting-place when you come to the spirit-world. We have in the spirit-land all you have in life: birds, fruit, flowers, paintings, books, and whatever else that can charm the taste or improve the understanding. Here all is beautiful, all is harmony and peace.

"When I turn to earth, alas! what wretchedness do I see! And yet, with it all, I feel happy and glad this morning. Is it because you have decided to visit France?*

"I was there last week, and O how my heart aches over the unhappy condition of my people; and how much they need my husband's presence! Do you notice how restless the Government is at present, and how the people suffer? O, we know their needs, and to my husband's strong arm are the people of France looking for deliverance.

"When you visit my country, you will find there is a deliverer expected; and now I say to you, my husband will fulfill that mission. Of his reincarnation I dream both day and night. Its success is the foundation-rock of all my hereafter. In his hands will be placed the welfare of his people—the glory of France and the heart of JOSEPHINE."

*I contemplate making a tour through Europe next season, and said to Josephine I would certainly visit the historic localities of France with more than common interest, especially those with which herself and Napoleon were identified.

After I had decided to write this book, and finding my purpose met with the approbation of the communicating spirits, I requested Josephine to write a letter or two specially for its pages.

I desired this, as the public, I thought, would be interested in any thing she might communicate respecting the after-life, and the conditions of the spirit-world. To this request she wrote the following reply:

(JOSEPHINE'S LETTERS, No. III)

"MY DEAR FRIEND,—You ask me to write something for the book. I will do the best I can. I never wrote much when on earth, nor have I accomplished myself in this particular since my spirit-life began. Indeed, I have written more to you than in all my other correspondence put together; so you can judge of the extent of my writing. I will furnish for your book a few ideas. You must arrange and dress them with presentable language for the public eye.*

"You desire me not to express my gratitude for the kindness you have bestowed upon me. You might as well say to the ocean, 'Hush thy sounds!' What is the music of the soul, if it be not gratitude? The grand old ocean feels it, and rushes with its gladsome waves upon the shore. That is its life, its gratitude, its joy. Next will come the wind, singing through your trees, and rushing wildly, with delight, over your house-tops. O, that is its gratitude to the power that gives it motion! The flowers you cultivate come smiling with their beautiful tints, and fragrant with their joy, to tell you the same story of their thanks. They all pay you for the work you do for them. And now word-writing and acts are the only

*It is proper to say that Josephine's modesty, in this particular, compels me to state that I have taken no such liberties with her writings as she here permits. I have omitted such parts of her letters as were too personal for general interest, and have edited her punctuation; but in no instance have I substituted my own ideas for hers, and rarely has it been necessary to borrow any new dress of language to make them presentable to the "public eye.

expressions I can make of my thanks, and, as I am a French woman, I must give vent to my soul, so full of gratitude. I will hold my peace, but I must tell you sometimes how grateful I am. . . .

"It has often been asked by those who entertain but imperfect ideas of the spirit-life, 'You tell us your homes are so beautiful, why do you leave them to come to this valley of shadows?' To such my reply is, I could not rest in ease and splendor when so many hearts are calling me to earth. *I am magnetically bound to earth, and can not free myself until sympathy deserts my heart, and every human tie is severed.*

"The souls of all men and women are crying for knowledge. Your people are starving for truth, such as the spirit-world alone can supply.

"Do you think I could idly fold my arms, as the oars cross over a boat, and let the waves of chance drift me to and fro? I have a mission more noble than that. I have come from my beautiful home to repeat the story, that I live beyond the earth—that I am the same Josephine Bonaparte, the same individual, that I was on earth; to tell you that beyond the tomb there are many bright faces and lovely forms to meet you with outstretched hands when you come to immortal life; to tell you that death is a beautiful angel, which disrobes you of your soiled garments, and clothes you in the beautiful dress of the spirit, as the Spring takes off the iron mask of Winter, and spangles the earth with sunshine and bright flowers.

"Remember, my friend, in all your earthly trials there is for you a crown of sunbeams across the waves of time. When you come over, you will not be a willing drone in the hive of progression. Soon the pathway to earth will be a familiar road. . . .

"The growth of spiritualism is far greater than is supposed. Its truths are falling among the people, silently as snow upon the earth. Some morning you will awake and find you have a white robe, and yet scarcely know from whence it came. Day and night your spirit-friends are wearing away the bulwarks of ignorance and superstition. They are instilling noble and pure ideas of life where all before had been darkness and misery.

"We do not desire to establish a new Church. The spirit-world will disfavor any organization not founded on individual freedom and universal truth. God gives his sunshine to all.

Let it penetrate your souls, and quicken into life the beautiful flowers of your spirits. You well know spiritualism is not to found a new sect or to establish a new creed. You may thank the spirit-world for all progress you make in knowledge and liberal thought. The power is exhausted. I can write no more.

"JOSEPHINE."

The following letter seems to have been written to expose the inconsistency of believers in Bible spiritualism, who reject similar manifestations in modern times:

(JOSEPHINE'S LETTERS, No. IV.)

"MY DEAR FRIEND,—Spirit intercourse is called 'a new revelation,' and yet it has existed in all ages of the world that have found a place in human history. In olden times, spirits were received by the inhabitants of the earth as honored guests; but to-day they are rejected as demons or as emissaries of the 'Evil One.'

"What has made this great revolution in the minds of men? Has the wisdom of modern days discovered all that was anciently good to be modernly bad? or have the laws entering into the constitution of nature, changed, so that to-day they invert the order of the things they formerly established? We are told by modern *savants* that the laws of nature never change. Then, why may not spirits return to-day, and hold conversation with the living present, as they did in the days of Moses and the prophets? Or was God so very partial to the Dark Ages, that he permitted his embassadors to visit those only who were ignorant of the facts which modern science reveals? Do not those who die to-day pass into the same spirit-land that those did who died centuries ago? And, if so, is their love any less for those they leave on earth than was that of the old Jews who returned to commune with their friends and kindred? O no! The law of cause and effect is unchangeable. If one spirit lives, all live. The law which develops the growth of a child is universal in its operation. Doubt this you may; but the fact will confront you forever. Do not draw your skeptical robes too closely, or you will make your form ungainly. Your better judgment tells you that the doctrine of immortality is true.

or why these longings, this unsatisfied feeling, this unrest of mind? Stand firm! The truth will uproot all error in your soul.

"I fear I have failed to interest you this morning; but such as I have, I give. I remain, your true friend,

"JOSEPHINE."

The following may be termed an interesting business-letter. It opens a chink, which, if it does not reveal specifically the purposes of the spirit-world, fairly intimates the character of their grand enterprise. The spirits applaud discrimination among their workers, and have intrusted Mrs. Hollis with one of their most important missions:

(JOSEPHINE'S LETTERS, No. V.)

"MY DEAR FRIEND,—When I entered the spirit-world, I was amazed as the spirits disclosed to me the greatness of the work they had undertaken to accomplish. To successfully carry out their purposes, old institutions of earth—many of them hoary with the age of centuries—had to be swept away; and, in doing this, the foundation of things seemed to be broken up, and nature itself convulsed.

"But the scales soon dropped from my eyes, and I began to see all this was for the best. The great Creator had set our feet in firm places, and established our goings forever. I now know that the foundation upon which we stand is rock, and no waves can wash it away.

"Every movement of the spirit-world is made in accordance with God's system of laws. All these will succeed in good time, as soon as the proper instrumentalities are employed to work them out. These are now being selected and set to work. All over the earth, men and women are engaged in doing the work arranged for them by unseen and unrecognized superintendents. We do not doubt our victory will come. All we want is workers; intelligent men and women who possess that priceless gift—energy, invincible determination, with a purpose fixed. This quality will accomplish any thing we wish—'t will snatch victory from the very jaws of despair.

"But few are qualified to do our work. Our best work is

reserved for a class of workers yet to be. Our medium will stand foremost among our grand agents, and to her we have intrusted one of our most important missions. Many are zealous in the cause of spiritualism who do it more harm than good. Still they serve to agitate the muddy waters, to liberate the offensive odors from the mire of society. But even here the bright sunlight of truth will finally penetrate, and these unclean places will be made pure.

"Our band are grateful to you for protecting our medium from the intrusion of the unthinking multitude. We are grateful for the discrimination and nerve evinced in excluding from our circles the presence of those who are uncongenial to the conditions through which we work. For these good services, we one and all thank you. JOSEPHINE."

As a "police detective," spiritualism promises to take high rank. Jim Nolan has stated many times that a criminal may be brought into the presence of Mrs. Hollis, in company with twenty innocent persons, and that she will, while blindfolded, designate the malefactor simply by touching his hand. A knowledge of this fact will be "cold comfort" to those who think they can depredate on life, character, and property, without detection and punishment. But, more, I have reason to believe that the spirit-world can reveal the name of a person who has been guilty of a misdemeanor or crime, if they deem it best to do so. I will illustrate this by citing a case in point.

The morning after Mrs. Hollis commenced her fourth engagement at my house, she received a letter from home, which, upon opening, was found to contain an inclosed anonymous letter, that had been written in Cincinnati and mailed to her in Louisville. She opened it at the breakfast-table, and, after reading it carefully, passed it to me, simply remarking, "You will be interested in that, Doctor!"

The letter was exclusively about myself. It was of the most scandalous personal character, dealing in defamation with the most reckless license. After reading it, I lost my appetite for breakfast, and became furiously annoyed.

I never refute lies, and do not fear them. There is something more than political wit in Ben Butler's grim declaration, that "he never enjoyed life until he lost his character." Reputation ought to be able to take care of itself, and when it must be looked after and watched and guarded every hour in the day, lest it do something very naughty, the cost of keeping it prim is really more than the thing is worth. But this letter annoyed me—not because of the charges it made, but because it was written by a cowardly assassin, who lay in ambush.

Any man is liable to be struck in the back, and it is sheer bravado to say he does not fear the stiletto. Society is full of *Thugs*, who are always to be feared ; those especially who control a depraved press. Their weapon is noiseless, but fatal. They strangle you under the guise of Christian fellowship. O, it were better to be accompanied by the ocean pirate or the midnight assassin! But my business now is to disclose how the spirits aided in dragging one of these cowardly miscreants from his hiding-place into the open light of day.

As I could not tell who had slandered me, I felt annoyed and restless. This was uncommon ; for lies ordinarily are short-lived, and I let them die. Mrs. Hollis, seeing me fretted, suggested that we should consult the spirits abcut the authorship of the scandalous letter. This we did, and "old Skiwaukee" came up to the work promptly. He had found out all about the letter, and the author of it; and after imparting all the information he had, and disclosing the writer's name, he supplemented his statement by declaring it as his opinion that "'em old dog was 'em dam old muscle-shell! *So!*"

As I was no longer in doubt, I felt easy. Such a scamp could not injure the reputation of any person, no matter what he might write, only by withholding his odious name. This is what he did. He knew that he was impotent to do harm if he were unmasked; so he became a concealed-character-ku-klux. I determined to circumvent this old slanderer, let him turn on his track which way he would.

Mrs. Hollis and I agreed to polish the "*shell*" of this old "trilobite." I said: "He has been guilty of these dirty tricks a long time, and it will be doing a good service to bring him to grief. Now, we will carefully remove from this letter our names, wherever they occur. Cut them out, so that no clew may be had of the person sending it. We will now tear the letter into little bits, leaving no piece of it large enough to write a monosyllable upon. Put these in an envelope. Now you write on this slip of paper as I shall dictate: 'Rascal! the whole spirit-world knows of your villainy! The avenger is on your track, and you can not escape him! Make your peace!' There, that will do; no signature; put it in the envelope, with the little pieces of his own letter. When he gets them he will know what it means, if the 'chickens belong to him. He will be a little more than surprised that they have 'come home to roost.' Now superscribe the envelope to this address; there it is, in the Directory. All right."

That same evening "Skiwaukee" reported progress; said the letter had been received, "that em old rat was sick;" and said, "What will em do? what will em do? I press em to come see em old chief. Said em come in mornin'."

True, the sickly old scamp came to my door the next morning, and I met him. He was much excited, and said he had received a singular letter from me, which he wanted some explanation about. "How do you know it came from me?" I said. He replied he discovered my name on some of the bits of paper inclosed. Whereupon I took him by the throat, and shook him. I then gave him my promise, that in the future, if he did not take more pains to conceal his lies, especially those that he felt it his duty to write about me, I would choke the "daylights" out of him. It was this affair, and another "cold-blooded" lie which Murat Halstead published in the Cincinnati *Commercial*, about the same time, concerning a spiritual *seance* held at my house, that induced the writing of the following:

(JOSEPHINE'S LETTERS, No. VI.)

"MY DEAR FRIEND, — I greet you again, as a faithful worker in the harvest-field of principle and truth. What you have written, the poodles may bark at, but it will strike home to the consciences of thinking men. The loving messages we bring will dwell in their hearts, and they will carry them, like waving banners, through every land.

"People often say, 'Why do n't Napoleon say something

worthy of himself?' Say to such that 'the greatness of a man is not measured by the number or the length of his speeches.' My husband's *executive* abilities were without a parallel in human achievement. Those people who think to put our work down, reckon without their host. The serpents who sting in the dark can not penetrate iron with their poisoned fangs. Their own venom will return to their craven souls, and destroy them. Ye who attempt to thwart us, beware how you take the step; for it will be the signal for your passing into nothingness. When the spirit-world is aroused, it never sleeps until the wrong is righted.

"We have no time to make idle promises. When my husband's face shines on any one, it means work. It will again appear in France with power, and thrill the hearts of millions with the resolution to liberate our beautiful country from the degradation of priestcraft and obscenity.

"We watch the progress of the book with great interest. It has an aggressive and fearless ring of truth about it, that will command the attention and respect of its readers. It will be bitterly assailed; but fear not.

"We stand by you, beloved friend. Good-bye!

"JOSEPHINE."

CHAPTER XII.

SEVERAL LETTERS FROM JOSEPHINE—EXTRAORDINARY STATEMENT OF MARSHAL NEY RESPECTING LOUIS NAPOLEON'S FATHER.

A FEW more letters from Josephine will not fail to interest the thoughtful reader. The seventh in the series will attract special attention, because it discusses a question of absorbing interest to a majority of thinking people. It joins issue squarely with the dogmas of sectarianism, and, in the spirit of true catholic charity, states plainly that the doctrine of separating loved ones in the spirit-world is a libel upon the Divine character:

(JOSEPHINE'S LETTERS, No. VII.)

"FRIENDS OF EARTH,—Time flies! Many years have sped since I left my earth-form, to become a dweller in the realms of truth and love. Great changes have taken place since then in the affairs of men, but the laws governing matter remain without variableness or shadow of turning.

"How few there are among you who comprehend the grand truths that are wrapped up in your being, or the glorified destiny that awaits you! Bound to earth by selfish passions, all your better nature lies asleep, and will, I fear, remain so until death transforms you with its loving touch, and opens to your soul's enraptured gaze the flowery portal of the spirit-world. Out of this stupor you must be aroused. Life has its practical lessons, which ye must be taught. The purposes of being must be understood, if you would fulfill intelligently the great mission of existence. The law of creation is motion; its manifestation, progress. Labor disencumbers the soul, and enables it to give forth higher expressions of its divine character. It is written on all things, Work is progression; idleness is rust and retrogression.

"Friends, the progress you make on earth will be aids to you when you enter the spirit-world. Divest your mind as much as possible of all corroding error. Stand firm in the pure atmosphere of truth and god-like principle. One of the first lessons you learn on entering spirit-life is, that knowledge is a power that can not perish. Nature wastes nothing; a force created will live forever; all knowledge gained by man on earth will be profitable to him after the death of his physical body.

"The Church condemns to eternal separation the spirits that have loved each other on earth, and makes them exiles from joy and peace forever. This dreadful penalty is attached to some error committed in earth-life—some law of nature disobeyed, some inhibited commandment of the Church disregarded. I come to tell you this is not so. You may have stumbled on the path, and while you were staggering under the weight of your errors, and the evils of misdirection, your more favored companions may have advanced beyond you; but you are not to be separated forever. You will outgrow all errors of earth-life in the spirit-world. You have committed no fatal mistake, no wrong which time will not rectify. The chasm of separation will again be closed, and again you will rejoin your friends, their equal in purity, their peer in wisdom, and their companion in love. These are the grand teachings of modern spiritualism. Death does not rob you of your loved ones. They are waiting for you on the threshold of their shining homes, and when you enter the spirit land they will guide you along flowery pathways to their sublime abodes. That will be the reward of your virtues and the triumph of your suffering.

"O, dear friends, it is our privilege to know these reunions will not be thwarted. Here there are no accidents, no mistakes; *law governs all.* Listen to the spirit-voices; they will teach you good and pure lessons, and bring joy to your hearts.

"The tiny 'raps' bring messages from your loved ones; but ye fear them, or affect to believe them not. Ye say they are

beneath the dignity of glorified spirits.* Do they not preach to you more eloquently of the after-life than all the pulpit-orators in your land? They assure you of continued existence beyond the grave. Faith you have, but not knowledge. O, faith is a dead form—an idol of clay, beautiful, but deceptive! Like moths sporting in a Summer-day, men and women, in a giddy throng of fashion, follow it. Being blind itself, where will it lead, but into spheres of vice, crime, and discord? The power fails.
JOSEPHINE."

Somewhat similar in character to the foregoing is the following letter, a careful perusal of which will show that the dogmas taught by creed-bound theologians are not in high favor in the spirit-world. We learn, when we enter spirit-life, that we must give up many conceits, which we were at special pains to acquire in this. Among the most worthless "rubbish" cast away as detrimental to spiritual progress, that will litter the road leading to the Temple of Truth, will be catechisms, surplices, crucifixes, chalices, holy candles, wafer-plates, and puddles of holy water. These will lie scattered, in bitter mockery of our fear and ignorance, all along our pathway:

(JOSEPHINE'S LETTERS, No. VIII.)

"MY DEAR FRIEND,—The whole world is trying to explain away the mystery of spirit phenomena, but, as yet, with indifferent success. A number of so-called scholarly men have advanced theories which only tend to show the poverty of

*And so they may be. Glorified spirits never condescend to address people of such inconsequential caliber. Those who receive inferior messages, find in them but the reflex image of their own instincts. Josephine ought to know that people who laud themselves by such remarks belong to the new order of "shoddy," who alone deal in such profligate dignity. What could these well-dressed idiots do—how could they live—if they did not themselves occasionally administer such a sop to feed their inordinate vanity? *O tempora! O mores!*
NEP.

their resources, and the poor material of which great men are sometimes fashioned. Those who make no claims to scholarship, think more clearly on this subject, in many instances, than the *savants.*

"It should be understood that the manifestations of spirit-power, now dawning upon your planet, are the legitimate result of ages of hard work in the spirit-world. The purpose is to establish, among the people of the earth, social, political, and religious freedom. To be thwarted in this design by a cramped and ignorant *theocracy*, is an exigency not to be tolerated hereafter. The path of progress must be left unobstructed. The underbrush and rubbish must be cleared away; the work of redeeming the world from ignorance and superstition must go forward; and all who oppose its completeness will be made to sink out of sight.

"The world has suffered by ignorance too long. The destiny of man will henceforth be better understood. Those who have misled the multitude by their fears, and built temples by the tribute of 'Peter's-pence,' will seek shelter in them from the maddened passions of an outraged humanity. Human nature can endure much, and is of long suffering; but there is a limit to the sublimest virtues.

"Spiritualism has taught more truth to man, respecting his *post-mortem* existence, in the last twenty-five years, than had been shed upon the world in the preceding five hundred. It has educated people to think without fear; and thought is the life-principle of the great center of intelligence. It has aroused the finer impulses of the soul into action, as the sun and dew quicken into life the beautiful flowers of the earth.

"The Churches have attempted to impede its progress by throwing their dark shadow athwart its shining pathway, but in vain. Men have become god-like, and now think for themselves. What kills the plant so soon as to exclude it from the sunlight? If it lives, it is only to maintain a feeble, sickly existance. So with man, when you deny him the freedom of reason and the sunlight of truth. He exhibits the unskilled accents of the babe, the tottering step of the invalid, the vacant stare of the demented. Day by day they are taught the dogmas of Church creeds. They are commanded to believe, until reason totters to its center, and existence becomes a purposeless blank and life a living curse.

"Into these dark abodes of ignorance and superstition spiritual light is now streaming, and fear is being banished from the minds of men. Stand firm, ye noble workers in the form! Back of the curtain of time there is great reward for ye who do your duty well. JOSEPHINE."

On the reception of the foregoing letter, I asked why the spirit-world did not develop good mediums in the Churches, where they would, like Oakes Ames's *pewter*, do most good; to which the following was given in reply:

"Around every one is formed a band of spirits, and, when in the Church, the magnetic influence from the members of the congregation go out and surround the medium. This forms a chain that holds the spirits back, and binds such to their old doctrines and dogmas. This is the reason that no good medium can attend an orthodox Church, and remain so. This is the cause of so many failures. JOSEPHINE."

These letters of Josephine were frequently suggested by conversations I held with Mrs. Hollis, or others in her presence. While a subject would be under discussion, raps on the table would indicate that the spirits had something to say on the question in dispute. Mrs. Hollis would then hold the slate under the table, where they would write their views freely. In this way I ascertained that, whatever was being said, was heard and understood by the spirits. One day we were discussing the subject of Napoleon's return to France, Mrs. Hollis having implicit faith in Josephine's prediction, and I hesitating in my loyalty to such doctrine. The slate was called for, when the following was promptly given:

(JOSEPHINE'S LETTERS, No. IX.)

"MY DEAR FRIEND,—We work by circles. The higher gives to the lower. So from the bright sphere of wisdom comes many of the directions I give you from spirits who have long since left the earth.

"Did the thought never occur to you, that those grand outbirths of *genius* which always startle the world, were but reincarnations of some brilliant mind that had lived before? Think of that.

"We are working very hard to free this first sphere of many errors that are choking out the higher truths. We depend upon workers to help us who are still in the form. To aid in tearing away the slavish fetters of creed from the human soul, and to arouse to active thought millions of Church-sleepers, is no ignoble mission. We have no time to trifle. . . .

"JOSEPHINE."

The following letter is somewhat personal; but in it is shown the disinterested character of the writer, so much so that it will be read with satisfaction on that account. It contains other points of interest as well, which will not escape the eye of the observant reader:

(JOSEPHINE'S LETTERS, No. X.)

"MY DEAR FRIEND,—All streams flow to the ocean. So it is with man, who is ever propelled by a grand law of his nature, toward the sphere of immortal life. Some pass along without thought, others with indifference, and some with dread approach the destiny that awaits them. Now, what we want to do, is to refine their coarse fiber, and put wisdom into their thoughtless brains. This will bring out the nobler attributes of their souls.

"All people need transplanting. The old ground becomes impoverished. Memory must live, but we do not want that memory to be darkened. It is pleasant, when people come to spirit-life, to possess the remembrance of something good.

"We have not rushed into this work without thought. Indeed, we never do any thing without first considering well. There are some spirits, like mortals, who will say or do any thing to please. This class do great harm; but it can not be helped. The same law that opens a pathway for one to return enables a million to do the same. Now, if you have noticed

HORTENSE

closely our communications, you will have observed that we have very often directed our medium to do many unpleasant things, such as almost took her breath at the time. In this way we do our duty, no matter whether it is pleasant or otherwise. We do not wish to cause mental or physical suffering, but if they are incidental to the discharge of our duty, we do not hesitate to inflict both. What we do is for the good which may result from our action.

"Remember, I gave up my beloved husband that France might have an heir to her throne. Ah, sir, no woman's heart ever suffered more than mine when making this sacrifice. I now see it was for the best, but could not think so then. Work on with a cheerful heart and a wise head. All will be well. The whole spirit-world are your friends and fellow-workers in the cause of justice, free thought, and truth.

"JOSEPHINE."

One of the most remarkable cabinet *seances*, which will hereafter be more minutely recorded, was that in which a number of French spirits materialized, and presented their faces at the aperture in the door of the cabinet. As they did this, their names were first audibly announced. When the beautiful face of Hortense Bonaparte was presented, I said to those in the circle, "That is the mother of Louis Napoleon, but I do not observe in the pictures of the son any resemblance to the mother."

As she retired from the light, the stalwart arm of Marshal Ney was projected into the room, and, picking up the pencil from the slate, wrote on it: "The conditions under which the child was begotten were not harmonious; so he does not look like either of his parents."

I audibly made answer, "Was not Hortense's marriage a love-match?"

"She loved the emperor more," he wrote,

"Still, would her platonic affection for Napoleon affect the organization of the child?" I asked.

"Napoleon," answered Ney, "was not much given to sentiment. His relation to Hortense was more than platonic."

"But the child was born in wedlock?" I persisted.

"O yes: and so have thousands been; but it is a wise child that knows its father."

"As I have but quite recently read the Life of Josephine, I remember she speaks of Hortense charging her with being over-zealous in bringing about a marriage that would separate her from the society of the emperor. I suppose Josephine had some cause for desiring her daughter's marriage?"

"That was unkind and unjust in Hortense to Josephine. Her mother would have made any sacrifice for France and the emperor. Her marriage to Louis was a diplomatic affair. It was arranged by the emperor himself, and only urged by Josephine on that account," wrote Ney.

"The relation you intimate as existing between Napoleon and Hortense was *pre*-marital, of course?"

"*Pre* and *post*. The time I specifically refer to was in the generation of Louis."

"Do you mean to say that the *first* emperor was the father of the *third*?"

"*As much so as of the second!*"

"This is not generally understood or believed. I never heard this statement before, nor have I ever seen it in print. I do not think many suspect what you have just said: though, of course, I do not know what people think; but there is so little personal resemblance existing between the *first* and *third* emperor, and their habits of thought and action are so dissimilar, that your statement stands in *vrai-semblance* to the facts, and may be fairly questioned."

"Are you quite sure you fully understand the law of geniture?"

"Certainly not! But, on the contrary, I am quite sure I do not understand it. The only thought I have on the subject is, that physiological science ought to prove the maxim of physical science true; that is, that 'like causes will produce like effects.' Do n't 'like beget like?'"

"Yes: but that implies the necessity of complete spiritual harmony, and perfect adaptation in the begetting relation."

"Now you obscure the whole matter. If you involve the subjects of temperaments, affinities, conjugalities, and the other *fogities*, in considering this question, I must beg leave to remain quiet, and receive whatever statement you make, without further interruption or comment."

"Please yourself best. The law of procreation can only express itself perfectly when the conditions are reciprocally harmonious. The emperor could not give a perfect expression of himself if there was not a corresponding receptivity. The germinal *third* emperor was more beset with dangers to life and limb than the daring leader of Lodi, or the coroneted victor of Austerlitz."

"Taking this view of the subject, Marshal, the begetment of a child in the likeness of its father is a *rara avis*, and to expect it to be a perfect type of both parents, is—well, to draw the first prize in a grand lottery scheme."

"You are apt in your conclusions. You now understand how the third emperor may be the son of the first, without possessing either the mental or physical characteristics of his father."

"I can understand that very well; but still the fact remains that Louis Napoleon was born in wedlock, and there is no testimony on record to invalidate the claim of Louis, the brother of the first emperor, and the husband of Hortense, from being the father of the present exiled Emperor of France."

At this juncture Ney began a most extraordinary oral statement of the intimacies of Napoleon and Hortense, in which he named circumstances, places, persons, giving dates which are historically correct, all tending to prove his declarations true. It was the most plausible circumstantial statement I ever listened to. He was proceding to clear up some obscure part of the testimony, when an audible voice in the cabinet said, "Stop, Ney, you have said enough."

Hereupon this remarkable revelation was brought to a close.

All this is given as an introduction to the following communication, which was received next morning:

(JOSEPHINE'S LETTERS, No. XI.)

"MY DEAR FRIEND,—Each day brings to light some hidden mystery of the past. Last night you were rather startled by the revelations made concerning my daughter. That which was disclosed to you is true and well known in the spirit-world.

"When there is entire compatibility of temperaments, and an interior love, these relations are well; but, if that does not exist, then no such intimacy should be maintained, as resultant organizations will suffer from inharmony and discord. The spirit, however highly developed it may be, can not express itself through an imperfect matrix. Those who are thus wrongly begotten may struggle and writhe under their unfortunate conditions, but they will ever suffer, while in the form, the penalties of the violated laws of the conjugal relation.

"So, in this instance, my daughter loved Napoleon; but there was not that mutual *adaptation* for a perfect expression of the procreative law. Therefore Louis is not an entire success. The flowers drink in the dew and sunlight, and become more beautiful and lovely. So should the soul-love and heart-sympathy be attracted. If the emperor had been to Hortense as the sun is to the flowers, their offspring would have been all that could be desired, and the necessity for another Napoleon being born in France obviated. The medium is exhausted. JOSEPHINE."

We will present but one more of these interesting letters at this time. A second series will follow, in connection with the phenomena occurring in the dark circles and the table-manifestations, during Mrs. Hollis's last engagement:

(JOSEPHINE'S LETTERS, No. XII.)

"MY DEAR FRIEND,—I will try again to give you some ideas to enlighten mankind. The only religion that will save the world from its sins, and raise it from its degradation, must find its way to the hearts of men through the filtering process of human reason. Science and philosophy will be its handmaids, and eternal laws and immutable truths its gospels.

"Deep down in the soul, there is an intense longing to know something of man's future life—to know really whether he is immortal or not. Churches have been founded to gratify these desires, but their speculations are unsatisfying. Wordy declamation will not feed the soul. It can only subsist on the bread of life, which must be leavened with knowledge. To a mother who has lost her child, the teachings of the Church can give but little consolation. Her heart aches the more when she is told it is God's will to take her darling away. The criminal sinks beneath a load of laws he never understood; and in his ignorant extremity he is told to repent, and put his sins on Christ, if he would be perfectly happy. No man born with the common instincts of justice in his soul, ever believed that story. He may say what he pleases; deep down in his spirit he accepts no such doctrine. He hopes it may be true; but that will not make it so. O, let it be understood, that when the spirit-world opens wide to your view, you will then learn that an eternity is too short to lose the memory of a broken law of nature; that a darkness will ever hover around the sin, until the spirit becomes pure and enlightened. All sin must be atoned for by the sinner. Reparation is the only acceptable repentance, saith the law. Sin and suffering go hand in hand.

"How many are hungering for light and knowledge, and yet how few there are who have the moral courage to grasp the truth when it is presented to them! They start in trepidation when it comes in the simple words of a mother, 'I still live and love you.' When in the form, these were welcome words that warmed your heart, and inspired your soul with love. Why should they be less so now? Laying aside the physical does not change their character. O no, my dear friends: your loved ones are still human, possessing the same love that filled their souls when they were with you in the form. Death has not robbed them of a single faculty. Their love has grown more intense, and they desire you to listen to their voices. O, my dear friends, you are throwing away golden opportunities when you reject us. Let us tell you of our bright homes, where you will one day come, and from which you may return to earth, if you desire to talk to your loved ones again. Listen, and treat us with common politeness. This is all we ask. The spirit-world will give you *knowledge* you do not possess. This is the savior you have been expecting so long.

"My dear friend, how grateful I am to you for your kindness! Accept the love and devotion of

"JOSEPHINE BONAPARTE."

CHAPTER XIII.

SPIRIT TELEGRAPHING—FRANK STEVENS'S MESSAGES WRITTEN IN TELEGRAPHIC CHARACTERS—NOLAN DESCRIBES SPIRIT TELEGRAPHS—INSPIRATIONAL IDEAS—BRIDGE-BUILDING—ROEBLING AS A MEDIUM.

IN Mrs. Hollis's second engagement, about the middle of November, 1871, at the close of a dark circle, held in the back room of the third story of my dwelling, the first sounds of spirit telegraphing were heard. I made a minute of the circumstance at the time of its occurrence, from which I extract the following:

"The usual manifestations had ceased, when the spirit of a telegraph-operator began to write by 'taps.' There was not a person in the room that could 'read by sound;' so whatever the import of the communication may have been, it was not understood. The experiment continued for a quarter of an hour, the 'taps' varying, as I have heard them, when the key of an instrument was being manipulated by a regular operator in transmitting messages. I make a record of this circumstance, with the belief that the spirits intend employing this means to communicate with their friends in the form."

After this manifestation had terminated, and before

the conditions of the circle were changed, I said to Jimmy Nolan, "What does all this mean?"

"It was an experiment in telegraphing," was his reply.

"By whom?" I asked.

"A spirit entered the circle by permission of our band. He brought a telegraph instrument, upon which he operated. He did not give his name, or speak while he remained."

"Had I known he was coming, I would have engaged the services of a 'sound-reader,' to receive his messages."

"This, I understand, was only an experiment, which will be hereafter repeated."

"Was it a success?"

"I don't know. The operator seemed to be satisfied, but said nothing."

This was about the substance of the conversation I had with Mr. Nolan at the time; he promised, however, to keep me advised if any thing important should be disclosed in that direction.

I began to reflect on this new method of communicating with the spirit-world, and fancied, if it could be accomplished, its success would mark a new and important era in the history of man. My notions, of course, were crude and vague, almost "without form, and void;" still, to my apprehension, these "taps" foreshadowed a new revelation of divine law, which, in its operation, would exert an elevating influence upon the destiny of the human race.

When the Atlantic cable was first submerged, great anxiety was felt for the success of the experiment. Men looked at each other anxiously, as if the *Great Eastern* contained their personal treasures. The success of the enterprise was felt to be important to all; and it was only after the electric pulse of the Old World throbbed through the heart of the New, that the painful suspense was broken, and the people shouted for joy. The names of FIELD and MORSE became immortal as their spirits. Their god-like intellects had struggled with the imponderable forces, and won another victory over ignorance, bigotry, and superstition, more potent for good and elevating purposes to the human family than all the pious pulpit platitudes that have sounded since the reign of Cæsar. Let their names and fame be enshrined in gratitude forever!

On the other side of the great ocean of Life there are grand spiritualized minds working out more intricate problems, for the uplifting of the human family, than any known to mortal. Having demonstrated the actuality of the after-life, they now seek to open communication between the two worlds, which will enable our loved ones, dead, to speak again. More than this, they seek to place the people of our planet in spiritual communication with those who inhabit the incomprehensible systems of suns and moons and stars, which scintillate, like tiniest nebulæ, upon the unmapped bosom of space. When they shall have succeeded in this, our poor groaning earth will for all time shake off its hideous nightmare of priestcraft, and kingly rule shall curse it never more.

The public notice I gave to these telegraphic "taps" attracted the attention of a gentleman in

Cincinnati, an accomplished "operator," who had long been connected with the telegraph business. In an interview with him, he suggested the propriety of placing a telegraph instrument in the dark circle, for the spirits to operate with. I did this, but they could not use the key any more than to give a "call." The spirits said a battery must be formed, and an operator taught before a success could be pronounced. My suggestion was to take time, but stick to it until completed. Before any headway could be made with the new experiment, Mrs. Hollis's engagement expired, and she returned to Louisville. Soon after, I forwarded an instrument to her, with the request that she would continue the experiments, and report to me from time to time the progress being made. I wrote also to James Nolan that there was a telegraph-operator in the spirit-world by the name of *Frank Stevens,* who, perhaps, would assist in carrying forward the work in hand. Stevens was well known in Cincinnati as a telegraphic expert, and a man of untiring energy. His name was suggested by one who knew him well.

The experiments continued almost a year without giving much satisfaction. It was not until the 30th of October, 1872, that Nolan wrote: "It will take us some time to get this thing to work. Do not feel discouraged. I think we will succeed; and, if we do, it will certainly revolutionize the whole system of telegraphing."

I had no thought of being discouraged; so I wrote in reply: "I am hale and hearty, with my 'first wind.' Go ahead, Jim, if it takes another year! Write no such nonsense to me! Success will compensate for all! Patience and perseverance will win! Get Stevens to aid you!"

On the 6th of November, just one week after Jim had written, Josephine wrote me as follows:

> "MY DEAR FRIEND,—We are very desirous that this new manifestation shall be given through our medium, and will make strong efforts to effect perfect results. We are trying to get our instrument in order. If we succeed, it will be one of the great sensations of the day, for by it we will bring some new ideas to earth in regard to telegraphing.
>
> "Yesterday I went to Franklin and Morse, and talked to them on the subject. They will join in the work, and are sanguine of success."

On the 12th of November, just one year from the time these experiments were commenced, Mrs. Hollis wrote:

"While holding the paper-frame under the table, this morning, I got these dots. You may get some one to tell you their meaning, if they have any. I was going to throw them in the waste-basket, but JIM insisted that I should send them to you:

.—— .   .—— .. —— ——   —.. ..   .. .—— ...

—... . ... —   — ..   ——. .:. ...— .   ...—

— . —— . ——. . .. .— .... —. ——.   .. —

—— .— ....   — .— —.— .   — .. —— .   .— ...

.— —— ——   — .... .. —. ——. ...   —.. ..

.—.   ... — . ...— . —. ...

I soon found an interpreter for "these dots," and placed the paper on which they were written in his hand. As he scrutinized the characters, I watched closely his face, to read thereon the purport of this mystery. I felt assured, before he spoke, that "these dots" were intelligible, and my anxiety abated. Still I was *curious* to know what they signified. Without speaking a word, he wrote with his pencil on the bottom of the paper:

"We will do our best to give you telegraphing. It may take time, as all things do.

"F. STEVENS."

"That's all," he said, handing me the paper again.

"Well, that is enough," I thought. It was the very thing I wanted. This writing was a success! but I decided to await further developments. On the day following the reception of "these dots," Mrs. Hollis wrote again:

"The instrument works well without my hands being near it, but whether it works intelligibly or not, I do not know. Come and see what you think of it. It is certainly very wonderful."

I accordingly arranged to visit Louisville on the 17th of November, and, in the afternoon of that day, sought to "interview" the spirits on the subject of establishing telegraphic communication between the two worlds. It turned out not to be a good time for "interviewing," as they not only refused to give me a tap on the key, but, by a provoking reticence, ignored the subject *in toto*. Several spirit-friends wrote letters of a personal character; but these were not exactly what I wanted. They did not make any allusion to the subject I was most interested in.

"Business is business," I remarked on the following morning, as we again sat to the table, "and I wish the spirits to make the best use of time, as I am on the limit." It was only a few minutes after this gentle reminder, that the following characters were traced on a commercial sheet, and flung from under the table:

—— .. ... — .— —— ... — .. —... .
.... .. —— —.. — .... . —— .. —.—. .... —
.—— . .— ... . —... ... . .— —.— .. —. —.—.
.— .—.— .— .... — .... —— .. ..— —.. ...
.. —.. .. —.—. —. .. ... .— —. ... .
.— —. —.. ... ..— .... — .. — .. .. —.
.—— ....— ...— . ... ..
—— .. —. —.—. .. —... ... .— ... . —..
— ....— .. .. —.

— . —— . —.—. ... .— .... —. —.—.
.—.— .. —— —— .— —.. —.. .— —. .. — ....
. ... —— .. —. —.— — .. — .... .
—— .. —.—. .... — .. ..— .. — ..
... . —— —— —... . —.— —— .— —..
— .. —... .. .— —— —— — .... .— —
.—— .. —— —— —... . .. —. — .... .
....—— . ... .. —. .. —— —— .. ...
— .— —— .— .. .— .. —..

.—. ... .— —. —.— ... — . ...— . —. ...

I am told, by a gentleman who is well qualified to know, that there are but few errors in this telegram, and that the characters are made with accuracy. To this gentleman I am indebted for the following translation of the communication:

"TO THE PEOPLE.

"I am trying to perfect telegraphing. It will only be one of the countless steps of a never-ending development, which began far back in the past, and is to extend through the infinity of future time. We will first give you raps, then will come the long messages of assurance there is life beyond this earth. What other doctrine is so reasonable? so logical? so consoling? so encouraging? What other can offer such powerful incitements to activity? We are putting aside the material that has covered the faces of the dead. We are bringing a purer atmosphere, causing the upturned eye of mortals to behold the

light. We are breaking away the clouds of ignorance and superstition which have so long obscured their vision.

"Telegraphing will add another link to the mighty chain. I shall be glad to do all that will be in the power of immortal to aid.

"FRANK STEVENS."

A few minutes after receiving the above address, another communication, in telegraphic characters, was thrown from under the table, of which the following is a translation:

"MY FRIEND W.,—I am glad to be able, in so short a space of time, to give these marks. I shall leave nothing untried to perfect this work. Many spirits with myself think it will be a grand and glorious achievement. My friends who knew me on earth will cheerfully attest that I was a man of energy, and I can assure you I have lost none of it by putting aside the physical. I never knew the word 'failure' on earth. I don't now. I am happy, and will often communicate with you. Good-bye! FRANK STEVENS."

"*November* 18, 1872."

These two communications were written in a space of time not exceeding ten minutes, on paper, in excellent characters, in a lighted room, while Mrs. Hollis was talking freely of her proposed trip south, to spend the Winter months. I made this statement to a young man—a telegraph-operator—who is *not* very modest in the estimate of his own ability, when he proceeded to enlighten me how these things could be done by the person holding the slate. Of course, I listened until he had finished, when I proposed to pay him a year's salary, not exceeding *five thousand dollars*, if he would get me two as well-written communications, of equal length, in the same space of time, and under precisely the same circumstances.

The proposition was made to reward him for his uncommon modesty. I will now make a similar offer to any telegraph-operator in the United States or Europe, and will modify it so as to make the amount *ten thousand dollars*, providing there is a forfeiture of *one hundred dollars* for every failure that attends the effort. I think this a good chance to any man of *ability* to make a small fortune if he has only confidence and modesty enough to try the experiment.

The interest excited by the reception of these telegraphic communications induced me to seek an interview with Jim Nolan on the subject; so the room was darkened, and it was only a few minutes after when he said:

"Doctor, you have the *writing?*"

"Yes: but will it ever amount to any thing?"

"Certainly! Why not? The time is not very distant when telegraphic communication between the two worlds will be as much established as it is now between Louisville and Cincinnati."

"Do you really think so?"

"Did you not receive two communications, written in telegraph characters, an hour ago?"

"I did; but—"

"That should convince you there are spirits here who understand how to handle a telegraph instrument."

"That's very true. But does it follow that you can establish conditions by which the instrument can be worked? The communications I received were written on paper, in telegraph characters, I admit; but could they be given through an instrument?"

"Doctor, it is no more difficult to telegraph a word than it is to write it. In both cases it requires practice. That which is needed here, is a band of electricians to sustain the communicating spirit, while he handles the key of the instrument."

"Will you succeed in organizing such a band?"

"To be sure we will."

"Will you be able to dispense with human mediums then?"

"O no; we can do nothing without human magnetism. We can not form a hand to work the key without it."

"It will be necessary, then, to keep a medium near, to supply the element with which you materialize the spirit-hand that manipulates the key?"

"That is it, exactly!"

"It is said, Jim, that all inventions, all the discoveries we make in science, are common with you in the spirit-world. Is that true?"

"Nearly so. We have them more perfect than you."

"Had you the electric telegraph in the spirit-world before it was discovered by Morse?"

"Yes: and as fast as we can find better mediums than Morse, we give our improvements. To him was given as much of the principle as he could make use of in constructing his machine. He was a medium of our will to that extent. Others have received additional information, and still further acquisition of knowledge will enable you to make still further improvements."

"I perceive, then, you impart your ideas or information by installments? Can you improve on our present system of telegraphing? or have you any thing better in the spirit-world?"

"Baron Swedenborg revealed a great truth to the world in his disclosures of the law of *correspondence*."

"I understand by this, that whatever exists on earth has its counterpart in the spirit-world."

"If you transpose your proposition, you will be more accurate."

"O, you would have me state it, that whatever exists in the spirit-world finds its correspondence here?"

"You are approaching exactness. Let me state it: 'Whatever you possess, exists with us more perfect than with you.'"

"Have you any thing more perfect than metallic wires for conveying electric currents?"

"Yes: we have electric currents without the wires. These are as appreciable to our eyes as your metal conductors, and the battery which enables us to transmit our thoughts is simply *will-power*. We not only send thoughts, but we *go* ourselves faster than you can conceive. Your metal conductors are simply the channels through which electric currents flow. We see these currents in the wire as you see the wire. We can outstrip them, as light moves faster than sound."

"I understand, then, that you make this distinction between our wires and their correspondence in the spirit-world. Over the first are transmitted electric currents alone, while over yours are thrilled electro-magnetic currents. Now, I am a little confused in apprehending this distinction. It sounds to me like 'tweedle-dum and tweedle-dee."'

"I can't help that! By the aid of electricity and Puck, you say, you can put a girdle around the world in twenty minutes; by the use of our electro-*magnetic* currents and *will-power*, I can make the trip myself in half the time."

"You are quick as lightning, Jim. We have no use for such celerity. But, tell me, do you think these electro-magnetic currents will ever supersede the metal wires we have in use?"

"The time is near when, with an improved instrument, these celestial currents will be utilized for the benefit of the world, and not only convey messages from city to city, but they will become channels for the transmission of thought between the natural and the spirit world."

"You are getting me a little befogged on this subject. Let me think a little. This doctrine of correspondence is a little new. Will it bear a general application?"

"Certainly! That is, whatever you possess, exists with us more perfect than with you."

"You strip us, then, of all creative power, and make us merely imitators?"

"Not exactly! It is only when you come in competition with the spirit-world that we surpass you. Man in the form has created nothing valuable to the world that is not found existing here. You model our ideas the best you can."

"Jim, have you seen the great suspension-bridge which spans the Ohio River at Cincinnati?"

"O yes; and have crossed it frequently with my medium and yourself."

"Well, is n't that rather creditable as a human achievement? You will admit that, to Mr. Roebling's brain we are indebted for this noble monument of his genius?"

"Do you know what a brain is, Doctor?"

"I have seen a brain!"

"Of a man?"

"Of many men, and horses too!"

"Well, the brain of a horse and the brain of a man, in substance, vary but little."

"You quibble, Jim. You know very well I meant Mr. Roebling's *mind*, not his material brain!"

"An intangible principle, which exists independent of matter, and expresses itself as intelligently through the brain of a bird as through the brain of a man. I will accept your substitution of mind for material brain, but wish to ask you a few questions, which may assist us to consider this bridge-building in a somewhat clearer light. First: What relation does mind sustain to matter? Second: Does mind exist independent of matter? And, third: Is mind so individualized that we can emphatically say it was Mr. Roebling's mind that originated the bridge?"

"It is easier to ask perplexing questions than it is to answer them. I fear, instead of simplifying the bridge question, you are making it more intricate. Still, I answer in general terms, that mind and matter, if not identical, are at least so intimately related that the destruction of the one involves the loss of the other. That is, I do not think they exist independent of each other; therefore they become unitized, 'flesh of one flesh, and bone of one bone.'"

"That is a monstrous doctrine you profess to believe. Let us examine it. Mr. Roebling, as you knew him, no longer exists. His mind, inseparably wedded to matter, has been buried with his brain and body. That means annihilation, according to the infallible laws of chemistry. The body becomes disorganized, and ceases to exist in a tangible condition. Your logic compels the mind to share the fate of the body."

"Jim, you have arrived at a conclusion repugnant to my feelings. All the instincts of my nature recoil at the thought of annihilation. I now perceive I have been entertaining a conceit—an undigested notion—which, like an iridescent soap-bubble, collapses when touched. Make clear to my understanding the knowledge you possess on this subject of mind and its relation to matter. I will listen more, and talk less."

"Death is the act of divorcement of the *mind* from the body. The body perishes; that is, its form is resolved into elemental conditions. Essentially, it is indestructible, but the mind pervading the body is eternal in duration. On earth, *mind clothes itself with matter; in the elemental world it clothes itself with spirit.* In its purest condition, mind is supreme intelligence; but when expressed through matter, its wisdom is less perfect than when it speaks through a spirit-form. It will thus be seen that there are two conditions or forms through which the Supreme Mind expresses itself. First: The earth, or material form composed of concreted elements called matter. Second: The spirit-form, which is really matter in its more sublimated or discreted condition. The latter form enables the expression of the higher truths, and transmits them to the coarser forms, which move on the elemental plane of life. Hence, the ideas of the natural world originate in the spirit-world, and the truths of the spirit-world emanate from the Supreme Mind. Perfect organizations are unfolded for the expression of purest thought. Faulty organizations—alas! the world is full of them—can not grasp the higher truths of spirit-life.

"I will illustrate my thought with the case in point. The suspension-bridge is but an actual expression of an idea—the tangible of the intangible; the materialized, immaterial thought. The thought was spiritual, and found its expression through Roebling's brain, as sounds are reflected through the bosom of the winds. Thus he only becomes the medium of the thought, not the originator—the inspired, not the inspiration. History is full of the grand achievements of men and women who have been but mediums for the outbirths of spiritual ideas. The natural world, you will now perceive, is a necessity of the spiritual world. It completes the circuit of unfolding and progressing life. Through matter, thus, the spirit-world proclaims its grandest truths. All men are mediums, to subserve some special purpose; but few there are who possess such fine-strung harmony in their natures, that the highest truths may, through them, find expression. Of such was Haydn, whose soul thrilled with spiritual harmonies, which found expression in his immortal 'Oratorio.' Raphael's spiritual vision opened upon the sweet face of the 'Madonna and Child,' before he transfixed them with enduring pigments upon the glowing canvas. Phidias gazed upon his 'Nemesis' and his majestic 'Olympian Jupiter,' as they lay dreaming in the unshapely blocks of marble, ere a chisel-mark was made or a hammer-sound was heard, fashioning them with dignity and expression. Shakespeare caught the inspiration of eternal verities, and marshaled them in deathless procession along the lines of his immortal verse. O, my dear friend, there is a world of beauty which the natural eye doth not see! It is a world of melody that the natural ear doth not hear. It is peopled with intelligences which but few understand. It is the source of natural life, supplying you with all that is true and beautiful and good."

"Now, Jim, stop this rhapsodizing. I have no doubt but you have spoken the truth; but we started to talk about material things, and here you have whipped me off into airy nothing, into the realms of intangible speculation. Please answer me this practical question: *Could this bridge have been built without Mr. Roebling's brain to superintend its construction?* Now, stick to the point squarely, and no dodging."

"I have already stated that brain-substance, essentially, is the same in man and beast. You mean the *mind* flowing through Roebling's material organization? Mind is impersonal."

"Well, if that suits you better, answer!"

"No: not that particular bridge. It would be

impossible to find another organization precisely like Mr. Roebling's, through which *mind* could so exactly express itself. The bridge embodied the highest truths which Mr. Roebling was capable of receiving at the time. But, one year later, he became the recipient of a new influx of ideas, which discovered to him errors that would have been corrected in the construction of another bridge. Man is eternally unfolding his faculties, placing himself thereby in more intimate relation with the causative world. The Mr. Roebling who built the bridge at Cincinnati was not the same gentleman who constructed the bridge across Niagara River. Organizations through which *mind* develops itself are changing day by day. The mind of Webster, almost god-like as it was, flowing through a different organization, might be stale, vapid, and commonplace. Or it might, under more favorable conditions, exhibit itself with such grandeur and strength that all its former achievements would be dwarfed in comparison. Mind will exhibit its quality whenever a medium is found, whether it be through the brain of a Webster or 'Blind Tom.'

"There are no two things exactly alike in the universe. All organizations of matter are individualized. That is the reason the suspension-bridge could not have been constructed by any other than Mr. Roebling's mind. I fear the distinction I make between brain and mind—or, the better statement would be, mind and matter—is a little obscure."

"No: your distinction is well made; still I can not surrender my brain-theory to your mind-theory without further illustrations. In the organization of the brain, is there not some center of motion wherein thought is generated, where there is a galvanic action of brain-glands by which all your spiritual ideas may be explained?"

"If there is such a self-acting organization in which a spring of intelligence spontaneously flows in the structure of the human brain, you should point it out, else you will be charged with the insincerity of following a devious fancy, rather than the guidance of a fact. The French writer, Descartes, advanced the thought that the *pineal gland*, which is a little soft, gray substance of a conical shape, situated just above the *quadri gemina*, was the seat of the soul and the center of mind. It is in this little gland—no larger than a marrow-fat pea—where the great creative power (of bridge-building) is born. Its tiny chambers become the picture-galleries of all the ideas you illustrate in matter. All thought, all passion, all impulse, all action, springs from this common center. Do you think Descartes was a philosopher, Doctor? But spare your breath, for he has presented the best theory for the material origin of ideas that has yet been essayed. It is the only demonstrated argument that has as yet been attempted."

"As I am not a follower of Descartes, I may speak of his *pineal gland* hypothesis with entire freedom. It seems absurd to my mind."

"And yet no more absurd than to talk about 'a change of heart,' which thirty thousand or more paid priests are doing all over your land, every day and night in the year."

"I fear you are irreverent, Jim. You have so little respect for the cloth."

"I fear so, too. I have but little reverence or respect for men or cloth, when they impede the influx of truth to the understanding of the world. It is good for us all that this 'pineal gland' theory is not true, else the old 'infallible' blatherskite would concentrate all his official cursings into one word, and call it *lightning*, with which pineals would be St. Bartholomewized in a jiffy, or be damned as 'flat as fips.'"

"Well, let the pineal glands go, and return to the bridge. I fear I do not understand you exactly. Suppose I admit the *idea* of the bridge to have been imported by Roebling through the custom-house of his brain: now that we have it in a materialized expression, have we not secured it for all time?"

"A prisoner you would make it? No: you have only secured the shadow of the idea. The idea itself is indestructible."

"But the bridge—"

"Is a mere shadow!"

"A hundred thousand tons of granite and iron?"

"Yes, a hundred thousand millions. Ideas are eternal, but matter has no permanent form. There are reciprocal forces ever at work building up new and destroying old forms. Children come, and men go. So granite and iron. The destruction of your bridge is only a question of time, which, measured by eternity, is but half a swing on the pendulum of the clock of the universe."

"And these forces will destroy my body?"

"What if they do?"

"But I—"

"Will live, like the idea of the bridge, forever! Your body is nothing but a crystallization of elements about the form of your spirit. It can't think! It is not you, no more than is your old coat!"

"But your logic annihilates my body; and that is all I know myself to be."

"You are to be pitied! You are startled by the thought of having your body annihilated. How does the annihilation of two cities impress you? Two have recently expired in flames.* Do you expect them to be reorganized as they were before their elements were liberated by fire?"

"But, Jim, there is a difference in the building material of a city, and the material of a human body?"

"Human bodies were burned with the cities. Did the fire discriminate in their destruction?"

"No!"

"Of course not! The same elements are found in building-material for houses that are found in the building-material for bodies. Lime in the stone, lime in the bone. When chemistry discovers an element, she calls it by name, and does not say it belongs exclusively to a cow or a dog or a pig-headed man; does *she?*"

"The body of a horse, I understand you to say, is composed of the same elements as the body of a man? What difference, then, is there between a horse and a man?"

"Mind! And that only in quantity, not in quality.

* The destructive fires of Boston and Chicago are here alluded to.

Thorough-bred horse-sense compares favorably with the 'scrub-sense' of the uneducated clod-pole."

"Jim, you have trotted around 'Robin Hood's barn' several times, and have got me in a perspiration. Will you please tell me just exactly, and in few words, what you are *driving at?*"

"Don't stultify the subject by 'lingo.' Do you not see that all my illustrations prove that ideas have a spiritual origin; that they are organized forces, seeking material expression to benefit the world; that *they* find you, not you them? Thus the ideal bridge found a medium for giving the best expression of itself *through* Roebling's organization. The telegraph found one in Morse. Steam begged of Fulton to utilize it for the benefit of man. The spirit sewing-machine could find no better medium at the time than Howe. And impersonal truths have poured their inspirations into the receptive brains of all men that have lived in the world since the morning of Brahma to the high noon of Walt Whitman."

"I understand you, then, to reverse the accepted order of things. All our great discoveries, you allege, are but inspirations from the spirit-world; that man creates nothing, only as he is acted upon by intelligence outside of himself; that he does not even discover law, but law discovers him?"

"Your statement is nearly correct."

"I fear this sort of spiritualism will find but few advocates?"

"That makes no difference in the status of truth. The multitude do not think. They follow the lead of the most noise. The 'still, small voice' is never heard by the boisterous rabble. Do n't talk to me about the *un-thinking* herd. One clear-headed, brave thinker, through whom the senate of the skies delivers its grand truths to the world is worth more to mankind than a million purblind, bigoted, creed-bound moles and bats, who chatter and grin about their creeds, their baubles, and their splendid churches."

"You would be crucified, Jim, for uttering such sentiments, if you lived in Cincinnati."

"I know that very well; but the truth would live without me. And yet Cincinnati is no worse than Boston, Baltimore, or Philadelphia. All cities are made up of money-changers, stock-jobbers, pawn-brokers, factors, venders and drinkers of lager-beer, butchers, soap-boilers, tobacco-dealers, shop-keepers, hucksters, and fashionable wine-drinkers. What appreciation can spiritual truths receive at such hands? Such people believe in the commodities they handle. Have they not stomachs to feed, backs to clothe, and respectability to maintain?"

"But, Jim, are they not happy?"

"O yes: 'tis true, and pity 'tis, 'tis true, that he is happiest who has most flesh and blood, the strongest sinews, and the stoutest stomach. But what of him as a spirit?"

"I do n't know!"

"Think a little! Good-bye!"

CHAPTER XIV.

A HOST OF SPIRITS—TWO PRIVATE LETTERS—COLONEL PIATT MYSTIFIED—A SINGULAR VISION—MOHAMMED'S AUTOGRAPH—JOSEPHINE EXPLAINS—NEY AND NOLAN TO BE SEEN.

ON the morning succeeding the remarkable interview recorded in the last chapter, I proposed leaving for home; but, before starting, I desired to say "good-bye" to those spirits who felt an interest in my movements. For this purpose Mrs. Hollis again held the slate; and it was only a few minutes when, from the frame, a sheet of paper dropped upon the floor; then another, and another, at intervals of three to five minutes. These were covered with written signatures, mostly the names of spirits that had at different times written or spoken to me. They gave no messages, but in this manner simply announced their presence. I have had one of these pages engraved as a specimen, thinking that the varied chirography might interest even the most casual reader. There are four capital J's that look as if they might have all been written by the same penman; but who is he? Yet the capital J in Mary Jordan's name is as unlike the others as possible. Excepting Josephine Bonaparte, John H. Bradley, James Nolan, and Daniel M'Dowell, the remainder are signatures of kins-people:

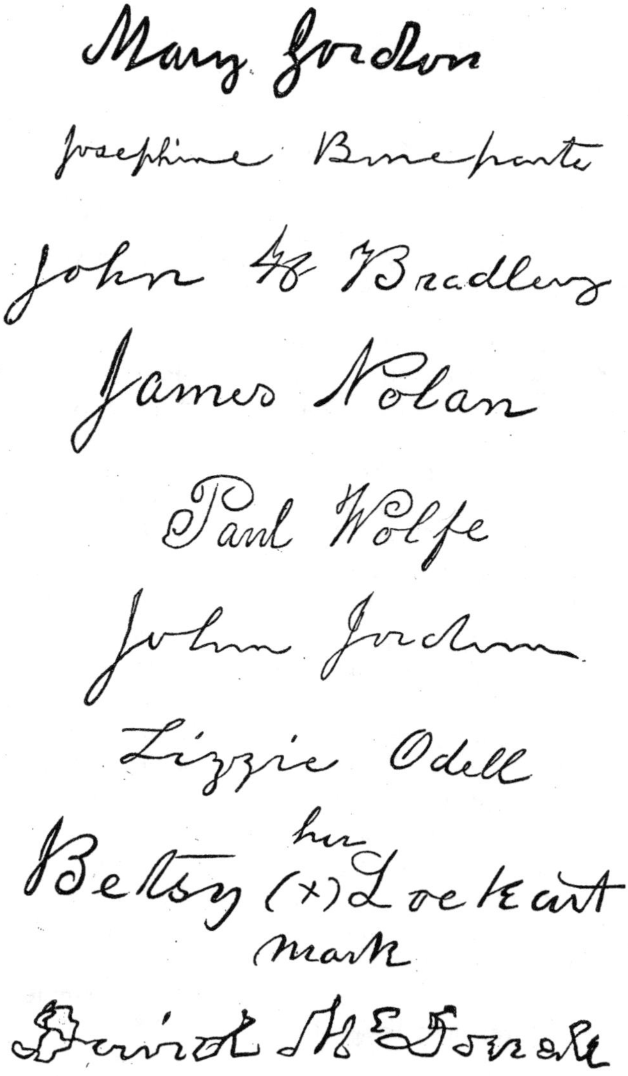

Mary Jordon

Josephine Bonaparte

John W. Bradley

James Nolan

Paul Wolfe

John Jordan

Lizzie Odell

her
Betsy (×) Lockart
mark

David McDonald

While we were examining these autograph sheets on the top of the table, almost continuous rapping was heard underneath, which we understood to be a call for the slate. Mrs. Hollis held it as before, and it was not more than five minutes when a letter was written, which purported to be from the wife of a congressman by the name of Goforth, living in or near Lafayette, Indiana. There was nothing in the letter that could be of the least interest to the public, and I only mention the fact because it occurred precisely in the manner stated. I mailed the letter to the M. C., by request of the writer, but have not heard whether it ever reached him or not. At the time, I had no knowledge of such an individual being in existence, but since then have been informed that a person of that ilk had really a habitation and a name in and about the vicinity of Lafayette. Alas for congressional honor!

"It seems to be a good morning for the spirits, Mrs. Hollis," I said. "See if there are any others who desire to say something." Again the slate was put under the table, and again we succeeded in capturing another letter. This time the communication was for Colonel Donn Piatt, Washington City, D. C., and, like the preceding one, was also of a private character. The letter was accompanied by a similar request, that it should be mailed to the given address. Of course, I obeyed instructions, and in due time received the Colonel's acknowledgments for the same.

The following extract from Colonel Piatt's letter contains the exceptionable views he entertains in reference to the spiritual origin of these mysterious communications. And yet he does not seem to be more satisfied with his own theory of "subtle characterizations" than with the startling facts which stare him in the face, and "will not down at his bidding." He writes:

> "For myself, Doctor, all that I can say is, that I am puzzled without being convinced. *I know that the medium has nothing whatever to do with the manifestations beyond furnishing the power, whatever that is;* but I must yet have other and better proof to convince me that the intelligence is from the spirits of the departed. The more I strive to convict my understanding, the more unsatisfactory it becomes. For example, the letter before me is not the voice of——. *The names mentioned, and the facts referred to, are startling; but those subtle characterizations that convince as 'soon as seen,' are wanting.*"

The italicized parts of the above show very clearly that Colonel Piatt's position is similar to that of many others who have had to deal with mental phenomena. He would have our friends speak, write, and think, just as they did before leaving the earth. It seems, however, in the vicissitudes to which the spirits are exposed in obtaining power to manifest their presence, that they do compromise in some manner their individual characteristics by which they were known as "soon as seen." Jim Nolan has said, many times, that when spirits return to communicate with their friends, as soon as they take on the conditions which enable them to manifest, they are influenced or limited in their expression by the mental and temperamental conditions of those constituting the magnetic sphere in which they work. For the time being, they are entirely dependent on those persons for their power to speak or write or think, just as a musician is dependent upon the instrument through which to give expression to his inward harmony. Had the colonel been present himself, by the introduction of a new element, the whole character of the communication he received might, and probably wou'ↄ, have been entirely changed, and those "subtle ʼnaracterizations" supplied that are now wanting. We experience a similar phenomenon in our intercourse with people. There are those in whose presence we are almost stifled to find words to convey our most familiar thoughts in an intelligible manner. Others become a source of inspiration to us, and by their unconscious aid we grow eloquent, elegant, and elevated in our thoughts, expression, and action. Public speakers especially have observed this difference in their audiences. The effect is obvious, but the cause obscure. In view of all the circumstances, my surprise is, not that the spirits are able to individualize so little, but so much. We expect too much and think too little ourselves. They do their best to manifest; do we to understand? May not our intellectual standard of criticism be faulty? Are we so clear in our apprehension that we see every effect in its right relation to the producing cause? "I see two objects," says the mal-formed optic. I can not see one, says the blind man. Both are right *wrong*.

"Go, wiser thou, and, in thy scale of sense,
Weigh thy opinion against Providence;
Call imperfection, what thou fanciest such;
Say here he gives too little, there too much.

. . . .

In spite of pride, in erring reason's spite,
One truth is clear, whatever is, is right."

By closely scrutinizing the ideas in the communications, however imperfect their verbal expression may be, we are always able to discriminate between a developed and undeveloped intelligence. Cultivated thought will exhibit somewhat of its quality or refinement, however much it may be restrained or modified by the conditions through which it is expressed. In the letter to Colonel Piatt this sentence occurs: "O, Donn, I believe those were our happiest days. It was the white-bread of life." I do n't know how that paragraph may sound to other ears, but it strikes me as being so refined in thought, and so exquisite in sentiment, that none but a highly cultivated intelligence could give such an utterance.

But whether the spirits whose names were attached to these letters really communicated them or not, is no part of my purpose to discuss. They came in the manner indicated, and, as neither Mrs. Hollis nor myself did the writing, it would interest me very much to know exactly who did, and how it was done.

But this was not all that occurred. While Mrs. Hollis and I were talking about the letters just received, she seemed to forget our conversation and lose all knowledge of her surroundings. Looking her in the face, she appeared to be dreaming, with her eyes wide open—an absent, introspective expression, that impressed me with a sense of listlessness or vacancy. I suspected that a *vision* had broken in upon her normal senses, as I had seen her in this condition before. I sat quiet for a few minutes, when she said:

"I see an extensive plain, a wide-spread, low, flat, singular-looking country. It seems to be an interminable, verdureless waste. There is no shrub, no bush, no tree, or any symptom of vegetable life, as far as the eye can reach, excepting along the banks of a turbid river, which stretches through the center of this muddy plain. The stream seems to be stagnant, and filled with hideous reptiles, who lash its dirty waters into boisterous waves. The banks on either side are fringed with leafless trees, from whose boughs are draped long reaches of decaying moss, descending to the water's edge. The monsters in the river make a most hideous and pitiful sound, as they flounder and furiously beat the waters into wildest commotion.

"There is a solitary man standing near the river bank. He is large, muscular, and of comely shape. He wears a turbaned sash about his head, and is covered with a scarlet mantle reaching to the ground. This he opens, revealing the costume of a Turk. Hanging to the girdle about his waist is a broad, crooked cimeter, or sword, which flashes in the sunlight. Over his forehead he wears a brilliant ornament in the shape of a crescent, which sparkles like fire. His beard is white and flowing to his waist. His complexion is olive, and his eyes large and intensely bright.

"He now points to the sky with his right-hand, and now to the earth. He speaks vehemently; but I can not understand what he says. He now strips himself of all his clothing, and flings them in the ugly river among the monsters. They wrangle and tear them to pieces. Extending his two hands, he says: '*Kingdoms rise and fall; nations come and go; but Allah rules forever. His truths are eternal. His laws are changeless. His eye never sleeps, and his hands are never idle. I come to help in his great work, and this day dedicate myself to his service.*'"

"How strange this is!" said Mrs. Hollis, as she seemed to recall herself as from a reverie. "What does it all mean?"

"You have been dreaming," I said, "and became a trifle rhapsodical."

"No: I have not been dreaming," she said; "but what I have told you, that have I seen. I don't suppose it amounts to any thing; but what do you think of it?"

"From the topography of the country you describe, I guess the river is called 'Styx.' Did those 'hideous reptiles' *roar you* like preachers, or slobber you like idiot editors, when they lie about spiritualists and spiritualism?"

"You are only joking!"

"I'm not good at divining. Your vision is very singular, and has, no doubt, a special and important significance, if we only knew how to translate or interpret it. Perhaps the spirits will tell us what it means. Please ask them."

Mrs. Hollis now held the slate again, and, as she did so, said: "I smell sandal-wood and odorous spices. Do you not smell the almost suffocating perfume?" Hereupon she began to cough as one who is stifled for breath, when the raps indicated the communication finished. The following edifying message was then found written on the paper, a *fac-simile* of which is here presented:

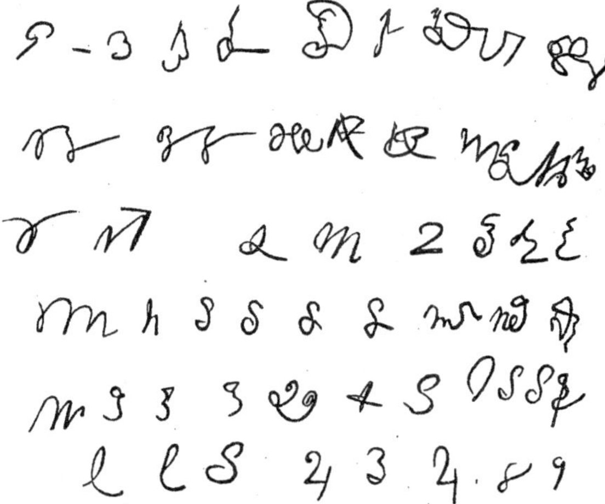

"Well, I can see nothing in all this but confusion worse confounded. Will the spirits please state what is meant by this vision and these characters?"

In reply to this request, Josephine wrote the following letter:

"MY DEAR FRIEND,—The vision described to you has an actual correspondence in the spirit-world. It is a type of the condition of the world under the teachings of a pagan religion, and the spirit described is Mohammed. His writings continue to exert a controlling influence over the minds of millions of his tawny worshipers. He beholds the error of his teachings, and the debasing effects they exert upon the lives of his followers, and has come to renounce them. He now disclaims his pagan worship, and enlists himself in the great work of opening communication between the two worlds. He has given his pledge of loyalty to the cause, and sealed it with his royal cyphers. Receive him with dignity. He is a great acquisition to the cause for which we all labor, and exerts a controlling influence over millions of spirits who continue to revere him in the spirit-world. JOSEPHINE."

It is my turn to ask, "What does all this mean?" Assuming the statement of Josephine to be true, what purpose is to be subserved by this vision with its co-related circumstances? If it is intended as a joke, the point is obscure. However, it is not my business to explain all I see and hear; but it is my business to record *facts* as they occur, for others to cogitate. Still this is no more a mystery than the reception of the letters for Colonel Piatt and *hundreds of others,* which come in the same manner.

Marshal Ney then wrote that he would try to materialize his entire form in the cabinet, when he next visited Cincinnati with the medium, and show himself with the door open.

Jim Nolan also wrote that he would be able to talk to me in the light, that I might see him during the conversation.

With these promises, the *seance* closed, and I returned home.

Here I will conclude this phase of manifested intelligence, which, for the want of a better name to express its character, I call "*spirit.*" If exceptions be taken to this, I will waive my assumption, providing a better designation is offered. "*Manifestations of the Devil*" has been suggested, by a clergyman of the Presbyterian persuasion, as a substitute; but, on weighing them both—the preacher and the devil—in the balance, they are found *even.* Give to the manifestations any name you please, but let it be reasonable. The subject requires plainness of speech. Sensible men and women demand it.

In the order prescribed for my writing, I will next record the phenomena I have witnessed in "*dark circles.*" In doing this, I must pursue the same course I have with the spirit-writing; that is, to present the facts, without strictly adhering to the chronological relation they sustain to each other.

It is of less interest to the general reader to know the exact time when a thing occurred, than it is to know that it really did occur, and *how* it occurred. The difference in time between Sunday and Saturday is not of much consequence. I am placing on record phenomena which occurred exactly in the manner related. Many witnesses could testify to these occurrences if they would; but as they will not voluntarily, they *shall on compulsion.* A large number of the witnesses I will call to testify, have the moral courage to do so voluntarily, and say openly, in no mincing manner, what they *know* about spiritual phenomena. Moral cowards shall be treated as such; and they will be known by their whining.

CHAPTER XV.

THE DARK CIRCLE—CHARACTER DISCLOSED—SPIRITS SINGING—CLAPPING HANDS—A GRIP—SKIWAUKEE'S TACTICS—ON A RAMPAGE—FLOATS THE MUSIC-BOX—MRS. HOLLIS LEVITATED TWICE—CLAIRVOYANCE—JIM NOLAN'S ELOQUENCE.

I HAVE already described, at page 125, the manner of forming a dark circle. It simply consists of three or four ladies and gentlemen going into a pleasant room, from which the light is excluded, with Mrs. Hollis, to witness spirit phenomena. That is a fair statement of the premises. There is nothing extraordinary in this to excite suspicion; and were it not for the manifestations which occur when Mrs. Hollis is present, the circumstance would not be worthy of special remark.

Sitting in the dark, in the momentary expectation that something extraordinary will occur, has a tendency to make the hearing very acute. Every sound, however trifling it may be, seems to be heard distinctly, amid the profound silence and darkness. No movement can be made to change the position of your feet or body, without the fact being made known by the now alert sense. I have, to test this sense in those in the dark room, upon several occasions, extended my hand forward, and moved it quietly from side to side. There was no noise, but simply gentle waves of the air, and yet this was appreciable, and excited inquiry.

A little experience in the dark circle will enable you to judge very accurately of the character of your company, by the *tone* of their voice. It is remarkable how you learn to sense almost their very thoughts, when in the dark. Darkness affords no facilities for concealment. If I desired to understand the true character of a man or woman, I could obtain all the needed information more readily by a conversation with them in a dark room than in a light one. It has, in fact, almost become a fixed conviction in my mind, that you can not fully appreciate the worth of your friend, until you interview him in the dark circle. Here he betrays the quality of his manhood, not in what he says so much as in the indescribable manner or tone he employs in speaking. If he "affects a virtue," or a style of speaking not natural to him, he might as soon proclaim it in so many words, to escape the harsher criticism which his duplicity invokes. In the dark circle, I have observed that persons who are very fastidious in their taste for dress, are sadly at a discount. Their gewgaws fail to divert the attention of the hearer from the speaker, and, notwithstanding the wealth of bodily adornment, there is a *poverty* in their expression, which "makes them (appear) poor indeed." "The costly ornaments and studied contrivances of speech" have no eloquence in the presence of the spirit-hosts. There must ring out the sound of true metal in every word and accent, or the base alloy or spurious coin is at once detected.

How sadly people deceive themselves, when they enter a dark room with the view to practice deception! A *young* man, to be smart, agreed with his companions before entering the circle, that he should be known as *Jones*. When he pronounced his assumed name in the dark, it was evident a lie had been spoken; and, a few minutes after, the spirits disclosed his real name, and refused to give any other test.

Spirits talk best in the presence of intelligent people. Like men, they can not display their powers of rhetoric or elocution in the presence of "sticks," no matter how fashionably dressed they may be. The dark circle very soon discovers all such people. They do very well to make up fashionable audiences for such peacock orators as *Gough*, where they exclaim, when he tosses up his coat-tails: "How beautiful! how delightful! how entertaining he is!" I say such people ought to keep out of the dark circle. They can not appreciate the philosophy of Nolan, or the stolid, matter-of-fact utterances of "Old Ski," who rises to the sublimity of scorn when he calls them "*papooses!*"

In most of the popular modes of worship, the services are begun with music. In our most fashionable places of worship this is a "hired service," and is paid for as any other entertainment. Exquisite music commands the best price. The prices paid are graduated to the quality of the voice. Richness, volume, purity, compass, are the desired qualities of sound to render the worship more impressive. The fortunate possessors of such gifts command good wages—they are staple endowments, and not grudgingly paid for. *Nose* singers are not in requisition. One organ with large pipes is worth more, in *devout* worship, than a whole congregation of *poor squealers*. The only thing that astonishes our pious devotees is, that the Lord should pay any attention to these *nose singers*, when he could be better entertained with the delightful operatic playing of Mr. Morgan. "We can," say they, "give him 'Opera Bouffe' in our cathedral, at one dollar a head, which is certainly very much more edifying than to hear a hundred poor devils drawling through their noses:

> "Come, ye sinners, *poor and needy*,
> Weak and wounded, sick and sore !"

What does he care about that class of people ? We never associate with them ; and if the Lord does not elevate his taste, and be a little more select about the company he keeps, he need n't come to *our church. We can get along very well without him !*"

As I was going to say, before the spirits begin to manifest in the dark room, as a general thing they request the circle to sing, or somebody to play a flute, guitar, or harp. Why they make this request, I do not quite clearly understand. Jim Nolan says it is because the electric vibrations of sound excite a freer discharge of magnetism from the medium ; and that music also has a tendency to blend the magnetic spheres of the individuals composing the circles. Both of these, he avers, are valuable adjuncts to the power for giving good manifestations.

"Sacred" music being a necessary appliance of worship, and not being able to supply the dreadful demand upon my limited ability, I invested a hundred dollars in a large, sweet-toned German music-box. It was the very thing—good, fashionable music, that would entice St. Peter from his post, if he were musically inclined. It answered the purpose, and gave satisfaction to the spirits.

But now commence the manifestations. During the singing, a number of spirit-voices will join the concert, which can readily be distinguished by the volume of sound, the clearness, purity, and precision of articulation. They will sing alto, air, and bass, sometimes without human aid of any kind. They prefer, however, to be assisted with singing or playing by some one in the circle. With no other person in the room but the medium and myself, I have heard the vocalization of the spirits for half an hour, and, though "unused to the melting mood," these "heavenly choristers" have moved me with their sweet voices, as neither Lind, Parepa, or Nilsson could do. The scientist takes no more interest in this phenomenon, however, than he does in the "cackle of a hen," and is ready to pronounce it all *flummery*. But not so fast, my Sir Oracle! I want you to disclose, just here, how that music was made, and by whom. You will, I fear, not make these discoveries with the aid of your square, compass, steelyards, and crucibles. Electricity and magnetism elude the grasp of figures. You can not define love with mathematics. You can not wrap up all creation in formulated problems. You gentleman of subtraction and division, multiplication and addition—I ask you again, and charge you to answer, *Who sings?* If any one entertains the thought that it is Mrs.

Hollis, she will, if your *bad* manners insist upon it, engage you in conversation while the music is also heard. These melodists sing at times more sweetly than Methodists at a love-feast.

On one occasion, Judge W. J. Berry and Captain Edward Air, of Newport, Ky., and myself, sat together two hours, in one of these spirit-concerts, during which time Captain Air, who is a fine vocalist, sang not less than twenty *test* songs, "old and new," in every one of which the spirits joined, frequently carrying the air, and supplying the forgotten words when the captain's memory was at fault.

This singing is a feature in the dark circle; and is so real, so life-like, that it is most difficult in thought to disassociate it from human vocalization. If every facility was not afforded to prove the absence of human aid in its production, it would be most difficult to believe in the spirit-origin of this pleasant and instructive phenomenon.

The next manifestation of the dark circle I shall notice, is the presence of spirit-lights. These, as a general rule, appear in the vicinity of the medium's head; and vary in size from that of a fire-fly to that of a man's hand. The small lights, like tiny rockets, fly in a straight line, from three to six feet, when they take a curvilinear course, and expire in different parts of the room. I have seen as many as ten of these small meteors glowing at the same instant, though never more than one of the large ones at a time.

The large light makes its appearance in a cloudy-looking haze, growing each moment more luminous until it becomes of a brilliant orange color. The lights float slowly about the room mostly in front of the circle. These spirit-pyrotechnics are seldom given, for the reason that they are very debilitating to the medium. Some persons affirm they see spirit-faces in these lights; but, excepting the single instance witnessed in the circle I attended in Louisville, I have no personal knowledge of such facts.

Equally noteworthy with the singing and lights, as occurring in the dark circle, are the manifestations of power which can only be exhibited in a materialized form of the spirit. During the singing, or before or after it, the spirits will touch your hand, take you by the arm, pat you on the head or knee, and clap their hands so loudly that you can hear them in the adjoining room. It occurred once, just as I extinguished the light, at the beginning of the circle, my arm was grasped with such a "grip" that the imprints of "old Ski's" huge, muscular fingers were ecchymosed under the cuticle for a week after.

Most generally, I observed, at the conclusion of the music, the spirits would clap their hands, if they made any demonstration at all. Many people have seen Blind Tom, the negro pianist, and will remember, at the conclusion of each performance, how jubilantly he claps his hands. This spirit hand-clapping is analogous—so it seems at least to me—to that of Tom's. I have heard as many as half a score or more spirits clap their hands rapidly at the same instant, in different parts of the room.

Millions of people have heard the spirit-raps; but not so many have heard them in the "dark circle."

They are quite a different article here from the little feeble sound so often heard at the table of a family circle. A green persimmon and a ripe pear could not be more unlike. Here the raps have volume, force, power. They startle you, when made near your head or heels, like the crash of a fore-hammer striking near you in the dark; you do not know but that some of the strokes are intended to brain you. This makes you feel decidedly uncomfortable. That is the way "*Skiwaukee*" takes the starch out of upstarts. I have heard such cry pitifully not to be hurt. After the old savage had scared his victim half out of his wits, he would soothe his agitation, with the tenderness of a woman's voice, by assuring him that he "won't hurt 'em papoose!" (baby.) I never knew "old Ski" to undertake a job of this kind that he did not succeed in putting his victim on his good behavior for the remainder of the evening. Sometimes he would put a reed-horn uncomfortably near the ear of the badly behaving gentleman or lady, and give it a sudden blow that would almost "split the ears of the groundlings!"

> "One blast upon his bugle-horn
> Could start a thousand men!"

How piteously they would plead to be let alone! Ski would then kindly tell them he knew they were cowards; that brave men were always men of sense, and knew how to behave themselves when they came to talk to the spirits.

Many persons have been profited by the lessons taught them by "old Ski," and will not forget him easily. FRED DOUGLASS said, when HENRY WARD

BEECHER'S defection from the abolition party occurred, and he had given in his adherence to the policy of ANDREW JOHNSON, " If I had Beecher on a plantation, and he was my nigger, and I was his master, I could, with a good limber raw-hide make him change back his opinions in twenty minutes." I believe Douglass; and so does "old Ski." If the raps fail to interest you, do n't go to sleep; for " Ski " has the horn. He will be very likely to disturb your "nap," by gently tapping your bump of veneration. He don't intend to hurt you, but simply to let you know that he is a phrenologist at times; and when he fails to find the bump of politeness on your cranium, he makes one with the big end of the "horn," you know! But, not to have a wrong impression entertained of "Skiwaukee," I declare him to be "y[e] most gentle savage;" and, in all that appertains to the quality of true manhood, the elements are so mixed in him that we honor ourselves when we call him *brother!*

A little spirit-child, "ANNA HANCOCK," a niece of Major-General W. S. Hancock, United States Army, cut, fashioned, and made, in a dark circle, a beautiful rosette, out of material which was taken into the dark room for the purpose; and, after its completion, pinned it nicely on the lapel of my coat, frequently touching my face with her little delicate fingers while doing so. In making this rosette, it was necessary to thread a needle with silk, and to stitch the fabric in a pitch-dark room. This child subsequently made a nice little doll-baby from materials placed in the room, which has excited the admiration and wonder of many ladies. She also made a regalia of rosettes, and hung them about my neck. Being only six years old, including both her natural and spirit life, I asked her who had taught her to do these things, when she replied, "*Miss* Josephine and grandmother;" meaning Josephine Bonaparte and my own mother. She thought to please me by calling her doll "Neppy." I have already intimated that the sense of touch sometimes leaves the imprint of spirit-fingers on your arm, which is sufficient to carry conviction, to the understanding of some people, that they have uncommon power in that way.

Carrying the horn about the room is mere child's-play for them. It don't amount to any thing as an achievement, especially when compared to the feat of carrying the music-box, which they have frequently done. It weighs twenty-three pounds, eight ounces. "Ski" will take this box, and float it about the room with wonderful rapidity, frequently a distance of twenty feet almost as quick as you can wink your eyes. This is always done when the music is playing, which serves to guide the mind to the locality of the box. It is quite interesting to listen to the transitive tones of this floating orchestra. Upon one occasion, the music stopped while the box was in transit, and the wonder was where it would be found when the light was introduced. It was found half under my chair and between my feet. The room was pitch-dark, of course. On another occasion, we had failed to throw a *red* blanket over the chair of the medium. This blanket the old chief claimed as his personal property, and its absence gave great offense to "Ski," who still retains his love and admiration for a "red article." He said it gave him strength, power to speak and act; besides, it was grateful to his feelings. He loved the red blanket. There was no excuse for not putting it in its wonted place, but carelessness. This put him in ill-humor, and a rampage was the consequence. In the room was a chest of drawers and a wardrobe, both of which were filled with sheets, pillow-slips, unseasonable clothing, table-linen, and other store-away things. He started on a hunt for his blanket. He commenced ransacking the bureau at the top drawer, and ending with the bottom. Things flew through the room like frightened pigeons, here and there and every-where, until the drawers were empty. He next went for the wardrobe, and gave it such an overhauling as it never had before, and will hardly ever get again. At last, almost on the very bottom of the shelf was found the much-prized article—the red blanket. The success of the search was pronounced with a guttural grunt, "Got 'em!" It was not loud, but deep. "Ski" was mad—mad as a "March hare"—and not to be trifled with in that way, much. When the light was brought in, the room was found to be littered with the contents of the drawers and wardrobe; and, what I have over-looked until now, the furniture of a wash-stand occupied a prominent place in the middle of the floor. He had given us a splendid display of his power and wrath; though that, I believe, was not the actuating motive. "Ski" will not wear *wings* for some time yet.

But the most marvelous manifestation of power in the dark circle is yet to be noticed. There were five persons in the room, including the medium. The conditions were unusually good. No public *seance* had been given for several days. The medium was rested. The *seance* I am about to notice was attended only by the several members of my family.

As soon as the room was darkened, "the birds began to sing!" I never heard such singing—the many voices blending in perfect harmony, clear, loud, musical, and bewitching. It was a love-feast of celestial melody, which we, one and all, enjoyed to the full capacity of our appreciation. This charming concert continued about twenty minutes, unassisted by a human voice, until it suddenly ceased, and Mrs. Hollis seemed to be surrounded by a multitude of spirit-voices, speaking quick, confusedly, and in an undertone. I could not comprehend what was being said; neither could Mrs. Hollis, who became alarmed, and asked me what they intended to do. I quieted her fears, with assurances that whatever they did, no harm would inure to her—to keep quiet, and offer no resistance to their will. What next transpired, I will copy from my note-book:

"A spirit-voice began to chant a part of the Episcopal service, and then improvised a rhapsody that was indescribably sweet and beautiful. This musical manifestation continued about ten minutes, during which time we commented freely upon the quality of the voice. The singing had but scarcely ceased, when an indescribable sound, resembling that which is made by a startled flock of birds, was heard, and coinstantial Mrs. Hollis, affrighted, was heard *over our heads, floating along the ceiling of the room!* She pleaded piteously to be let down! "Don't let me fall! Please don t hurt me! O, do let me down! Please let me down!" This aerial flight continued only for a minute, during which time I ordered her to clap her hands against the ceiling, and mark the wall with the pencil she had in her hand; all of which she did. She no sooner touched the carpet than she sprang forward into the arms of one of the ladies, begging us not to permit the spirits to carry her up again. Several efforts of this kind had been previously made, but never with such success. It always frightened her, notwithstanding she felt assured no harm would befall her. Ordinarily she was a courageous woman, but this lifting unnerved her.

"I can not tell, Mrs. Hollis," I said, "what object they have in view, in levitating you in this manner; still I feel assured they will not injure you." As I said this, Jim Nolan spoke in a more than usually sympathetic voice, saying:

"Why, Doctor, we could not be induced to hurt our medium. She is to us as precious as your eye to you, always an object of our deepest sympathy and most tender care. What could we do without her? *If she were lost to us, we could not replace her among a million of women.*"

"But, Jim, what's the use of this manifestation? If it is only pastime, you ask her to make too much sacrifice for your pleasure."

"We seek to show our power, and, by that means, convince of our presence. We could float her like a feather, if she were entranced. But to this she objects; and we prefer to float her while she is in the full possession of her faculties. If she would submit to our wishes, we could in six weeks carry her over the heads of an audience in good light, to be seen by all, while she held conversation with the spectators. O no! we will do her no injury, nor will we permit harm to come to her. We guide her footsteps, and guard them from peril. We know her every wish, and seek, when it is proper, to gratify them."

"But, Jim, why do you permit her to suffer so much with terror, when you lift her? A fancied danger causes as much mental suffering as a real peril. Imagination can kill or cure, as its power may be directed."

"It is not from apprehension of personal harm that her terrors arise, but from the peculiar condition of her mind, after depriving her physical system of its magnetic relation to the brain. In this de-magnetized condition of the body, the will-power becomes abeyant, when the faculties of the soul, alarmed and disordered, start up as in a hideous dream. We want gradually to overcome this condition; we will then be able to lift and float her at pleasure."

"But why," I interposed, "do you disturb this magnetic relation of the brain to the body, when the consequences of doing so will plainly thwart your efforts and distress the medium?"

"We can not succeed without doing this! Besides, the distress is not real," he replied; "the panic is unpleasant, but it passes away as soon as the magnetic relation of the brain to the body is re-established. By intercepting this magnetic relation, the body becomes more buoyant, and if completely broken off, the spiritual forces would express themselves with such power, that its avoirdupois would be almost destroyed. It would 'take to itself wings and flee away.'"

"Do you mean literal wings, such as Raphael's cherubs have?"

"O no! I only wish to symbolize the celerity of spirit-action, when not harnessed in the service of human magnetism."

Before the conclusion of the *seance*, Mrs. Hollis was again lifted to the ceiling, and floated through the room. She made pencil-marks on different parts of the plaster, indicating the direction of her aerial movements. When the light was restored, the pencil and right-hand were covered with lime-dust, as well as the sleeve of her dress.

Though the name "dark circle" conveys the idea of entire obscurity from sight, this impression is erroneous, as many persons can testify. Mrs. Hollis in the dark room not only sees the persons composing the circle, but also the spirits manifesting, whom she describes with accuracy, and calls by name. This power of clairvoyance is one of the most interesting studies in the whole range of spirit phenomena, and excites our admiration most when we give it most thought. But few persons have attempted to account for this wonderful clear-sight. I have my theory, and will briefly state it.

In the anatomical construction of the human eye, two chambers are necessary to perfect the visual law. These are known to anatomists and opticians as anterior and posterior, or front and back, chambers. They are filled with aqueous, crystalline, and vitreous humors, through which are transmitted images upon the membranes, which serve as mirrors to reflect them upon the sensorium. These are called the sclerotic, choroid, and retina.

The uses of these several organs are: first, to reflect images along the optic track to the *sensorium;* and, second, to *exclude* solar rays, by a process of filtering, from entering the picture-gallery of the soul. However paradoxical it may seem, we are nevertheless indebted to darkness for all the pleasure we receive through the sense of sight. I will give a familiar illustration of this proposition.

The *camera obscura* is fashioned after the structure of the human eye. It has its anterior and posterior chambers; also lenses, to correspond to the humors of the eye. The posterior chamber, in both cases, is *dark*. Over the back wall of the back chamber of the eye is spread a dark-colored secretion, through which the almost invisible fibers of the optic nerve are woven. This finds its correspondence in the sensitized plate of the photographer. It is not necessary to trace strictly the analogy of structure any farther; so we will present the more interesting details of the phenomena.

Artists tone down the light while a picture is being taken. So the circular band of muscles which forms the pupil of the eye contracts and tones down the light on the first lens, that it may be almost or entirely lost on the second, leaving the background *black*. Hence, darkness is an absolute condition of vision. Solar rays falling in a direct vertical line upon the sensitized retina of the eye, would destroy its quality, and paralyze it forever. The action of the sun upon the whole structure of the eye is to lessen rather than augment its power.

The converse of this proposition is equally true. In the absence of solar rays the integuments of the eye become so highly sensitized, that they develop a more perfect luminous condition than they can in the face of day. Thus the *dark room* becomes to the eye what the dark tube of the microscope becomes to sight, an augmenting power which reveals the wonderful phenomena of millions of creatures in a dew-drop. The telescope, in like manner, with its lenses and *dark* chamber, assists the eye to penetrate space so remote, that the added power makes the senses ache. Telescope the earth, and from the bottom of a well you may see stars at the high noon of day.

To sit in a dark room several hours every day, for a year, the humors and attachments of the eye become so sensitive to light, that their sensibility becomes painfully acute. But sit in a dark room for only *one* hour, once or twice a week, for six months, and what will be the effect on the optic structure? The testimony of those who have patiently put themselves under such a discipline is to the effect that darkness at first makes the whole nervous system excitable, and the effect is quite painful. But after a while, the system becomes tranquil, when the brain begins to idealize most vividly. Between "dreaming and waking," the room grows light, the outlines of furniture, and at length the face of "the old clock," can be distinctly seen. Persevere in the dark baths, and not only will the dark room become light, but, under the scrutiny of the new vision, the human form becomes transparent as glass, with the action of every organ in its complex structure distinctly appreciated. The brain, heart, arteries, and glands are seen, brilliant with flames of life, and more beautiful than auroral splendors. But now "the wonder of wonders" is revealed! Intangible, incomprehensible space becomes *peopled* with living forms. Be calm, and the faces of old friends will be seen, and their voices will again be heard. Thus the spiritual sense of hearing and seeing become unfolded, and thus a latent power we little thought belonged to us, disclosed. But to return to the phenomena of the dark room.

You may test the clairvoyant powers of "old Ski" or Jim Nolan—but especially the former—by holding in your hand, in a dark circle, any article you may wish, and ask him to name it. He will do it, if he is at all familiar with its name or use, thereby proving conclusively that, in the entire absence of light, the power of vision remains good. A lady, who thought to please "Ski," promised to present him with a fine red feather, designating an ostrich plume as the gift. "Ski" was much pleased, and reminded her several times, during the evening, of the promise she had made. She forgot all about it when she next visited the dark circle, but "Ski" had not. She was severely reprimanded for her neglect, the old chief saying, "Em squaw lie!" She pleaded forgetfulness, but promised not to forget again. She brought the feather the next visit, but made no allusion to the fact, not even after she entered the dark room. She now quietly placed the feather in her hair, and while in the act, "Ski" gave a shout: "Em squaw bring em! em nice squaw!" But, alas for the short-lived reputation of the squaw! when "Ski" gave a closer inspection to the article, he discovered a fraud, and felt indignant at the deceit. He scornfully rejected the gift, saying: "Squaw bring em old *chicken*-feather! Do n't want em old *chicken*-feather! old chicken-feather squaw!" He had made an intelligent discrimination between an ostrich-plume and a very beautiful chicken-feather of his favorite bright-red color, *in the dark*, to the surprise and merriment of every one present. But mark the feeling he displayed! He will also tell the exact time by your watch, or, as stated, name any article of dress or toilet you may call his attention to, in the blackest atmosphere.

Marshal Ney wrote to me at the table, that if I would sit in a dark room with the medium, for three or four mornings, he thought he would be able to draw a picture, while I held the medium's hands. Of course I consented; and, procuring the necessary paper and pencils, Mrs. Hollis and I took position beside a table in the dark room, on which the articles lay, I taking her hands in mine. The sitting continued half an hour or more, but with no other result than a few straggling marks. Three trials were given on three consecutive mornings, but with very little better success. On the fourth morning, we had resumed our usual position but a few minutes, when we could distinctly hear the pencils moving rapidly over the paper. In half an hour after the light had been extinguished, the signal was given that the *seance* was closed. The room was again lighted, when the accompanying picture was found to have been drawn during the time we had sat in the dark. (See next page.) As a work of art, this picture has no merit whatever. If it symbolizes any occult idea, it is quite valueless to me. I am told some of the emblems belong to Masonry. I have no knowledge of this—am not a Mason, and believe Mrs. Hollis is not—but the picture is interesting when viewed as a spirit production, and as being executed in a dark room.

But spirit conversations are the most interesting features of the dark circles. I have already spoken of these, and reported interviews which I had with my mother, Jim Nolan, Josephine, Marshal Ney, and others. The reader, however, may want more exact information in regard to their occurrence.

When persons first visit the dark room, especially if there are strong influences antagonizing their power, the spirits are unable to talk for some time. Those who belong to Mrs. Hollis's band can speak freely almost from the moment the singing ceases; but your own friends require more time to master the situation. What difficulties they have to surmount before they can manifest, I have already hinted; but this subject, I am well convinced, is but little understood. The spirit of a person who died with a lingering disease, in whom the strength gradually wasted before death, I have observed, exhibits a voice so feeble as almost to be indistinct. The victims of pulmonary phthisis experience the same feebleness and difficulty in talking

We shall ever love you
as our friend we thank you for
your patience in geting this
good bye

M Ney

that they had before passing into the spirit-world. I have heard them cough, to remove what seemed to me secretions from the air-tubes, that they might be enabled to speak more distinctly. They often allude to this disability, and deplore their want of strength with sincere regret. To my questionings they reply that it is only when they come into the circle-room that they feel the infirmities of the body-life; and this only at the beginning of their visits.

The gradual increase of power to talk is quite noticeable as they appear from time to time. They get accustomed to the situation, and, like old hands at the business, can "hew close to the line" without making mistakes.

The spirits forming the band that controls Mrs. Hollis's circle, of course speak without impediment, loudly and distinctly. Jim Nolan has spoken to me two hours without exhibiting the least symptom of fatigue or exhaustion. He never grows weary; his endurance would sustain him for a month, if the medium could supply the requisite power. Jim Nolan speaks loud enough to he heard distinctly in every part of the largest public hall in the city of Cincinnati, and when I say he could entertain as many thinkers as could be seated in the hall, with his grand ideas and compact reasoning, I but iterate a fact that is well known to hundreds of the best minds of our country, who have been amazed at the splendor and rapidity of his thought, the profundity of his logic, and the grandeur of his eloquence.

CHAPTER XVI.

CABINET FOR THE SPIRITS—EXCITEMENT IN HADES—WONDERFUL PHENOMENA—MY MOTHER'S FACE, HAND, AND VOICE—FACE OF THE EMPRESS JOSEPHINE—SPIRIT-FLOWERS—SPIRIT PLAYS THE HARP—MARSHAL NEY IN UNIFORM, MATERIALIZED.

THE extraordinary manifestations I am about to record began on the 25th of May, 1872. The time was near the close of Mrs. Hollis's third engagement. I spoke to Mrs. Hollis several times about constructing a cabinet—something similar to the one used by the Davenport Brothers, in giving their public exhibitions—simply as an experiment; but she seemed to think the results would be an expensive disappointment. Hence, she advised against it. Nolan and Ney took similar views; and Josephine gave timid counsel—not committing herself either for or against the experiment. I had no alternative but to back down or go ahead, and I could n't back down.

Accordingly, I gave my idea of a cabinet to MR. JOHN H. BROWN, a well-known mechanic on Third Street, near Central Avenue, with an order to materialize it as soon as possible. He did this to my satisfaction, and brought it to my house, and placed it in the center room, on the second floor of my rear dwelling. The following diagram will show the position of the room and cabinet, where the manifestations occurred:

North blank wall—36 feet.

A. West room, used as reception-room. B. Consulting-room, in which the cabinet was placed. C. East room; office for writing, etc. D. Entrance doorways to cabinet-room, with transom lights. o o o. The position of chairs for spectators when witnessing spirit manifestations. E E E. Doorways. H H. Halls. SS. Stairways from first floor. W W. Windows. □. Music-box.

The cabinet is fairly represented by any ordinary full-sized wardrobe, six feet high, five feet wide, and two feet deep. The back and two ends were factory-planed one-inch pine boards, tongued and grooved. The front had but one door, three and a half feet wide; in length, the whole height of the cabinet. In the center of the door, about four and a half feet from the bottom, was cut a diamond-shaped hole, about eight inches in longest diameter. This aperture was covered on the inside by a thick piece of cloth fastened over the top, and permitted to hang down loose over the opening, and several inches below it, in such a manner as to effectually exclude the light from the interior of the cabinet. In the cabinet was placed a chair for Mrs. Hollis. This completes the appointments of this much-talked-of structure.

Mrs. Hollis entered this little dark room—for

that is all it really is—on the 25th of May, 1872, for the first time, in the presence of myself and two lady members of my family. I closed the door, and she fastened it on the inside with a wood-button. Her exclamation was, "How very dark!" After being seated a few minutes, she asked me to sing. I began to choral the "Old Folks at Home:"

"Away down on the Swanee river."

But before I had proceeded far, there was a regular plantation racket in the cabinet, which convinced me "the old folks" were not "at home," but the young folks were having a "high old time" in their absence. My first impression was, that Mrs. Hollis had gone daft; and the impulse to tear the door away, to liberate her from her insane asylum, was very strong. In the din, however, I could hear her speak; so I bated my zeal to demolish until I had more evidence of its necessity. The fact is, I expected to see that cabinet fall to pieces; for it was banged, and pounded, and shaken, with an uproar and confusion of noises, from every part of it, that was startling and dreadful to hear. There could not have been less than half a dozen spirits hard at work in that cabinet, for fifteen minutes; and yet not half so many could get into it, had they been in the form. The racket continued about twenty minutes, when a lull occurred, and Mrs. Hollis came out. Under the closest scrutiny, I could not discover the least excitement in her face, or any evidence that she had been at work. She seemed rather languid, and looked pale.

"Did you ever hear such a confusion!" she said;

"the cabinet was full of spirits, and they were wild with excitement!"

"Could you see them distinctly?" I asked.

"No: they were more like shadows. I could only get glimpses of them occasionally."

"Was Ski among them?"

"Yes: he stood beside me, and told me not to be afraid, I would not be hurt."

"And did you have no fear, Mrs. Hollis? It was almost terrifying. I thought the cabinet would be battered down about your head."

"At first I was afraid they would hurt me; but the old chief's assurance satisfied me all was right."

"Will you go in again?"

"If you desire me."

"Why, certainly; but I hope the spirits will be less violent in their demonstrations. They 'out-banged Bannegar.'"

Mrs. Hollis again entered the cabinet, and the door was closed. I assured her the cabinet was a nice place to sit in, and entirely free from danger. "It's all right; only be cheerful; be happy if you can; good-bye!" I said, as I shut the door. I expected, of course, a re-enactment of the first sitting; but fifteen minutes elapsed without giving the slightest symptom of any occurrence appreciable to our senses. I was on the point of starting in on the "Last Rose of Summer," when a noise in the cabinet began to attract my attention. This gradually increased, until it seemed as if two or three carpenters were at work sand-papering the inside of the cabinet. This continued about five minutes, when there was a slight motion to the cloth over the aperture in the door, which increased, until finally it was pushed aside, and a large brown hand was projected through it. It remained in view about twenty seconds. I called to Mrs. Hollis as much to ascertain her position as to inquire if she saw the hand. She replied from her place: "I can only see a haze about the aperture. I can hear spirits talking, but can not see any."

The hand was not like Mrs. Hollis's; and while I was speculating as to whom the proprietor might be, it was withdrawn, and *two* little hands, such as might belong to a child two or three years old, were quickly presented. While looking at these, a *third* hand—the same large brown hand—appeared the second time, and seemed to hover above them, "keeping watch and ward" over these helpless ones. This concluded the first of Mrs. Hollis's cabinet *seances*. It was held in the evening.

On the following morning, we again visited the cabinet room, bringing the music-box. This I placed on a little stand, and set to playing. It was a decided improvement on my vocalization, and it so seemed to the spirits; for Mrs. Hollis had entered the cabinet but a few minutes, when they began to play a *rub-a-dub* accompaniment on the boards, the noise sounding as if made by muffled drumsticks. After they had ceased, a peculiar, sharp, explosive noise, as when a table-cloth is shaken violently, was heard for a few seconds. Then of a sudden a yard and a half of Brussels carpet, which had been placed on the floor of the cabinet, rolled tightly, was shot swiftly through the aperture into the middle of the room. I should have premised, when Mrs. Hollis entered the cabinet, I placed with her a small tin horn, a French harp, and a bunch of flowers. These were ejected in quick succession after the carpet. Wondering what next would come, the curtain was suddenly drawn aside, when through the aperture was projected into the room, the long, muscular naked arm of *a man*. It was of full length, the shoulder articulation being exposed to view. The hand, when it first appeared, was closed, but it opened and shut often; and, when doing so, the muscles were seen to enlarge and lessen in the fore-arm. The elbow articulated freely, flexing and extending with apparent ease; and the arm swung around, reaching over the top of the cabinet. From the development of that arm, I should think it belonged to a man not less than six feet in height. I looked at it closely, and was not more than six feet distant from it. When this arm was withdrawn, Mrs. Hollis came out of the cabinet for recuperation. As on the day before, she seemed to be exhausted of her vitality; her face was pale, and she complained of languor. In reply to my inquiries, she said she could see nothing but a hazy atmosphere about the aperture of the cabinet, when the cloth would be pushed aside; and, though she could hear distinctly the spirits talking, she could not discern them.

Subsequently, I asked Jim Nolan to explain to me the condition of the medium when in the cabinet, which he did, to this effect: "The medium," he said, "had a horror of being entranced; so we permit all her faculties to remain uninfluenced, excepting her sight. We influence the optic-nerve during the time, so that no impressions of the eye are transmitted to the sensorium. Examine the pupils of her eyes as soon as she leaves the cabinet; they will be found preternaturally large and morbidly sensitive.

"Why do you make this discrimination against or in favor (which ?) of the optic-nerve?"

"It is necessary that the medium be perfectly calm while we materialize the arms and hands. If she could see, she would not maintain this passive condition. Music has a tendency to tranquillity; that is why we desire it."

Observing the dexterity of the arm, hand, and fingers that were projected through the aperture, it occurred to me that there might be sufficient intelligence guiding them to write a letter. Up to this time, spirit-writing had all been done in the dark. Here, now, was the hand and arm exposed—*could they write in the light ?* I'll soon ascertain. I procured a large walnut bracket, and fastened it on the outside of the cabinet-door, so that the top was an inch or two under the aperture. On this I placed a slate and pencil, and, as soon as the arrangement was completed, Mrs. Hollis entered the cabinet.

I started the music-box to play, and had scarcely resumed my seat, when the same muscular arm we had formerly seen was projected, full length, into the room. There was no noise this time in the cabinet preceding the materialization. "Order reigns in Warsaw!" thought I. The arm now swept almost the entire front of the cabinet with its reach. The fingers ran along the little cornice, as if manipulating the keys of a piano, and continued to wander around in this manner for a minute and a half, when they picked up the pencil, and proceeded to write as decorously as though it were a common occupation. While the writing was going on in full view, I called to Mrs. Hollis, who made answer from her remote part of the cabinet. She did not know what was being done, and reiterated her former statement that she could see nothing but the smoky atmosphere at the aperture.

After two minutes, the writing was completed, when I took the slate from the shelf and found the following communication upon it:

"God bless you, my fellow-worker in the cause of liberty and truth. I greet you this day: 'Well done, thou good and faithful servant!' Work on; your reward shall be great! When the world asks, 'Who is your control?' tell them the words I said to Dumas long years ago, 'I am the rear guard of the Grand Army;' for so it really is. We are a host, and you shall have the cross of honor. My voice never went forth to the Grand Army of France, to cheer it on to victory, as it does to you! Work on! Be firm! You are the front of that army, and I the rear. It can not fail.

"Yours, in truth and honor,

"MICHAEL NEY."

This was a singular communication, to be sure, but entirely too personal for my appreciation. I could not understand why I should be designated for such distinction, and was not conscious that I was at all deserving of the decoration promised. I was, however, much interested in the fact that the spirit-world could thus hold communication with the natural world; and I was particularly gratified with the success of the experiment, and as being the *first* to witness this startling phenomenon.

I transcribed the message, and replaced the slate for further developements. As I was placing the pencil on the slate, within twelve inches from my face *three hands* were presented at the aperture. I looked at them curiously and closely; they were strange hands, belonging to adults; and on one was worn a large, plain gold ring, on the finger next to the little one of the left hand. The light was such as to enable me to examine the texture of the skin. They remained on exhibition about half a minute, and were then withdrawn. I had scarcely resumed my seat, when the large arm again appeared and wrote:

> "We can do no more this morning; our medium is exhausted! We will try to show you a face to-morrow.
>
> "NEY."

"Very well," I said, "you'll see me to-morrow at Philippi! Keep your engagement, and I will keep mine."

Punctual at the appointed time, our little circle assembled in the cabinet room. As soon as the music started, Mrs. Hollis entered the cabinet; when, as the door was closed, hands were exhibited at the aperture. I should think there were as many as ten materialized, in as many minutes, some of which were projected into the room, but at least half the number retired after barely getting an exposure to light. They were single at first; then two, three, and, finally, five hands were finely materialized at once, four of which belonged to children. These were all open, with the palms to the front. The fifth hand was large, and moved over the tips of the fingers of the children, touching them gently, as I conjectured, to impart to them strength.

Mrs. Hollis complained of exhaustion, and took a recess for half an hour. So interested in watching the manifestations was I, that when she entered the cabinet again, I neglected to start the music, of which fact I was reminded by a spirit saying, distinctly, at the aperture, "Start the music!" The table on which the music-box was placed, stood not more than two feet from the cabinet. I proceeded to wind it up, and was just turning to resume my seat in the circle, in doing which I had to face the aperture. *As I did this, I beheld my mother's face in the opening of the cabinet door!*"

"Why, mother," I exclaimed, "is it possible!"

I riveted my gaze upon her for twenty seconds, during which time she smiled, bowed, and pronounced my name. The curtain then swung between her face and me. All in the room saw and heard the same as I did. I was not more than two feet from the cabinet and aperture.

I am not given to illusions, and rarely dream when asleep, much less when awake. I am a very cool, quiet man in emergencies, and was never more so than upon this occasion. Every person in the circle saw this face; but I only recognized it. It was my mother's face. She recognized me, and called me by my given name. To make assurance doubly sure, I said, "Mother, please materialize your *left-hand,* and present it at the aperture!"

In a very brief space of time a left-hand appeared at the opening, *with the forefinger shut at the middle joint.* My mother had just such a finger on her left-hand. When a child, she received a burn which contracted the tendon, and fixed the forefinger of her left-hand permanently in that position. I did not require this additional proof of my mother's identity; but, as it came, it was "a confirmation, strong as Holy Writ."

It is not necessary to say any thing about my sensations on this occasion. The reader is only interested in the bald fact, and such I give. *I was glad to see my mother's face again;* and speak of it now simply to vindicate the integrity of my senses. To those who charge me with giving undue prominence to this manifestation, I have but this to say: I respect my own judgment on all occasions, caring little for the applause of men, less for their criticism, and least for their censure.

After the materialization of my mother's face and hand, Mrs. Hollis came out into the room and remained for half an hour. She was much interested in the manifestations, and regretted that she could not see them as we did. When she returned to the cabinet, I placed with her a bunch of flowers and a French harp. The door had scarcely been closed, when Ney's long arm came out into the room, and began to ambulate in front of the cabinet. This he continued to do for several minutes, when he wrote on the slate: "*Josephine will salute you this morning!*"

Scarcely had his large muscular arm been withdrawn, when a more feminine and beautiful arm and hand were projected. The arm was covered with a sleeve of tulle or illusion, from above the elbow to the wrist. Here the delicate fabric was gathered into a band, fastened with a narrow ribbon of a pale cherry color. Beyond this gathering, partly covering the hand, was a small ruffle formed by the end of the sleeve. The hand was slenderly and symmetrically formed—two of the fingers being ornamented with jeweled rings. A spirit-handkerchief, looking like gossamer, was held and gracefully waved several times in a sweep of a foot or eighteen inches. The hand then retired, and in a few seconds reappeared, holding the flowers I had placed in the cabinet. These were subsequently distributed by this hand among the members of the circle, as souvenirs of the occasion. When the last flower had been given, the spirit-hand picked up the pencil, and wrote:

> "MY DEAR FRIEND,—There is much I would like to say to you, respecting the reincarnation of my beloved husband. I will write you more fully when the medium has been rested. These materializations are very exhausting to her. I will try to show my face before the medium leaves for home. You aid us very much, for which our whole band are grateful. We shall always esteem you our good friend. JOSEPHINE."

At the conclusion of this writing, I went forward to remove the slate, and as I did so, Ney's hand came out, and patted me on the arm and the back of my hand almost caressingly.

I was about resuming my seat, and had retired half the distance between the cabinet and the chairs, when the curtain covering the aperture was put aside, and the dim outline of a face presented. It was quite indistinct, and remote from the opening; but it gradually came to the front, and grew brighter and brighter, until every feature was distinctly limned, and the tint of the skin and the color of the eyes discerned. The face wore a pensive expression, and the large dark eyes seemed sad. The hair was gathered up in bunches, looped with strings of pearl, and studded with brilliants. It was Josephine, following, so soon, her promise with its fulfillment. She could only maintain her best materialization for a few seconds, when she seemed to retire from the front to the rear of the cabinet, fading, fading, fading, into utter darkness.

After an interval of a few minutes, her hand appeared through the aperture, holding a phantom flower. It remained for a few seconds, then retired, when another, and another were presented quickly in succession. These "celestial exotics" were plainly presented, but could not be identified.

But a few minutes had passed, when there appeared at the aperture the lower part of a man's face, plainly seen from below the eyes to the chin, which was covered with a heavy beard. A French harp was held to the mouth, and the notes sounded several times, though no tune was attempted. These could be distinctly heard in the adjacent rooms. It was subsequently stated that Jim Nolan was the harpist.

After this unique concert was over, and the cloth had fallen over the aperture a few minutes, the door of the cabinet was suddenly pushed open, when, to my utter amazement, I saw, as plainly as could be, for an instant, the form of a man standing beside Mrs. Hollis. His head was uncovered—large and full round face. He wore a military uniform, with medallion decorations upon the breast of his coat. I could see him only for a second, and was in such a line of observation as to obstruct the view of others in the circle. When the light fell upon him, he melted into air, as melts

> "The snow-flake on the river;
> A moment white, then lost forever."

CHAPTER XVII.

A NEW CABINET AND NEW PROGRAMME—CHARLES REEMELIN—PURCELL AND MANSFIELD—CORRY—PARENTS RECOGNIZING CHILDREN—CHILDREN RECOGNIZING PARENTS—OLD FRIENDS—THE TESTIMONY OF WELL-KNOWN CITIZENS—WRITING—SPIRITS CONVERSING THROUGH THE APERTURE—F. B. PLIMPTON AS AN INVESTIGATOR—HIS ABLE REPORT.

THE cabinet *seances*, recorded in the last chapter, ended Mrs. Hollis's *third* engagement in Cincinnati. The following morning she started for home. I now wrote a statement of the manifestations that had occurred in her presence, and published it in the *Cincinnati Commercial.* My object was to direct public attention to the subject, and, if possible, enlist more general interest in the marvelous character of spirit-phenomena. In this, I but partially succeeded. The chief editor of the *Commercial* very soon discovered himself to be neither friendly to spiritualism nor to the investigation of its phenomena. He was master of the situation, and with as wayward a fancy as if he swayed an empire.

Under such circumstances, "discretion is the better part of valor;" so my best policy was to "Sage nichts so lange als der verdammte hanswurst faselt."

Give him scope, and he and his corps of sniveling correspondents will soon *dangle*. And they did. To mention spiritualism in the presence of some people, is like displaying a red flag before a wild steer, or throwing water on an animal with hydrophobic proclivities; they get mad—*very* mad. In fact, they take on duodenal cramps and epigastrical spasms of the brain. "Why this is thus," I can not exactly tell! It is as perplexing a problem to me as spiritual phenomena itself. I only notice the fact because it is a fact. These people are generally the escapes from lunatic asylums, or the inmates of pagan Churches, in which the milder forms of insanity are popularly manifested as devotion.

So much had been printed that was alike "foolish and false" respecting the spirit-manifestations I had publicly recorded, that I deemed it necessary to have Mrs. Hollis return again to the city. I did this to enable me to cite other witnesses to the facts when I came to make my final report, which I now had decided to do in the present form. Her fourth engagement commenced on the 20th of August.

As I had disposed of my cabinet, it was necessary to construct another; but this time I directed Mr. Brown to put up a close board partition across the end of the cabinet room, four feet from the north wall. In the center of this partition a batten-door was hung which opened into the room; and in the center of the door a circular aperture was made, twelve inches in diameter, four feet and a half from the floor. This was covered with black cloth hanging on the inside, to make the chamber perfectly dark. When completed, the interior dimensions of this cabinet were ten feet long, seven feet high, and four feet deep. The door fastened on the inside with a wood button. Under the aperture, on the outside, the bracket was adjusted to hold the slate. This was the new cabinet.

As soon as it was completed, Mrs. Hollis entered for manifestations. The members of my family only were present; among these a lad fifteen years old, who had never been in a spiritual circle, and who had but recently come to the city. Several hands were presented at the aperture in the course of fifteen minutes, when, after a lull of ten minutes, my mother's face appeared. I said nothing while the materialzation was taking place, nor did I give it recognition until the lad referred to exclaimed, "*Look, uncle; see, there is grandmother!*" This boy was reared by my mother, and was quite competent to identify her familiar face. The spirit seemed to be gratified with Tom's presence and recognition, as she smiled, and pronounced his name in such audible tones that all present could hear it. She remained at the aperture *two minutes*. Several other faces, besides a number of hands and arms, were shown, when the *seance* came to an end. It was evident the power to manifest had increased rather than diminished in the new cabinet. I therefore at once decided to invite a number of representative people to witness the manifestations, and examine the conditions under which they were produced, with the understanding that such persons would make a fair written statement of what they saw and heard, over their own signatures, for public use.

The invitation was given in the *Commercial* of

August 30, 1872, of which the following is about the substance:

SPIRIT PHENOMENA IN CINCINNATI.

TO WHOM IT MAY CONCERN.

Editor of Commercial:

SIR,—You have published several articles recently, over the signature of "Nep.," in relation to spirit phenomena, which have attracted attention. The statements contained in those articles were of such an extraordinary character as to elicit a great deal of unfriendly criticism by yourself and correspondents.

I now propose to afford a limited number of intelligent men and women an opportunity to witness similar manifestations at my dwelling, on condition that, over their own signatures, they will make a written statement of what they see and hear appertaining to the same, for public use.

To facilitate this object, I propose to form several circles composed of three persons each, and give from four to six sittings to each circle, all to be subject to the rules governing the formation of circles, which are known to establish the best conditions for spirit manifestations.

To enter these circles, there shall be no discrimination between Jew and Gentile, Pagan and Christian, editors and preachers, but representative men and women of all classes shall be welcome, "without money and without price."

To stimulate the wavering to engage in this good work, *I promise that in a lighted room will be realized the presence of our supposed dead friends, who will* WRITE, SPEAK, AND SHOW THEIR FACES SO AS TO BE RECOGNIZED.

If these manifestations are frauds, now is a most propitious time to "smite them, hip and thigh!" There shall be no effort attempted to protect them from the closest scrutiny.

This invitation brought letters in response from about two hundred *representative* (?) men and women, all willing to *come and see* these wonderful things.

The Queen City may well be proud of her jewels I did not think the crop so prolific. Some of them signatured themselves with an X; and others (E. A. among them), claimed to be such because they scribbled occasionally for a newspaper.

> "O, wad some power the giftie gi' us
> To see oursel's as ithers see us!
> It wad frae mony a blunder free us,
> An' foolish notion."

I discovered my mistake. My intention was to engage the attention of such men as Mr. John B. Purcell, Mr. Max Lillienthal, Mr. Edward Purcell, Mr. Thomas Vickers, Mr. Charles Reemelin, Mr. E. D. Mansfield, Mr. F. B. Plimpton, Mr. Granville Moody, Mr. Wm. M. Corry, and one or two others who really occupied positions which commanded the respect and confidence of a limited number of their fellow-citizens. To most of these gentlemen I was personally unknown; and when I spoke of my intention to call upon them for the purpose indicated, I was assured that I would be denied by every one of them. I could not see why it should be so; for truth seeks neither place nor applause, bows at no human shrine, but only asks a hearing. When men deny this, they openly manifest their own error, and write their own condemnation.

On a careful inspection of my list of representative men, I found so little homogeneousness of character among them, that I gave up the conceit of getting them together in a common circle. The next best thing to be done was to select three or four, and handle them the best I could.

I found, in my intercourse with people who had

adopted Church creeds for their guidance in spiritual matters, that they were either afraid to investigate spiritual phenomena, or were ready to zealously condemn without examining it at all. I therefore began my operations with Mr. Charles Reemelin, who, I understood, was not at all trammeled with dogmas or fettered with creeds. I drove to his residence, near Dent, and found him superintending the gathering of grapes in his vineyard. After introducing myself, I stated the object of my visit as briefly and fairly as I could. Mr. Reemelin is not a man to be trifled with; and it is plainly written all over his face that he entertains decided opinions, whatever they may be. He said: "What is the use of talking about seeing spirits, when there are no spirits to see? You can't see a thing that is not. A woman told me she expected to meet her husband in heaven, and I said, 'Madam, you would n't want to look at him after he is rotten; when the breath leaves the body, that is the last of the man.'"

"But, Mr. Reemelin," I said, "that which you say *can't be, is! Come and see.* You limit possibility to the operations of your own mind. The impossible to you, may be the possible to others; we are all students yet, and have much to learn. I would like you to see these manifestations, and know what you think of them afterward. Your opinions before seeing them are of no value. After you have seen them, that which you may say will have some influence with other men."

"This is all a trick, a species of jugglery, got up for a purpose. I heard of a ghost-story in Germany—"

"Mr. Reemelin," I interrupted, "allow me to introduce you to Mrs. Hollis, the spirit-medium. Talk to her about the trick."

Mr. Reemelin changed the topic of conversation, and spoke to Mrs. Hollis of his grapes, his family, and some friends with whom she happened to have acquaintance. We left him about sundown.

This interview with the great free-thinking Charles Reemelin convinced me that "the pride of opinion" made a man as intolerant a bigot as if he had no opinion at all. If he is not fast settling into fossilism, it is because I could not engage his mind with the grandest thought that has been given to the world.

"I fear your representative men will all fail you," said Mrs. Hollis, as we drove homeward from our fruitless visit to the sage of Dent. "You will hardly get *a circle* to suit you."

"I have given up the idea of *a circle*. If we can only get one or two to begin with, we will go ahead. I will next try Mr. W. M. Corry. He has been a member of the Legislature, when it was more honorable to be such than at present; and, as an independent journalist, has won a national reputation. Colonel Piatt says he is the bravest thinker in America, and also the finest parlor orator. From what I have heard, the impression on my mind is, he is a materialist in belief; but, I hope, not so bigoted a one as Mr. Reemelin."

"Your original idea, I think, is impracticable," said Mrs. Hollis; "if you could get all your representative men to come together in one circle, there would be so much personal antagonism, I fear, the spirits could not manifest. Harmony is an essential condition."

"There is not so much *personal* antagonism as you think. If Purcell and Mansfield, who are about the same age, were placed, like Selkirk, on a solitary island, where the sound of church-going bells were never heard, how long do you suppose their personal antagonism would be maintained?"

"Until they became hungry!"

"Exactly! The bishop would forget his infallible dogma, and swallow gopher on Friday; while Mansfield would soon consider him as one of the elect, and be as fraternal as was Tam O'Shanter with Souter Johnnie, when they were 'fou for weeks thegither.' It is their devilish creeds that disunite them, and 'break up nature's social union.'"

"It will always be so!"

"No, it won't! Nature will develop men too large to sit in pews, and too noble to be fettered by creeds. To these the door-way to the spirit-world will be open, and the dread and mystery of death will be removed. Such men are now living, and their number is increasing day by day."

"Will we hold a circle to-night?" asked Mrs. Hollis, as she adroitly gave a new direction to the conversation.

"Yes: I forgot to tell you I have invited some friends to the house this evening; and I suppose they are there by this time."

It was eight o'clock before we got home, where we found awaiting us, MR. W. W. WARD, MRS. ROSEANNA C. WARD, and MR. GEO. W. SKAATS. With these, and several members of my family, we soon visited the cabinet-room, and Mrs. Hollis entered the dark closet.

It was only a few minutes after the door was closed, when a large, muscular hand presented itself at the aperture, which at first seemed shadowy, but gradually grew to be as substantial looking as one of flesh and blood. It remained a minute or more, and was then withdrawn. Very soon after, my mother's head and face, with all the details of her head-dress fairly delineated, appeared at the opening in the door, and remained two minutes. After bowing, she retired, and was followed soon after by the materialization of a head and face of a young woman that had not appeared before. Mrs. Ward instantly recognized the spirit as Anna Clemfort, and spoke to her. The reply and acknowledgements were made by bowing the head and rapping loudly on the inside of the cabinet. Mrs. Ward herself is a fine clairvoyant, and has often seen, while in her supersensuous condition, the spirit of Miss Clemfort, looking exactly as she presented herself at the aperture. As this spirit retired, another face and head of a beautiful woman appeared, and bowed to Mrs. Ward. It was one who had stood by her as bridesmaid many years before. Mrs. Ward called her by name; in response to which, she smiled, bowed her head, and rapped, as the preceding spirit had. It was not long before the aperture was again filled by another head and face of a lady, evidently of the Society of Friends, for she wore a plain cap. The materialization was good for half a minute, during which time the spirit was recognized as MRS. RACHEL

FISHER, by Mr. Skaats, to whose family, during her natural life, she was quite well known.

It was but a short time after she had retired, when the head and face of Mr. Thomas Eller, the father of my nephew, appeared at the orifice in the door. All these were presented in good light, and, as they were strongly individualized, could not be mistaken.

A hand was now projected into the room, and wrote upon the slate:

"We do not wish to tax the medium's strength any more this evening. Good-night! NEY."

This concluded the *seance*.

When Mrs. Hollis came out of the cabinet, her pulse was sixty, her face pale, her hands cold, and she spoke of a general feeling of languor. She was, to superficial inspection, the least excited person in the room.

The next *seance* I shall notice was held in the evening of September 3d. It was attended by Mrs. Angeline Madison, Dr. A. J. Hazelwood, and Mr. G. W. Skaats, and two members of my family. In five minutes after Mrs. Hollis entered the cabinet, hands of various sizes began to appear at the aperture; some were projected into the room, but most of them appeared at the opening only, inside the cabinet. This exhibition continued for a quarter of an hour. Following this digital display, was the head and face of a sweet little girl, who was immediately recognized by Mrs. Madison as her own child. The materialization was very good, and continued for a minute. The mother's heart was filled with joy, at meeting her darling again. Following closely was the beautiful face of another angel child, radiant with love-light and smiles. Mr. Skaats at once recognized her as his little daughter.

It is no part of my business to preach, but I may be indulged to say, that to be present when these angel visitants return to show their shining faces, and to assure parents that there is life beyond the tomb, is a most exquisite privilege. I envy not the head or heart of the man who can ask, "Of what value is all this?"

Seemingly as a guardian to the little girls, the motherly face of Mrs. Rachel Fisher appeared almost as soon as the last one had retired. She was instantly recognized by Mrs. Madison and Mr. Skaats, to whom she bowed her head several times in token of satisfaction. As she passed from the light, the face of an old and well-known citizen appeared, which was at once recognized by Mrs. Madison, Mr. Skaats, and Dr. Hazelwood, as being Mr. R. A. Madison. He was better known to old citizens of Cincinnati as "'Squire Madison." Mrs. Madison was his niece, Dr. Hazelwood his grandson, and Mr. Skaats his kinsman by marriage. The materialization was good, and the light sufficient to distinguish every feature of his face. No more faces were presented during the evening, but a *peculiar* hand was projected into the room, and wrote on the slate:

"Andrew, beware of following in the footsteps of ——! The wine-cup is fatal!"

To this message no name was signed; but the hand was recognized, and both the message and the hand sufficiently indicated the identity of the author.

The voice of a child was now heard in the cabinet, addressing Mrs. Madison as mother. The conversation that ensued soon disclosed the fact that the living and the so-called dead were again in communion with each other, with only the thickness of cloth separating them. The interview lasted about twenty minutes; and when it concluded, the *seance* closed.

On the morning of the 5th, I was agreeably surprised by a call from Mr. F. B. Plimpton, whose attention had been arrested by the publication of my Card in the *Commercial*. Mr. Plimpton is well known as an editorial writer on the *Commercial*, in its literary and scientific department, where scholarly and scientific attainments are required to fill the position well. I had never met this gentleman until he presented himself at my door, and, to the best of my recollection, had never before seen him. He said:

"Good morning, sir. Are you Dr. Wolfe?"

"That is my name, sir. What is yours?"

"Plimpton."

"Of the *Commercial*?"

"I represent the *Commercial* as a reporter this morning, and am here to witness the phenomena, an account of which you have published as occurring in the presence of Mrs. Mary J. Hollis."

"You are welcome. I will afford you every facility in my power to carry forward your investigation of these strange occurrences. I am as anxious to know the truth of these marvelous manifestations as yourself. Do not be in a hurry in making your report or in forming conclusions. Examine closely, patiently, and perseveringly; and at any time, if you think

I can be of assistance to you, command my services. Come when you will, as often as it may please you, and stay as short or long a time as your convenience will permit; you shall be welcome."

I now introduced Mr. Plimpton to Mrs. Hollis; and of what followed the ensuing five days may be ascertained by reading the report he gave through the *Commercial*, which is here appended.

THE BORDER LAND.

AN EXPERIENCE WITH THE SPIRITS.

It was a condition of the *seance*, which I was invited to attend at the house of Dr. N. B. Wolfe, No. 146 Smith Street, that I should make faithful report of what I saw and heard, or—if it better please the reader—what I seemed to see and hear; what, if any thing, was failure, and what, if any thing, success. Mrs. Mary J. Hollis, of Louisville, Kentucky, an unprofessional developing medium, but notable for the extraordinary character of the manifestations made through her, was the temporary guest of Dr. Wolfe.

It is the purpose of this writing to fulfill that condition. It is proper, however, to say at the outset, that spiritual terms and phraseology will be used by the writer as simply convenient, and to add, personally, that in the capacity of a reporter he records only witnessed phenomena, indifferent whether they help or hurt the cause of spiritualism. In that capacity, he has no theories to advance, no opinions to state, no conclusions to publish. He has but one duty to perform: "to report proceedings," as he would, if detailed, those of a convention, mass-meeting, or any public affair.

I.

SLATE-WRITING.

The first sitting took place on the 5th of September, and commenced at nine o'clock A. M.

I was conducted to a chamber-room on the second floor of the house. It was furnished as such rooms ordinarily are. The window, looking south, had inside lattice-blinds, through the slats of which the morning sun looked cheerfully in, making the room "light and as a lily in bloom." This condition remained unchanged throughout the sitting.

A light walnut toilet-stand, without drawers or compartments—a simple oblong wooden top, on slender supports—was brought from an adjoining apartment, and placed in the center of the room. A plaid-green and black-worsted shawl was thrown over it, and a light checked carriage-robe spread over the shawl, and falling to the floor on all sides of the stand. Upon the stand was placed a six-by-ten school-slate, which was carefully sponged off, and a bit of pencil half an inch long, and whittled so small that it was difficult to handle it, and almost impossible to write a legible word with it.

These arrangements completed by myself, and again examined in detail and in general, to detect mechanical hocus pocus, if there were any concealed about the stand, Mrs. Hollis entered the room, and seated herself at the right and about eighteen inches from the stand. Dr. Wolfe was on the left, and not less than three feet away. My own position was at the end fronting both, so that every motion could be observed.

Taking the slate, on which was the bit of pencil, in her right-hand, and lifting the stand-cover with her left, Mrs. Hollis projected the slate and hand to the wrist under the stand, letting the drapery fall around it. At no time did she change her position, nor did any part of her dress or person, except the hands, when used to project or withdraw the slate, come into contact with the stand or its covering.

Some minutes elapsed, during which a lively conversation on social subjects was kept up. There was time to take personal observations of the medium. Mrs. Hollis is of middle age, but looks younger than she is; of good form; rather stoutish; has lustrous black eyes and hair, and regular and pleasing features. Her manner is rather retiring, always modest—that of a cultivated, sensitive woman, who has, however, been enough in society to acquire an easy and graceful self-possession. On this occasion, she was dressed in a light morning-wrapper, tastefully but plainly trimmed.

In the midst of the conversation, a scratching sound, as of a pencil drawn across a slate, was heard. I narrowly watched, during this and subsequent writing, the portion of the medium's wrist exposed between the sleeve-cuff and the stand, but could detect no motion of the muscles; on the contrary, they had assumed a fixedness or rigidity which comes of supporting a weight in one position for a space of time.

Suddenly the sound ceased; the pencil dropped with a click, and rattled over the slate as though it had been lifted some inches and let fall upon it. This was the signal, in each instance, that the communication was finished.

The first writing proved to be only a signature, written in an irregular, running hand, in which our family name was *phonetically spelled* "Plymton," nearly its old English form. John tried repeatedly to communicate, but with discouraging success. James Plymton came next, and "Elizabeth *Plimton*, of Farmington," (after it was suggested to John that we spelled the name differently now,) but none of them was able to go further. They were possibly repelled by the assurance that they were all unknown to me.

When the slate was next withdrawn, there was written on it: "I am Willie Potter, son of Dr. Potter. Do you know me?" Willie was told that I had not the honor of his acquaintance. In reply he wrote, and with some rapidity, "I was always with my pa in his buggy, and thought every body knew me."

The question was then orally put: "Is any one whom I know with you?"

"Yes," was the reply in writing; "your aunt Mary, and she says that—"

Here the pencil dropped. There ensued a series of confused answers, as if the spirits were considerably "mixed" as to identity. For example, I wrote a question on one side of the slate, and, turning it over, handed it to Mrs. Hollis, who passed it under the table. The answer was, "Yes, my son," which was entirely irrelevant. As, again, "Emily is with me now."

The following intelligible communication was next received:

"Your friends are here, but not able to write.

"M. D. POTTER."

This specimen of so-called spirit-writing I preserved for comparison. It seemed at the moment that there was a resemblance between the signature and Mr. Potter's, as I remembered it. A subsequent comparison, however, showed a material difference. In his life-time, Mr. Potter never varied the form of writing his name. To those familiar with it, it was as instantly recognized as that of Mr. Spinner, on the United States treasury-notes. He wrote a deliberate, decided hand, plain, firm, business-like, and very characteristic of the man himself. The capital "M," in the slate-writing, was constructed radically different. He never so wrote it. The "D" had some general resemblance. The "P" and the final "r," in the Christian name, were unlike his.

It may be that the pencil (which, as I shall show, is taken between the fingers of what is called a "materialized" hand) was too small for manipulation, and modified the writing. This was suggested by another experiment. The point of a lead-pencil was broken off, and the point again broken; the smaller and almost infinitesimal part was placed on a sheet of white paper, and put under the table. A few words, of no importance, but purporting to have been written by Mr. Potter, were written, but the writing was as labored as that of a school-boy just mastering his pot-hooks; showing that the instrument employed by the spirit-hand modifies the writing as it would have been if held by a hand of flesh and blood.

Next came a request that I should be at the cabinet the following morning, at eleven o'clock, and then this:

"We want to stop all manipulation now.

"JOHN PLYMTON."

The sitting was over.

It was noticeable that the writing—for example, of John—was consistently characteristic, first and last, and each was distinctive from the other. Nothing of conceivable human interest was imparted, and in the only instance where it was possible to trace a resemblance of writing, the experiment was a failure. The spelling of a name phonetically was not creditable to a spirit of intelligence. That there was no mechanical fraud or ambidextrous jugglery in the slate-writing, I was entirely satisfied. Those who seek to solve the mystery must give it patient investigation. To denounce it as trickery, intentional deception, and humbuggery, is simply to display dense ignorance or unsavory prejudice. I have thus been minutely particular because of what follows.

II.

THE CABINET—MATERIALIZATION.

THE cabinet, as it is called, is on the second floor of a brick building, in the rear of the dwelling-house. It is in a small middle-room, between what appeared to be two consulting-offices, with doors opening into each, and transoms above them admitting enough light to read coarse print, or to see local color. A carpet on the floor, a book-case, three or four chairs, a small stand, upon which was a Swiss music-box, constituted the furnishing. The cabinet was on the wall side of the room. A space, about the size of an ordinary clothes-closet, had been partitioned off, from the ceiling to the floor. The door opening into it was peculiar only in having an aperture something higher than a man's head cut into it. This aperture was round, and perhaps twelve or fifteen inches in diameter. A curtain of dark cloth, falling on the inside of the door when closed, shut out the light from the cabinet. A few inches below the aperture, and on the outside of the door when shut, was a plain wooden shelf, on which were placed a slate and small pencil.

I carefully examined this contrivance, sounding the wall. The brick wall of the building formed the one side, the board partitions the opposite side and the ends. With the exception of a strip of carpet on the floor and a wooden chair, it was absolutely bare. Not a nail or nail-hole was visible, nor was it possible that there were traps or concealed openings, doors, panels, or other pantomime contrivance about it.

The palm of Mrs. Hollis's right-hand was deeply marked, in my presence, with burnt-cork. As I vacated the cabinet, she entered, closing the door after her. I had hardly time to cross the floor and take a seat by the side of Dr. Wolfe, who had wound up and set the music-box in play, when an open hand appeared at the aperture, the palm toward us; it moved twice slowly from right to left, and disappeared. Other hands followed with like demonstrations. Presently another presented itself, palm open toward us, then turning slowly down, groped over the slate on the shelf below, and, finding the pencil, began to write, holding it between the thumb and forefinger. The writing occupied a full minute, and the hand was visible quite another. Elevating the pencil some inches, it was let fall on the slate, producing t' ~me rolling sound I had heard during the slate-writing *seance*. Again displaying the open palm, the hand was withdrawn. The messages purported to be from a sister, long an invalid, who died some years ago, and was couched in phrases of affection such as she frequently used during her life-time.

Some time now elapsed. The music-box continued to play. The eye, accustomed to the half-light of the room, easily took in all objects. The local color of the paper on the wall, the figures in the carpet and its texture, were readily perceived. I was informed that the spirits preferred this softened light for cabinet materialization. The time seeming tedious, Dr. Wolfe said the spirits were engaged in materializing a face. Soon after, an apparition—at first indistinct, then brighter and more defined—appeared at the aperture. It was a female face ; but it was known neither to the doctor nor myself. Asked if it was one of my friends ; it nodded a reply, and withdrew.

Again some time elapsed, and another face appeared, but so dim that we were only able to make out the outlines of a man's face. "You must do better than that," said I, "if you want to be recognized." Two other efforts were made, the last so successful that I involuntarily exclaimed, "Potter!" and instantly a roll of sharp knockings, while the face was still visible, sounded along the partition. When the face disappeared, the knocks were rapidly repeated with intense emphasis. The face was life-size, had the compact full forehead, the hair brushed away from it after the manner in which Mr. Potter wore it. The mixture of gray in the hair and chin-whiskers was visible. Dr. Wolfe did not recognize it till the name was mentioned. This manifestation lasted three minutes.

Presently another face appeared. "Who is that?" said Dr. Wolfe. "It is a woman, wearing a cap," he added. I thought of all the grandmothers and aunts I had known. There appeared to be great difficulty in the materialization of this face. Three or four times it appeared, but was told it could not be made out. Again it came forward. What the doctor had mistaken for a cap was the hair, combed down over a very high forehead and drawn plainly over the tips of the ears. The large, serene blue eyes, the oval of the face, the retreating chin, the languid expression about the mouth, the light color of the hair, were unmistakable characteristics of the face of an invalid sister who died ten years ago in the northern part of Ohio, who was never in Cincinnati, and of whom no picture is in existence, except an old faded daguerreotype, taken, perhaps, sixteen years ago. The peculiar mode of wearing the hair was due to protracted illness; it was put up in the readiest way an invalid could do it with comfort to herself.

Next appeared the face of a female, recognized by Dr. Wolfe as Lizzie Odell—a pretty, full face, with a profusion of black curls, and a cherry-colored ribbon bound across the forehead at the edge of the hair, and running back over the ears. Lizzie smiled, nodded twice, and passed on.

A hand again appeared, took up the pencil, and wrote. It was a communication purporting to be from my sister. Two other messages were written by the same hand. The last time it appeared, after writing and dropping the pencil, it was suddenly projected into the air, high above and forward of the aperture in the door, displaying the fore-arm bare to the elbow, and so sharply clear and tangible that the modeling and veining of the arm were distinctly seen. It was so unanticipated that I confess to have been startled. I had been prepared to see hands and faces, but this was a sensation. Swaying to one side and the other for the space of thirty seconds, it was withdrawn.

A rap on the wall indicated the conclusion of the *seance*. Mrs. Hollis came out. The black spot in the palm of her right-hand was unaltered. In every instance the right-hand had been shown, with open palm, to show us it was not marked. The cabinet was as it had appeared before the sitting.

I had abundant leisure to observe these apparitions. The hand and arm could not have been those of Mrs. Hollis. The fingers were long and delicate, the arm fair in shape, but slender; the texture was that of a blonde, which Mrs. Hollis is not, and the modeling was that of a girl's rather than a woman's arm. Hands were shown much smaller than the medium's. By no possibility could they have been hers, and there was about them what seemed to me a soft filminess, as distinguishable from a living hand, as to the eye the outline of a distant snow-capped mountain is distinguishable from the fleecy, sun-illuminated clouds which surround it, and through the rifts of which the snowy summit is revealed. It seemed to me, also, that there was a constant effort, especially in the case of faces, to maintain the status of materialization, as if the tendency were to dissolve and "melt into thin air." At moments when the materialization was most perfect, there was a curious glow upon the face, not destroying, but rather heightening, the effect of local color in the hair, eyes, and skin.

I have thus endeavored to state plainly what I saw, or supposed I saw, and to give the reader as clear and intelligible an idea of the phenomena as it is possible for me to convey.

III.

THE DARK CIRCLE—A SPIRIT INTERVIEWED.

THERE are three forms of manifestation through this medium: slate-writing, materialization of forms, and vocalization. The last, and said to be the most difficult, takes place in a room from which all light is absolutely excluded.

The dark circle was appointed for the evening of the same day. It was given in a sleeping-room on the third floor of the dwelling-house. Bed-quilts were tacked over the two windows. Four chairs were placed against the wall, between a bed, over which a mosquito-bar was drawn, and a wardrobe containing a lady's dresses. Upon the dressing-bureau was the music-box. An ordinary speaking-trumpet of tin stood by the door; a chair was placed in the center of the room. Dr. Wolfe, myself, and two ladies occupied the chairs by the wall, and the medium that in the center of the room, about eight feet from us.

The night was intensely hot for the season, and this room under the roof, from which the air as well as the light was excluded, was oppressively close. The fans, with which all were supplied, were kept in unceasing agitation. I could hear that of the medium whenever, during the sitting, there was a moment of silence.

The music-box was wound up by Dr. Wolfe, and set to playing, and the lights were turned off. A conversation was kept up between Mrs. Hollis and all of us while awaiting some manifestation. Presently there was thumping and pounding on the floor in various parts of the room, sometimes unpleasantly near, suggesting the propriety of taking care of tender corns. It ceased, and now voices were heard in the room singing snatches of the opera-airs which the music-box was playing, and in remarkably good pitch and time. They were not the voices of the persons about me, I knew. They did not come from the direction of Mrs. Hollis' chair, and they seemed to proceed from a source much higher than her head, and to float about the room. It was an unworded song, unless a language unfamiliar to us was used.

The music-box having exhausted itself, there was a space of silence, and presently there was a hoarse vocal effort at speaking, but not clear to my ear. Then an infantile voice was heard, which Dr. Wolfe recognized as that of a child who had died at six. At his request, she sang a verse of the song, "I want to be an angel," in company with him. It was a child's voice, unmistakably, in its limited vocal power and range, immature tone and accent and articulation of words, and very near to us.

Again, the hoarse voice, as of a man speaking through a trumpet, was heard. It announced the presence of James Nolan. He was described as materialized, speaking through the trumpet, which he held in his materialized hand, and as visible to the medium, who also described several spirits standing by us.

This communicative gentleman, after an introduction to the strangers of the party, and a familiar "How are you, this evening?" to Dr. Wolfe and the medium, undertook to explain some of the mysteries of spirit manifestation. For the space of an hour he was pretty smartly plied with questions by all of us, the medium not unfrequently joining in the discussion with him. I was in no position to take note, as the reader will readily imagine, and have to rely upon memory for an outline of the conversation.

He was asked why it was necessary to darken the room after such fashion.

He said: "You have noticed a ray of sunlight passing through the slats of a window-blind, and filled with fine particles of dust. Well, so the atmosphere is pervaded with electricity. Light increases its activity, and makes it difficult, almost imposible, for us to control it. This force, in its refined form, surrounds the human body, and passes in currents over it. It is least active in darkness, and hence you fall to sleep easier in a dark than in a light room. Does this seem reasonable to you?"

It was admitted to be at least plausible.

The conversation was continued at great length; but I shall not attempt to report it in detail. The conditions of the spirit-world were inquired into. Was it light always there? Yes. Do you take cognizance of what transpires on the earth? Yes: all men and women are attended by their own spirit-friends, who see their good and bad acts, try to impress them with good impulses, seeking to elevate them; feel sorry for them when they fail to control them, and rejoice when their progress is toward that which is good and pure and lovely. Then you feel as we feel—have emotions, passions, joys, sorrows? Yes: but we have no sickness, no death. And you have volition and the power to pass from place to place? Yes: with the rapidity of thought.

The question of moral responsibility was raised by a lady of the party, growing out of some remark of Nolan's touching inherited temperaments and dispositions. Nolan maintained that whatever is, is right, quoting Pope's language, and practically denied moral responsibility for what is done in the body. He was pretty sharply examined on this head, and said much which has formed the matter of speculation, reasoning, and analogy among thinking men, into which I shall not enter.

He gave an interesting account of himself. Was born, he said, in Harrison County, Indiana; went to Gosport; enlisted in the Fifty-fourth Indiana (I think he said); served three years; was with General Pope at Island No. 10, and went with Sherman in his famous march; was taken sick with typhoid fever somewhere near Atlanta; was sent back to Nashville, and died in the Maxwell House, then used as a hospital; was insensible some days before he died; saw his spiritual leave his physical body, but still seemed unconscious of the change till two or three of his comrades, who had gone before, came to his side and said, "Well, Jim, you have come over;" whereupon he replied, "Good God! am I dead, then?" to which they answered that he was.

An incident of this conversation I must not omit. He asked me if I had not invited a Presbyterian deacon to be present that evening. I could think of none. "Didn't you ask a man named Reed to come?" I then remembered to have met Mr. Reed, of the *Gazette*, by chance that day, in Fountain Square, and said I was going to a *seance* that night, inviting him, in a jocular way, to accompany me, to which an equally jocular reply was given. Jim had possibly confused the "truly good man" of the *Gazette* with his wicked partner.

Nolan's question surprised me, as the incident had wholly passed out of my mind. I had not mentioned it to any person, whatever Mr. Reed may have done.

At the conclusion of the conversation with Nolan, I heard a voice not much above a whisper, seemingly within a foot of my ear. It announced the presence of my sister. My mother, she said, and a very dear aunt (whose name she gave, and one that could have been known to but one person in the room besides myself, and she an utter stranger to the medium, Dr. Wolfe, and the other lady) were present, but could not talk. She did not use the trumpet, and articulated with difficulty and in so low a tone that it required attentive listening to catch her words.

The heat in the room by this time had become stifling, and, to the relief of all parties, bodied and disembodied, the *seance* was brought to a conclusion.

All that had been said by Nolan concerning the spirit-life, the laws and conditions of manifestation, the difficulties to be overcome, the subtleties of the medium which they employ—called by him refined electricity, by many animal magnetism, by others odic force—the positive and negative characters of this force, the power of mind over mind in the body, and of spirit over mind under certain favorable sympathetic conditions, was familiar to me from investigations made more than twenty years ago, and dropped after satisfying myself of the assumptions of mesmerism and clairvoyance.

This dark-circle business is least satisfactory of the three modes of manifestation. You have to depend upon the single sense of hearing. There is reasonable opportunity for trickery and intentional deception. Yet if what I heard at this *seance* was ventriloquism, I have no hesitation in saying Mrs. Hollis is the most extraordinary ventriloquist in the world, and is endowed with as many voices as Orator Puff. She has capacity not only to direct her voice to all parts of a room, to advance and retire it, but to speak in her natural voice at the same moment she speaks ventriloqually, not only articulating different words at the same moment, but constructing different sentences, and conveying entirely different ideas upon subjects wholly irrelevant to each other.

The reader can draw his own conclusions. He may pronounce this so-called spiritualism illusion, trickery, jugglery, sleight-of-hand, the work of the devil or his imps ; it is a matter of total indifference to me what he thinks, or how much he believes or disbelieves of this statement. Having never been troubled by dreams, premonitions, illusions, prophetic monitions, apparitions, ghosts, or other evidences of indigestion or disordered nerves myself, I do not believe I have suddenly fallen into a condition in which I may not credit the reasonable evidence of my own senses as to what I see and hear. But how these phenomena come to pass, it is not the business of a reporter to explain, if he could, while employed in that capacity. My duty is discharged, and the conditions fulfilled.

"And so you are going to make a report of this stuff?" said a friend.

"And why not?"

"And intend to publish the statement?"

"And still, why not?"

"And subscribe your name?"

"And yet again, why not?"

"But what good will come of it?"

"I don't know; I have nothing to do with consequences."

"But you will be sneered and laughed at."

"Very well; I am but a reporter of things which have taken place. In this, as a matter of good faith, and a guarantee that I do not seek to tax incredulity, or practice upon the popular love of the marvelous, I have no hesitation to attest it in the best form that a man having respect for his reputation for veracity, can give it."

As an act of good faith toward the reader, I depart from the impersonality that ought to characterize journalism, in this single instance, and subscribe myself respectfully,

F. B. PLIMPTON.

CHAPTER XVIII.

PLIMPTON—CORRY—PRIVATE SEANCES—RECOGNIZING FRIENDS—SPIRIT-FLOWERS—BUCHANAN READS, AND SPEAKS AUDIBLY—A SPIRIT PRINTS HIS HAND IN FLOUR—ABOUT CONDITIONS—"A BET"—GEO. D. PRENTICE—COLONEL PIATT—TRANSFORMATION—ILLUMINATED SPIRITS.

MR. PLIMPTON'S report was read with amazement by those who had previously treated the whole subject with ridicule. It was copied in several papers, and awakened general interest in the subject of spirit phenomena. It was the voluntary testimony of one who had spoken and written effectively *against* spiritualism. His mission was to persecute, when he began to investigate—to punish Mrs. Hollis and myself for daring to invite the public to examine the manifestations. The fact was quite patent that Mr. Plimpton's hostility to spiritualism amounted to a persecution of those who believed it, and his check was almost as sudden and unlooked-for as as was that of the infatuated Saul who fell by the way-side.

After the publication of his article, Mrs. Hollis and myself invited Mr. Corry to examine the phenomena, which were now beginning to challenge so much public attention. Mr. Corry is a cool, deliberate man, with very little "speculation in his eyes" or conversation. Still he is not a bigot, and, in this particular, is unlike Reemelin. He is a progressionist, but moves slowly. "Be patient!" is the axiom around which his whole system of philosophy revolves. He seems to move only on compulsion, if his understanding is not clear. Nature never designed this man for a leader—though he is a brave thinker. He can plan a fight well, but will lose the battle by tardy movement.

Mr. Corry consented to join Mr. Plimpton in the further investigation of spirit phenomena, in the presence of Mrs. Hollis; and while these two gentlemen are prosecuting their researches, I will record the results of a few *seances* given to other well-known citizens.

On the 12th of September, Mr. Charles Graham, Mrs. Mary Graham, and their son "Freddie," entered the cabinet-room to witness manifestations. The interior of the cabinet was first carefully examined, and then Mrs. Hollis's right-hand was blackened with burnt-cork before she went in. The door had scarcely been closed upon her, when a large hand and arm seized the pencil, and wrote on the slate:

"We will give you uncommonly good manifestations to-night! A large number of spirits will appear!"

At the conclusion of this writing, the pencil dropped, and the hand was held open, with the palm to the front, for inspection. It was a clean right-hand, almost transparent, without any trace of burnt-cork to be seen. I could not desire a more conclusive test to prove the materialization of a spirit-hand. It was certainly not more than ten seconds after the door was closed, that the clean hand appeared. Only half a minute after the writing, a brilliantly illuminated head and face of a lady were so clearly seen at the aperture, that the color of the eyes and hair could easily be distinguished. Her dark-brown hair was looped up Pompadour, with a cherry-colored ribbon. It was the sweet face of my cousin, Lizzie Odell, who had appeared several times before. When she left the aperture, the matured face of a woman appeared, whom Mrs. Graham recognized as her sister, Mrs. Elizabeth Parker. The spirit bowed, and retired. Very soon the curtain was again drawn aside, to show the face and head of ROBERT GRAHAM, a sturdy old man, who was at once recognized by his son Charles. This materialization lasted two minutes, during which time father and son saluted each other by words and bows. My mother next appeared, but only for a few seconds, though a good materialization, when she was quickly followed by the head and face of a young girl, who was immediately recognized by Mr. and Mrs. Graham as a long-buried daughter. Following the fading-out of this face, were presented two baby hands and arms, partly projected through the aperture. These had scarcely been withdrawn, when the familiar but sweet face of *Katie Kerns*, the medium's sister, came fully in view, and maintained a good materialization for *four* minutes. The next face presented was a strongly individualized one, whom Mrs. Graham instantly recognized as her half-sister, Mrs. Celia Rix, saying, as she did so, "There is no mistaking that face!" Immediately after she had retired, Washington's face came forward to the light, and remained a minute. He had scarcely retired when the long, muscular arm of Ney was projected through the aperture, holding in his hand a spirit-painting or portrait of Napoleon Bonaparte. This I was permitted to closely inspect. I am not an art-critic, and know little beyond the fact that when a painting, no matter whether it is a portrait or a landscape, pleases me, I say so. This picture of Napoleon pleased me. It was most exquisitely colored—the flesh-tints being soft, natural, and life-like. I inspected it closely for five minutes before it was withdrawn. On a subsequent occasion this portrait was presented, when I examined it with a lighted stearine candle, which I held not more than six inches from it.

The face of an elderly woman followed the withdrawal of the portrait, which Mrs. Graham recognized as her mother. The light was good, and the materialization faultlessly presented. Following this one was the bright, smiling face of little Anna Hancock; after which, that of a negro girl, by the name of *Caroline*, who had been an attached servant to the medium. Her color was that of a quadroon. She had barely retired, when the face and head of Josephine Bonaparte appeared, her dark hair strangely arranged with strings of pearls. She remained perfectly materialized four minutes. After she had retired, Mr. Buchanan and Mr. Douglas presented themselves several times at the aperture. They were quickly followed by a lady's face, which Mr. Graham pronounced to be his sister-in-law, "Jessie." · This spirit remained three minutes at the aperture, and nodded several times to Mr. Graham.

Jim Nolan now spoke at the aperture, thanking us for the conditions that had enabled so many good materializations to be made. They had exceeded all preceding efforts in number and completeness of detail. He then projected his arm into the room, waving a spirit-handkerchief for several minutes. This closed the *seance.*

This circle was distinguished for the number of materializations that had taken place, being no less than sixteen, six of which were the recognized friends of Mr. Graham and his wife.

The same parties, with Mr. J. A. Tyler, of Newport, Ky., formed a circle, a week after. Mrs. Hollis was in the cabinet only a minute or two, when a jeweled hand appeared, holding a flower, which looked like a camellia or japonica. The light was sufficient for a most critical inspection ; still, I availed myself of the privilege of examining it with a candle. It remained perfect for a minute, when it began to fade. I then placed my hand in front of the light, throwing its shadow upon the flower, which enabled it to revive somewhat ; at least, the shadow would arrest its decline. But for the complete renewal of its form and beauty, it was withdrawn to the interior of the cabinet ; it would soon appear fresh-looking and perfect again. This process of renewal was repeated five times, and the last time green leaves were added to the stem upon which the flower was supported. My attention during this exhibition, was about equally divided between the flower and the beautiful arm and hand of the spirit sustaining it. Both were inspected closely, and both claimed an equal share of admiration.

The next materialization was a pond-lily, so perfect in its size, form, and constituent parts, that I almost fancied I sensed its perfume. I examined this flower with the same care I did the first, and had ample time to satisfy myself that the material from which it was formèd was not the same we find in the natural flower. This floral exhibition was closed by Josephine waving a spirit-handkerchief, as if self-applauding the success of the manifestations.

Scarcely had the handkerchief been withdrawn, when a face appeared at the aperture, which Mr. Graham identified as BETSY PARKER. Then followed, at intervals of a few minutes each, the presentation of Lizzie Odell, an unrecognized lady, a little boy, and MRS. SARAH RIX; which latter spirit was immediately recognized by her daughter, Mrs. Graham. Following closely in the order of time, two faces of children appeared, which their parents, Mr. and Mrs. Graham, recognized as Walter and Emma.

For the first time was now presented a perfect and full materialization of the head and face of Elwood Fisher. This spirit had made several attempts to show himself to his friend Mr. Corry, but never with entire success. Mr. Corry's anxiety, I think, was the cause of his failure. He now materialized in good light, and maintained his form a minute and a half. This face of Elwood Fisher is a remarkable one, evincing power and will of an uncommon degree. He has an immense head and ponderous brow, much like Webster's; and yet the face reminded me more of John C. Breckenridge's.

After Elwood Fisher had retired, several faces

appeared, which were recognized as spirits that had manifested before; and when a lady's appeared, and nodded to Mr. Tyler, she responded to the name of SARAH PARISH. After her, Mr. Tyler's wife came to the aperture and remained long enough for complete recognition. She subsequently wrote a letter to her husband, on private affairs, which gave him much satisfaction.

Following this spirit, very soon, came Mr. Buchanan. He maintained his materialization so long and firmly, that I had time to fetch an autograph letter, framed and hanging in the east room. I handed it to him, and asked if he remembered writing it. He received it from my hand, and withdrew about half a minute. When he reappeared, *the view of his face was changed from a full front to a profile.* He held the letter before him, as if reading. Perhaps a minute elapsed, when he retired, and almost instantly reappeared, full front face, handing me the letter. As he did this, he said, audibly, "I remember it very well, Wolfe; it is a letter of introduction to Forney!"

This manifestation of Mr. Buchanan will arrest the investigating mind by its more than common interest and significance. It will be noticed that *two views* of his face were presented; and yet he could not rotate his head, to do this, in the light. I have seen the spirits change position during their appearance, but not to turn round. To the charge that these faces are flat, these materializations of Mr. Buchanan are sufficient refutation. The letter was evidently read by Mr. Buchanan, for he announced *audibly* its character. The materialization was one of the best I have seen, and, with one exception, the speaking as good as any I have heard.

After Mr. Buchanan retired, Mr. Douglas, Mrs. Jessie Graham, Mr. Robert Graham, David Wolfe, and CATHERINE HOLLIDAY appeared, *seriatim*. This latter spirit identified herself to Mr. Tyler, as being from Natchez, Miss. He remembered her well, after she referred to corroborating circumstances. This closed the exhibition of faces for the evening. The remainder of the time was consumed by writing messages, on the slate, to Mr. Tyler and Mr. Graham.

The *seance* was remarkable—eighteen spirits having materialized, besides the flowers, hands, arms, and writing. It lasted two hours, and left Mrs. Hollis very much exhausted.

September 14th was set apart for Mr. Corry and Mr. Plimpton to hold a dark circle; but Mr. Corry not appearing, it was decided to change the programme for the evening, and have a cabinet circle, with Mr. Plimpton and my whole family present. The evening was quite inclement; so we expected but indifferent manifestations.

It was not five minutes after Mrs. Hollis was closed in, when the spirit-hands began to appear at the aperture. These varied in size; one, especially, was noticeably large. This was Marshal Ney's, and seemed to possess more power than any of the others. I asked if it could leave its impression in a plate of flour, if I placed one on the bracket. The reply, by raps, was, "Yes." I filled an oblong steak-dish with flour, and set it before the aperture, *sideways*. This position was not favorable to receive a good impression. The spirit-hand changed the position of the dish, and commenced a kind of magnetic manipulation over the surface of the flour, which lasted several minutes. It then retired for a dark-bath, but in a few moments appeared again, and settled on the dish, till the hand and fingers were buried in the flour. It remained there half a minute, when it rose, carefully, to a vertical position, exposing the whole palm-surface of the hand to view. It was thickly coated with the adhering flour, not dust, but thick spread, as if the hand had first been wet. The flour began to dribble off, beginning at the points of the fingers, and wasting toward the base of the hand. The remarkable character of this manifestation was, that the fingers and hand wasted as the flour fell away, the same as if they had been formed of snow, and melted under the heat of a midday sun. At the conclusion of the *seance*, there was not a hand in the circle that could fill the well-preserved matrix in the flour ; and Mrs Hollis's hand could very little more than half fill it. I requested Mrs. Hollis to leave the impression of her hand in a plate of flour, and the two compared about as well as a lady's slipper and an Irishman's brogan. Following this experiment, Lizzie Odell appeared, with her hair very tastefully secured with the usual light cherry ribbon, and, after smiling and bowing, retired, to make room for the sweet but pensive face of Mary Plimpton. There was a bright light about her head, which at first was mistaken for lace ; a closer inspection, however, discovered it to be a spirit-halo. She could only materialize about thirty seconds.

In this connection, this seems to be a good time and place to say something on the subject of cabinet and writing conditions. I have observed that any mental or emotional excitement among the members of a circle has a tendency to disturb or destroy the conditions through which the spirits manifest. As in the case of Elwood Fisher, he has never, in all his efforts, been able to materialize fully in the presence of Mr. Corry; but in the presence of my family, or in the presence of Mr. Vickers, and others, he has materialized well. Is it because Mr. Corry *wants* to see him, that he can not do it? We can see the effect of one positive man's will over another who is magnetically negative to him, but do not understand just how it is. In this instance, the will to assist seems to produce the opposite effect intended, disabling rather than aiding the efforts of the spirits.

I am quite aware how much incredulity this statement may excite in the mind of an inexperienced reader; but the fact remains, and will compel us to recognize it at last. But few people have any proper appreciation of the delicacy of the conditions through which manifestations are given. These can be so disturbed by the most trifling and seemingly inconsequential circumstances and causes, that the spirits can no more manifest through them than they could in a slaughter-house or distillery. I have heard the spirits command Mrs. Hollis, peremptorily, to wash every bit of pearl-powder from her face, when she had been silly enough to "whiten up" to receive company, alleging that they could not give manifestations while her skin was pasted over with such trash. She is also required to keep her hair loosely done up, entirely free from oil or perfume of any kind. The odors of some flowers are odious to the conditions; and a hankerchief, rank with the extract of pole-cat or frangipanni, will so stifle the spirits, that they are quite incapable of manifesting. A camphor and chloroform liniment applied to a strained ankle in the morning will unfit the medium for manifestations in the evening. A drop of onion-juice or touch of asafetida upon the frame of the slate will disable spirits from writing. So, also, the presence of some persons with repulsive magnetisms and discordant minds will utterly unfit the medium for the delicate uses of the spirit-world. The spirits utterly refuse to manifest in the presence of intoxicated persons, and they dislike the odor of tobacco. It may now be understood why the spirits will manifest much better in the presence of some persons than they can in that of others; and also why the experience of one man may not corroborate the experience of another. Opportunities may be similar, but conditions as varied as temperaments. It follows that, mentally and physiologically, men may be so constituted that the spirit-world can not reveal itself to them. Of course, they can no more help their hapless condition than the leopard his spots, or the Ethiopian his skin. Nature, through violated physiological laws, puts her stamp of disability upon some organizations, so that they may commiseratingly be called "cripples," and treated as such, when they essay to deal with spiritual affairs. A monstrosity of this kind, to make his deformity the more obtrusive, wanted to *bet* five hundred dollars that the spirits could not manifest in his presence! I think it a safe bet; and the rascal, with as much certainty, knows he would win, as if he were playing with loaded dice.

But to return to the point of digression. Mary Plimpton had left the aperture but a few minutes, when the following spirits appeared, in the order of naming: M. D. Potter, James Buchanan, Stephen A. Douglas, Mrs. D. P. and son, Anna Hancock, Sarah Powers, Josephine Bonaparte, "Caroline," and George Washington. There was a spirit of a fair-haired lady, who could not be recognized, and she gave no name. Josephine presented the same portrait of Napoleon we had before seen, which she said was a most difficult materialization to accomplish. Sarah Powers wore a beautiful red flower in her hair, on the left side.

The remainder of the evening was occupied by the spirits writing messages to their friends. Of these, the following seems to be the only one possessing any public interest:

"I come from the bright land of peace to greet you, my friends! Beyond the ken of mortal eyes I have found a world of wondrous beauty. There I am no longer a suffering man, but a glorified spirit. All is well with me.

"GEORGE D. PRENTICE."

Mr. Prentice was requested to state his feelings when dying—whether conscious or not? In reply he wrote:

"When the shadows of death were over me, my breath, little by little, sank apace. The phantoms of destiny gathered thick and fast around me. I felt, like a limed bird, powerless to arrest my doom—the approach of the dreaded messenger. As an unworthy servant of His will, I prayed God's mercy; take me hence; thy will be done forever."

Again, as soon as the foregoing message was transcribed, Mr. Prentice was asked if he wished to say any thing more, when he quickly wrote:

> "Farewell, my friends. You will soon walk with me the broad road of progression. Fear not the dip of the oar that bears you over the river of death, for it brings you to the land of peace. GEORGE D. PRENTICE."

This concluded a very interesting *seance*, which lasted two hours. It was intended to hold a dark circle during the evening; but, as stated, Mr. Corry not appearing, the cabinet entertainment was substituted.

Mr. Plimpton and Mr. Corry had now become deeply interested in the phenomena which they day by day witnessed, and were regular and constant in their attendance, dividing their time about equally between the writing, the dark circle, and the cabinet manifestations. I made no engagements with the public for *seances* that would at all interfere with their investigations. My desire was to afford them every facility to examine the premises, and to assist them to discover the exact means Mrs. Hollis employed to produce these wonderful "tricks."

One evening, without announcing their intention, these gentlemen introduced COLONEL DONN PIATT, the well-known writer and satirist, as an investigator. I requested COLONEL PIATT to join the party of representative men, and give the subject a thorough sifting; which he consented to do. He was introduced to Mrs. Hollis, who became so much agitated that I almost despaired of the success of the circle that evening. The colonel's reputation as a satirist was a great bug-a-boo to her.

This trio—Plimpton, Corry, and Piatt—formed an able circle, to investigate the phenomena and discover fraud, if any existed. Neither of these gentlemen entertained friendly views of spiritualism, but rather a feeling of hostility, believing, as thousands do, the whole affair to be a cunningly devised system of deception. As their purpose was to examine the phenomena for public use, to which end they took minutes of that which transpired in their presence, I will in due time submit their personal statements, instead of my own, respecting the results of their investigation.

I will here report the occurrences of a *seance* which my family and Mr. Plimpton witnessed, a few evenings subsequent to the holding of the circle just reported.

Mrs. Hollis had been closeted but a few minutes, when a strange object was projected about six inches through the cabinet aperture into the room. After a close inspection, it proved to be the elbow of a flexed arm. It remained in this position about a minute, when the whole arm was suddenly extended into the room. The arm was symmetrically formed, and almost transparent; of a delicate rose-tint, and entirely nude. It remained four minutes before it was withdrawn, and then only to reappear, after a few seconds, covered with a sleeve of white tulle or illusion. This remained on exhibition a minute, when; presto! the arm retired, and reappeared, in a few seconds, dressed in a rich black silk over the first, the white protruding an inch or two from under it at the hand. Different positions were now given to the arm and hand, which, to an artist's eye, would have been deemed exquisitely graceful. The manifestation continued three minutes, when the arm was withdrawn, and quickly reappeared, clad in a green silk wrapper, fitting more closely than the black sleeve, and in the hand was held a phantom handkerchief, which was waved, like "a banner of beauty," half a dozen times before our astonished eyes. Another transformation, quickly succeeding the last, was the substitution of black lace for the former sleeve-making materials; the handkerchief still being retained in the hand. Very soon the arm was divested of all covering, and, as at first, extended into the room. The hand opened and shut rapidly, making an "awful fist" for a woman. If William Horace Lingard had been a woman, and in the spirit-world, I would have ascribed this transformation entertainment to his genius; but as he is neither a woman nor "*dead*," so far as I know, unless it be in "trespasses and sins," the show was a trifle mysterious.

It was only a few minutes after, that the same comely hand held by the stem a beautiful, pure white, and strangely shaped flower, resembling in size and form a "Spring sparrow, with wings extended." The leaves seemed vibrant with life, and I almost fancied I could hear the hum of their tiny motion on the still air. Our inspection of this "gem" continued about three minutes.

The next materialization was a spirit-lily. This was much admired, as it is always a graceful beauty; and on this occasion every part of its structure was perfectly presented. Following this was a cluster of violets and a purple morning-glory. These were followed by a delicate-pink flower, resembling in shape the blossom of the Virginia creeper. All of these were nicely materialized, and strangely beautiful. The next flower presented was a rose, about twice the size of our jacqueminot—colorless and phantom-like. The last single flower presented was a huge pond-lily, which filled the entire aperture of the cabinet. It was the most imposing representation of the floral kingdom displayed during the evening.

It was followed by a vase filled with flowers. This was held in the left-hand of the spirit, while, with the right, the flowers were picked out one at a time, presented to our view for inspection, and again replaced. This was a most interesting ceremony to witness.

As a fitting *finale* to this entertainment, little Anna Hancock first showed her smiling face, then her little hands filled with rosebuds. This floral exhibition was followed by the materialization of a number of faces, among which were Anna P., Katie Kerns, my mother, and sister Emma Francis—the two latter at the same instant. When they appeared, both were in profile—mother being nearest the aperture. That which I deemed noteworthy in these materializations was that sister's face was the most brilliantly illuminated, though most remote from the light in the room. Subsequently I was informed that the power to illuminate varies as much as temperaments in the form. All spirits can materialize, but all can not illuminate. This was a new thought. My mother spoke twice while at the aperture, pronouncing distinctly first my name, then my nephew's. After they had retired, Mary Plimpton gave a prolonged and beautiful materialization, frequently nodding to her brother, but unable to speak. After her, Mr. Potter, of the *Commercial*, and Lizzie Odell, appeared; which closed the *seance*. Mrs. Hollis was then liberated after a two-hours' confinement in her prison-house; and as she came out, I could not help scrutinizing her closely to discern, if possible, where and how she concealed about her person the many flowers and delicate fabrics which had been so handsomely presented through the aperture.

The weather was warm, and Mrs. Hollis wore a thin dress; not even a stuffed "bustle," or "pannier," wherein such articles as we had seen, could have been kept. I employed a lady detective—a room-mate of the medium—to discover the hiding-place of her "traps," and promised, as a reward of her success, an "Antwerp silk;" but even that did not bring a satisfactory reply. The answer was, unless she *swallowed* them, there was no other cunning place of concealment.

CHAPTER XIX.

COLONEL PIATT REPORTS—HAS THE FUN KNOCKED OUT OF HIM—DISCOVERS SOMETHING TOO SACRED FOR HALSTEAD, THE "BRUTE," TO TRAMPLE ON—HE SAND-PAPERS HALSTEAD'S NOSE, AND DRAWS "BLUD."

COLONEL DON PIATT was the second member of the representative circle to make his report to the public, through the columns of his Washington paper, *The Capital.* It will be seen that this brilliant writer, humorist, and satirist, began his investigation of spirit-phenomena, as Mr. Plimpton had, under the belief that Mrs. Hollis was an impostor, I her confederate, and the manifestations a fraud. Of course, they had predetermined the whole affair. Their intention was to make an *awful* example of somebody, as soon as *somebody* was discovered trying to impose upon the credulity of the people.

The announcement of this intention did not scare or surprise me in the least. I knew my men better than they knew me. I was well aware there was no fraud intended; and that I would rather assist in exposing trickery than aid in concealing it. If any man denounced me on suspicion, I would treat him as a poltroon and calumniator. The peer of any good citizen, why should I accept affronts, or be subject to insults, for presuming to investigate the claims of modern spiritualism, any more than I should be for exercising the same right in making choice of a religion?

I invited investigation, that the public might obtain, through representative men, reliable information respecting the facts of modern spiritualism. To the prosecution of this object Colonel Piatt gave eight days, devoting seven hours each day to the study of its phenomena. The time was not sufficient to witness a tenth part of what I have seen; but he could spare no more. He saw enough, however, publicly to acquit the medium of fraud; and of his humor and jesting he says, "All this ends when a coffin-lid is lifted from a loved face; and, after many years of longing grief, the well-remembered features return to us."

The following is the published statement of Colonel Piatt, dated Cincinnati, September 25, 1872:

AMONG THE SPIRITS.

I WAS sitting in the editorial room of the *Commercial*, talking to one of its versatile editors, who answers to the name of Plimpton, and who ought to be known throughout the country as one of our most accomplished journalists, and who is known to a wide circle of friends as the best sort of a fellow, when William M. Corry, late of the *Commoner* and Kentucky Resolutions, and now for all time the most brilliant conversationalist ever endowed with breath, came in, and immediately opened a conversation concerning a message that he had received the night before from his grandfather, long since deceased and quite forgotten. This message, it seems, came in the shape of advice, directing William to drop the *Commoner* and stick to bricks. This was certainly good sense, and showed that the grandfather's head was level, if not brilliant. I thought the gentlemen were joking, and put in my little jest accordingly.

There has always been something extremely ludicrous to me in the spiritual business. At best, it seemed a sort of rat-hole revelation and an unseemly attack on furniture. I had known the little Foxes at an early day, when they were quite pretty, plump as partridges, and as full of the animal as they claimed to be of spirits. Through these little girls, we used to interview St. Paul and Julius Cæsar. They were both represented to me as small men, with bald heads and hooked noses. Julius had a good deal of a stomach on him, which came, I suppose, on account of his unbounded ambition; at least, that is what Queen Catherine said of Cardinal Wolsey. I soon discovered, however, that my two friends were in earnest, and not in a frame of mind suited to joking. They went on to tell me, first one, and then the other, of the wonderful things they had witnessed at a Dr. Wolfe's, on Smith Street, in the presence of a medium, called Mrs. Hollis, of Louisville, Kentucky. I was, of course, interested; and, when invited to accompany them that night to a *seance* at the house of said Wolfe, under the direction of the said female medium, I readily assented.

At eight o'clock, we were at the house of the doctor, a charming residence on Smith Street, just out of Fourth. I was introduced to Mrs. Hollis, quite a handsome, dark-eyed brunette, weighing about a hundred and forty, and some thirty-five or forty years of age. Like the little Foxes, she is personally attractive; but, unlike my former mediums, I found her quiet and unassuming, and rather diffident. Aside from her personal attractions, the chief characteristic that impressed me was the exceedingly frank and honest expression of her face. A judge of human nature would dismiss all suspicion of fraud, after taking one good look at her kind, gentle countenance.

We were at once conducted through a long porch to the rear building, where, between the library and laboratory, the doctor had erected for Mrs. Hollis what was called the cabinet. It consisted of a partition run across one end of the small room, in the center of which was a door, and in the center of the door a circular opening twelve inches in diameter and about four feet from the floor. This aperture was covered with black cloth, while on the outside lay a slate with a minute slate-pencil upon it. The doctor made us examine the walls and floor to satisfy ourselves that there was no machinery about, while in the cabinet there was nothing but a common chair. Into this cabinet went

Mrs. Hollis; but, before so doing, the doctor blackened the palm of her right-hand. The door was closed, fastened on the outside, and we then sat down to the rattle of a large music-box that had borne about as much music in it as a tin-pan covering an insane bug. The gas-light shone through in a dim way from the adjoining rooms on either side, and we sat watching that dark spot upon the door, like three terriers gazing into a rat-hole. In about ten minutes, a delicate, white hand appeared, that seemed to waver and flicker before us and then disappear. As it went down, it seemed to melt into darkness. Directly the hand came back, and again went out as before. The third or fourth time, it seemed to grow steadier, reached out, seized the pencil, and wrote something with easy rapidity. It then opened so as to show the white palm, and disappeared. The doctor seized the slate, and we all rushed into the other room to read this message from the spirit-world. It was to the effect that some fighting character felt certain that he could whip somebody a second time. I thought the message was addressed to me, and so said, with the opinion to the ghost, that it couldn't be done; but it turned out subsequently to have been addressed to Mr. Corry, from a venerable defunct, who, in the remote ages of Cincinnati, had thrashed his (William's) grandfather, and, unwilling to clasp hands over the bloody chasm, was prepared to fight again.

This message, with the subsequent ones, accorded with my sense of the ludicrous, and I quite annoyed my friends with my levity. After receiving four or five messages, a luminous ball, very dim, appeared at the aperture, grew lighter, resolved itself into a head, with the features clearly defined, and, for a second, gazed at us from the opening. Mr. Plimpton told me that that was his sister Mary, dead some years, and was very striking in its resemblance. After this, came a message addressed to me, purporting to come from a cousin deceased some time since in Boone County, Kentucky. Then came another face, appearing and disappearing like the other. After this, we saw the late President of the United States, James Buchanan, that was so like the common lithograph head of the old Pub. Func. that my sense of humor grew stronger than ever. I thought that if James Buchanan, dead these many years, had only got so far as Smith Street, Cincinnati, he was as slow in the spirit as he used to be in the flesh. It seems, however, that Dr. Wolfe had, at one time, been the private secretary of the solemn old pump, and through life quite intimate with him; so that his appearance was not so extraordinary as it otherwise would have been. We then had the pleasure of seeing Stephen A. Douglas. Stephen came, I suppose, because Buchanan did, and my doubts overtook my fun when I saw that the bow each gave in response to the "good evening" of Dr. Wolfe, was precisely that which would come from a crayon sketch on a paste-board if the upper end were dipped forward suddenly.

I had made up my mind that the whole affair was an ingenious, innocent sort of fraud, when the luminous appearance at the opening resolved itself into a head that so shocked me, that, for a second, my heart seemed to stop its action. I was so surprised that, for a second, I was stunned, and my first feeling was that of indignation at what struck me as a wanton outrage. This was not, however, well defined, and the moment I could reflect, the fact forced itself upon my mind, that probably I had deceived myself. My sight is quite dim, from over-use, and I had only caught a glimpse of what had so startled me. It was too sacred a subject to be trifled with, and I determined to investigate the matter closely, and if I found any fraud in the business, to make an example of one medium, at least.

The face appeared but once afterward, and then more indistinct than before; so that nothing was given me upon which to solve my doubt. I had enough, however, to satisfy me that there was something more in this than is generally attributed to such manifestations.

To tell the honest truth, I had gradually settled into that unhappy state of belief, so common to this materialistic age, that we possessed nothing in the way of spiritual life that could be administered upon after death. This had been jammed into me by being knocked on the head, when I found, by actual experience, that as the physical ceased to operate, that part of me which thinks, wills, and remembers, ceased to exist also, and all was blank until the blood began to circulate, and the material engine got under way again. For thousands and thousands of years that chin of death has been tied up, and the napkin folded over the mouth, never to be removed by any message from the world beyond. So, like the more eminent theologians of our day, I had come to the unpleasant conviction that all there was of it we could feel, taste, hear, smell, and see. And yet, through this rat-hole came what purported to be facts, upsetting my settled opinions, and putting me all at sea upon this subject.

It is a common error for us to reject a truth because it does not come to us in a dignified and imposing manner. All the miracles of Christ failed to overcome the disbelief of the Jews, that grew out of the melancholy fact that the Messiah had come up out of Nazareth, and had been born in a manger. Newton got his idea of a great law from the falling of an apple, while Franklin with his kite identified the lightning. And so this startling disclosure of a great truth is as likely to come when least expected, in an obscure way, as others have done before.

With this spirit of skepticism, and with no belief in any thing, not even myself, I entered upon this investigation. I do not propose to go into the details of it, for others are at work upon them; but I can say in brief, that at the end of a week, in which I gave from five to eight hours daily to the investigation, I was forced to the conclusion that if I had not been holding intercourse with the dead, I had, at least, been in communication with a mysterious intelligence, outside the humanity subject to the laws of flesh.

Mrs. Hollis gave me, for example, a *seance* to myself, in which I was to receive communications in writing. I repaired to the house at ten o'clock A. M., and, in broad daylight, we two sat down by a small tea-table, over which the medium threw a woolen cover, and, giving me the slate, she requested me to ask any question, either mentally, or to write it. I did the first. She placed the slate under the table, and, while talking about other things, held it there with her right-hand. By means of a mirror that was hung accidentally in such a way that I could see her entire person, I noticed that her left-hand rested in her lap. In a few minutes I heard the pencil drop upon the slate, and, bringing it out, sure enough, I found written upon it an answer to my question. This continued for two hours and a half, in which time I asked forty-one questions, and received the same number of answers. In some respects these were not satisfactory; that is, I could not realize that the person who purported to be in communication with me would send precisely such messages. They were answers, and they were reasonable, but in the answers I could not feel the source indicated. There was one peculiarity which struck, and somewhat annoyed me. Every question I asked was a test, while nearly every answer was an avoidance of the test. And yet, while this was going on, quite unexpectedly, and, of course, unasked-for, the most conclusive evidences would be given.

There was a circumstance that occurred that amazed me, for it was so unexpected. I had written a message upon the slate that I did not wish the medium to see; and so turned it down, putting the pencil upon the upper side. In this position she placed in under the table. We heard the pencil drop directly, and, fetching out the slate, found no writing. Turning it over, however, under my written interrogatory was the response. The spirit had written it on the under-side; and the medium told me of a fact that I immediately put to the test—that the writing would go on upon the upper side, with the slate pressed to the bottom of the table.

The most striking manifestations were made in the dark, when the voices of the spirits became audible to us. The spirit whose face I had seen—and, by the by, this had been repeated to me until there could be no question about the resemblance, at least, if not the identity; for I had procured a powerful opera-glass that revealed to me the very color of the eyes and hair—this spirit whispered to me long messages that could be heard by others, which fact saved me from the doubt as to whether my imagination had not played me false. But the most striking and conclusive manifestation was in an interview between Mr. Corry and his former friend, Elwood Fisher. This was introduced by the medium asking if any one knew Elwood Fisher, and giving a description of his personal appearance. Mr. Corry said he would be glad to communicate with his friend, but asked for some evidence that it was Elwood Fisher he conversed with. Elwood, the Friend, then began:

"Does thee remember the little store on Fifth Street?"

"Yes, very well," responded Corry.

"Does thee remember the first time thee saw me there, sitting on the counter?"

"Very distinctly."

"Does thee remember taking me to thy father, who expressed an approbation of me?"

"I remember it all."

"Does thee remember Daddy Bassett, with his long queue, and ruffled shirts?"

"I do; and I have not thought of him these thirty years."

And this sort of thing continued, it seemed to me, for nearly an hour—this talk of the two friends over the events of their lives, in which the one from the spirit-land sought to convince the other of his identity, and succeded, beyond doubt. While this was going on, Mrs. Hollis informed me that quite a stout gentleman was examining my arm, lately twisted in a buggy-wheel, who claimed to be a surgeon, and called himself Jesse Judkins. She described him as a merry gentleman, fond of his jest. Poor Jesse! no truer word was ever said. After these whispered communications, that we were assured would grow stronger, and become more distinct, we had a talk with Jimmy Nolan. Jimmy spoke right out, very like a man talking through a horn, which I have no doubt he was doing, for there was a tin horn in the room; and having decided that the medium was honest, this strange, hollow voice, speaking to us in a familiar way, with ease and fluency, had a very strange effect. I could not help asking Jimmy, however, whether Greeley was going to be our next President.

"That I can not answer, sir; and you know as much about it as I do. I can only say that he seems to have a first-rate chance."

I wish I could write more at length upon this interesting subject, but I find myself, since making the attempt, shrinking from the task. I am not ashamed, as many are, of my experiences, or afraid to avow my convictions; but, unfortunately for my testimony, the proof came to me in a shape too sacred for common use. Dr. Wolfe had invited this lady to his house, after what I understand was rather an unfortunate experience as a medium, at Cincinnati, for the purpose of calm, careful investigation of spiritualism generally, and this lady's power and honesty in particular. Of all the prominent men invited in the city, two only could be found possessing interest enough in the subject to look into it and report the results of their investigation. I happened, accidentally, to make a third. I join heartily in the report which says that the medium is above all suspicion, and I can add my conviction that the intelligence with which we communicated was beyond, if not above, the experiences of material humanity. D. P.

This report of Colonel Piatt was extensively circulated through the press of the country, and variously commented upon—not always with commendation. Among the journalists who did not read it with complacent feelings, Mr. Halstead, of the Cincinnati *Commercial*, may be distinguished. This man exhibited so much zeal and ignorance in his denunciation of spirit phenomena, and its claims to public confidence, that Colonel Piatt deemed it necessary to rebuke the "brute" by the publication of the following card:

MANIFESTATIONS AT DR. WOLFE'S.

To the Editor of the Commercial:

IT seems absurd in any one to exhibit feeling in a discussion of the reality or humbug of the manifestations at the house of Dr. Wolfe. But this wrath or indignation is natural, when you reflect that to question one's conclusions, after a careful investigation, is to attack one's understanding in the most aggravating manner. The doubting party says, in so many words: "Here's a precious ass; he believes a Punch-and-Judy show to be a manifestation of the spirits!" This aggravation is not alleviated when the party making the attack confesses that he or she has not looked into the business; or, starting to investigate, is satisfied with the first glance that reveals beyond question the shallow humbuggery that has taken in the other fools.

I incontinently admit that in the preparations and surroundings there are much to excite suspicion, and the rat-hole revelations provoke one's sense of humor. But all this ends, when the coffin-lid is lifted from a loved face, and, after many years of longing grief, the well-remembered features return to us.

Now, under this state of fact, ridicule becomes insult; for if the thing is a fraud, there is no punishment sufficiently severe or degrading for the perpetrators of the outrage. If, on the contrary, there is any truth in the manifestation, a right-minded person will see that to attack it with sneers and laughter, is to trample, like a brute, upon what one holds to be sacred.

I am, through temperament and intellectual training, a skeptic. Possessed of a keen sense of humor, I am given to jesting. I was startled out of both by what I saw and heard in this so-called Punch-and-Judy show, and, after eight days' careful investigation, I was driven to the conclusion that, whether the spirits of the dead had appeared, spoken, and written to me, or not, the medium, Mrs. Hollis, had nothing whatever to do with the business, beyond being present at the manifestations. What the evidence was that brought me to this finding, is exclusively my affair. I could not, if I would, force it upon the public. But as I never yet recognized a truth I was afraid to avow, or shrank from the defense of a course, or a creature, through dread of ridicule, I assure you that any attempt to account for these strange things by a charge of fraud and collusion is a wrong to an inoffensive, unassuming woman; and a refusal to investigate what is considered of enough importance to print columns about, is a wrong to ourselves.

All I wish to say, however, can be put in one sentence. I am not satisfied that I saw the faces, heard the voices, and read the written messages of the dead; but I do know—for it would be a miracle, were it otherwise—that the manifestations were not the result of any fraud, design, or even effort on the part of the medium. D. P.

CINCINNATI, *October* 6, 1872.

CHAPTER XX.

EXTRAORDINARY CONVERSATION WITH JIM NOLAN, IN THE LIGHT—A NUMBER OF DISTINGUISHED FRENCH SPIRITS—CALLING DISTINGUISHED CITIZENS TO TESTIFY—PARENTS RECOGNIZING CHILDREN—THE DEAD SPEAK AND WRITE AGAIN.

JIM NOLAN said, on several occasions, he would be able, before the termination of the engagement, to talk to me twenty minutes, while he stood before the aperture, with his face fully in view. Still, one morning, when he wrote upon the slate he wished me to go to the cabinet-room for that purpose, I confess I was a little surprised. He said the medium was in excellent condition, and I should not apprise her of his intention. I gave my promise to be *inter nos*, and, so pledged, went to the cabinet-room.

This imposed silence, I subsequently ascertained, was for the purpose of keeping the medium passive. Had she been apprised of his intention, her anxiety or agitation would have been sufficient to defeat his purpose by dissipating the power he employed. Mrs. Hollis has much to learn, and a great deal of discipline to receive before she will, of her own accord, establish conditions through which the spirits may best manifest. Both Nolan and "Ski" have often written me to do certain things without permitting the medium to know their object until after it had been accomplished. To her credit, however, it must be said, that she rarely opposes their wishes, when her compliance does not inconvenience her too much. Like most people, Mrs. Hollis, when she is commanded to do a thing, wants to know the motive in view, before she implicitly obeys—asserting that she is no longer a child, and will not consent to be treated as such. Still, she is the most patient and passively obedient woman to the wishes of the spirits that I have known. Their word is law, but she requires the reason of the law; yielding an intelligent subjection, but not indulging in an unreasoning faith. "I walk with my eyes open," she said, "and will not be led."

As requested, I went with Mrs. Hollis to the cabinet-room, and as I was pushing the door to, after she had entered the cabinet, a voice spoke distinctly, "Stand still!" It was Jim Nolan's voice, I knew; for I had heard it a hundred times. I obeyed the command, standing about two feet in front of the aperture, upon which I fixed my gaze. About five minutes elapsed before the cloth was put aside, when, far back in the dark chamber, was discernible the outline of a man's head. It approached slowly to the light, until it was plainly seen, though it wanted the spirit-halo to brighten it, as I have seen with many. The light, however, was sufficient to discern the color of the eyes and hair. The skin of the face was sun-tanned and dark, while the beard was brown-black and full. From my position, I could have "pulled him by the nose" if he had been a lying spirit, and would have done so had I detected him in a fraud. I looked steadily in his eyes for a minute, when he defended himself from my aggressive stare by shading them with his hand. He seemed to be perplexed or confused, and, in a hesitating, stammering manner, at the beginning, said :

" Do—you—see—me,—Doctor ?"

" Certainly I do," I said ; " I see you very well."

" Do I look like a mask ?"

" Not much ! You look more like a man."

" I feel so just now."

" I hope it is a comfortable experience," I said.

" It is not ; I feel my old fever again."

" Do you mean the fever with which you died ?"

" Yes : the old hospital-fever. "

" And will it kill you again ?" I asked.

" No : but it makes me feel very uncomfortable ; and, when I retire, I w ll, in some measure, be as infirm in the spirit-life as I was when I entered it from the hospital."

" You are speaking better. Please tell me : do all spirits, when they return, take on the conditions of the disease with which they died ?

" Mostly so. If they remain long materialized they do ; but if only for a short time, then they do not suffer with their old disorders."

" Does that account for the difference in the displayed power of materializing by different spirits ?"

" Partly. Some spirits can not materialize at all, with all the instructions and aid we can give them. Others are diffident and incapable without aid ; and others, again, materialize without embarrassment or effort. The conditions surrounding the medium have very much to do in influencing the power to materialize, and in maintaining the organization."

"Why is it that some spirits speak, and some do not?"

"It requires a completely passive condition to speak—a power but few attain. Perhaps never before has a spirit been able to speak so long in the light as I have upon this occasion. I am getting sick, and must soon retire."

"This is really wonderful!—the living and the dead again exchanging ideas. Who will believe this, when I make my report?"

"Neither fools nor bigots!"

"And I fear a great many who would take offense to be thus classified will be incredulous."

"Does that disturb you?"

"Not very much; but it is not pleasant to have one's integrity impeached by the world."

"Do you remember the story I told Vickers?"

"I do not: what was it?"

"A German fable about a man, a boy, and an ass."

"I believe I recall it now. It was to the effect that a man who sought to please every body, succeeded in pleasing nobody. Instead of riding the ass, the ass rode him."

"You have the *juice* of it. Keep that in mind. Be true to yourself, you can not then be false to any one. I must now leave you. There are a number of distinguished spirits here, who will materialize after the medium has rested awhile. Good-bye."

After ceasing to speak, Jim Nolan remained at the aperture, stroked his beard with his right-hand several times, made an effort to whistle, "winked very wickedly" three or four times, opened and shut his mouth twice, displaying tongue and teeth, and then vanished. This remarkable inverview continued twenty minutes.

Mrs. Hollis now came out of the cabinet, for fresh air and recuperation, after giving the most remarkable spirit-manifestation that I have yet found recorded in the literature of spiritualism. The time was exactly twenty minutes from the beginning of the materialization to its fading out. The voice at first, as already stated, was slow, hesitating, and feeble, but a gradual amendment in all these particulars supervened. He was at his best vocalization when I said, "You are speaking better," and rapidly declined after replying, "Neither fools nor bigots."

MR. THOMAS WICKERSHAM, of Memphis, Tenn., a gentleman of fine poetic temperament, after an interview with Jim Nolan, apostrophizes him thus:

"THE ANGEL, JIMMY NOLAN.

"GOD bless thee, Jimmy Nolan, and bless thy spirit-band!
My soul salutes thee, angel, a guest from Summer-land.
I hear the spirit-voices; they whisper in my ear;
I know I am immortal; departed souls are here.

Thy coming, Jimmy Nolan, is wonderful to me;
My fervent prayer is answered, my soul from doubt is free;
I thought not, in my weakness and gathering despair,
That God would send an angel in answer to my prayer.

Thy presence, Jimmy Nolan, as messenger of truth,
Is 'fulgent with the glory of an immortal youth;
It floods with light that river—the unseen country's bourne—
Streams through the secret portal, bids mortals cease to mourn.

In wonder, Jimmy Nolan, I here confess my soul
Before an unseen power, of mystical control.
Who will believe this marvel—that I, with mortal breath,
Have talked with thee, immortal, beyond the gate of death?

In myst'ry, Jimmy Nolan, our friendship thus began;
Though not thy Brother Mason, I am thy brother man;
In faith, in works, in worship, in love and holy prayer,
"We meet upon the level, we part upon the square."

In duty and in kindness we ever work and toil,—
Not with that emulation that seeks the victor's spoil;
But with high aspirations, in common brotherhood—
Our great reward for action, the joy of doing good.

We own that mystic worship the ancients used to know,
Beside the sacred Ganges, in ages long ago;
That worshiping in spirit, with souls in sweet accord,
When sitting down in silence to wait upon the Lord.

We know not by our wisdom what is that wondrous power
That renders every lover oblivious of the hour.
It fills and rules all creatures in earth and heaven above;
Therefore the loved disciple has written, "God is love."

Not in the crowded temple, not where the priest attends,
But from our secret closet, our fervent prayer ascends.
And prayer thus breathed in secret, like incense upward rolls;
Joy fills the waiting angels; their hearts pray for our souls.

O, may that Holy Spirit, heard in the wild-bird's song;
Heard in the voice of waters that, gushing, foam along;
Heard in the angel-voices, that cease their music never,—
Become a light to cheer us, to hover round us ever!"

Before Mrs. Hollis entered the cabinet again, several members of my family came into the room to witness the remainder of the manifestations. As soon as the door was closed, the hand of Marshal Ney was projected from the cabinet, and, seizing the pencil, wrote upon the slate:

"1. Napoleon.	4. Hortense.
2. Cardinal Richelieu.	5. Maria Antoinette.
3. Josephine	6. Charlotte Corday.

7. Madame Lafayette.	10. Rousseau.
8. Talleyrand.	11. Madame De Stael.
9. Murat.	12.

"These spirits will appear in the order they are numbered.
"NEY."

I had scarcely time to make a minute of the above, and replace the slate on the bracket, when the cloth at the aperture was lifted, and a full, fair-lighted face of Napoleon appeared. It was, of course, instantly recognized; and after a half minute he spoke quite distinctly, though evidently with an effort, "*Vive la France!*" Having said this, he instantly vanished.

The cloth did not fall over the aperture again before the great cardinal appeared just opposite to where the emperor had retired—the head, large, angular, and almost square, with unusual breadth between the eyes; a close-fitting black velvet cap, with a fringe of gray hair below it; the eyes large and prominent; and the mouth wide, with their lips compressed. He wore a full, thin beard, several inches in length. He had upon his neck a chain, to which was attached a crucifix.

No. 3. A beautiful oval face, with large dark eyes, prominent nose, small mouth and chin; hair confined with strings of pearls; and a crown, sparkling with brilliants, worn upon the head. The neck and breast were almost literally covered with strands of pearl, from the center of which a medallion likeness of Napoleon was suspended. It was richly set in brilliants or costly stones.

Following Josephine, was her daughter Hortense; her hair lighter than her mother's, done up in short

JOSEPHINE

curls, with features much like her mother's; also wearing a likeness of Napoleon on a necklace of brilliants. As she was finely materialized, I said to those present: "That is Hortense, the mother of the present Emperor of France. I do not observe the pictures of the son bear any resemblance to the mother." If the reader will refer to page 241, it will be seen what these simple remarks called forth.

No. 5 appeared, after the long colloquy with Ney, with head and neck well developed; hair very black, and combed smooth, and close to the face. No ornaments.

No. 6 looked like a sick person, in a reclining position, far wasted with disease; the face pinched and shrunken, and very pale, with the eyes closed. Lips seemed colorless; a white bandage was worn round the head, which, Ney subsequently said, was put on by request of the unhappy woman, a few minutes before her decapitation, to prevent her beautiful hair from being draggled with blood.

No. 7 was a plain, republican face, but finely materialized and life-like. The face was oval like Josephine's, but more gross, Her chest was a marvel of beauty, well seen, the dress low. She wore a medallion likeness of Napoleon on a necklace, larger than either of those worn by Josephine or Hortense.

No. 8 has a singular-looking face, with a hawk-like nose, an aggressive crook on the end, bearing a strong resemblance to the nose of the late William H. Seward. The hair was grizzly and gray. The general expression of the face was "foxy," cunning; which I did not like.

The materialization of No. 9 was fine; but the style of dress decorations and curly hair would be more befitting a prince of coxcombs than a prince of men. The angles of this fellow's mouth were puckered up in the most contemptuous manner, though the face seemed the very picture of repose. I should call him a game-peacock, who wore his decoration for holiday display, but laid them aside when he went into a fight.

The other materializations were not distinct, as the medium complained of exhaustion, and asked to be relieved.

It will now be asked. "Do you really believe the faces presented at the aperture belonged to the persons whose names were announced in connection with them?" To be candid with the reader, I must say the question is impertinent. What I believe or disbelieve should not affect my statement in this matter. I simply record what I saw and heard. The spirits I have mentioned appeared in the order I have given, and in the manner described. If there is any doubt about their identity, pass it over, and interest yourself in the major proposition, "How came they there at all?" They were not automatons manipulated by Mrs. Hollis. Of that I was well satisfied. I am not easily deceived. At least, I was all the time on the lookout for the presence of fraud. There was none in this case: I assert it at the risk of my reputation! The conversation with Marshal Ney was, to say the least, a most wonderful disclosure! Is it possible that Mrs. Hollis can do every thing, and know every thing, and conceal herself so well as to defy detection in her frauds? I will call other witnesses to the stand. I may be deceived, but surely all can not be.

On the 4th of September, Mrs. Augusta Stone, Mrs. Jennie Paul, and Mrs. Apoline Smith had a cabinet *seance* with Mrs. Hollis. She entered the cabinet, and, in a few minutes after, the spirit of a young lady materialized and appeared at the aperture. Mrs. Stone and Mrs. Paul, almost at the same instant, exclaimed, "Lizzie Donaldson!" Following this spirit, was an old lady with a peculiar head-dress, which was recognized without difficulty as Lizzie Donaldson's mother—Mrs. Paul, Mrs. Stone, and Mrs. Smith, all attesting to the recognition. Who next? Why, Miss Amelia Drewer, of Stockbridge, Massachusetts. How do we know? Mrs. Smith says so. Several other spirits were presented, but not recognized.

The next witnesses had a cabinet *seance* on the 7th of September. They are Mr. D. H. Hale and his son, Clinton B. Hale, from Indiana.

These gentlemen had been in the cabinet-room but a few minutes, when a young lady, giving her name as Melvina, appeared at the aperture, and Mr. Hale recognized her as his daughter. The young man claimed her for his sister. Daniel Hale, an uncle of Mr. Hale, appeared, and wrote a characteristic message, saying, "I am here, thank God!" Mr. Hale says he recognized his uncle. A little girl appeared, and gave her name as Emma Beam. She was but five years old—an adopted daughter of Mr. Hale. He says it was she. A young lady appeared, after this child, and wrote:

"Dear Mr. Hale: how kind you were to me!
"JENNIE BILLINGS."

Mr. Hale wept, as he recognized this face as belonging to one whom he had assisted in her poverty. With the knowledge that our good deeds are thus remembered, a belief in this kind of spiritualism won't make people uncharitable. The daughter Melvina then wrote a private letter to her father and brother; and, after several other unrecognized faces had retired, the *seance* closed.

Mr. Robert Mitchell, Mrs. Robert Mitchell, and Mr. Stephen H. Burton had a cabinet *seance* with Mrs. Hollis, on the 9th of September. Quite a number of spirits appeared, flowers were materialized, and arms and hands presented. Among the spirits, General Joseph Wright, of Indiana, and Mrs. Harriet Mitchell, were recognized.

Mrs. Maria J. Lemon and Mrs. L. A. Chandler engaged a cabinet *seance* with Mrs. Hollis, on the 10th of September. The aperture was soon made interesting by the face of Mary L. Andrews, which was quite familiar to Mrs. Chandler. Mrs. Lemon's sister, Lizzie Tucker, then appeared, and brought with her Mary Fairchilds, the daughter of Mrs. Lemon. The next face presented was one familiar to Mrs. Chandler, which she called Adeline Durant.

September 12th was set apart for a cabinet *seance* for Mr. W. G. Morris, Mrs. Matilda Withers, Mrs. Mary J. Ball, Covington, Kentucky.

To these persons a number of spirits appeared, giving the names of relatives accurately, but were not recognized. Among them a boy, who wrote:

"Grandma: I will show you a better picture of myself, to-night, than that old faded photograph is.
[Signed,] "CHARLEY."

The grandchild came, but was not recognized. The name and circumstances were given correctly. The only *seance* where there was no recognition. "No one so blind as *she* who will not see."

The next witnesses are MR. RUFUS SLOCOMB and his wife. They came for a cabinet interview on the 17th of September. Fifteen good materializations were given in the presence of these witnesses; among them, their daughter CELIA, a lad, and CLARA RESOR TAYLOR were distinguished very readily. Celia wrote several messages of a private character to her parents, besides exhibiting a variety of flowers.

On the 19th of September, Mr. Samuel R. Bates and wife and Mr. Edward C. Urner had a cabinet *seance* with Mrs. Hollis. Eleven very fine materializations were given, among which were quickly distinguished Mrs. Elizabeth Bates (by a portrait), Mrs. Lilly Gaylord, Miss Catherine Urner, and Mr. Philip Grandin. This last spirit wrote to his daughter, Mrs. Bates:

"Don't cry, my dear child; I'm very happy!"

Mrs. Elizabeth Bates appeared four times at the aperture. She wrote:

"Samuel, you do not remember me. You were an infant when I passed from earth!"

The following communication was written to Mr. Urner:

"MY SON,—I have made *five* efforts to show my face, but could not succeed. Give my best love to your mother. I am ever near her. George and Catherine are with me. I am very happy. This is my first writing. I will be able to do better after a while. I see you every day. BENJAMIN URNER."

A *seance* was engaged by Mr. Joseph Abrams, Mrs. Zerlina Cahn, Mrs. Fannie Hellman, and Misses Louisa and Jennie Cahn, for the 20th of September. In the presence of these witnesses there were *ten spirits* materialized and presented, besides hands, flowers, and handkerchiefs. Among the spirits were JULIET LEWIS, MRS. JULIET BLOOM, MRS. CAHN, SARAH DREYFOOS, ANNA ABRAMS, and ISADORE DREYFOOS. These were recognized by the witnesses. Mrs. Cahn wrote to her daughter, Mrs. Hellman: "Out of the dark waters of sorrow joy will spring!" Anna Abrams wrote a note to her father.

On the following day, September 21st, Mr. William Sumner, Mr. S. Harvey, Mr. Sidney Omohundro, and Mr. J. C. Moore visited the cabinet-room, and saw at the aperture ten spirit-faces, among which were a sister of Mr. Harvey, and his little boy "Joey;" Mrs. Samuel Shock, of Columbia, Pennsylvania, and J. Moore. The first three were recognized. There were also presented hands, arms, flowers, and spirit-handkerchiefs during the hour and a half they sat in the room.

On the 22d of September, a cabinet *seance* was given to General Rees E. Price, Mrs. Price, Mr. Rees Price, Mr. John Price, Mrs. Mary M'Duffie, Miss Estelle Matson, and Mr. Rees M'Duffie. In their presence, twelve spirits appeared at the aperture; among whom were James Price, Judge Matson, Miss Sallie Price, Annie Price, Grandma M'Duffie, Mary

Whipple, and "Uncle John." These were recognized, and some of them wrote messages to their friends. There was also a fine display of spirit-flowers, arms, hands, and handkerchiefs.

Captain James Drouillard and Mrs. Florence Drouillard, of Cumberland Furnace, Tenn., and Miss Marie Drouillard, of Gallipolis, O., had a *seance* on the 29th September, in which eight spirits appeared at the aperture. Among these, Mrs. Drouillard's mother, Uncle Chambers, Emma Robb, and Sadie Drouillard were recognized. General M'Pherson, a personal friend and comrade-in-arms, was also recognized by Captain Drouillard. Jacob Hornberger wrote his name, which was recognized, and then Charles Campbell wrote:

> "My wife, child, and I were killed by the accident on the railroad, near Nashville, when the bridge gave way."

The name and circumstances were recognized. Mrs. Drouillard's mother wrote to an old servant, "Dear old cooky, God bless you!" after which, the following message was written, and the author identified:

> "My Dear Florence,—I am often with you. Jimmy is so glad to have you come here. O, darling child! our dear ones are all here; we have a beautiful home, and we are so glad to tell you..
>
> "Your devoted Aunt Kit."

Another message was as follows:

> "Dear Cousin Florence,—Tell my dear wife I am happy. I tried so hard to write to my friends, but was so cold I could not. The papers were found near me. Jimmy."

It was stated, in explaining the last message, that

this person froze to death, and that he essayed to write something by which his body might be identified when discovered, and his people apprised of his fate.

After projecting several hands, arms, and flowers, the *seance* closed.

On the following day, Mrs. Robert Mitchell and Miss Lizzie Couden visited the cabinet-room, and witnessed the materialized faces of eighteen spirits. Among their friends and acquaintances appeared Edith Couden, Mrs. White, Mrs. D. P., Henry Chase Couden, William Craig, James Craig, Governor Joseph Wright, of Indiana, and Captain Pogue, of Madison, Ind. Arms, hands, handkerchiefs, and flowers were also displayed at the aperture.

Mr. J. W. Hardman, of Louisville, Kentucky, had the most prolific cabinet materialization that was given. There were twenty-six faces well distinguished, in good light, besides a number of arms, drapery, jewelry, flowers, and handkerchiefs. He recognized a number of friends and acquaintances.

Rev. Thomas Vickers began his investigation of the phenomena in the cabinet-room, on the 2d of October, but had been in the dark circle previously, and also at the writing-table. As he will make his own report, the next, and last, cabinet *seance* I will record, was held on the 5th October.

This circle was composed of Mr. F. B. Plimpton, Hon. Fisher Ames, U. S. Minister to San Domingo, Miss Maggie Baker, Mrs. M'Kee, Mr. Andrew De Ford, Mr. John Price, and three members of my family. Quite a number of spirits appeared; but they were those mostly who had materialized before;

among them, Elwood Fisher, James Buchanan, Stephen A. Douglas, Katie Kerns, my mother, Lizzie Odell, Mary Plimpton, and M. D. Potter. The spirits recognized were, Sallie Price, Emma De Ford, and Mrs. Helen M. Willet. Others came to the aperture, but their recognition was not so well pronounced. There were also fine materializations of arms, hands, handkerchiefs, and flowers, making the occasion an interesting one.

For the present, I will close my citations of witnesses, but continue the testimony in the ensuing chapter.

CHAPTER XXI.

REMARKABLE INTERVIEW — ELWOOD FISHER IDENTIFIES HIMSELF TO MR. CORRY — JIM NOLAN IS PHONETICALLY REPORTED BY BENN PITTMAN — THE MARRIAGE QUESTION FROM A SPIRIT STANDPOINT — NOLAN'S VIEWS ON A VARIETY OF SUBJECTS—"THOUGHT INDICATOR."

IT often occurred to me that a phonetic report of the remarks of Jim Nolan, in the dark circle, would afford matter of much interest to the reading public. The same thought occurred to Mr. Plimpton, after interviewing Jim two or three times. *But could it be done in the dark?* That was the question of interest! I commissioned Mr. Plimpton to engage MR. BENN PITTMAN for a trial, if he thought well of the experiment; and it was agreed that CORRY, PLIMPTON, PITTMAN, and myself should interview "*Jim*," on a certain day, with the stated object in view. Mr. Pittman, it is hardly necessary to say, has a reputation coextensive with the country, as the most accomplished expert in his profession; still, it was an untried experiment to report a protracted conversation in a room so dark that you "could not see your fingers before your eyes." To master the situation satisfactorily, was a matter of some anxiety to us all, but especially to Mr. Pittman. Writing in the dark was sufficiently embarrassing; but to report the words of a spirit was an added novelty, not calculated to quiet his nerves upon the occasion.

At the appointed time, the parties named were all present, and, with Mrs. Hollis, entered the room. Before extinguishing the light, the room was carefully examined, and no concealed confederate was found. The door was then secured; and, after Mr. Pittman arranged his writing appliances, sitting next to Mr. Plimpton, I next to him, and Mr. Corry next to me, the light was put out. Mr. Pittman has made a most faithful report of what followed, which is here appended:

AN ACCOUNT OF A SPIRIT SEANCE

HELD IN THE DARK:

Being an Interview with the Spirits of Elwood Fisher and James Nolan. by Hon. William M. Corry, F. B. Plimpton, Esq., and Dr. N. B. Wolfe.

PHONETICALLY REPORTED BY BENN PITTMAN.

AFTER a few minutes' desultory conversation, Mr. Corry said: "Do you see any spirits, Mrs. Hollis?"

Mrs. H. "Yes: but not very distinctly. I see a peculiar light around your head."

Q. "What is it like?"

Mrs. H. "An illuminated atmosphere." (Taps of the horn on the floor.)

Q. "Do you wish us to sing?" (Several quick raps.)

Mr. Plimpton sang, "Oft in the Stilly Night," and was accompanied by a female voice, I supposed to be Mrs. Hollis's, and inquired if it was she.

Mrs. H. "I never sing; am not able to carry a tune!"

Dr. W. "I have never heard Mrs. Hollis sing or hum a tune, since she has been an inmate of my family."

Mr. Plimpton sang, "Ye banks and braes o' bonnie Doon," with a female voice accompaniment, said to be a spirit-voice.

Mrs. H. "There is a spirit standing beside Mr. Corry, in

plain clothes. A Quaker, I should suppose. He has his eyes closed. He stands with his arms folded across his breast."

C. "Does he announce his name?"

Mrs. H. "He will speak to you."

C. "I will be very glad to have a communication."

A. (A whisper.) "William, I am glad to meet thee!"

C. (To the spirit.) "Is it well with thee?"

A. "It is well."

C. "Will thee pronounce thy name?"

A. "Does thee remember thy Faneuil Hall speech, when I told thee I thought I should have to save thee, like Actæon from his hounds?"

C. "I remember it very well. The crowd was raging, fighting, yelling, and stamping, to prevent me being heard; but I did not not care whether they heard me or not. I made my speech, and it was printed. Can thee make thyself audible to this circle, so that every syllable can be heard, as if thee were on the rostrum where we admired thee so much?"

A. (A whispered reply.)

C. "Thee holds me in too high estimation! What is thy reason for thinking so?"

A. (A whispered reply.)

C. "It may be a mistake, but it is ingenuous."

Spirit. "I thank thee for it. I know thou art a true friend."

C. "Of that there can not be the least doubt in thy mind."

Spirit. "I know thee will never betray." (Low whispering, heard by Mr. Corry only.)

C. "*Thee has identified thyself perfectly to me*, and to those who were at the last sitting. Can thee relate any circumstances by which thy identification would be made absolute? Thee knows what a yearning I have to establish the fact; and how the world scoffs at the imperfect evidence which is presented in these investigations."

Spirit. (Whispers). "Palmetto—cause—not lost—Vallandigham. Farewell, William!"

C. "Farewell, Elwood!"

Dr. W. "Mr. Corry, do you recognize that spirit?"

C. "Yes: that is Elwood Fisher."

Mrs. H. "Near you, Mr. Pittman, I see a spirit who gives his name as William Glenn. He says he died on Fifth Street, between Smith and John, of disease of the brain. He gives the names of his children as William, George, David, Anna, and John. He was a partner of M'Gregor in the lock——. I can get no more. I see the name of Joseph Langdon. Mr. Corry, I see the name of Barnett, and a small foot. What does it mean?"

C. "Do you get his initials?"

Mrs. H. "G. W. are given."

C. "G. W. Barnett was celebrated for having the smallest feet of any man in town."

Mrs. H. "I see an old man, very much stooped, his clothes much worn; looks as if in distress. He gives the name of John Clingman."

C. "I knew him very well. He was a hatter."

Mrs. H. "He says, Yes; his daughter Eliza is living on his place. He can not tell where his son John is. I thought you was n't coming, Jim." (Spoken in an under-tone.)

Jim Nolan. "I only stood back to give them old fellows a chance. How are you, Mr. Corry?"

C. "Quite well, thank you, sir!"

Spirit. "How are you, Mr. Plimpton?"

P. "Very well; I'm glad you've come, Jimmy."

Spirit. "Thank you, sir! How are you, Doctor?"

Dr. "Tip-top, Jim! Hope we'll have a good time this morning."

Spirit. "I hope so! How are you, medium?"

Mrs. H. "I am not feeling very well to-day."

Spirit. "I'm sorry for that, but can't help it."

P. "Jimmy, we have Mr. Pittman here to report your conversation. Any thing you have to say, we will be glad to hear."

Spirit. "You had better indicate the topic upon which you desire information, Mr. Plimpton. You have a preference, of course."

P. "In a former conversation, you said, when death takes place, we are provided with spiritual bodies. Can you tell us something about these spiritual bodies?"

Spirit. "I did not say you were *provided* with spiritual bodies. You have them all the time with you. Your spiritual body dwells in your natural body, and is of the same shape, and only a trifle smaller in size. The natural body is like an old garment over it. When you lay that aside, the spirit steps out like a new-blown flower! You are then free, sir, from al. physical defects."

P. "What is the first consciousness after the spirit is freed from the body?"

Spirit. "I felt as if I had stepped out of an old pair of boots. I did not know I was dead. I thought I had shaken off an old garment. I never dreamed I was dead, until my comrades told me."

Q. "How long have you been in the spirit-world?"

Spirit. "About six years."

Q. "Where did you die?"

Spirit. "In the hospital, in Nashville, Tenn.

Q. "You were a soldier, then?"

Spirit. "Yes: I enlisted in Company K, Fifty-ninth Indiana Volunteers, and served until my death. I was at the surrender of Vicksburg."

Q. "How did you get to Nashville?"

Spirit. "I was with Sherman on his march to the sea. At the Etowah River I was taken sick with typhoid fever, and from that place was sent back to Nashville. The Maxwell House was then a hospital, and in it I died."

Q. "What were your sensations when dying?"

Spirit. "It was like going to sleep. You may remember some thought you had before sleeping; but when passing into sleep, you are oblivious. So, in passing into death. My mind had been very active. I thought of every incident and circumstance of my life. I could see and hear all that ever transpired with which I was associated. I remembered jokes, fun, and frolic, and enjoyed them as I did when first I heard them around the camp-fire. We had a Dutchman in our company that was always taking care of things. He would permit nothing to go to waste. One hot day, in June, we had a hard march through the swamps, in Mississippi, and 'the boys lighted up,' that is, they threw every thing away that could be dispensed with. The line of march was literally strewn with blankets, shoes, caps, canteens, and other traps. Several car-loads of valuable goods were thus wasted. The Dutchman tried to carry all he could find, but he found too much. The pile on his back grew higher, higher, until it loomed up like a pack-saddle on an elephant. Under this load he staggered for several hours, sweating and blowing. He spied the shining blade of an army ax lying in an out-of-the-way place. He could not resist the temptation; so he went for it, with the exclamation, "Ich muss diese axt haben!" As he stooped for it, he fell, and it almost broke his heart when he found he had to leave the ax, and traps he had carried for miles. It became a rallying word with the boys—"Ich muss diese *Reb* haben!"

Q. "Is it possible that you could think of this anecdote while dying?"

Spirit. "It was before I died. As already stated, dying, to me, was going to sleep. You are not conscious when you slumber, and you have no memory of the exact time you became unconscious. The clock strikes ten; that is the last you remember. When it strikes eleven you do not hear it. I remembered the anecdote—a hundred of them—and went to sleep like a tired person."

Q. "When you awoke, how did your new situation impress you?"

Spirit. "I felt as if I had but arisen from a slumber, a trifle bewildered. I did not feel sick; that surprised me most. *A faint suspicion passed over my mind that something had occurred,* but could not tell exactly what. My body was lying in the cot, and I recognized it. That was strange. Looking around, I saw three of my old comrades, who had been killed in the trenches before Vicksburg. I buried them; and there they were. I looked at them in amazement, and they at me. One of them said, 'Hallo, Jim! have you come over?'

"'Over!' I said, 'over where?'

"'Why, here; in the spirit-world, to be sure. It's a mighty nice place, old fel.'

"This was too much. Almost in agony, I exclaimed, 'My God! I am not dead!'

"'No, you are not dead, Jim, but you are in the spirit-world. If you have any doubts about it, look there at your old body.'

"My body was there, *sure enough;* and in less than an hour I saw it carried from the place I left it, to a shuffle-board, that slid it into a wagon below. I followed it to the grave, the only interested spectator at the funeral. I returned to the hospital, and saw the surgeon, the nurses, and the cots in the room.

"It was some days before I went to the spirit-world. I went to my mother, in this world, first. I remained with her until after she received the news of my death. Then I got a singular longing for rest. I seemed to walk the atmosphere, or rather sailed through it, like a bird with wings extended. I can not tell how long it took me, but I think in five minutes I was told I was sixty-two and a-half miles above the earth. Do you understand me, Mr. Pittman? In five minutes.

Q. "What was your first experience in that world?"

Spirit. "I was just going to relate that my soldier-friends never deserted me, singular as it may seem to you, during the time from the period of my death until I went to the spirit-world. I never saw any relatives, only my soldier-friends, though I had several sisters and brothers and grandparents in the spirit-land. I seemed to step on veritable ground. An old lady them came toward me, saying, 'Jimmy, you have come home.' I looked again and again at her face, and then I said, 'O, grandmother, is this you?' 'Yes, dear boy,' she said. Then I walked with her over actual ground, where there were flowers and trees, and I noticed birds in the limbs; I heard them singing. We walked a distance, and came to a dwelling. I went in. She told me I must rest now. I lay down on the lounge, or couch, and slept for hours. From the time of my death and my return to my mother, I have no recollection of sleeping until that moment."

Q. "Did that house appear like our houses?"

Spirit. "Yes, sir: it was just as tangible to me as your houses are to you. But there seemed to be pillars instead of walls, and the light shone straight into the house. It was perfectly white. There were flowers and vines twining around it; there were musical instruments in it; books, tables, and many things."

Q. "How high was it?"

Spirit. "It was only one story, but we have houses with five and six stories."

Q. "Are the houses already provided, or do you construct them?"

Spirit. "Some construct them themselves, and some have them constructed. I never built a house, but I have planned them. In the spirit-world you can create all that is beautiful that your spirit desires."

Q. "How far is it possible for our aspirations to be realized?"

Spirit. "Every holy and pure aspiration of your soul will be realized to the fullest extent, and all the beauty that you desire to create in this world, you will create in the spirit-world; for that portion of you will live and grow forever."

Q. "Now go back to your sleeping experience in this house."

Spirit. "After I awoke, I found myself surrounded by some twenty or thirty friends, some I had never seen before; and I asked the question, 'Am I in heaven?' The answer was, 'You are in the spirit-land.' 'Then,' I said, 'I suppose I can rest forever.' At this there was a smile passed over the countenance of each one. I was puzzled for a moment or two, when one stepped forward, and said, 'If you were to rest forever, you would not go beyond what you are. The spirit-land is no place for folded arms; you have a greater work to do than you ever dreamed of.' Immediately after my death I resolved, if it were possible, I would return, and convince the world of the after-life, because I was a materialist, and believed in no hereafter."

Q. "Did you form that resolution after your death, or before?"

Spirit. "Immediately after, sir, as I stood in the Maxwell House, looking on my body."

Q. "Now, as to these spiritual bodies—do they grow in stature, as we grow here?"

Spirit. "Children do; children arrive at maturity of size."

Q. "But do you grow old?"

Spirit. "Well, no, sir; not in personal appearance."

Q. "Have you seen the spirits of any men of note, in the spirit-world; say, Michael Angelo, Shakespeare, or Swedenborg?"

Spirit. "I have seen Shakespeare."

Q. "How old, judging by our standard, did he appear to be?"

Spirit. "About twenty-seven."

Q. "Have spirit-bodies a spirit-anatomy?"

Spirit. "Yes, sir: if you ask a man who has lost his limb, he will tell you that he feels it still. The physical portion of that limb is gone, but not the spiritual portion. He will tell you that his foot actually grows cold; and physicians will tell you it is only the nerves that give him that sensation, but that is a mistake. If you were a clairvoyant, you would see the missing limb to be as perfect as the other."

Q. "Is it made use of in the same way, if the limb is taken off?"

Spirit. "Yes: it moves with the other foot. There is no

deformity from our stand-point. I assume, sir, that all spirits are born with equal capacity. Now, gentlemen, I shall have to explain. Take, for illustration, an idiot; you will say that such spirit is born with inferior endowments. I say no! It has a diseased organization which can not work perfectly, and therefore it gives forth an imperfect expression. Do you understand me? You know, gentlemen, that if you have a bad piece of machinery, it turns out bad work. So it is with the machinery of the human brain; if it is imperfect, it gives forth an imperfect impression.'

Q. "I would like to ask about your opportunities for mental culture since you left the body. What have you learned in the spirit-world that you did not know when you were here?"

Spirit. "Well, sir, I could not tell you all."

Q. "Tell us one thing you have learned."

Spirit. "I have learned that I am immortal."

Q. "Did you never suspect that here?"

Spirit. "No, sir, I never did. I used to think I would believe it when I saw it."

Q. "Can you tell us something more that you have learned, since you left this world?"

Spirit. "I was twenty-two years old when I passed from this world, and all I have told you this morning is what I have learned since I left it."

Q. "Now, come back to your spirit-life, and tell us how, in the first place, you came to find this medium, and how it is you work through her. Could you explain the process to us, so that we can understand it?"

Spirit. "I will try, sir; but it will be rather a difficult matter. You want to know how I first found her. Well, I knew her husband in the army; and, as I visited all the men of my regiment, I went to him, and I found a wonderful attraction about her house. I remained there for weeks, and tried to give manifestations. She saw them, but did not pay any particular attention to them. I found that I could get particles from her body that I could materialize a hand with, and after she had retired, I could lay that hand on her head so that she could feel it. That was the first. After I found that I could materialize my hand, I thought I could my whole body; and I came so that I could materialize the organs of speech, when the room was darkened after night, so that I could whisper; which I did, and frightened the family very much."

Q. "Why is it that you require darkness?"

Spirit. "By all spirits and mediums you will be told that darkness is negative, and light positive. You notice a ray of sunshine entering a darkened room, through a crevice; the room seems to be filled with dust. Well, sir, that motion is electricity and life in the atmosphere. Light keeps it in motion, and in that light we can do nothing. But when the room is dark, and there is quiet, we can gather those particles, and form hands and bodies."

Q. "Then you need those electrical particles?"

Spirit. "Yes, sir: the atmosphere is filled with life, just as water is."

Q. "In what sense, then, is it necessary, if you can gather these particles from the atmosphere, that you should have a medium?"

Spirit. "Well, sir, why does brown sugar have to be refined to make it white? It arrives at this condition by passing through a medium; so we pass the electricity we gather from the atmosphere, through our medium, and refine it. Then it becomes human magnetism?"

Q. "Then magnetism is nothing but refined electricity?"

Spirit. "That is it, sir; yes."

Q. "And when it is filtered, you call it magnetism?"

Spirit. "Yes, sir."

Q. "And you have to remain in what is called her magnetic sphere, when you speak or materialize?"

Spirit. "Yes, sir; and I can not go away from it."

Q. "If you did, could you then materialize?"

Spirit. "I could not speak, sir."

Q. "For what length of time can you speak?"

Spirit. "As long as the medium can supply the materializing element. That is my power—as steam moves machinery."

Q. "Will you ever be able to speak in the light?"

Spirit. "Quite recently, with my face fairly seen at the aperture in the cabinet, I spoke to Dr. Wolfe for twenty minutes. The doctor can attest to that fact."

Dr. W. "You did; and a very interesting conversation we had."

Q. "Why couldn't you speak to me as well as the doctor?"

Spirit. "We could, if you supplied us with the magnetic element he does."

Q. "How extensive is this magnetic sphere about the medium?"

Spirit. "It varies. Sometimes it is not more than two feet; but sometimes it extends ten feet, according to the condition of her health."

Q. "Are you now on a segment of that sphere?"

Spirit. "She is not in a very good condition this morning for manifestations. I am only a short distance from her."

Q. "Do other spirits assist you in materializing?"

Spirit. "Yes: we assist one another."

Q. "Can you see us when you are in an unmaterialized condition?"

Spirit. "Yes: better, sir, than I can when materialized. I can see no more, as a materialized spirit, than a clairvoyant."

Q. "In an unmaterialized condition, is this room dark to you?"

Spirit. "No, sir."

Q. "There is one question I want to ask further. I see, in these manifestations, that you require the assistance of music. In what way has music any effect or influence?"

Spirit. "It really does not do us any good. It only concentrates the thoughts of the parties present, and makes them more passive."

Q. "Then, if we could be harmonious without the music, you could manifest yourself as well?"

Spirit. "Yes, sir: sometimes we have music that is not very pleasant, but still it tends to harmonize the sphere of the circle."

Q. "Have you a clearer consciousness of the great Creator than we have?"

Spirit. "O no, sir: we don't believe in a crowned God, in a king. One thing I was going to say, gentlemen: I presume you know that you all make your own God? I have frequently remarked, '*An honest God is the noblest work of man!*'"

Q. "That is, each of us creates an ideal, which we imagine or think is God?"

Spirit. "Yes, sir."

Q. "And the higher our conception of him, possibly, the nearer we approach to it?"

Spirit. "That is it, sir."

Q. "Does that Creator manifest himself to you specially in any way, that you are conscious of, in the spirit-world?"

Spirit. "O no, sir: only as you are conscious."

Q. "You remarked, the other night, that there were spheres beyond or higher than ours. What is it that divides you from those spheres?"

Spirit. "Conditions!"

Q. "How do conditions distinguish the spheres?"

Spirit. "Now, Mr. Plimpton, one question I will ask you: You meet, on the street, a drunken, miserable, mean, degraded wretch; what is it that divides you from that man, but your condition?"

Q. "Certainly, I understand that; but you do not quite comprehend what I was trying to get at. You say that when you entered the spirit-world, it was about sixty-two and a half miles from the surface of this earth; that then you entered into what was a real world to you, with its mountains and valleys, and all the incidents of reality. What I want to know is, if those spirits who go from you, and return to you, and tell you of what they have seen and experienced—whether they go, also, to an entirely different sphere, a new-created world to them?"

Spirit. "Yes: you have a world, and you pass from your condition to ours, just as we are preparing to pass to a world beyond our spirit-land; that is, from one condition to another still higher."

Q. "Will this go on indefinitely?"

Spirit. "Well, sir, I am told there is no end to progression; but men in their infancy can not help putting an end to all things."

Q. "If spirits are so anxious for the welfare of people, why do not such men as Howard, Wesley, and Swedenborg, or men whose whole lives were given up to the instruction and elevation of their fellow-men, come to us and give us the benefit of their spiritual experience?"

Spirit. "They do try; but there will be no material change for the better till the conditions are changed, and till the laws and systems by which you are governed are done away with."

Q. "What law, specially, will be changed?"

Spirit. "Your marriage law."

Q. "When will it be changed?"

Spirit. "I can see no prospect at present."

Q. "Is any change desirable?"

Spirit. "O yes, sir; and I will say this: that your conventional marriage is the root of all evil."

Q. "But people should marry?"

Spirit. "Yes, but not without knowing each other, and be held together for life."

Q. "Give us your best thoughts on this subject."

Spirit. "I can scarcely give you my thoughts; but it is my opinion that if a man and woman are married, who are not suited to each other, the sooner they separate, the better. Let me illustrate my position: A young man is enamored with a young girl who has been brought up in the lap of luxury; and they are married. He is determined to be a great man, if wealth will make him so, even if, in his ambition to attain that end, every good feeling within him is crushed out. They are married scarcely a year, before they learn one thing—that they are separated in affection thousands of miles, although living under the same roof. The loveless wife soon learns deception. She has to steal from that man what she actually needs. After he has retired, and gone to sleep, she will search his pockets for a dime or half a dollar, to get some little needed thing. They live together year after year, but in her heart of hearts she feels that, if there was no law to take her in hand for it, she would take his life, to rid herself of the one she positively hates. She raises a family. I ask you this question, gentlemen: do you wonder that thieves and murderers are the result of this kind of marriage? I think you require law in the present day; but I am not speaking of low conditions, but of the very highest. I have looked through the world often, and seen the misery from inharmonious marriages, and I have almost come to the conclusion that it is sinful to remain in those conditions. It may, perhaps, surprise you, but I think people should live together for a year, so as to know one another before marriage. I would like to know, gentlemen, how many men there are in this city who act, in the presence of a young lady, as they appear to us; and how many ladies are there who appear before gentlemen as they do in the presence of each other. We are frequently charged with bringing mischief from the spirit-world, in separating men from their wives; but we only discover the mischief, do not cause it."

Q. "In the spirit-land, do you communicate with each other in a language that is articulated as ours is?"

Spirit. "Yes: it would be a disagreeable thing to live in a world where there were no sounds."

Q. "If you died without a knowledge of the French or German language, could you acquire a knowledge of either, in the spirit-world?"

Spirit. "I could, sir, by impression."

Q. "Then it would be difficult to have any secrets."

Spirit. "There are no secrets. I am going to tell you something that is coming, and that will do away with all crime. The two worlds are ever drawing nearer to each other. You know, gentlemen, people are afraid of their deeds being known. They are not afraid to act, but if they thought that their acts were seen and known, they would try to act differently from what they now do; and then there would be no criminals. Hence, there would be no deception between those who are to be married; and if there were none but harmonious marriages, that would bring about harmonious children. Now, I will ask you one question. If one of you were tempted to steal, would you not look up and down the street first, to see if any one saw you, before committing the deed? And if you knew their eyes were upon you, would you do it? It is just as natural to avoid eyes as it is to live. Do you see, if you had a real vivid consciousness that a spirit-friend was by your side, you would avoid, or be restrained from, doing many things that you now do? Let me ask you, if you knew that your mother's eyes were upon you, would you do any thing that would grieve her?"

Mr. P. "It would certainly operate as a restraining influence."

Spirit. "I will tell you one thing. My medium is impressional. You may bring five criminals and five good men into her presence, and blindfold her, and let each one take her hand, and if she does not detect which are the good and which the bad, I will never come back and speak in this world again. People never have thoughts with regard to her that she does not comprehend at once."

Mr. P. "I want to ask you a question, a little personal in its nature. My mother spoke to me, and I have no doubt it was her voice, but I have never seen her face. Now, do you think you could assist her to materialize?"

Spirit. "I do not know, sir. I will try, before my medium goes home."

Q. "Have you any inventions or instruments in the spirit-world that we have not?"

Spirit. "All the inventions you have come from the spirit-world. I stated this to Dr. Wolfe, when speaking of the electric telegraph and big bridge. [See page 247, chapter xiii.] We have an instrument now ready to be given to the world, as soon as a proper medium is found to receive it. It is called a 'THOUGHT INDICATOR.'"

Q. "How does it act?"

Spirit. "It in an instant indicates thought."

Q. "Does it do this by means of symbols, such as our letters?"

Spirit. "It does it by means of characters. The instrument I speak of will be used on earth in sixty years from now. You will not live to see it; but remember what I have told you."

Q. "How does this instrument work?"

Spirit. "It indicates thought on paper as rapidly as if done by electricity—as rapidly as we think."

Q. "Are such records now made in the spirit-world?"

Spirit. "Many of our finest writings are given in this way."

At this point of the interview Mrs. Hollis complained of feeling exhausted, and Nolan, after thanking us for our patience and enterprise, became silent. The *seance* was ended.

CHAPTER XXII.

SPIRIT PHENOMENA SEEN BY HON. WM. M. CORRY—SPIRIT-WRITING, TALKING, AND MATERIALIZING—A TROUPE OF OLD CITIZENS COME TO THE FRONT—ELWOOD FISHER INTERVIEWED—SHOWS PART OF HIS FACE—ASTOUNDING MANIFESTATIONS.

HON. WILLIAM M. CORRY'S report of his experience with spirit manifestations will attract special attention, as he is widely known throughout the country. This is the third report in the series, given by representative men, and bears upon its face the characteristic ingenuousness for which its author is distinguished. Without further introduction, his report is subjoined:

SPIRITUAL MANIFESTATIONS.

W. M. CORRY'S STATEMENT OF HIS EXPERIENCE.

FIRST SEANCE.

I WENT to Dr. Wolfe's, No. 146 Smith Street, at his request, last September, for a spiritual *seance*, there being much discussion of the subject in the city.

It was ten A. M. when Mrs. Hollis seated herself at the side of the small stand, with a light cloth on it, in the center of the room, and I sat near her, at the end of the stand. There was light enough to see objects distinctly, and to make notes. She held a small slate, on which was a bit of pencil, in her hand, under the stand. The whole arm, above the wrist, was visible, and the other hand hung by her side. She conversed on ordinary topics with me, while in this position, for ten minutes, when I heard the pencil fall on the slate. She immediately produced the slate, and there was nothing on it but a mark like the letter V; the pencil was there, and I requested the spirit who made the mark to write me a message.

After a few minutes' delay, came the following, which is my first communication. It was in two lines, thus:

"John Corry.
"William."

I then wrote, "Describe yourself, so that I can identify you."

The answer was given: "William Corry, your father. I am here."

This took five minutes, at least.

I wrote again: "Please write a sentence about any thing you desire to say."

Five more minutes elapsed, when came this answer: "I respect your standing *firm* to your party."

The word *firm* was underscored.

Prompted by this allusion to politics, as I had just suspended my weekly democratic newspaper, the *Commoner*, I put this question: "Ought the *Commoner* to be continued?"

In about three minutes, the answer was: "No, I fear not."

The answer not being positive, I repeated the question, thus: "Should the *Commoner* go on?"

In other three minutes, the answer was given: "Let the *Commoner* go. Make brick."

The writing was not clear, and I said: "Write plainer, please. Why should the *Commoner* stop?"

After the usual interval, the answer was: "Make brick, William."

This was the end of the conversation, at that time, with what purported to be the spirit of my father. It is proper to explain the injunction about making brick, by saying that I am in the business of manufacturing pressed brick, under George C. Bovey's patent, by steam machinery, and have, for several years, been giving it attention, thought, time, and money. This is the first encouragement I have received from any quarter; the living appearing to have a holy horror of brick-machines. I may add, however, that if the dead had also been against me, it would be some time yet before I would give it up, such is my confidence in the invention and my associates. I make this statement to show that my own mind has been full of the subject of brick-making, which some may think explains the paternal injunction.

The *seance* went on. The next message was from another spirit, who wrote, "Do you remember Joseph Gest?"

I inquired, "Are you Joseph Gest, the old city surveyor?"

The prompt answer was, "Yes."

I inquired again, "Why do you ask?"

The answer came: "He wants his daughter Clarissa."

I asked: "What does he want with her. Will he write to her?"

No reply.

I continued: "What have you to say?"

The answer was: "I want thee to tell her I am here."

I inquired, "Have you any thing to say to her?"

In a couple of minutes, this came: "Tell Clarissa that my wife and her father, Dr. John M., are here."

I could not make out the doctor's name; the whole message being badly written, and the name, although it was on the slate, was not legible. I asked to have the name made plainer, and wiped out the message. In a minute or so, the slate was produced, with the word "*Moore*," in very plain characters.

I then asked, "What more do you want, and who are you?"

In two minutes, the answer was: "I am Joseph Gest."

I then asked, "What have you to say?"

The reply was: "Thee knows Erasmus?"

I answered: "Yes: have you anything particular to say about Erasmus, or your wife? She is dead."

At the usual interval, the answer was: "Yes, no. Tell Clarissa, that my wife and the doctor are with me."

I continued: "What about Erasmus? I told you I knew him?"

After three minutes, the answer came: "He must take care of himself."

I then asked, "What do you mean?"

To this, no answer was made. Mr. Joseph Gest was a city surveyor many years, and he died here, not long since, at an advanced age. He and his family were Quakers, and used the plain language in conversation. Clarissa and Erasmus are two of his children; and, on inquiring of the latter, he told me, what I never knew before, that the name of his grandfather was *Dr. John Moore.*

In a few minutes more, the noise of the writing on the slate was heard, and, when it was shown, there was written quite across it, in a bold hand, the name of "Lafayette Neville."

I inquired, "What have you to say?"

The answer was: "I am glad to see you, William."

I asked: "How can I serve you? I will be glad to do it. Do you want to send any message to your widow?"

The answer was: "Only say to Caroline, that I am happy."

"Any other message?" I asked.

No answer. I knew Mr. Neville well; and Caroline is his widow's name.

Next, there was an illegible writing. I said, "Write that over."

The answer was: "You have Dr. Curtis's house."

I asked, "What of it? and what do you want to say?"

The answer came: "Are you not"—illegible.

I requested to have the illegible word written plainer.

The answer was: "Are you not afraid of ghosts, there?"

I inquired, "What do you ask that for?"

The answer was: "The doctor (word illegible) men."

I asked: "Please answer plainly. What is the middle word?"

"Dissected. He cut me up. I am James Nigger."

"What do you mean by 'Nigger?'"

Answer: "Colored, I mean."

By this time we had spent an hour and a half, and there was a lively knocking, which made Mrs. Hollis inquire if there were any more spirits wishing to communicate. The reply was by the single negative knock.

SECOND SEANCE.

In the first *seance* which I have described, there were no adjuncts at all discernible; but in the cabinet *seance* the musical box is wound up at the beginning, and never ceases to play till the end.

I was present with Mr. Piatt and Mr. Plimpton at a cabinet *seance*, held at Dr. Wolfe's house, but in another room, which has been arranged for the convenience of the medium and the visitors. It is on the second story, in a small room, between two others which are lighted with gas. At one side of this room, a thin board partition has been run up, from the floor to the ceiling, about two and a half feet from the wall. We examined, and found nothing but a chair for Mrs. Hollis to sit upon. The light was turned low, but not so that we could not distinctly see each other's faces and forms, and the furniture. The doors communicating with the two end rooms were nearly closed, to exclude the light. Mrs. Hollis's right-hand was marked in the palm with burnt-cork. She entered the cabinet, and shut herself in, the door having, at the height of four feet, a round aperture, of a foot in diameter, over which a piece of square cloth hung down, inside. I do n't think this cloth was ever lifted, but I am told the doctor believes otherwise. The musical box was playing, and soon a hand and wrist appeared quickly at the aperture; then another, and another. All these hands were feminine in appearance, and moved about freely, up and down, forward and backward; but always, when one disappeared, it showed the palm the last thing, and there was no mark on it. The hands were all right-hands, and each withdrew before another appeared. They looked natural, and I asked, several times, to touch them, or be touched by them; but the doctor, who was always present, did not consent, although he said that he had done it himself, and it could be done.

A hand took up the bit of pencil lying on the slate, which was placed on a shelf just under the aperture, and wrote: "Judge Burnet"—that, and nothing more. We asked if Judge Burnet would communicate, but there was an answer in the negative by knocking. Dr. Wolfe himself asked the questions generally during the sitting, although every one felt at liberty to converse and to ask explanations of the spirits.

A hand came out of the aperture, in plain view, and wrote a message on the slate, picking up the pencil and holding it just as any body would. The message was: "Major Ben, I can whip 'em yet!"

Some one inquired, "Who are you?"

The hand came out again, and wrote the monosyllable, "Barr."

Mr. Piatt thought he understood the question, and that

it was to him, but he asked, "Was that message directed to me ?"

The hand came again, and wrote, "Sam B. Keys will know."

Mr. Piatt asked the spirit to be more particular.

The hand came again and wrote, "I was his relative."

Mr. Piatt inquired, "Are you Sam B. Keys?"

The hand then wrote, "Major Barr."

I thought the message was not probably to Mr. Piatt, but might be for me; so I related that, among other manly qualities of Major Barr, in his early days, was a propensity to fight; and that on one occasion there had been a great battle between him, a merchant, and my grandfather, Thomas Fleming, a farmer of Butler County, in the Lower Market House, about a quarter of beef, in which both were worsted. While I was telling the story, there was a vigorous knocking within the cabinet, which, as I understand it, indicated approval.

James Buchanan, ex-President, next appeared, and was recognized by me and the rest. He is a constant guest at Dr. Wolfe's. The well-known head and the white cravat and hair came forward. Dr. Wolfe greeted him with, "Good evening, Mr. Buchanan!" which was recognized by a nod, and in a minute or two he retired, having advanced to the aperture, and receded several times. The appearance was precisely that of a large lithograph portrait. A hand on the slate followed, and wrote, "Corry spent three days at Wheatland." Mr. Buchanan came again and again. Stephen A. Douglas also put in the same appearance and pantomime, the action of the two heads, the only part visible, in each instance, being perfectly characteristic.

The next I saw distinctly a female head, which I recognized as the late Mrs. Donn Piatt. The hair was worn after her taste, and the expression was exactly like hers. She came several times, but very timidly and faintly. It was her side-face.

Then followed Lizzie Odell, who was a relation of the doctor, and generally comes to the cabinet *seances*. She was recognized by Mr. Plimpton, as well as the doctor. Her hair was held up from her forehead by a cherry-colored ribbon.

Mary Plimpton, the deceased sister of Mr. Plimpton, came next, and was greeted and recognized by him. She lingered, and responded, by her action, as if she loved to be there.

Then the hand came out and wrote on the slate. It was simply, "Donn Piatt."

Mr. Piatt, attributing this message to his wife, asked orally if she had any thing to say?

The hand wrote, "Fenton Lawson," a well-known citizen, long since dead. Then, "Mary Piatt."

"Have you any thing you wish to say to me?" repeated Mr. Piatt, orally.

The answer was: "I am happy; you must not fear to come."

He added, "Have you any thing else to say?"

"No!" was immediately written by the hand on the slate.

Mr. Piatt asked orally, "Is there any one else who wishes to communicate with me?"

The answer was by the hand, written as usual: "Do you—" but the rest was illegible; and when Mr. Piatt requested an explanation, the hand wrote again, "Come to-morrow, Donn."

Another hand now wrote a message. It was simply, "William Corry."

I asked orally, "Have you any thing further to say to me?"

The hand appeared at once, and wrote upon the slate this message: "William, let the *Commoner* go; you have lost enough!"

I asked again, "What further advice have you to give?"

The hand wrote again, "Go on with the brick."

I inquired, "Will that be profitable?"

The hand wrote again, "You will make money with the machine."

Another hand wrote, "Morgan Neville."

We asked if he had any message. There were affirmative knocks—several of them—and then the hand wrote, "I gave my children no money, because I thought it best."

With this communication, that cabinet *seance* terminated, at half-past nine P. M.

THIRD SEANCE.

MR. PIATT and myself, with Dr. Wolfe, had a dark *seance* for conversation with the spirits. It was at ten in the morning; but the chamber in which it took place was made perfectly dark, by padding the doors and windows. Not a ray of light was admitted, although after a while it was said that lights flitted about. I never saw the phenomenon but once, and then faintly.

After three minutes, there were knocks heard, and the tin horn, which stood on the floor, was moved about. We all talked freely; Mrs. Hollis as well as the others. The music-box was playing. Mrs. Hollis described several persons—spirits—who were in the room. One was a large man, of jovial bearing, who was leaning toward Mr. Piatt and examining his arm, which had been hurt recently by an accident. Mrs. Hollis gave his name directly as "Jesse Judkins." Mr. Piatt inquired what he was doing; to which she replied that it seemed to be about his injury, which he was attentively examining, but smiling all the time.

Just then, there was a faint utterance, like a female voice, so low that it required very quick ears to detect what was said. I distinguished the words at last: "Ella is better; she will get well."

The message was supposed to come from the former Mrs. Piatt to the present.

Then the voice feebly said, "Don't you know—" The rest was inaudible.

Mr. Piatt said: "I can't hear you. Speak louder, please!"

Another effort, but fruitless.

Mr. Piatt said, "Try again."

The voice said, "Mary Meeker."

Mr. Piatt replied he did remember her very well; and he remarked to me that she was a little girl in his family years ago, and was a medium.

My notes were taken in the utter darkness, and the lines crossed, and other difficulties, make them imperfect:

"Tell Ella I love her; and that, of all the hats she wore last Winter in Washington, the one I liked was the pink one with the white plume. The white plume cost twenty dollars. Good-bye!"

James Nolan, familiarly called *Jimmy*, now seemed to seize the horn, and began to talk. He gave us his history: That he was born in Harrison County, Indiana, and at nineteen went into the war with the first volunteers, a private in Company K, of the Fifty-ninth Regiment, which was commanded by Colonel Courcy, or De Courcy. His captain's name he gave, I think, as M'Bride. He served four years; was at the siege of Vicksburg; and, finally, on his march to the sea, under General

Sherman, he was attacked with typhoid fever, and was sent to Nashville to the hospital, now the Maxwell House, where, after a short illness, he died. He said he lingered round his remains while they were warm, and saw himself laid out and dressed for the grave by his comrades. It was just like putting off an old garment. He was surprised at the ease of the change, and could hardly think he was dead. He said he exclaimed, "Am I really dead?"

In a future conversation, at which Mr. Plimpton and Mr. Pittman, the celebrated phonographer, assisted, *Jimmy* explained these matters, and his subsequent career in the spirit-land, at great length. A note was taken of it all, which I expect to see in print. It is interesting. I can state that the impression he made on me was not that of a light, ordinary young soldier, but of a man of truth, sincerity of purpose. He said he had the strongest desire to persuade men of the future state; that he devoted most of his time and energies to the work; that it could not be done but by a process of materialization, which he explained; and that he was drawn to Mrs. Hollis's house and herself, because he had served with her husband, and become attached to him in the army. It is only possible to communicate with the world's people by the instrumentality of a medium, to whose sphere he had to confine himself in order to be heard. He appeared at all the dark circles, as they are called, where the spirits hold their oral communications; and he was always in a pleasant mood, and made himself popular, if that word can be so applied. I leave him here for the present; for I was most anxious to talk to my mother, if possible, and with my friend, Elwood Fisher, for whom I had always felt an attachment so ardent that it seemed to many romantic; but as I had seen no man then or since that I thought equal to him, I will probably never change.

The medium, Mrs. Hollis, said that she saw a tall lady dressed in black, wearing a cap, who seemed to have lost her teeth, standing by me and looking at me. But she was unable to speak. Mrs. Hollis said she saw another lady there, who was tall, slender, and a younger person than my mother.

I asked who it was, but she could not talk. A voice, however, very low, said, "That is my wife!"

I thought it was my friend Fisher who spoke; and I asked him why my mother did not speak to me.

He replied that *he* could only do so with great difficulty, and after his best efforts; that speaking was a new thing to them, and had to be learned. "*Thee has no idea*," my friend said, "*of the extreme difficulty of articulation by the spirits!*"

"Does thee remember Elizabeth Fisher?" he asked.

I said, "Yes: thy mother."

"Does thee remember the little store on Fifth Street, where thee saw me the first time, sitting on the counter? Does thee remember taking me to thy father's office on Main Street, after a while?"

I said I did remember these things, and that my father had as high an opinion of him as myself; and from that time Mr. Fisher was always cherished in our family, and made perfectly at home. He was our greatest favorite; and I thought him superior to the college-boys with whom I studied Latin and Greek. It was on my daily walk across Fifth Street Market Space, to and from college, that I found out my life-long friend. I should observe that he was the friend of Mr. Piatt also; and that at this sitting he spoke to him several times; and that he bade him farewell when he left.

He asked me if I remembered "Judge Bassett," of whom I have not once thought for thirty years.

I replied I did.

"Thee recollects, then, his brown clothes and his ruffled shirt?"

Again, he said, "Thee remembers the Brimstone Corner?" (Fourth and Plum,) which was a Methodist church of former years. I replied I did; and then he said, "The Friends' meeting-house on Fifth Street is turned into a lager-beer saloon!" Then suddenly he asked, "Does thee remember the white kids?"

I asked, "What kids?"

He added, "Those Joseph Benham wore, when he delivered the address to Lafayette?"

"I did remember them," I said; and the spirit of my friend, if it was he, seemed pleased with the reply. His tone of voice denoted that feeling.

He continued, "Does thee remember the old German woman that Lafayette recognized in the crowd as the person who had carried him milk when he was imprisoned at Olmutz?"

I said I did not, and asked him if he did.

He replied that his "mother told him the incident, which seems to be one of my own recollections."

"Thee remembers Harriet Benham—Mrs. Prentice?"

"Yes," I said, "I knew her all her life."

He merely said: "What a singular woman! Amelia Nolan, thee knows her?"

I replied: "Yes: very well. She is thy sister-in-law."

He then said that "she was an excellent woman," adding, "But thee knows my opinion of her, and also of her husband."

There was a pause after this strange interview. Mr. Piatt, as well as myself, was deeply impressed with the inexplicable nature of it, without, however, comprehending it. The spirit, very audibly, said "Farewell" to him, and then took leave of me in these most impressive words: "*Farewell. I will stand by thee while time lasts for thee; and when thee comes over, I'll be the first to greet thee.*"

FOURTH SEANCE.

22d September.—Mr. Plimpton, Dr. Wolfe, Mr. Piatt, Mrs. Jordan, and myself, went into the cabinet-room at eight o'clock P. M. A large hand appeared at the aperture—then a hand and arm, the hand with a gauze veil over it. Then again, with a lily of large size, and perfectly white. Afterward, a hand came, and closed and opened; and then, again, another was thrust out into the room, waving a handkerchief. Then a hand attempted, several times, to grasp the pencil, but failed to do so. At last, a message was written on the slate, from Joseph Gest. It was:

"William, tell Erasmus Canby; he will understand you."
"JOSEPH GEST."

Then another: "Thee knows, William, that facts are facts." Again: "Tell Erasmus, his uncle, James Canby Moore, is here." And, finally, he wrote on the slate: "I want thee to startle him out of his heathenism."

In explanation of this message, I may say that, after the first interview with his father, I had conversed with Mr. E. Gest, and he had avowed his partiality for Buddha and Confucius.

The next appearance was a little boy's head and face. "*Is it Charley?*" *the lady asked, who thought it was her little son.* There were knocks of affirmation.

Then my friend Fisher presented his forehead and eyes, as usual. I requested him to show me his whole face.

The hand wrote, "William, thee sees my face."

I replied: "No, not distinctly—only a part of it. Let 's see thy whole visage."

The hand wrote again, "The *soul* is too long."

In explanation whereof, I may say that Mr. Fisher used to assert, playfully, that he believed the chin to be the residence of the soul. It was the distinguishing feature of man; no animal had it but the horse, he said, and he and man were always friends; and the Centaurs were actually man and horse—half and half.

A lady's face appeared, which was not recognized; but we requested her to write the name. There was no answer. A pair of very small baby-hands appeared, and seemed to be quivering at the aperture for over two minutes; then they faded away.

Mr. Fisher again showed his forehead and eyes.

I said, "You did better before; try to show thy face entire."

The hand wrote on the slate, "William, I can 't do better."

Dr. Wolfe's mother then came to the aperture, and the doctor bade her "good evening," and she nodded, and withdrew. Then Lizzie Odell, wearing the cherry-colored ribbon in her hair.

There was a vigorous knocking in the box, which the doctor said was a demand for more music. Indeed, he asked the question, and was answered affirmatively. The music-box, however, gave out. The knocks became violent, and the doctor proposed to sing. He started the African melody of the "Swanee River," and when that had been sung by the company, "Bonny Doon" succeeded. Hand after hand came to the aperture, to the number of five or six, and some of them tried to use the pencil, but without success. This was attributed to the cessation of the music.

At length, a hand wrote a message, which was for Mr. Piatt, and in these words: "Dear, hand in the slate." That was done at once, and soon the slate came out again with "P. Grandin, John H. Piatt, Louise Kirby Piatt, Mackie, your darling."

We requested further manifestations, but were answered, "No," by knocks which the doctor interpreted; and, on the slate it was written, "The time has been so long," and also, "It is too late."

A hand, supposed to be friend Fisher's, wrote. "William,

thy mother would have given her face," meaning, if nothing had happened to retard the manifestations. That face was precisely what I wanted to see, as it would be proof positive of the verity of the portraits; but I never got it, nor the whole face of my friend Fisher.

Mr. Piatt received this message: "My dear, take care of yourself and Ella. I will often write you tests." The last word was scarcely legible, and Mr. Piatt requested it plainer, when it was written as above—tests—in very plain character.

So the *seance* terminated. The accidental failure of the music having embarrassed it, from first to last, as the doctor informed us. The effect of the music is said to be most decidedly upon the spectators, to concentrate their minds, and exclude wandering thoughts. The spirits seem to be very partial to it; but it is of no other consequence to them than to predispose the audience to receive and appreciate their communications.

FIFTH SEANCE.

3d October, A. M.—I went with Dr. Curtis; and it was suggested by Dr. Wolfe that the slate-writing should come first, and then the cabinet scenes. As soon as we were seated, Mrs. Hollis holding the slate under the table, there was written upon it the name of "Mary Curtis," the doctor's mother, whose full name was Mary Ann.

He asked, "Have you any other name?"

"O yes: there are others here," was the response on the slate.

Mrs. Hollis then said: "Does any one present know Dr. Atlee? I get that name, but nothing else."

We both replied that we knew Dr. Atlee well. He was several years a resident of this city.

Another message was written on the slate:

"Well, Dr. Curtis, thee stands it well!

"WILLIAM JUDKINS."

He was the father of Jesse and David Judkins, and a good physician here for many years.

Mrs. Hollis observed that she saw a tall, slender man in the room, near the doctor, wearing a brown overcoat, and bald; but she said he did not give his name.

The slate then showed the name, "Elizabeth Curtis," that

of his present wife. The doctor said, "Refer to some incident between us alone, which none know but ourselves." "I am near you—Mary Ann." Then, "I am, every day." The next name was "Harriet Ann Curtis, your own dear wife." Soon after, a message, "This is a very happy morning!"

The doctor then asked her what benefit there was in these communications? The reply was, "I saved you years of doubt by them."

Then, "Elizabeth can be a good medium." Pretty soon afterward, "Good-bye!"

I think there had been no music during the writing part of this interview.

We now adjourned to the cabinet. Mrs. Hollis walked with us, and spoke of ordinary things to Dr. Curtis, Dr. Wolfe, who joined us, and myself. She directly took her seat in the dark recess, completely out of sight, and there were loud raps for music. The box was set a-going. A hand appeared through the aperture holding a flower. I asked Dr. Wolfe's permission to touch it. He said the spirits did not allow it. They would touch his hand—pat it sometimes—but that was all. It would offend them if I attempted to grasp it, and we should have no more manifestations. I asked him to put the question to the spirits, which he did, but the knocks answered, "No!" Then a hand appeared, and picked up the pencil and wrote down these words, "We are sorry you can not touch it." A hand then wrote on the slate, "Look if you can see color?"

I asked the spirit of Mr. Fisher if my sister Alice was here. The reply came, "Alice is here." Then we had the face of a lady, who was not recognized by any of the party. Then, an old lady's face and head, with a cap on, said by Dr. Wolfe to be his mother. Then Lizzie Odell, with her hair tied up with a cherry-colored ribbon, which was plainly to be seen and distinguished. Then Miss P. Then a beautiful girl's face and head. The hand came through the aperture and wrote on the slate, "Harriet, my dear, as a spirit." Dr. Curtis thought it was his deceased wife materialized. There was then a face which obscurely showed itself, and might be taken for my sister Alice; but she made no answer to my question.

I now asked Mr. Elwood Fisher to show me, if possible, his entire face. The reply was, "William, thee knows I will make a great effort!"

He showed his forehead, as he had done before, but with the eyes open, and not shut. I could see the whole head, and down to below the eyes.

The hand wrote upon the slate: "William, thee was the companion of my boyhood, and the staunch friend of my manhood. When all others deserted, thee stood firm. I honor thee for this above all men."

Again he wrote, "I have followed thee through all. Stand firm to the P!"

"What P?" demanded Dr. Wolfe. "Is it Palmetto?"

There was an affirmation by knocks; and the hand appeared again and wrote, "William, thee knows."

I presume the allusion was to South Carolina and her doctrine, she being called the Palmetto State. Mr. Fisher had named his Indiana farm, near Patriot—to which he was devotedly attached—"Palmetto."

The hand wrote again: "Thee has entered upon a new field of thought. It will lead thee out of the briers and thistles, and make thy pathway pleasant in thy declining years."

The slate was taken into the cabinet, and shortly came out with a long message as follows, purporting to come from my friend Fisher:

"If all the wishes of thy friend could be realized, thy life would be one of great pleasantness. I was thy friend while time lasted for me; and when thy footsteps echo through heaven, then I will clasp thy hand. Now for eternity—fear not to cross the river. I, thy friend, will be there first to greet thee. Farewell! Peace be with thee!

"ELWOOD, *thy devoted spirit-friend.*"

And then the *seance* was concluded, and Mrs. Hollis came out of the cabinet, appearing to be fatigued; but she descended the stairs with us, and conversed as freely as the rest.

Mr. Corry closes abruptly; he makes no "summing up of his opinion;" he discharges the whole subject without a word of comment; and, too, when the reader would consider his opinions golden. Mr. Corry's thoughts belong to himself, and his discretion in not obtruding them upon the public is worthy of approbation. He has made a faithful report of the facts as they came before him, and that was all he was expected to do; he made no promise to do more. The casuist has the whole field of speculation to himself. He can rise to explain as much as suits his purpose, "without let or hinderance." Mr. Corry grants full permission, and rests upon the facts. There are no shifts in his testimony. He states only what he saw and heard, and the reader must judge whether he has done it well or not. He has spoken fearlessly, and in no uncertain sense, that which he knows to be true. He does not hesitate to declare his conviction that he conversed with his old friend, Elwood Fisher; that his identification was complete. This admission will constitute a new epoch in the mental life of W. M. Corry. "*Tempora mutantur, et nos mutamur in illis.*"

CHAPTER XXIII.

SPIRITS WRITING GERMAN AND FRENCH—VICKERS CONVINCED THAT THE MANIFESTATIONS WERE NOT FRAUDULENT—MRS. HOLLIS COULD NOT DO THE WRITING—THE TEST OF A. P. C.—A GERMAN FABLE—ELWOOD FISHER— SPIRIT-HAND LARGER THAN MRS. HOLLIS'S—CAN MAKE NO DISCOVERY OF FRAUD—A HEIDELBERG PUPIL SPEAKS TO MRS. VICKERS IN GERMAN.

REV. THOMAS VICKERS was the fourth, and last, of the representative men to examine and report upon the phenomena occurring in the presence of Mrs. Hollis. He began his investigations after the others had concluded theirs, and at a time when the medium's mental condition—on the eve of leave-taking—was unfavorable for good manifestations; still the phenomena he witnessed were of such a startling character as to convince the investigator that they were not the result of trickery or fraud, practiced by either Mrs. Hollis or myself, and that on some other hypothesis must a rational explanation be founded.

Mr. Vickers admits the insufficiency of the time he had for a thorough examination of the principles underlying the phenomena, and hence he is still open to conviction. Every man has his own discretion, of course; but I respectfully submit whether additional facts will not produce additional perplexity of mind. Enough is as good as a feast.

"Mrs. Vickers," he says, "was addressed by a voice in German, calling her by her given name. To the question, as to where the person speaking had known her, the reply came, 'In Heidelberg.' The name given was that of a former pupil." To this may be added Mr. Vickers's remark, "That he was morally certain there was no deception."

SPIRIT MANIFESTATIONS,

AS SEEN BY REV. THOMAS VICKERS.

DR. N. B. WOLFE:

DEAR SIR,—You were kind enough, in the latter part of 1872, to afford me the opportunity to witness some of the "manifestations" that were occurring in your house, "in the presence of Mrs. Mary J. Hollis." In return for this kindness, I cheerfully comply with your request, to make some report of what I saw and heard. You will remember that, unfortunately for the prosecution of any extended investigation, I did not become aware of Mrs. Hollis's being in the city until very near her departure; so that the *seances* in which I could participate were few. It is, therefore, not surprising that the result was not, on the whole, so satisfactory to myself as I could have wished. Still there are some things of importance to which I can testify.

I was present at five sittings in all. Two of these were devoted to slate-writing, two to the dark circle, and one to manifestations from the cabinet. I need not describe the accessories of these sittings; this has been done so minutely and so accurately by my friend Mr. F. B. Plimpton, in the Cincinnati *Commercial* and the Washington *Capital*, that it is unnecessary to go over the same ground again.

For some reason or other, the communications which I received through writing on the slate were, so far as their matter was concerned, very unsatisfactory indeed. At the first sitting, which took place in the morning of September 28th, there was considerable writing done, but to little purpose. The first communication which came, consisted, apparently, of eight words; only the first four words of which were legible. These were as follows:

"*Bin gern so hier.*" *G.*

It was suggested that the remaining words might be written over again, when, after a slight pause, the following was written:

"*Vous vous portez bien* *J'espere.*"

I then inquired whether these were the words which had previously been illegible, and received the answer, "No: the first was German." Upon inquiry as to whether I had read the first communication correctly, it was answered, "You did." I then asked whether I had interpreted the signature (*G*) correctly, which was attached to the German words; and the response was, "Yes, G." On requesting that the name represented by this initial, be written out in full, I received the following: "Thomas Vickers."

Q. "Is that the name of the person communicating?"

A. "Yes: and your name."

Q. "What relation is he of mine?"

A. "William Vickers."

Q. "Will the person who signed the first (German) communication give his name in full?"

A. "Elizabeth Vickers."

Q. "*Der Schreiber der ersten Mittheilung mœchte seinen vollen Namen geben.*"

A. "Yes."

Q. "Will he do it?"

The name that was written in answer to this question was illegible; it seemed to be "Minna Genlis." A request was made that it be written over again, but the second time, it was less distinct than before.

Q. "Can you not give this name more distinctly?"

A. (What seemed to be) "Gustav. Yes."

Q. "Give the last name."

A. "Conrad." (With an indistinct surname.)

Another attempt was made to write the name, but with no better result. The name seemed to be "Richer." On asking whether that was the name, it was answered affirmatively. Two further efforts were made to write it, resulting, each time, in an illegible scrawl. It was then suggested, by Mrs. Hollis, that I write something upon the slate, addressed to a friend, without permitting her to see it. I wrote the following:

"*Wenn irgend einer meiner Freunde da ist, so mæchte er so gut sein, seinen Namen anzugeben.*"

The slate was then held under the table by Mrs. Hollis, for a considerable space of time, but no response came. I afterward wrote the same request, in English, as follows:

"If there is any one of my friends here, let him be good enough to give me his name."

To this there was, for some time, no response; finally, there came an illegible line of three words, with the signature, "Thomas Vickers." I then wrote upon the slate, without allowing Mrs. Hollis to see it, the following:

"Is A. P. C. here?"

To this there came, after a pause, the answer:

"P. C. is here."

This induced me to put the question in a plainer form, by writing out the surname in full. In each case I turned the slate upside down, before giving it to the medium, and she placed it under the table, in the same position. The last questions and answer were as follows:

Q. "Is A. P. C——y here?"

A. "Yes: A. P. C——y is here."

Q. "Have you not something to say to me?"

A. "Can 't write."

This ended the sitting. I have given you here an exact report of all the writing that was done. At intervals during the *seance*, Mrs. Hollis described some persons whom she saw about me, but none of them in such a manner that I could recognize them. In the beginning, she asked me whether I was a German, saying, at the same time, that she saw many Germans around me. I replied that I was not German, but understood the language. The remark, hereupon, that she often received communications in German, led me to ask some q .estions in that tongue.

From the nature of the above report, you will see that if the spirits had undertaken to play at cross-purposes with me, they could not have done it more successfully than they did.

I certainly was in a position to appreciate the remark made by you toward the close of the sitting: "One of the peculiarities of this thing is, that the thing you want you don't get." Nevertheless, I am free to confess that the fact of any writing at all being produced, under the circumstances, was sufficiently astonishing. I watched Mrs. Hollis very narrowly during the sitting, and was morally convinced that it was done without fraud on her part. I think it impossible that she could have done the writing herself, without my discovering it. Her left-hand was in view all the time; she held the slate with her right, with nothing to rest it upon. The room was well lighted; no accomplice could have been present. What, then, produced the writing? I do not know; and I have no theory to offer.

The next sitting was on September 30th, in the dark circle. There were, if I remember rightly, seven persons present in all, including Mrs. Hollis and yourself. I shall not attempt to give a full report of this occasion, for the reason that nearly all the communications came to other members of the circle. There was considerable singing, which, so far as I could judge, did not proceed from any one in the circle. I heard very distinctly a voice speaking in German, in a loud whisper, with the Rev. Dr. Max Lillienthal, who sat at some distance from me. The voice purporting to come from James Nolan was, although somewhat hoarse, perfectly natural; so much so, indeed, that it was difficult to realize that the speaker was not in the flesh. One singular utterance of his is worth particularizing. Several of us were taking notes, although the room was in utter darkness. All at once the voice said, "Take care how you cross your lines!" When I came to look over my notes afterward, I found that, in running lines between the sentences, I had, previous to the caution, crossed out some of the words. The voices that attempted to communicate with me were very weak; and I was unable to identify, beyond the possibility of a doubt, those from whom they purported to come. I asked for the full middle name of the "A. P. C." who had written upon the slate, but was unable to obtain it.

The following *seance* occurred October 2d. Mrs. Vickers and I were the only persons present, excepting the medium and yourself. It was intended to devote the sitting wholly to "materializations," but it turned out, quite unexpectedly, that considerable writing was done. Before Mrs. Hollis entered the cabinet, I examined the form and size of her hand very carefully; the palm of it was blackened. The room was sufficiently light to enable us to see all the objects in it distinctly. It was proposed at first to do without the music; very soon, however, a hand appeared at the aperture, and wrote upon the slate: "We want the music!" The music-box was started, and directly afterward the following was written:

"You remember the old man and his son and the ass?"

We did not remember. The writing was continued:

"They were riding double-first, and were told by the people it was cruel."

After we had read this, the slate and pencil were taken in at the aperture. When put out again, we found the following:

"The boy got off. The old man was told he was a brute to let the poor boy walk, and so on, until they drove the ass to please the people. So you may do, if you listen to every one."

This was followed by the words:

"It is a German fable. Do you remember it, Mrs. Vickers?"

After this, a face appeared at the aperture, but not clearly defined, and keeping much in the background, toward the side. There was some resemblance to a very dear friend of mine. But still the face kept so much in the shade that I could not feel certain about it. The use of an opera-glass did not help the matter. Apparently the face made several efforts to come nearer, for the purpose of showing itself more distinctly, but without success. The slate was then resorted to again, and the following was written:

"O Thomas! it is I. A. P. C."

After this a face appeared, which was announced to be that of "Elwood Fisher." Then a number of baby hands were shown, the fingers were opened and shut, and the hands moved about in various directions. Then quite a number of faces appeared in succession, eight or ten in all. None of them, however, were recognized either by Mrs. Vickers or by myself. Some of them were very distinct and life-like. Arms were also shown, and moved about. In regard to these latter, it must be said that they were masculine and sinewy; and I could not conceive them to be those of Mrs. Hollis. So, also, of the hand which did the writing. It was much larger than that of Mrs. Hollis, and of an entirely different shape. Unless all evidence of the sense of sight be delusive, it could not possibly have been hers. Of course, it would have been an additional satisfaction if the request which I made, to be allowed to take hold of it, had been granted. Still, I am bound to say that, after careful examination both of the cabinet and of the room where the dark circle occurred, I could discover no indications of the probability of fraud. I do not think there was any.

The last two sittings took place on the 5th of October, in the morning. The first of them was devoted to slate-writing. The first question which I put was written on the slate in the same manner as at the first sitting: "Is any friend of mine or of Mrs. Vickers's here?" After the lapse of thirty minutes, this answer came: "Spirits are here." I then asked, "Can you give the names of any?" In about half an hour more, we received the following: "Thomas and Lena Vickers, good morning." Mrs. Vickers then wrote, without permitting Mrs. Hollis to see it, a question in German. When the answer came, after long waiting, it was wholly at random. These were all the direct communications we received, during two hours. Mrs. Hollis described various persons as being present, but we were unable to recognize any of them. She also said that she saw written, in bright characters, over my head:

"Mine was a love that died not with my breathing, but through all eternity it will grow brighter and brighter."

I was somewhat astonished at this, for the reason that these identical words had been uttered, by one of the spirit-voices, to another person at the first of the dark circles at which I was present. I heard them distinctly.

It was concluded, after this, to try the dark circle. We proceeded to the room used for that purpose. After some preliminary music, Mrs. Vickers was addressed by a voice, in German, calling her by her given name. To the question as to where the person speaking had known her, the reply came: "In Heidelberg." The name given, was that of a former pupil. I was again addressed by a voice purporting to come from "A. P. C." On asking for the full name, the first and last were repeated, with great distinctness, ten or a dozen times; and, finally, as it seemed to me, also the middle name. I was very persistent in trying to get the name, for this reason that I was certain that no one in Cincinnati, except myself, knew what the middle initial stood for. The rest of what was said by these voices consisted of expressions of interest and affection. Again, several spirits were described by Mrs. Hollis; but they were not recognized.

In conclusion, I can only say that I witnessed at your house, phenomena which I am unable to explain. I am morally certain that there was no deception in the production of them; still, I am not thoroughly convinced that they were produced through the agency of disembodied spirits. What the future may do toward convincing me of this, I do not know. I can only wait for further revelations. Thanking you for your kindness,

I am, very respectfully, yours,

THOMAS VICKERS.

CINCINNATI, *June* 17, 1873.

This closes the last report of the four representative men who engaged to investigate the phenomena which occurred in the presence of Mrs. Hollis, while a guest in my family. How well they have accomplished their work, the intelligent reader must determine. These statements are made in compliance with terms stipulated in my card of invitation; but the gentlemen were left free to represent the facts of the manifestations, whatever they might be, as to them seemed just and proper.

Personally, I had no acquaintance with either of these gentlemen, until they entered my house to examine the phenomena. But, like most of my fellow-citizens, I knew them well by report. I had every reason to believe that Mrs. Hollis would not receive any favor at the hands of these keen-sighted men, if found guilty of practicing a fraud. With that understanding, I invited them to investigate.

What they saw and heard is now before the reader. It was my desire to have published these reports in the Cincinnati *Commercial;* but after Mr.

Plimpton's statement appeared in that journal, the editor debarred the others by saying: "We have had enough of this thing! It 's making these men too d—d conspicuous."

It was "more in sorrow than in anger" I listened to this terrible profanity of Mr. Halstead, of which I fear the "recording angel," with no "dhrop in his eye," made a note. I had always esteemed brother Halstead a truly moral and sweet man, and, next to Uncle John Robinson, the most pious man in Cincinnati. The story is fresh in my memory, how with his little hatchet he hacked his father's tree, and then told his pa, with tears in his eyes: "*I can not tell a lie! Deacon Smith did it!*" It was so cute of the little rascal to put it on Smith, and I always loved him for cutting that tree.

But since he has taken to imprecation, I fear he has wrought a great change in my love. It grieves me to think he has excluded himself, by his horrid profanity, from the fellowship of the good, pious members of the Young Men's Christian Association. I hope they will pray for him.

On my bended knees I said: "Brother Halstead, the 'd—d conspicuous' fellows to whom you allude, investigated spiritual phenomena, as representative men, and the public expect to read their reports in your paper. This fact ought, in some degree, to excuse that 'conspicuity' to which you take such profane exceptions. Does n't thee think so, sweet Hal?"

It was asking too much! An awful frown gathered upon his brow (such as Jove is supposed to wear when he launches a thunderbolt), as he made this reply, in tones that would have mellowed the bellowing of a buffalo bull, "*I'll make you sorry you have had any thing to do with it.*"

Whatever others may think of this upstart's menace, Mr. Murat Halstead evidently entertains a high opinion of his own ability to make people *sorry.* At times he believes the sun rises and sets only by his behests, and that it illumes no other object than the Cincinnati *Commercial.* Thus fooled and flattered to his bent, this addle-pated newspaper scavenger presumes to determine what shall be joy and what grief to those who sneer at his pompous drivel. If he can make any body "sup sorrow with his horn-spoon," why do n't he do it? The fact is, "the wish is father to the thought," but his courage is impotent as Bob Acres'.

Halstead's knowledge of spirit phenomena has been acquired while *snooting* among his exchange-papers for "copy items." If he were not a sniveling mountebank, he never would have entertained the silly conceit that he could make me sorry for having examined the law and testimony upon which the facts of Spiritualism rest.

"The *beagle's* bark 's more baleful than his bite."

Intercourse between the natural and the spirit world is as much a truth as telegraphic communication between Europe and America. It is utterly inconsequential to the fact, whether time-serving editors, priests, or politicians recognize this truth or not. They are fleeting as Summer clouds; but the verities of God endure forever.

CHAPTER XXIV.

MANIFESTATIONS IN MEMPHIS—ON THE THOMPSON DEAN—IN NEW ORLEANS—ALONG THE RAIL—MRS. HOLLIS'S RETURN TO CINCINNATI—A REMARKABLE INTERVIEW WITH FANNY WRIGHT.

THE manifestations that occurred during the fifth engagement with Mrs. Hollis did not vary much in character from those that have been recorded. It would be, therefore, monotonous to repeat, in detail, that with which the reader is already familiar. The engagement was a success in affording a large number of ladies and gentlemen the opportunity to witness the startling phenomena which have excited so much interest among thoughtful people.

The *seances* were given mostly to persons who might, with propriety, be called representative men and women. My object was to make the best use of the stipulated time, by presenting the *facts* of spirit intercourse to the skeptical mind—not including in such either bigots, fanatics, or fools. There are two classes of skeptics which require to be intelligently discriminated, else injustice may be done both; and I may as well designate their leading characteristics in this place, to avoid all obscurity on the subject.

In general terms, they may be distinguished—the skeptic with brains, and the skeptic without brains. The first is governed by reason, and takes a thoughtful survey of conditions and things, and arrives at conclusions after exercising the legitimate powers of mind upon the subject considered. The second simply says: "I'm very skeptical! I don't believe every thing I see! Your eyes may deceive you!" etc. These latter are sagacious poodles, who have, according to Darwin's theory, developed in human forms. Whenever practical, I always exclude this latter class of bipeds from the circles; not that I have any thing against them—for they are well enough in their place—but it is a waste of time to encourage such people to investigate spiritual phenomena by their peculiar mental processes. My experience in the formation of circles convinces me that good manifestations can only be had in the presence of enlightened, free-thinking people; and that the most intelligent spirits are stifled by fashionably dressed imbeciles.

To a clairvoyant's vision, it is seen that every man and woman gives out accurate expression of their spiritual conditions by the character of the magnetic aura that surrounds them. This spirit atmosphere has color and density, and by these qualities the character of the spirit's development may at once be determined. An individual in an undeveloped condition is surrounded by a dark aura, graduated in color to represent the degree of ignorance that still holds the faculties of the soul in bondage. Spirits and mortals alike gather no inspiration in the presence of such unwholesome people. It is best to avoid them; for they neither impart nor receive benefit by associating with those unlike themselves. It is not doing a man a good service to place him in wrong relations to his fellow-men. That is why I exclude a large number of people from the circles. A well-dressed woman—that is, one who had a superabundance of costly silk goods festooned about her poor skinny skeleton, in the most *killing* style—came to my door, and inquired if "the fortune-teller" was in! Of course, I had to inform this almost idiotic creature—this manakin of fashion—that she was slightly in error respecting the character of Mrs. Hollis's mediumship. She wanted to find out whether Sam Snigglefritz was not in love with her. I told her to ask Sam's priest, that he would be most likely to confess his folly to a fool or knave. It is to be hoped that spiritualism will never become fashionable; and when it begins to build churches, and crystallize stupid dogmas into creeds, then it will no longer be spiritualism, but *sectism*, and be deserving of the execration of all good men.

By a judicious discrimination in forming circles, allowing those only to enter them who could comprehend the importance of spirit intercourse to the world, I have reason to know, many persons changed their views during the month of November, who now rejoice in the possession of knowledge which time can not corrupt nor moth destroy. These *seances* could have been continued during the entire Winter; as the interest in them grew more intense, the more they were understood. Mrs. Hollis had, however, accepted engagements for the Winter in the South, principally in the cities of Nashville and Memphis, Tennessee. These engagements were made at the suggestion of the spirits, for a purpose they subsequently explained; the object being to remove some errors from the mind of the medium, which operated against the purity of their control. They insist that the best mediums are those who have developed out of wrong mental conditions. The folly the spirits sought to arrest in this medium was the habit she had of thinking and speaking of Southern people as if they were superior to their fellow-citizens in other sections of our common country. The fact was, simply, that her whole mental structure was so much warped by politics and poisoned by prejudice, that she was unfitted for their high purpose, and failed to do their work acceptably.

After a short stay in Nashville, she began a two-months' engagement in Memphis, under the auspices of Captain James Holmes and his accomplished and talented wife, Mary J. Holmes, in whose family she became an honored guest. Here, the same, or similar manifestations to those I had witnessed in Cincinnati, occurred in the presence of some of the most intelligent people of that city. The leading newspapers of the place, the *Appeal* and *Avalanche*, opened their columns daily to the discussion of the wonderful phenomena, until the subject of spirit intercourse was talked about, as it never had been before, by all classes of people, in every situation of life.

In the midst of the excitement, I precipitated a visit to Memphis, to compare the manifestations occurring there with those I had witnessed in the Queen

City, and, if possible, discover any human agency that might be employed in their production.

"Slate-writing" and "dark circles" were given at the dwelling of CAPTAIN HOLMES; but the *cabinet seances* were held at the residence of MR. M. H. BALDWIN, a well-known architect and highly esteemed citizen, who had been convinced of the verity of spirit intercourse in the presence of Mrs. Hollis. The cabinet was simply a plastered wardrobe, an adjunct to a well-lighted chamber on the second floor, the door of which had been removed, and a temporary one adjusted, with a hole cut in the center, about four feet from the floor. Before this aperture, scores of intelligent men and women assembled, to stare, with surprised senses, upon the forms, faces, arms, and hands of their loved ones, who came for recognition, waving welcomes with handkerchiefs, and presenting for inspection flowers that had bloomed in gardens above. The excitement over these manifestations grew wild and bewildering. That was the most unfavorable circumstance I noticed. If there ever is a situation that requires a clear head and deliberate judgment, it is just such a one as this. The claims presented are, that the lost are living, that they have never died, that they return to demonstrate the truth of immortal life: in short, that there is no death, under its old definition; that there is no devil but that which we make in our distempered imaginations.

I found all these *seances* largely attended by the most capable people of Memphis, most of whom had become convinced of the ingenuousness of the manifestations. Mr. William L. Vance and wife were prominent among the attached friends of Mrs. Hollis, made such through her wonderful mediumship.

At the conclusion of Mrs. Hollis's engagement in Memphis, a number of ladies and gentlemen tendered her a complimentary passage to New Orleans and back, on one of the floating palaces of the Mississippi, proposing to make it a pleasant spiritual picnic. I was invited to join the party in their *bon voyage*, and accepted the invitation, thinking something might "turn up," in an unguarded moment, by which a clew to the manifestations could be obtained. I wanted to see this thing from different stand-points, cost what it might of time, money, or personal comfort.

The distance from Memphis to New Orleans is eight hundred miles by the river, and from New Orleans to Louisville, by rail, is fourteen hundred miles. All this distance—twenty-two hundred miles—I traveled with the medium and her friends, with the single purpose to discover, if possible, fraud in the manifestations. On the boat, almost a week—morning, noon, and night—the manifestations of spirit-presence were similar to those I had witnessed at my own house, and again in Memphis. They occurred in the main saloon, in private state-rooms, in "texas," up aloft in the presence of the pilots at the wheel, Wallace Lamb and Sobeski Jollie.

Information of her coming had preceded the arrival of Mrs. Hollis at New Orleans; and when the steamer was lashed up to the wharf, conveyances for herself and party were awaiting them. A suit of rooms had been engaged for manifestations, but these she declined, as she was the invited guest of Mrs.

LIZZIE SAXON, at whose dwelling she gave, during the short time she remained, manifestations of the same startling character I had witnessed on the boat, at Memphis, and in Cincinnati. The marvel and mystery were the same.

Most of our party returned north with the medium, through the Cotton States, by rail. As we sped along fourteen hundred miles, the spirits would write interesting matter about the places we were passing and the persons we met.

It will thus be seen that neither time, place, nor circumstance prevented the occurrence of these manifestations in the presence of this strangely constituted woman.

While *en route* for home, Mrs. Hollis informed me that the spirits had accepted invitations from distinguished persons abroad, to visit Europe, and that she would start on her voyage about the first of June. I then arranged for her final visit to Cincinnati about the middle of March, to remain until the first of May. I did this mainly to carry forward a line of experiments at the writing-table, which began to interest my mind, though I well knew the public would be exacting in their demands for private *seances*.

That no time might be wasted in advance of her coming, I employed Mr. Brown to take down the partition in the middle room, as I intended the whole space for a materializing cabinet. To fit it for this purpose, my instructions to him were to take out the two upper panels of the door opening into the west room, and hang them on hinges, and cut a hole in the south one similar to that in the door of the partition.

This being completed, the west room would constitute the audience-chamber for witnessing the phenomena. When the panel of the door was opened, there was an aperture forty inches in length and ten inches wide. This would enable spirits to show more of their forms, and, if need be, accommodate a larger number to exhibit themselves at the same time.

The question was now, could the spirits materialize at so large an aperture? When the door was opened, the interior of the room was flooded with light. It was almost equivalent to inviting them to step out where we were. Would not the bright light, streaming through this opening into the dark chamber, destroy the conditions, or so modify them as to render materialization impractical? There was no cloth to cover the opening. When the panel swung back, the channel for inflooding light was clear. The audience could see a large part of the interior of the cabinet-room plainly. The bug-a-boo objections raised against the medium being locked up in a cabinet, or being concealed behind a partition, were now mostly overcome. If the medium appeared at an opening of the door large enough to reveal her entire person, she would under a strong light, be recognized at once by discerning men and women. So could the spirits be.

Mrs. Hollis arrived on Saturday, 15th. On Sunday morning, during the clatter of church-bells, she entered the middle room, and sat to the south of the door opening into the west room. I then hung a bracket on the outside, to lay the slate on, as I did before, and shut her in.

I began a conversation with her at once, and in a

few minutes, while we were talking, the north panel of the door opened wide, and a large, muscular, flesh-and-blood-looking arm reached out of the middle room, and wrote on the slate:

"Napoleon has had many existences, extending back for thousands of years. He was a Roman Emperor during the time Jesus lived on the earth; and Jesus himself was the reincarnated Moses. These facts have only been communicated to Josephine and myself, within the last two months, by Richelieu. Napoleon was born the last time, to flash like a meteor across the path of the French people, and mark it with blood. It is this bloody path that forms the magnetic chain that binds him to France, and which will cause him to reappear, as its savior, in the beginning of the next century. I have much to say to you on this subject, at some future time. Let the medium rest to-day. NEY."

I thought this rather a singular communication to write to me. The reincarnation of Napoleon did not concern me much, or, as Toots would say, "it is of no consequence" to me whether Napoleon reincarnates or not. It is exclusively his own business. If he has a predilection for reincarnating, I shall not mar his pleasure, unless he crosses my path. Napoleon is welcome to all the enjoyment reincarnations bring him. But why inform me about it? If the object was to put the prediction on record, that had already been done. Josephine did that, in French, some time ago; and I have no doubt the French people will be looking for the advent of the new century and the reincarnated "little corporal" with a great deal of pious impatience. The intimation is, that Napoleon had previously existed as Julius Cæsar. I'm sorry for that! Cæsarism is at a discount in this country. My prophetic soul! I now understand why Louis Napoleon wrote the Life of

Julius Cæsar. Admitting Ney's account of his geniture, it was the instincts of the son tracing his lineage along the genealogical tree. But Josephine says that Louis was not a success! That's a little rough on her grandson. Did she mean as an historian? I wot not!

On the 17th of March, being St. Patrick's day in the *evening*, my family and Mr. Plimpton waited upon the spirits in a dark circle. As soon as the light was extinguished, Mr. Plimpton's mother requested him to sing an old favorite hymn; in doing which, she accompanied him. He had forgotten some of the words, which she readily supplied. After the singing, the spirit-mother and the living son held quite a long conversation about the different members of their family, and the affairs thereof; and then his sister Mary conversed with him about ten minutes.

Jim Nolan now obtained the control, and saluted all present in his usual manner; after which, he spoke of the progress spiritualism was making among the thinkers of the world, and of the improved conditions which enabled them to manifest. He said: "There are those now living who will see spirits fully materialized in the light, standing on the platform, addressing thousands of people in audible tones. Spirits are making proselytes, through their mediums, every-where among the leading intellectualists of the world." He then described the relation he sustained to the medium, and the existence of an electro-sympathetic chord, through which he was made concious of her every wish, no matter where she might be. He next spoke of the book of the Rev. Samuel Watson, "The Clock Strikes

One," and said: "Watson is in a transition condition; he can only utter such truths as harmonize with his theological education. Gradually he will take in new ideas, and then he will be brave enough to give them utterance."

After Nolan concluded, "Old Ski" announced himself, and had a talk with Mr. Plimpton.

It seems he had been visiting Mr. Plimpton's house, and making notes of every thing he saw, which he described with entire accuracy, not forgetting his "squaw," who, he said, was in need of some medicine, which he prescribed.

Ski had barely retired, when I was addressed by Lizzie Daly, who had lived in Baily's Court, near my residence. Lizzie was an Irish Catholic girl, and an object of sincere pity to all who knew of her bodily affliction. She came to thank me for assisting her brother Pat to get back to Ireland, and for some trifling favors she had received from my household. After her, David Wolfe and Sarah Powers addressed relatives in the circle, when Jim Nolan bid us good-night.

On the 18th of March, Mrs. Hollis received a note from Mrs. G. W. Coffin, living on Broadway, saying she was confined to her bed from the effects of a painful accident, and requesting a visit. Mrs. Hollis decided to call upon her friend in the evening of the same day, and invited me along. She now met, for the first time, the venerable mother of Mrs. Coffin, Mrs. Nancy Martin, widow of Mr. Jonas Martin, who had been a public man in Cincinnati for many years. This venerable lady, in the eighty-first year of her age, was deeply interested in spiritual phenomena, and had read most of the standard works on its philosophy. For the first time, she now had the opportunity of meeting a medium, and expressed a desire to have a dark circle. I had never, until now, met either Mrs. Martin or her invalid daughter; so Mrs. Hollis and myself were strangers alike to Mrs. Martin, and to Mrs. Coffin I was personally unknown.

The windows were closed, and the room made dark. Almost as soon as the light was extinguished, a child, giving her name as "Olive," spoke, saying she was "Mussy's" great-grandchild, that "Harriet" was here, "and my two grandpas — Grandpa Misener and Grandpa Martin." She also said, "My two uncles, both named *Charles Coffin*, are here;" supplementing that one of them had changed his name to Martin Coffin since he came to the spirit-world. This was all the child could say; after which, Jim Nolan began:

"Mrs. Martin, there is a spirit here who says he was an officer in the Prussian army—a nephew of the Duchess Amelia—and says he was your husband."

"What is his name?"

"He gives the name as Colonel Misener. There is also present a woman who gives her name as Francis Wright D'Arusmont, author of 'Altore' and 'A Few Days in Athens,' who sends her love to you, and her compliments to Mrs. Judge Gholson. She will speak to you this evening. There is a spirit who gives his name as George Neff. He says his daughter lives near you, and has no communication to send. There is another lady near you, who gives the name of Febbiger, and wishes it announced without comment. Another great-grandchild gives the name of Jennie. Says she is Olive's sister."

All these names were recognized by Mrs. Martin, who expressed her great gratification for the privilege of living to see the auspicious dawning of spirit-commumication with the people of earth.

Jim Nolan then said, "Mrs. Martin, spirits will soon be able to materialize in the light, and address audiences in public halls and churches, just as lecturers and preachers now do." He then said, "Good-night," and retired.

It was only a few seconds after he did so, when a strangely earnest voice said :

"My dear friend, this moment is the happiest of my life, and is a compensation for all the misery and suffering I endured while in the flesh. It was you, my steadfast friend, who remained by me after my own flesh and blood deserted, and closed my eyes after I had left the form. O, how my soul goes out in gratitude to thank you for your steadfast love!

"You told me truly there was individual life beyond the grave; but I could not comprehend it. It was my thought, and I so expressed it many times to you, that all there was of life was in works; that the reward of human improvement was here—not hereafter—for death meant annihilation by absorption, or oblivion, in the great center of life. But, my dear friend, to-night I redeem the promise of my covenant with you, made twenty years ago, and return to tell you that I, FRANCES WRIGHT PHIQUEPAL D'ARUSMONT, still live, as much an individual as when you knew me as your friend on earth. I came to tell you that the spirit-world is as much an actuality as the one on which you live, and to say I am ever near you, and will be so to the end of your earthly existence. When you come to our bright abodes, I will be among the first to meet you and give you welcome, my steadfast friend!"

These remarks were delivered with a calm, deliberate emphasis that I had never heard before but once. I remember to have heard this remarkable woman speak, while in the form, in 1835, at Chiquis, near Columbia, Lancaster County, Pennsylvania; and this delivery was in that same emphatic style. I then heard her advocate "the universal education of youth, on the basis that human-kind belonged to one common family."

Mrs. Martin subsequently informed me that herself and Mrs. Judge Gholson were the only persons present when this historical woman closed her earthly career. She said the covenant to which she alluded had actually been made between them, and that she had closed her eyes after death. She narrated the following anecdote of the illustrious woman: A few minutes before she died, she requested Mrs. Martin to pass her a hand-mirror from the mantle. After surveying her features for a few minutes, she fixed her hair back of her ears, and returned the glass to Mrs. Martin, saying as she did so, "Thank you, my dear friend!" In a few minutes her spirit left the body, and the ear of Fanny Wright could no longer be pained by the harsh criticisms of an un-Christlike pulpit, or the calumny of a venal press.

Shortly after the spirit of Fanny Wright had

spoken, another voice was heard, in an audible whisper, to say: "My dear wife, I am here, and am so happy to meet you! My children are all here, and we come to see you often. You were a good wife to me, and will soon be with me. I have a beautiful home prepared for you. It is very difficult to speak. Good-bye! Bless you, my dear wife!"

This closed the *seance.*

On the 20th of March, a dark circle was formed by Mr. William Ringgold, Mr. Perry O. Ringgold, Miss Emma Ringgold, Mrs. Edward Webster, and Mr. Geo. M. Finch. Jim Nolan complained of the gentlemen in this circle being saturated with the unpleasant odor of tobacco, and refused to talk. Several spirits addressed their friends in the circle, giving a number of names, which were recognized. A long silence followed, and the circle was permitted to adjourn without the usual "Good-night" being given. Mrs. Hollis complained of the turn things had taken in this circle, when Jim promptly came to the front, and wrote:

"Have faith in us! We know what is best. These people came for fun; and our silence will be a rebuke to them. Good manifestations would have been wasted to-night. They got enough—and just what was needed, though not what they wanted. They will get better manifestations next time."

CHAPTER XXV.

WONDERFUL PHENOMENA—MATERIALIZING IN THE LIGHT—A SINGULAR VISION—COWEN, THE MURDERER, RELEASED—HUGHES'S MURDERERS IN BAD COMPANY—BABIES.

A DARK circle was formed, on the 22d of March, by Mrs. Clark Williams, of Mount Auburn; Mrs. W. P. Neff, of Clifton; and Mrs. Rufus Slocomb, of this city.

Jim Nolan opened the *seance*, and spoke for twenty minutes, announcing the names of a large number of spirits present, who dictated messages of love to friends in the circle; after which, he retired. Celia Slocomb then conversed with her mother, for twenty minutes, on family matters; after which, "Eliza," Mrs. Williams's daughter, spoke to her, in the most filial manner, for fifteen minutes. She said she kneeled by the side of her darling mother, in prayer, morning and evening, and tried to make her feel her presence; that she placed flowers, every day, in the little room which had been set apart, in the house, for spirit-communion, when her mother retired to it. She then spoke intelligently of family affairs, and expressed her satisfaction with what her mother did in reference to certain business transactions. Throughout, the spirit evinced unusual elegance of language and purity of style. She spoke very distinctly.

Mrs. Neff's son Frank then talked to his mother about some articles he prized, giving instructions how they should be taken care of, or distributed among his brothers and sisters, to whom, also, he sent messages of love. Clark Williams then conversed with his wife, in most affectionate terms; after which, the circle ended.

On the evening of the 22d of March, Mr. Plimpton and my family assembled in the west room, and Mrs. Hollis entered the center one. It was twelve minutes after, when a white lily was exhibited at the north panel aperture. It was six inches in diameter. I approached to within five feet of it, and, in the strong light, could distinguish the most delicate fibers of the plant. A few minutes later, a pink rose was shown several times; after which, *two* flowers were exhibited, in good light, for a minute,—all of which I inspected closely.

These were soon followed by a naked arm, seen to the elbow, being projected into the room. In a few minutes it retired, and reappeared covered with a delicate fabric, something like illusion. In another few minutes, the arm was clad in a rose-pink satin sleeve, fashioned after the bishop pattern. The sheen of the satin was brilliant. The edge of this sleeve was trimmed with white narrow lace, fastened in pleats. Mr. Plimpton played the melodeon while this arm was exhibited, and, to our surprise, it beat exact time to the music.

Anna Hancock then presented her spirit doll-baby, which she called "Neppy," and this was immediately followed by a fine materialization of Mrs. Sarah Powers, who nodded to her daughter in the room. Scarcely had she retired, when a familiar, but unrecognized, form and face of a beautiful young woman almost filled the aperture of the north panel. She stood about two feet away from the opening, but in a direct line with it. The light was good, so that the spirit could be distinctly seen. Her hair was tastefully arranged, and banded with what seemed to be white and red chenille. This spirit remained perfectly materialized four minutes, during which time I scrutinized it closely. It did not retire, but began to fade, gradually growing indistinct, until it was lost in the faintest outline of its original form. At this juncture, a faint gleam of light began to be reflected over it, which grew lighter and lighter, until it seemed to be a shower of silver spray. The spirit began to take on its form and shape again, when suddenly a band of spirits, all invisible but their hands and arms, surrounded the central figure, and began to fan it rapidly with a flaming light, under which operation it soon regained its lost brilliancy and life-like appearance. These streams of light seemed to emanate from their finger-points, and were not unlike the lurid rays seen in the arctic sky. I now observed the spirit-face was invested with a white gauzy veil. This was put aside by a spirit-hand, when the whole aspect of the face and head became so life-like that I could scarcely realize the presence not to be human. This materializing process was repeated six times in the space of twenty minutes. It was a startling manifestation, and one which, perhaps, was never before witnessed by either man or woman, while in the form. It was an interesting occasion.

Subsequently, it was stated by the spirits that this was the most successful effort they had ever made to materialize in the light. They were well pleased, and expressed the hope to be able to give a materialization with the entire door wide open, or, at least, with "the gates ajar." The spirit thus brought so prominently to notice was a matured and beautiful female, seemingly about twenty years old. It was said I had seen her before, in a vision, at which time she promised to meet me again. As already stated, her face looked familiar; but I was so dazed with the novelty of the operation that I failed entirely to recognize her. No sooner, however, had she finally disappeared, than I recalled her image as connected with a strange experience in my life; and, as it is somewhat of a spiritual character, I will relate it to the reader, hoping the lesson it taught will be as profitable to others as it has been to myself.

Many years ago, in sleep, I had a vision of a secluded valley, which was filled with flowers of the most bewildering beauty and richest perfume. The slopes of the surrounding hills were covered with blooming trees and trailing vines. Here, in a deep shade, I sat, listening to the hum of bees and the silvery clink of dripping waters. The air was laden with delicious odors, which fed the senses with a thousand delights. Gorgeously plumed birds sported among the trees, chasing each other with gladness, and singing sweetly their songs of love. It was a retreat of sylvan beauty, and all that marred my enjoyment was my companionless condition.

A sense of isolation swept over my being, until I became indifferent to the charms about me, and lamented my unhappy lot. As I did this, suddenly there stood before me a beautiful woman, with a most queenly form. As I gazed in her eyes, I felt a thrill of joy pervade my entire being. She spoke no word, but, with downcast look, contemplated the untidy dress she wore. This now attracted my attention, and I began to realize that my sister-visitor was clad in rags, soiled, and repulsive to my feelings, and disfiguring to her faultless person. Her hair was beautiful, but tangled and uncared for. She wore an expression of sadness on her face, which awaked my deepest sympathies. I thought she looked appealingly to me for pity, and as I was going to express my sorrow for her condition, she faded from my sight.

My situation now became more unendurable than ever. Solitude was doubly irksome since I had looked into the eyes of my unknown friend. My spirit was seized with a feeling of unrest, and that which seemed to give most occupation to my mind was the thought of the repulsive and untidy dress of my strangely beautiful companion. While engaged in the contemplation of this subject, unconscious of the presence of any one, a graceful shadow fell upon the lawn beside me, and, turning, I saw approaching my charming visitor again. But what a transformation! She was completely changed; her tattered and soiled garments were gone, and in their stead, she was clad with graceful and well-fitting habits about her peerless form.

> "Grace was in her step, heaven in her eye,
> In all her actions dignity and love."

I could utter no word in her charming presence; seeing which, she spoke, "In which attire do you love me most?" Her words thrilled me with a strange happiness; and I said, "As you are now!" She made reply: "Then purify your thoughts, elevate your tastes, chasten your desires, and make me beautiful forever. I am now clad as you would have me; but as you saw me first, so have you made me. My soiled rags are but the reflection of your impure desires, your ungoverned passions, and your unrefined spiritual nature. Watch yourself, my dear companion, and think of what I tell you. *You will see me again!*" Whereupon I awoke.

> "When like a passing thought she fled,
> In light, away!"

I need not be told that this was a sentimental dream. I know all about that. It was a pleasant dream; and I think it has been a profitable one to me. I only introduce it now to say, that the spirit, so singularly materialized in the cabinet, bore a striking resemblance to the one I saw in the vision. She gave no name; but simply announced that I had seen her before, in a vision. Whether there is any thing in it or not, it is a pleasant little episode in a man's life; and as we do not understand every thing connected with our "sleeping and waking," there may be something more than wayward fancy in it. Who knows?

Soon after the spirit we saw materialized had retired, a very singularly dressed head appeared. The forehead was very low, and receding from a point scarcely an inch above the eyebrows. There was intelligence in the eyes ; and, from the rich ornaments worn in the ears and upon the neck, and also the peculiar head-dress, I should judge a person of rank had come to the aperture.

The manifestations were very good in this *seance;* but the materialization of the spirit I had seen in the vision was the finest witnessed by me in the presence of Mrs. Hollis.

On the morning of the 23d, Marshal Ney wrote :

"The room is charming! We are preparing batteries, and do not wish the public admitted until all things are in readiness. We will advise you at the proper time."

On the evening of the 23d of March, a dark *seance* was given to W. H. LINDSEY and GEORGE JOHNSON, of Louisville, Ky.; WILLIAM RINGGOLD, WILLIAM DE FORD, F. B. PLIMPTON, MISS LIZZIE COUDEN, and four members of my family.

A large number of spirits attended this circle, among whom "Nelly Butler" and a black man, a former slave to Mr. Lindsey's mother, spoke to him. John Lindsey, Mary Graham, Alice ———, John W. M'Allister, Thomas Carse, and John W. Keats were announced, and recognized by him.

The spirits of A. B. Whiting, George Johnson, and an Indian chief by the name of "War Eagle," announced themselves to Mr. Johnson, the last making quite a display of his power, claiming Mr. Johnson as his medium.

Mr. Plimpton was addressed by his sister Mary, his mother, and M. D. Potter.

Miss Couden was spoken to by the spirits of Edith Couden and Alice Clymer; after which, the presence of Eliza A. Couden, Henry Chace Couden, George V. Couden, Emma Couden, and Thomas Craig was announced, and recognized.

The spirit of John Ringgold then carried on a confidential conversation with his brother, when Mrs. Hollis startled the circle by the announcement of the presence of a dark and undeveloped spirit, from whom she apprehended mischief. So excited and fearful did she become, that she demanded the light to be struck and the circle broken up. There was a feeling of terror pervading the minds of all present, and a panicky stampede became imminent. By assurances that no injury could come to any of us, quiet became restored, when was heard an abject voice pleading piteously for permission to speak to Mr. Ringgold. Mr. Ringgold said, "Certainly, speak out!" Still again and again, however, the voice pleaded, and begged him not to be offended for speaking to him. Mr. Ringgold assured the spirit that where no offense was intended, none would be received, and that he should speak freely what he had to say. The voice then tremblingly began by saying:

"I am John W. Cowen, who, many years ago, was hung in this city for murdering my wife and children. You are the only one in the room who saw the victims of my jealous rage and cruelty, though perhaps all have heard of the circumstance. You remember the ghastly gash made by the hatchet, which I had previously sharpened for the dreadful work. I was insane with jealousy when I committed the unnatural deed, and took two drams of whisky to nerve me for the occasion. My wife was peeling an apple when I struck her. O, she was innocent, and I killed her without cause!"

This confession, delivered loud enough to be distinctly heard by all present, in that dark room, had a startling effect. The spirit was asked if his wife and children were with him.

He replied: "No: they are in a different sphere, higher! I have never left the earth, and could not, until I had proclaimed my wife's innocence."

"This confession has been of some service to you, I suppose?" said Mr. Ringgold.

"O yes! I can now rise to higher conditions. To-night I will leave the earth, and pass to the second sphere!"

After saying how grateful he was for the permission to confess his guilt, and proclaiming the innocence of his wife to one who had seen his victims, he bade us farewell.

Mr. Ringgold confirmed what the spirit said as to his seeing the wife and children of Cowen after they had been murdered. He was at the time but a lad, and, like hundreds of others, visited the scene of the tragedy.

After Cowen had gone, Annie Hancock sung one of her little songs alone; and then my friend Lizzie Daly again addressed me. Jim Nolan then announced, by name, the presence of my mother and father. John Jordan, Charles Odell, Hannah Odell,

Nathaniel Odell, Lizzie Odell, Betsy Lockard, Peggy Lockard ("who lived over the hill"), John Lockard, "Grace," Isabella Jordan, Emma Frances Jordan, and *Thomas Ewing* (I think Thomas *Eller* was meant): all of whom, excepting the last named, I recognized as kinspeople.

After this, Emma De Ford spoke to her brother, and announced the presence of her father, Washington De Ford, and George De Ford, Mary Barns, and Captain Air, the latter sending a message to his son Edward.

The father, mother, and grandfather of a member of my family, and also Nelson Atchison, announced their presence. A number of names were given to others of my family, among which David Wolfe, Grandfather Reigel, Thomas Eller, and Willie De Huff were recognized.

In all, there were sixty-six names given at this circle; but the chief interest centers in the confession of our contrite brother, Cowen.

On the morning of the 24th of March, while sitting at the breakfast-table, I asked Mrs. Hollis to enter the cabinet room. After she had done so, I was informed, by a spirit writing, that an unusual manifestation would be given at the aperture. I waited patiently twenty minutes, fingering the keys of the melodeon, when the north panel was thrown open, and little Anna Hancock came to the front, so as to be plainly seen from her waist up. She was beautifully dressed in colors. Her face was in repose, no muscle seen to move. A few seconds after her appearance, and while she still remained, another spirit stood up behind her, looking over her head. The face was more matured, but still child-like—a girl of twelve or fourteen years of age. Her hair was blonde, while Anna's was black; both were wavy, the blonde's reaching to the shoulders. She subsequently gave the name of "Grace." While these two spirits were in view, a third appeared very distinctly, standing back of Grace, taller and more womanly. Her hair was tidily put up, and very dark, displaying a most beautiful head, neck, and shoulders, I at once recognized "Nackie Haynes," a young lady of great personal charms, who was well known and beloved by a large circle of friends in this city and Mount Auburn. The three figures were beautifully materialized, standing one back of the other, and remained distinctly in view for ten minutes. They then began to fade; but very soon streams of magnetic light were showered upon them, when they again revived. This materializing process was repeated several times before they finally melted from view.

In the evening of the same day, my family were in the west room, and Mrs. Hollis in the center. Again the north panel was opened wide, and after witnessing a display of electric light, which seemed to illuminate the interior of the room, three heads came to the aperture, well materialized, almost in the position of those who had appeared in the morning. Anna Hancock and Grace were two of them, but the third was not Nackie Haynes. It was a different style of face, the head of a different shape, and the dark hair was kept up by a gold band. I noticed these spirits seemed to be closer together than before, leaving half the aperture unoccupied;

and while I was conjecturing the cause of it, three other spirits appeared and occupied the vacant space. Here was a tableau of six spirits, finely materialized, all in view at the same instant; and, to give additional interest to the occasion, the beautiful child "Grace" changed her position, and turned her face from one side to the other several times.

This group continued in sight five minutes, when one at a time retired, until but one was left. It was she who wore the gold band on her head. She remained, and *talked.* It was Josephine Bonaparte. She said, in reply to my remark that she seemed different from the rest, "*Mine is flesh and blood; theirs, illuminated faces!*" She remained at the aperture alone twelve minutes, extending her arms, kissing her hand to those present, and frequently changing the position of her person. It was the most satisfactory materialization I had witnessed.

On the following evening, March 25th, a dark circle was formed by Adam Fox, Mrs. Charlotte F. Miller, George P. Miller, Belle A. Miller, Mrs. Anna Standish, Emma Smith, and Belle Wilson.

Thirty-five spirits were announced by name, most of whom either spoke or sent messages to their friends in the circle. The communications were of a private character, and quite satisfactory to those to whom they were addressed.

The same parties had another *seance* on the following day, to which were added Edward Miller and wife, Mrs. Jabez Miller, Ida, Maud, and Thomas Miller, and George Fox. Forty-one spirits were announced, or spoke, upon the occasion.

On the 27th of March, Mr. Plimpton, Mr. Melville Bonham, the well-known public reader, Mrs. Charlotte F. Miller, and four members of my family, had a cabinet *seance*. There were fifteen good materializations, among whom Letitia E. Landon, the gifted authoress, appeared, and spoke to Mr. Bonham ; and Anna Williams, who was recognized by Mrs. Miller. Mary Plimpton, Lizzie Odell, and Josephine Bonaparte were among those who came to the aperture.

In the evening of March 27th, a dark circle was formed by J. W. RYLAN and wife, HENRY NUNOS and wife, C. L. DUNBAR and wife, and two other people unknown.

After the light was extinguished, a spirit made the request that all should leave the room but the medium and Mr. Rylan, as she had a *private* communication to give him. It was his sister " LOUISA." Mrs. Hollis requested that I might be permitted to stay ; but this was denied : so we all left. We were absent about half an hour, when we were again admitted ; and, during the remainder of the evening, ten spirits spoke, and gave some astonishing tests.

The dark circle, on the 30th of March, was composed of Dr. J. B. Buck and wife, George W. Skaats and wife, W. W. Ward and wife, W. T. Winchester, and four members of my family.

The lights had been put out but a short time, when Mrs. Hollis became excited by the presence of three " dark spirits," who stood at the door, trying to enter the room. They were announced as the three men who had been executed for murdering Hughes ; and their object was to make a clean breast of their guilt, as Cowen had, that they might improve their condition. It sounded so much like a fair business transaction, that I advocated their cause; but the medium and Nolan put their veto on it. If these unhappy spirits really wish to confess their fault that they may be forgiven, why should they not be permitted to do so? Doctors of moral monsters tell us,

> "While the lamp holds out to burn
> The vilest sinner may return."

These ignorant brothers want to get out of the "bad place;" and I think this wish arises as much from an instinct of goodness in their nature as from a desire to escape the tortures of an ecclesiastical purgatory. But whatever the motive, let us, in the great name of humanity, help them.

When the circle became composed, some very fine singing by the spirits was given; after which, Nolan spoke and conversed with different members of the circle, for half an hour. He was followed by Dr. Bigler, who gave a message, for his wife, to Dr. Buck; and then Father Baker, Mrs. Ward's spirit-guardian, spoke most eloquently of the grand mission of Mrs. Hollis, and her approaching tour in Europe. Several other spirits spoke, but were interesting only to those addressed.

On the 31st, A. M., when before the cabinet, a nun wearing a white bonnet, appeared at the aperture, and chanted "*Excelsis Deo*," beautifully. At the same place, at noon, Miss Maggie Baker being present, her nephew, Harry Willett, appeared; also a baby, a fat, chubby one, about three months old, which had to be sustained by the materializing spray. It was then wrapped up in a spirit-cloth, which looked like fine white crape.

Mr. John Whaley had a dark *seance* on the 31st of March, at which his wife spoke, and twenty-five other spirits were announced by name.

The first of April was appointed for Hon. Frederick Hassaurek, Rev. Henry D. Moore, Mrs. Nancy Martin, and F. B. Plimpton, to form a dark circle. There was a heavy thunder-storm prevailing at the time these parties entered the room, which continued during the sitting. Jim Nolan said the agitation of the elements would prevent a number of spirits present from speaking. Of these, he gave seven names to Mr. Moore, which he recognized ; to Mrs. Martin he gave the names of ten spirits, all recognized ; to Mr. Plimpton, ten names ; and to Mr. Hassaurek, two. As none besides Nolan could speak, the *seance* was soon closed.

After the storm had subsided, Mr. Plimpton, Mrs. Martin, and my family, entered the west room, and Mrs. Hollis the center. She had scarcely closed the door, when an arm and hand were projected through the open panel, holding the branch of a bush containing leaves and flowers, as fresh and natural-looking as if just riven from the parent stem. After two minutes, it was withdrawn a few seconds, and reappeared with the hand muffled in a gauzy veil. This was again removed, and the bare hand, holding the flowers, appeared, with a handkerchief grasped at the same time.

Magnetic light then almost illuminated the inside of the cabinet, when a nude baby was fully presented in the panel-opening. It was then covered with a gauze-like veil; and again, nude, lying on a downy pillow, within an arched canopy formed by the gauze. It next appeared at the aperture on the shoulders of a blonde-haired boy. A number of spirits were presented, after this, in good light, when Mrs. Martin's beautiful daughter "Harriet" came fully in view. She remained six minutes, fully materialized, and repeated the words, "Mother! Mother! Mother!" She wore a pink illusion head-dress, folded like a veil, through which her dark hair could be distinctly discerned.

After several other spirits had shown themselves, a young woman, wearing a bridal veil, stood at the aperture a few minutes, and then lifted the veil at arm's-length, forming a vista through which you had to peer to see her face. She then turned the veil aside, and it hung down as far as could be seen. Her clear bright face was now perfectly revealed, and she raised her hands to her lips, and threw kisses to each member of the circle. The spirit was not recognized. The veil again descended over her face, and she retired from sight. After several manifestations of hands, handkerchiefs, and flowers had been given, the same baby was again brought to the front, supported in the arms of a nurse. She seemed to be very fond of it, frequently kissing it, and toying tenderly with it by playing bo-peep, touching its nose, lips, and cheeks, in the manner mothers generally do with their helpless darlings. The whole scene was so life-like that I could hardly think of it as a spirit-manifestation.

At the termination, Mrs. Hollis came out, feeling languid and exhausted.

CHAPTER XXVI.

PRIVATE SEANCES—MANY WITNESSES—NOLAN—SKIWAUKEE—FOUR LETTERS FROM JOSEPHINE, ETC.

THE 2d of April was set apart for Mr. Alfred Gaither, Joseph Rhodes, and L. C. Wier to interview the spirits—first at the writing-table, in the morning, and in the dark circle in the evening. The writing I did not see, but was present in the evening circle.

The premises were carefully examined, and found all right. Mr. Rhodes proposed to lock the door, which proposition I amended by suggesting that he should watch it on the outside. The door was made secure, and the light extinguished. Jim Nolan began to speak, in a few minutes, and very soon had Mr. Rhodes "in a spirit" on masonry. These brothers of the "mystic tie" satisfied themselves that they were both "all right on the goose," when, first to one, and then to the other, Jim addressed Wier and Gaither.

The spirit-friends of these gentlemen now began to talk, and were questioned closely by them, in order to be certain of their identity. For instance: when the spirit of Mr. Gaither's uncle announced himself, Mr. G. requested him to state, in exact terms, where he was born, where he died, and when; all of which questions were correctly answered. This spirit announced the presence of his (Mr. G.'s) aunt Maria, stating that she died of cancer in the stomach, and when, and under what circumstances.

Mr. Rhodes was then spoken to by his four-year-old son, who inquired about his hobby-horse, and the whip his pa had bought him, also about a number of his playthings which his ma had put away.

Mr. Wier had with him a small telegraph instrument, which he carried in his pocket; with this he made a peculiar call, it being personal to Frank Stevens. The spirit thus solicited, responded at once; but stated that he was unable to manipulate the key, in his present condition.

Quite a number of other spirits were announced, and one spoke to Mr. Gaither, rather in a menacing manner, in reference to the method of his sudden taking off. It was *Sim Reno*, the express-robber, who was hung in New Albany Jail, Ind., by a vigilance committee. Because Mr. G. was an official of one of the companies robbed, Reno fancied his detectives had a hand in the matter, and so expressed himself.

The same gentlemen, with their wives, and Miss Gaither, had another *seance* on the 6th of April, and received some very fine tests of the presence of their friends in the spirit-world. They were of a private nature.

On the 3d of April, Mr. William L. Vance, of Memphis, and Mr. James B. Speed, of Louisville, Ky., had a dark sitting with the spirits. There were over forty present, whose names were announced to Mr. Vance, and recognized as among his family relations and friends, some of whom, he averred, had not been spoken of for thirty years.

Eighteen spirits gave their names to Mr. Speed, recalling to mind individuals who had long since passed to the "land of the leal."

To myself, James Collins, an old resident of Columbia, Penn., my native place, and Mrs. Margaret M. Scott, of the same place, spoke. The latter requested me to write to her husband, Thomas A. Scott, the distinguished railroad-manager, and inform him that she wished to speak to him in the presence of this medium. I wrote to Colonel Scott, stating her wishes, but fancy he regards my service as one of questionable sanity.

A dark circle was formed on the 6th of April, composed of Rees Price, Jr., and wife, Mrs. Sallie Price, Miss Clara Matson, Mrs. Mary M'Duffie, John Price Rees M'Duffie, and George M'Duffie.

By request, Miss Matson sang, "You'll remember me," and was accompanied by her spirit-mother. Jim Nolan then spoke for half an hour, on the actualities of the spirit-world, and man's universal heritage—happiness. He finished by an apostrophe to Death, stating that it was the flowery portal, through which humanity passed from low to higher conditions of being. He left, after pronouncing a benediction.

Grandma M'Duffie then spoke to her daughter-in-law. Thomas M'Duffie gave admonition and advice to his two sons. James Price conversed with his mother, and Mrs. Matson with her daughter. Sallie Price talked to her brother John; and Rees Price and wife received a beautiful communication from their spirit-daughter. At the conclusion of the *seance*, Anna Hancock sang two nursery-songs very sweetly.

On the evening following this *seance*, a dark circle was formed by Mr. Plimpton, Benjamin E. Hopkins, Mrs. Lucy Chandler, Henry Mosler and wife, Mrs. Charlotte Miller, Miss Emma Ringgold, and Mr. William Ringgold. The evening was very sultry, and the manifestation feeble and unsatisfactory. It was made plain to me, that to assist the spirits to communicate, circles should be formed of families. When thus constituted, a dozen individuals will each receive more satisfying testimony of their friends' presence than two can, who are utterly strange to each other. It is said to arise from the blending of the family sphere into a homogeneous condition, which the spirits can penetrate more easily.

The spirits often reproved me for not observing more discretion in the formation of dark circles. On one occasion, they had so much difficulty to speak, that Josephine wrote, the next morning, the following comments on the *seance:*

JOSEPHINE'S LETTERS, No. XIII.

"My Dear Friend,—Your circle, last night, was of little value, either to spirits or mortals. Such unprofitable circles discourage us, and jar on our sensitive natures more than you can understand.

"And yet our work must go on, even among such undeveloped people. The earth is full of them. But how insignificant they seem, and how unworthy of the efforts we make to elevate them! Without our assistance, they come to the spirit-world in an almost idiotic condition; and here they must be cared for as helpless children.

"Some of these people disgust us, and we feel like leaving them to their gross ignorance and impurity. But this we can not do. Swine need feeding, even though we must work in the mire to do it.

"When we look at our mediums, their number and conditions, we feel that the work of elevating mankind will require the lapse of ages. Go into your large and splendid business places, and listen to the thoughts of your great men. They soon betray the tinsel material of their minds; their conversation is puerile and disgusting; not an idea do they entertain above their sensual wants, or that which their brute instincts do not originate.

"Remember, my dear friend, that you are only reaching a few of these people, and perhaps the best of them. But these will serve as propaganda to fire the remainder, until their trashy institutions shall be swept from sight; and the quicker the better. The storm is gathering, and it must break, when these stubble reputations shall be consumed by the billowy flame of a more enlightened intelligence. Men will cease to be bigots, and truth will purify the atmosphere that now hangs loweringly over the mental condition of the world. Where churches now flourish as centers of miasma, poisoning the minds of men, flowers of free thought and progress will spring forth to grace the earth, and make glad the heart.

"You will live to see much of this grand transformation. The storm that will effect this change is so near, that the flash of the lightning may be seen, and the mutterings of the thunders of discontent distinctly heard. . . .

"JOSEPHINE BONAPARTE."

With all the care I could exercise to select people for the circles in the dark room, I did not entirely satisfy the demands of Josephine. Many who consider themselves of much importance to the world would not feel highly flattered to learn the opinions the spirits entertain of them, after an hour's interview in the dark room. Of a number of influential representative men, who constituted a circle on the 8th of April, the following was written on the succeeding morning:

(JOSEPHINE'S LETTERS, No. XIV.)

"MY DEAR FRIEND,—Last night, as I listened to the silly conversation of those learned men and women, the *Sympamthmm** of my ear was pained, as the slave's back is under the lacerations of the master's whip; and deep in my soul the cry went up, 'O Lord! how long must this continue?' I felt that the beautiful messages we had brought, with so much painstaking, from the spirit-world, to improve the condition of these people, were 'love's labor lost;' and that the flowers of truth would wither and perish in their barren souls.

"We often ask of each other: 'What will be best for such people? What will do them most good?' But the response is always given in perplexity and doubt. No matter how well developed spirits may be—how far they have risen from the sensual plane of earth-life—when they come to communicate with such people, they must be confined to the spiritual and mental conditions of those they address; for powers to communicate are limited to the inspirational capacities of those with whom we are. We are like the sensitized plates of the photographer, upon whom the mental condition of the circle is reflected. Such people quarrel like children with the pictures taken of themselves; and, truly, we esteem this dissatisfaction as the glimmer of a merit in them.

"Is it not pitiable that spirits of a high order of development should be compelled, that they may do good, to take on the mental level of men and women who have barely passed the condition of animal existence? This we must do, else we can not fulfill the purposes of our beneficent mission, though at times we feel self-degraded and disgusted by the work we essay.

"You have had some such feelings yourself, when you have attempted to benefit people, but found such conditions surrounding them as to paralyze your best directed effort, and thwart the purposes you have in view. You feel that time has been misemployed; and yet, what are you to do?

* This word being entirely new, I thought it best to present the writing of it in *fac-simile*. The word signifies the spirit-organ of the tympanum of the natural ear.

"We are compelled by the laws of progress to assist the undeveloped people of earth to rise from lower to higher conditions, before we advance to higher spheres ourselves. What is the reward for the sacrifices we make? The spirit-world is full of ignorant people, who are objects of pity, and who call out our sympathies and aid to instruct and advance. O, if the inhabitants of earth could only realize how important it is that they should make the best use of their time in improving their rudimental life, while they have the opportunity, there would be less worship and more work among them! To promote this end is the main purpose for establishing intercourse between the two worlds. When men know how to make the best use of their time, both for the present and future life, they will cease to do wrong, and learn to do right.

"My kind friend, these low conditions of the human family are much to be deplored, but can be improved only by making sacrifices, and engaging actively and persistently in the stern duties of life. Let us work together, and the more we accomplish, the sooner will we inherit the reward of peace.

"JOSEPHINE."

A number of private circles were given, in which no matter of public interest was evolved. Most people seek interviews with the spirit-world, to obtain information of the well-being of their personal friends, mostly of their own family. In this way, the more important information pertaining to the real conditions, laws, and usages of the spirit-life is unsolicited and withheld.

It is true, that to converse with our friends again, after they have passed the boundary of human life, is a gratification and privilege that can not be too highly estimated; still a *knowledge* of the laws appertaining to spirit-life is a *power* which originates, and perpetually maintains, a pleasure for the soul, unknown to those who prefer to interview personal friends rather than progressed philosophers. Indeed, these are the distinctive characteristics of the investigators of spiritualism. One seeks to establish its truths or falsities by the testimony of his personal friends; another gathers truth, through the processes of reason and intuition, from the testimony of enlightened witnesses.

A private circle, in which many excellent personal tests were given, was formed by John G. Brotherton, Mrs. S. Ryder, John French, Mrs. H. French, and James T. French, all of whom were spoken to by their spirit-friends.

Another circle was formed by Joseph Kinsey and family, Thomas Kinsey and family, Samuel R. Bates and wife, and Benjamin E. Hopkins and family, in which a number of good personal tests were given.

On the 7th of April, a circle was formed by Dr. J. B. Buck and wife, Mr. Robertson and wife, Miss Cluff, Dr. Walton, and Dr. H——. The voices were quite low—sometimes indistinct—in this circle; and the spirits pronounced their names with difficulty. Still a number of good tests were given; and, but for the strange conduct of Dr. Walton, who seemed to be ignorant of the proprieties of a spirit-circle, the manifestations would have been much better. The following note was written on the slate next morning:

"O, the dearth of spiritual people! How much the great world needs this light! And yet, when we meet such as partly composed the circle last night, we feel that the work we have undertaken to perform is almost incomprehensibly great. Your circle last night was exceedingly unprofitable to us.

"JOSEPHINE."

On the 9th of April, Elias L. Lewis, John M'Kinney, Ephraim Holland, and Edward Henderson had an interview with the spirits. All these gentlemen, I have been informed, were pronounced materialists in belief. They are all bankers in good standing, I believe, never having dishonored *a check* of their own issuance, so far as the public are informed. Mr. Henderson is not a banker, but a city editor on the *Commercial.* One of these bankers compromised himself with the public, on one occasion, by clothing and feeding, at his own expense, a number of emigrants, who had reached our city in midwinter, almost naked and hungry. He did this without conferring with the municipal officers, Deacon Smith, or the Young Men's Christian Association. On another occasion, of his own free-will and accord, he remitted more dollars than all the churches in the city combined to the president of the "Orphans' Home," with the request that they should be expended by him in making the little ones happy on the natal day of Jesus Christ. He had the audacity to subscribe the name of "Santa Claus" to his lawless note. I'm told of similar *tricks* by the remainder of them.

The spirits like to talk to such men; and when Mr. Lewis, by request, sung *a hymn,* a spirit-voice joined him. At the conclusion of the music, Jim Nolan challenged Lewis and Henderson, in a mysterious manner, and found them to be "all right" as brother Masons. Lewis made several mistakes, which "Jim" pointed out at once, showing himself "bright," and they quite "rusty." These members of the "brotherhood" were a little confused by the examinations Jim gave them, and said that no woman could talk of the mysteries of Masonry in that style. These four men questioned Jim, first one, then the other, in the most embarrassing manner; and sharp they were in wit; but Nolan was clear to perceive, and quick in repartee. It was a "fair fight" for the maintenance or surrender of old opinions.

"This is the most astonishing event of my life!" said Lewis. "That voice speaks of my friends, and calls them by name, with as much familiarity as I could do. It describes, with entire accuracy, the form and presence of one long since placed in the coffin, and delivers a characteristic message. What does all this mean? Is it possible we live after death, and the way has been made clear for the dead to return and speak to their friends again?"

Jim Nolan now announced the given names of every member of the circle, which had been purposely withheld until thus disclosed. A voice then said to Mr. M'Kinney: "Brother John, I am so happy to see you! I am so happy! so happy! O, I am so happy to see you! *I am not blind now!* O, I am so happy!"

"Well, why do you cry so, if you are so happy?" said the brother, almost stifled with emotion.

"O, dear brother, we are all here! Father and mother, and sister ——, and brother ——, are all here, and are so happy! Bless you, dear brother, for coming here to-night!"

After the excitement had subsided, Mr. M'Kinney had a long conversation with what purported to be the spirit of *a blind sister*. The conversation related to different members of the family, living and dead, and was of so private a character as to make its publication inexcusable.

"Who was that talking to you?" I said to Mr M'Kinney.

"It was my blind sister!" he replied.

"Then she is not dead," I said, "but living."

"It seems so!" was his thoughtful reply.

A female voice now spoke to Mr. Lewis, addressing him in a manner that was peculiar to a young lady whose memory was still fondly cherished.

"Who calls my name?" said the interested man.

She gave the name of the young lady in question, and proceeded to identify herself in the most unmistakable manner. A long undertone conversation here followed, which resulted in establishing the belief that he had really been talking to his "loved and lost." I said, "What do you think of it, sir?"

"I am dazed! I do n't know what to think of it! This is wonderful—this is wonderful! That voice has been silent many years, and I never expected to hear it again! And yet here it is, awakening strange echoes in my soul, which I had thought asleep forever!"

"As a proficient ventriloquist, do n't you think Mrs. Hollis could have spoken to you in the manner you have heard?"

"Ventriloquism does not divulge the secrets of the heart. No mortal could disclose to me what my ears have just heard."

Another spirit now spoke in a peculiar old man's voice, a trifle reedy. It was addressed to Mr. Holland, and purported to be the ancient head of the family of Hollands. After giving his name, he was recognized by his son, in a manner that placed the fact beyond question.

"He speaks just as the old man used to speak!" said Holland. "That's the old man, certain! I could tell him among a thousand, and *bet* on him!"

Quite a lengthy conversation ensued, in which facts upon facts were given, until Holland "threw up his hand" at the complete identity of the *pater-familias*.

The medium's strength being exhausted, the spirit-friends of Mr. Henderson did not succeed in giving any audible manifestations—at least, what was said was in an undertone.

The circle was broken up at half-past ten P. M., and the bankers came out from the presence of their spirit-friends, wiser than when they entered.

On the following morning, the appended letter was written at the table:

(JOSEPHINE'S LETTERS, No. XV.)

"MY DEAR FRIEND,—I listened last night to every word that was uttered, and weighed each well. There was more of the true ring of pure metal in that circle than in any you have had for a week.

"Deep down in the hearts of these men, there is a longing for testimony of the after-life, which the Church does not present. The voice of a loved one, speaking from the borders of the Summer-land, has a power to move them in an indescribable manner. Their whole natures are permeated with love, as flowers with fragrance. When the voice of the lost was heard again, the holy and pure feelings of childhood came back, and rushed over their souls, like a mighty flood of waters over its encumbering banks.

"It is more pleasing to talk to these men two minutes than to religious bigots two hours. Church members may pronounce against this class of people; but had they not better strive to become as good as they? In their want of charity, they blind themselves to the good qualities of their fellow-men, and set up arbitrary standards of morality; but I tell you, my friend, there was more divine truth in the souls of those five men than is sometimes found in a whole congregation of fashionable worshipers. I felt like giving them my hand, to assist them to a higher position on the ladder of spiritual progress.

"That which was said last night has done much good. It was as seed sown upon rich, well-prepared ground. The chords of their souls have been touched, and the music will thrill their beings for evermore. The door of their inner life has been opened, and the light of a new day will enter. Be thankful you have assisted to lead these men out of darkness into light.

"I am with you in all good work. JOSEPHINE."

On the 10th of April, Milton Miller and wife, Joseph Smith and wife, Mrs. Anna Standish, and Adam Fox formed a circle, and interviewed the spirits.

Nolan began, and spoke for three-quarters of an hour. Mr. Miller's sister Belle conversed with him a few minutes; after which, Mr. Fox's mother and brother Robert conversed with him in reference to family matters. Mrs. Standish's father addressed her, and Mrs. Miller's son George gladdened his mother's heart with his presence. It was a good test circle; but no principles were discussed.

On the 12th of April, Benjamin Hopkins, wife and son, John French, wife and son, and Miss Mary Sackett had a dark circle, and a good one. Hopkins and French presented some fine leading questions in spiritual philosophy, which delighted Jim to answer at length.

On the 13th of April, A. J. De Ford and his mother, Charles Graham, Mr. Plimpton, John Price, and the members of my family, held a dark circle.

Mr. Plimpton's sister spoke to him several minutes about family matters, and said she would write him a letter on the following Wednesday, which she did. He was then requested to sing several favorite hymns, in which the spirit mother and sister joined. Jim Nolan then spoke for an hour, first in reply to questions put by the circle, and then to announce the names of forty spirits present, all of which were recognized. The new name of Letitia B. Wolfe was given, as an inhabitant in the spirit-world, who had never been born into life in this, but as an embryo.

Jim remarked: "I have never mentioned this fact before, but it is proper you should know it: that when persons over seventy years of age pass to the spirit-world, they rarely come back to the earth; and if they do, still more rarely do they become interested in the local affairs of men. But when persons pass to the spirit-world before they attain that mature age, they continue to feel an interest in human affairs, and engage actively in the enterprises of men. Their zeal abates as they approach the three-score years and ten, when they turn their faces from the natural world, and begin their journey along the stellar heights of the spirit-land."

The reason he gave for this was that the magnetism of the spirit became refined in character, losing its earthly grossness. The dreams and visions of youth and age are accounted for on a magnetic hypothesis. Through magnetic changes, the law of progress unfolded its power, and gave expression to the phenomena that had so mystified the minds of men. The wisdom of age was but the simple outgrowth of the spirit's early magnetic conditions. Physical life could only be maintained while the magnetism of the spirit was gross. As it became etherealized, the attachments to earth grew feeble—the attractions to the higher life strengthened and intensified.

After Jim had concluded his rigmarole, "old Ski" announced himself with a prolonged halloo-oo! Being greeted by all present with a hearty welcome, the old chief spoke in saddened voice of the massacre of General Canby by the Modoc Indians. He deprecated the act as "bad," and that Jack and his men would be routed out of the Lava-beds, captured, and put to death. Said the word *Modoc* signified "much big injuns;" that is, a large tribe.

Nackie Haynes then reminded me of the fact that while she was an invalid, she would not permit me to speak of spiritualism to her. She alluded to the pleasant drives we made through Clifton, Avondale, and Walnut Hills, and spoke characteristically quick. Said she was happy, and was now realizing the truth of what I had said about spirit-life.

James M'Cammon spoke to John Price, and sent a message to his father and mother, to whom he had both spoken and written in the presence of Mrs. Hollis. Mr. Price's sister also spoke to him.

A son spoke to Mr. Graham. Lizzie Daly said her father was a medium for materializing flowers.

Mr. Plimpton was spoken to by Colonel Robert Lachlan, late of Mount Auburn; and my family were also addressed.

The *seance* closed, and those composing the circle were delighted with the communications they had received. On the following evening, Josephine had something to say, and here it is:

(JOSEPHINE'S LETTERS, No. XVI.)

"MY DEAR FRIEND,—The *seance* on Sunday was good, and we were truly glad. There is so much discord through the week, that a little harmony on Sunday repays us for our trouble and suffering. There is so much to antagonize our efforts, that it is with great difficulty we can deliver our messages correctly. Our spirit-forms are so sensitive and film-like, that the harsh sound of a human voice repels us, and sometimes renders us incapable of giving any evidence of our presence. In the circle we hear voices sometimes, that strike the sympamthum of our ear as the jar and rattle of a boiler-yard assail yours. We sink under this boisterous din; and it is with the greatest difficulty we manifest our presence. How few understand this!

"In one of your recent circles, a sensitive child called its father's name, who exclaimed, in terrific tones: 'Who is that? What do you want? If you have any thing to say, *proceed!*' Well, the child could n't *proceed!* It staggered under those harsh expressions, as if it had been struck in the face! Consider, we are like sensitive plants, and suffer accordingly.

"Again I say, your circle was good; for all was harmonious. Your hearty welcome sustained us. Mr. Plimpton was in sympathy. Mr. Graham has a sturdy, honest voice. Madame De Ford displayed in her tender tones the affectionate nature of her mother heart; while her son's manly voice was its fitting echo. JOSEPHINE."

CHAPTER XXVII.

SPIRIT-HAND ON TOP OF A TABLE—A CURIOUS REVELATION BY JOSEPHINE—SPIRITS WRITING IN THE ROOM—BRUSH MY HAIR—PLAY THE DRUM—EAT AN APPLE—MRS. LEWIS--SPIRITS EAT CAKE AND DRINK WINE — SPIRITS PUT THEIR HANDS IN FLOUR—THE NEEDLE-TEST—JOSEPHINE EXPLAINS PHENOMENA — WATCH - TEST — JOSEPHINE IN A DARK CIRCLE — NOLAN WRITES WHILE I HOLD THE PAPER--BEATS THE REVEILLE AND "THREE CHEERS"—DRUM-STICKS — EXPLOITS WITH A FINGER-RING—JOSEPHINE AFTER CHURCHMEN.

IN the twilight of the evening of the 14th of April, having returned from a drive over the Clifton hills, I requested Mrs. Hollis to hold the slate for communications. While waiting for the writing, I observed spirit-hands playing with the fringes of the cloth covering the table, which hung half-way to the floor. This discovery suggested first one thing and then another, until the phenomena hereafter recorded were all exhibited in the manner and form as stated.

I held a new, crisp bank-bill five or six inches distant from the spirit-hands, and said, "Can you reach it?" A hand came out its full length, and carried it under the table. My hand was touched by the spirit when it grasped the bill. The handling of the bill under the table could be distinctly heard, by the crisp noise it made. After a few minutes, the hand came out, and dropped the bill, neatly folded, on the floor. The same bill was again taken from my hand when I held it a foot from the table; thereby exposing the spirit-hand and fore-arm, very distinctly, to view.

After that, I laid my *porte-monnaie* on the table, and said, "Can you reach the pocket-book?" The spirit-hand pushed the cloth out and up, until it rested in the hollow of the flexed arm. The *porte-monnaie* was reached, and taken under the table. A number of other articles, in like manner, were taken from the top of the table, affording me ample opportunity to examine the arm and hand, not more than ten inches from my face. They seemed semi-transparent, as china-ware when you interpose it between your eyes and the light.

The spirits asked, by writing on the slate, for a handkerchief. One was given, and rejected, because it had been perfumed. Another without perfume was substituted, and carried under the table, where it was tied firmly with knots, and then thrown several feet from the table, to the floor.

All this was done while Mrs. Hollis sat beside the table, with no part of her person under it, but her right-hand, in which she held the slate. Her back was to me, and her position was such that it would be physically impossible for her to have used her one hand to produce the phenomena I witnessed; and yet they transpired as described.

I was given to understand that it was Josephine Bonaparte's hand I had seen, and that she desired to say something to me in the dark room. I went to the dark room, and in a few minutes a voice began to sing, with much pathos, a French stanza. It was subsequently said to be a favorite song with Napoleon, and that the voice I had heard had sung it to him a hundred times. The voice was more clear than any I ever heard. Its ring was like the tintillations of fine metal, and could be heard in any part of the largest hall in Cincinnati. Josephine next said (for it was she that sang) that the public had never been apprised of the true relations existing between herself and Napoleon. Being a medium, she had been guided by spirits to Napoleon, and became his wife, under their instructions, to assist him in carrying out his grand mission on earth. This she did by revealing to him, while in an entranced condition, the measures he should adopt for the betterment of the *Human Race.* France was simply the battle-ground for the success of grand principles that exerted their influence on the destinies of all nations, and even the lives of all people. The said spirit-intelligences organized the emperor's campaigns, and most of his battles, through her mediumship; and so successful were these plans that Napoleon thought he bore a charmed life, and called himself "The Man of Destiny." In speaking of her own life, she said, before she left the island of Martinique, she foresaw that she would become the Empress of France; that when imprisoned by Robespierre, and informed she must die the next day, in deep trance she saw the tyrant overthrown, and her ultimate release and triumph. She spoke of the change that came over the affairs of Napoleon when he threw himself into the arms of the Church, and consented to be guided by its counsels. 'T was that that sealed his fate, and brought disaster upon the cause it was his mission to uphold. To finish the work he then began, she said, her dear Napoleon must again appear in the flesh, and again become the central figure in the family of the race. She then declared his reincarnation already begun—that in thirty years he would appear in France in his grand mediatorial mission, and that before the brilliancy of his new achievements all his former acts would pale their ineffectual fires. With a promise to watch over my sleep, she bade me "good-night."

In the twilight of the evening of the 15th of April, I again requested Mrs. Hollis to hold the slate under the table. I had it now surrounded with a valance of black calico, reaching to the floor, as a substitute for the shawl. At the end of the table next to Mrs. Hollis's back, I made a flap opening in the muslin, about six inches square, serving as the aperture did in the cabinet. It was really a dark chamber, with no part of Mrs. Hollis's person in it but her right-hand, and in that hand she held a slate.

I now placed a chair against the valance, under the opening, to serve a purpose similar to that of the bracket. On this chair I placed a slate, and requested the spirit to write, while I sat, leaning on the table, with my face not twelve inches distant. In a few seconds, certainly not more than a minute, a man's right-hand, with a heavy, plain gold ring on the finger next the little one, came out and wrote:

"This is the best arrangement you have made; we will give you good tests at this table. NOLAN."

While the writing was taking place, I blew my breath on the back of the spirit's hand, when it stopped, and turned up the palm in the direction from which I was blowing. I considered this a protest, and blew no more, when the hand finished writing the sentence, and withdrew. This hand was not the same that had exhibited such dexterity in removing articles from the top of the table, on the previous evening. This was Nolan's hand, the other Josephine's.

I now placed a large horn-handled hair-brush on the chair, more with the object of testing their strength to lift it than with any other definite purpose. It was quickly taken under the table, and rattled around for several minutes. It was then projected through the aperture, held by the hand of Nolan, and a motion made, which I construed into a desire to brush my hair. I removed the chair, and placed myself in a favorable position before the aperture, by sitting on a stool, and leaning my head forward to the opening. The hand and brush began to operate on my head, first brushing my hair to one side, then to the other, and then back, until each particular hair stood resolutely on end, like quills upon the fretful porcupine. The pressure on the brush was unpleasantly hard to the scalp, and I made the remark that, perhaps the work could be as well done if the brushing was performed with less emphasis. The observation had a good effect; for the shampoo, thereafter, was pleasant.

While this operation was going on, the arm was over my head, and I had an opportunity of looking into the dark chamber from which it proceeded; but, beyond the edge of the table, I could see no arm.

The materialization seemed to terminate at a point an inch or two above the elbow. I could not see Mrs. Hollis's hand under the table, nor the slate, but her wrist, fore-arm, and elbow were all exposed in the now gas-lighted room.

Jim Nolan, the improvised spirit hair-dresser, had been a head drummer in the regiment in which he served. This fact suggested my next experiment, which was to place a tin pan upside down on the chair before the aperture, and mount it with a pair of small drum-sticks. I had barely completed the arrangement and resumed my seat, when, as if anticipating my purpose, two hands seized the drum-sticks, and began to roll and tattoo on the pan, with as much glee as a four-year-old displays with his first nursery drum. It was not real first-rate music, and I so informed the drum-major, who was not slow to reply that he "could not make a good whistle with a dog's tail, nor a silk purse from a sow's ear!" It was the best he could do ; what more could I do ?

"That's a fact, Jim," I said ; "you did very well, considering all things ; besides a great many disadvantages you labor under, which, I fear, I do not consider. How you can make your hands and arms, and use them at all, without having a discernible body, chest, or head, makes me groan to think of it ! But I'm not so much interested in your affairs as in Mrs. Hollis's. I have more anxiety to know how she could form the *two* hands, and perform with the *two* sticks, than any thing else. If neither yourself nor Mrs. Hollis can explain how the thing is done, perhaps somebody else can, and, of course, reproduce the phenomena. I wish they would undertake it in my house. I promise a good reward for the service, if it is as well done!

There was a large red apple on the table, which I placed on the chair, and asked Jim if he was forbidden to taste thereof, lest he might know good from evil. He wrote in reply, "Where ignorance is bliss, 'tis folly to be wise!" Still he grasped the apple, and carried it out of sight. It was a 'cute trick of Jim's, to make a quotation that put me off my guard, and allay all suspicion of his intention to commit *petit* larceny. The Italian value of the apple was five cents, and its weight about eight ounces. I made no remonstrance to the act of its "taking off," believing it would be returned in "apple-pie" order, when it ceased to entertain the spirit-culprit. I was partly right; yet not wholly so. In five minutes after it had been taken under the table, one-half of the apple was placed upon the chair, but the other half was not. I looked for the missing part under the table, in Mrs. Hollis's sleeve, and every-where I thought it could possibly be concealed; but "nix cum 'raus!" Half the apple had been consumed, leaving an irregular or uneven surface, as if it had been sucked off—not rough, as if bitten or broken. The meat of the apple was firm and juicy, and remarkably well preserved for a wintered apple.

Of course, I felt mystified, and asked Jim what he did with the four ounces of apple.

"I dissolved it by a chemical process!" he said; and continued: "It is now in the atmosphere of this room, excepting so much of it as has escaped up the chimney-flue, out the door, or has been breathed into your lungs."

Jim knows; and I rest the case upon his statement! I don't know what useful purpose may be subserved by recording this fact; still, while one reader may find it devoid of interest, another may find something in it to think about.

An hour after the foregoing experiments, John R. Whaley and Mrs. Elias L. Lewis, with Mrs. Hollis and myself, formed a circle in the dark, and, after singing a song or two, the spirits began to talk. Mr. Whaley's wife spoke to him about family affairs; after which, thirty spirits—old Kentucky friends—were announced by name, some of whom colloquied as Elwood Fisher had with William M. Corry. A number of half-forgotten circumstances were recalled by them, and many personal incidents of long ago revived, which precluded the possibility of deception in the matter. While Mr. Whaley and Mrs. Hollis were in conversation, and Mrs. Lewis and myself were exchanging remarks, a *fifth* voice addressed Whaley, respecting some long-forgotten fact, which settled his mind on the ventriloquial question. One of the spirits gave its middle name as "*Alabama*," which was not a common name.

Mrs. Lewis was spoken to by several of her friends, but on subjects that were purely personal and private.

On the following morning, these comments were given in regard to this *seance:*

(JOSEPHINE'S LETTERS, No. XVII.)

"MY DEAR FRIEND,—The circle last night was pleasant to us. They appreciated what they received. We so often have our words rebound, that our power becomes destroyed. We can not talk to some people, because they wo n't let us.

"Mrs. Lewis has a finely developed spiritual organization; her whole nature responds to our approach, like the Æolian harp to the slightest motion of the air. She has a quick appreciation of spiritual truth. Really, she lives more with spirits than with mortals. Spirits can stay near her, lay their heads on her breast, look into her eyes, and find love and sympathy in her soul. O, what happiness to meet such natures! 'T is sunshine to us, and brings forth the finer attributes of our being.

"Mr. Whaley's heart is moved by generous impulses. This attracts his old friends to his presence. They can approach and enter his genial sphere. *All generous natures can be approached by the spirits, but selfish ones keep them far away.*

"I can not write you a long letter this morning. I will tell you why at some other time. JOSEPHINE."

Dissipating four ounces of a juicy apple under the table, so that no particle of the substance could be discovered by the eye, induced me to repeat the experiment, with a four-ounce slice of pound-cake, on the evening of the 16th. I held this on the top of the table, and requested the spirits to take it from my hand, which they did. It was, of course, taken under the table, and, after an interval of five minutes, all the cake was replaced, excepting "a big bite out of it," perhaps one-fourth of it, gone. This missing fragment, it was alleged, had been reduced into thin air, just as the apple had; though it was said that eggs, butter, flour, and sugar, baked, were a trifle harder to dissolve than apple-juice. This remark suggested to my mind that fluids might be more readily evaporated than substances. So I placed a wine-glass, two-thirds full of sweet "White Martha" wine, on the chair, and said, "Are you thirsty?"

The reply came promptly, from under the table, in the shape of Jim Nolan's hand, which took the glass carefully around the rim, and passed it out of sight. I have often seen men put themselves on the outside of a glass of wine, but never before had I seen a table do it. In the present instance, the glass was swallowed with the wine. This, however, was returned in three minutes, *dry*, with no symptoms that "ever a dhrop had been in it, to be shure." The room was full of wine-odor, which was pleasant enough, but when the table was lifted aside, and the examination made, no evidence of a "spill" could be found.

The next experiment, at the table, was with a dish of flour. This I placed on the chair, and requested Jim to make in it the imprint of his right-hand. In two or three minutes, a slender, delicate hand, as unlike Jim's as could be, came out, and, after hovering over the flour a few seconds, retired again. In five minutes it reappeared, and settled deep in the flour, leaving a perfect imprint of itself in the soft, snowy bed. The flour fell from the hand; but it did not dissolve, as I had seen it at the cabinet. I then procured another plate of flour, by request; and, this time, Jim "put his hand in it" like an old stager. The matrix left was half as large again as the first; and this experiment closed the table entertainment. After first closely inspecting Mrs. Hollis's hand, to discover any flour-dust there might be upon it, but in vain, I requested her to place her hand in the imprints, which she did, and in the first there was room enough to receive two hands the size of her own; and in the second, enough and to spare. The imprint which she subsequently made of her hand, in flour, was smaller, and entirely different in structure.

On the 17th of April, CAPTAIN EDWARD AIR and JUDGE BERRY, of Newport, Ky., had a daylight sitting at the table, when the hands came out and handled pocket-books, knives, a match-safe, knotted and untied handkerchiefs, and did a number of other strange things, literally under their noses. These gentlemen were slightly perplexed by what they saw.

Another half-hour was spent at the table, in the twilight of the evening of April 17th. I procured a paper of fine needles, containing twenty-five in number, "No 5, Royal Grooveless Sharps," and placed it, with an unbroken No. 80 spool of cotton-thread, on the chair. I said, "Can you see to thread a needle, in the dark, under the table?"

The spirit-hand took up the paper of needles and spool of cotton, and retired with them under the table; and, in five minutes, again replaced them on the chair. The spool had been unwound ten wraps, and by counting the needles, four were missing. I said, "What have you done with the missing needles and thread?" A spirit-hand was now projected, holding the ends of a double-thread between its thumb and forefinger; and at the lower part of the thread were four needles, the thread being passed through their eyes. I took hold of the needles, when, with a dexterous movement, well known to seamstresses, the retained ends of the thread were evoluted about the finger-point, and a returning knot made. This in good light. The length and quality of the thread corresponded with that which was missing from the spool, and the four needles were exactly of the size and quality of those that remained in the paper. If the reader will think a minute about this experiment, it will be found less insignificant than at first appears. Remember, Mrs. Hollis had but one hand under the table, and with that hand she was supporting a six-by-ten slate. If she had had both hands disengaged, under the table, in the dark, her patience would have been sorely tried to accomplish so much, even in a much greater length of time. I have no desire to magnify this experiment into undue importance, but simply to say that it was utterly impossible for one hand to do it; therefore there must have been two hands to handle the needle and thread, eyes to see, and head to understand and guide the operations. If these premises are granted, the presence of a being possessing all the attributes belonging to mortals, is a legitimate inference. If the advocates of unconscious cerebration can apply their theories to meet the case in point, they have permission to rise and explain.

I next placed a quire of paper on the chair, and a lead-pencil, and requested a communication to be written. Several different-sized hands attempted to take up the pencil, but did not succeed well. Twice it was picked up, but suddenly dropped again, as if it had been hot. Then came out the beautiful hand I had so often seen and touched, and, taking up the pencil, wrote "Josephine." This was soon followed by the words, "God is Love." The writing was hurriedly done, and unlike the chirography displayed in her lengthy communications written under the table. It is only just to say that the flame of gas was flooding the room with light, and a reduction of the supply was asked for. I turned it down, when Ney's hand appeared, and wrote, "We are working for principles, not men." It then retired a few minutes, and, when it again appeared, wrote: "Truth lives, error dies! Stand firm, all will be well!"

On the 18th of April, in the morning, after breakfast, I asked Josephine, who was announced at the table, to explain to me, as well as she could, how it was the apple and cake had been dissipated, two evenings ago. In answer, she wrote:

(JOSEPHINE'S LETTERS, No. XVIII.)

"MY DEAR FRIEND,—There has been much said and written upon the subject of disintegration; and yet I do not think the people understand it any better for what has been said or written. Indeed, the finite mind can scarcely grasp a subject that requires such fine analytical powers to explain as the one you have suggested.

"All organized matter has a principle of death within its form. That assails the bond of organization, and destroys it. When this coherent bond is riven, the particles composing the organization are at once liberated, and disappear. Thus, fire, as a dissolvent, destroys the bond of union, and liberates the elements of organized substances. Chemistry is the handmaid of death, ever changing forms, reducing old ones, and creating new.

"The substance of the apple was held together by the law of elective affinity, the same that pervades the universe and sustains all organized matter. It governs growth, or development, causing the sap to ascend, and to flow from the trunk to the branches of the tree. Here the same law awakens the bud and blossom into life, and finally unfolds the luscious fruit. Day by day, the homogeneous particles organize cells of growth, until the fruit has attained its mature size; when waves of heated electricity pass through the new organization, enduing it with fragrance and color. The waves of heated electricity continue to thrill the new organization, until the procreative law is perfected in the offspring; then the bond of union is broken, and the apple drops to the ground. The dear old mother-tree matured it in her bosom, until the conditions of independent life had been attained, when she reluctantly consented to the separation.

"The apple thus gradually developed from elements found in the atmosphere, was held together by elective laws. We passed through the organization a dissolving chemical so potent that the original substance was instantly resolved and absorbed into the great reservoir of elements. The chemistry of a natural law would have accomplished the same result; but we desired to exhibit, in a special sense, the power of the spirits in this *miraculous* (?) manner.

"The same power can be exerted in the destruction of human bodies; but we are careful, in all the relations we sustain with mortals, not to injure them in any way.

"I have but imperfectly represented this subject to your understanding; still I hope my desire to please you will make some amends for any lack of knowledge I may have displayed.

"JOSEPHINE."

The experiments at the small table grew in interest each succeeding circle, more so than the last. In the twilight of the evening of the 18th of April, after Mrs. Hollis had taken her position at the table, I first stopped my watch, and then turned the stem communicating with the ratchet that regulated the position of the hands on the dial-plate, several times. I did this with the case shut, so that it was impossible to know exactly the position of the hands, after I had ceased turning the stem without opening the case. Without doing this, I placed my watch on the chair, from which it was soon removed by the spirit-hand to the slate under the table. I now said, "See what o'clock it is by the position of the hands on the dial, and write the time on the slate."

In a few seconds the watch was replaced on the

chair, and I requested Mrs. Hollis to put the slate on the chair also. This she tried to do; but, holding the slate in her right-hand, and sitting with her right side against the table, she could not present the slate at the aperture at her back without rising to her feet and passing around to the other side of the table, and then only by leaning over the table. Let any one try the feat, and see what a noodle he'll make of himself.

The slate was produced, and on it was written, "Nineteen minutes to twelve!" I now opened the watch, and found the hands pointing to the figures thus written. The experiment was repeated several times, and always with entire accuracy.

Thus it will be seen that the hand receiving and replacing the watch belonged to an organization that had intelligence enough to open and shut the cases; and eyes to see the exact time, and education to write it in good, legible letters. And all this under the table, and in the dark!

A dark circle was held in the evening, attended by a number of ladies and gentlemen from Newport, wherein good manifestations were given. Still there was so much discord in the circle, that the following comments were written upon it the next morning:

(JOSEPHINE'S LETTERS, No. XIX.)

"My Dear Friend,—'Sunshine and cloud' alternates in the circles you form for us. Where we have one of pleasure to us, there are ten from which we gather no inspiration. The circle last night was so dreadfully material that Jimmy refused to speak. He says he will not meddle with family matters; and therefore will stand aside in silence, and allow their own friends to tell them 'how old they are,' and 'when they were born!'

"There are some mortals who are so ignorant that they scarcely know more of existence than the animal that munches its corn. They eat when they are hungry, and drink when they are dry. To talk to such people, we feel to be a damage and a detriment to ourselves. And yet, we are told, we must aid each other! But how do they aid us? In what manner do they return good for good? It is impossible for us to be interested in their little family matters; and when they come repeating these things day after day, and month after month, is not a little impatience excusable occasionally? Besides, is it not seemingly throwing time away?

"We are obliged to give manifestations to the world, and it would be a great pleasure to do this, if we had always good conditions to receive us; but it is the fewest number who can comprehend the importance of our mission; or who understand the philosophy of spirit-intercourse.

"I am not complaining in any petulant spirit just now, but am simply stating the facts as they exist. The knowledge that great results will arise from our labors is the most sustaining thought we have to encourage us. If in two hundred years we can look back and say, 'We began in this great work: we prepared the way for the higher development of more exalted spirits,' that will be sufficient reward.

"Spirits that return are not evil; but the neglect of opportunities to improve their condition compels them to come back to receive lessons in wisdom. We listen to them talking to their friends—repeating the same things over and over again. Do you wonder we get tired, even as you do, and not feel happy with their lively rattle?

"I have complained enough this morning, and fear you will begin to esteem me unamiable. I beg you will pardon my discontent. I feel that I may speak to you of these things, without the imputation of wrong-doing, as we are both working for the same beneficent end, through the same experiences and instrumentalities. JOSEPHINE."

It was written on the slate, on the evening of the 19th of April, that Josephine was in France, and had been for six hours. It was Nolan's writing; so I asked him to show his hand. This he did very promptly, extending his hand and arm at least twelve inches, seizing my hand as he did so with considerable force. I then held a bundle of paper near the aperture in the valance, with a pencil on top. I said, "Can you write while I hold the paper?"

Nolan picked up the pencil and wrote:

"Receive us; we are your fellow-men."

Again he wrote:

"I still live. Yours truly,
"JAMES NOLAN."

At the conclusion, the spirit dropped the pencil; and, after patting my hand, retired.

There seemed to be a superabundance of spirit-power at the table. They rapped very much, and projected their hands through the valance a number of times. The raps began to roll like the beat of a drum, and finally the *reveille* was beaten, I think, without the omission or addition of a single tap. Then followed a desultory beat, which he informed us meant "three cheers!"

Nolan now requested the music-box to be brought in the room, and placed on the table. It was set to play, and Nolan drummed an accompaniment to each of the pieces, in the style of an accomplished drummer. This performance mystified me. I knew there were no sticks under the table, and the sounds were too sharp for fingers to produce; so I said, "What are you drumming with?"

"Drum-sticks!" he wrote on the slate.

"But you have none!" I said.

"I have materialized a pair," he answered.

"Can you show them?"

Rapped: "Yes!"

"Will you?"

"Yes!" by raps.

In a few seconds a pair of drum-sticks, about one-fourth the usual size, were projected four inches through the aperture. I requested him to show them entire; but he wrote, "Can't do it!"

I then obtained a ring from Mrs. Hollis, with a diamond set, and put it on my finger. Holding it in front of the aperture about four inches, I said, "Can you take it off?" The hand of the spirit took hold of the ring with its thumb and two fingers, and, by dint of wriggling and pulling, succeeded in getting it off. In a few seconds the spirit-hand appeared with the ring on the index finger. After this, it was shown several times, and then held between the thumb and finger; seeing which, I extended my hand. The spirit then, with considerable effort, replaced it on my finger. I wanted to remove the ring from the spirit's finger, and asked if I might do so. He wrote:

> "I can not explain the law forbidding it; but to grant your request would destroy my power for the remainder of the evening!"

He then seized the chair in front of the aperture, and first drew it close up to the table; then, with a sudden push, forced it to the middle of the floor, several feet distant. This closed the manifestations for the evening.

On the next morning, Sunday, April 20th, while the streets were thronged with church-going people, the following letter was received:

(JOSEPHINE'S LETTERS, No. XX.)

"MY DEAR FRIEND,—I have passed most of the last thirty-six hours in France; hence I did not write to you yesterday. But I am here again to give you a letter this morning. I fear I bring you but a poor offering as a reward for your kindness and painstaking with us; but it is a happiness to me to do this.

"While looking over the land, this beautiful Spring morning, I could not help thinking how like a pawnbroker's-shop the whole city appeared. Women pawning the sensitive germs of their souls, regardless of their value, simply for the love of display. For diamonds and rich lace, they sacrifice every great and good impulse. They are so steeped in all that is artificial, that they can not rise above it. Hence their misery and discontent. Dress has become their master; and when they realize their degradation, they affect humility, and pawn their poor starved souls to the Church. But the Church affords no relief; on the contrary, its very life depends on keeping up this extravagant passion for dress. Fashion rules the Church, as well as tyrannizes over the soul.

"There is a germ of divinity in the soul, however, which neither Church nor fashion can destroy. It may be necessary to bury the body in the ground before it develops itself, as you do the seed-corn before it can show the vital spark wrapped up in its organization. When this is done, it will spring out of the old body with gladness, rejoicing to be released from the bondage of Church and State.

"Death to the seed-corn develops the life-germ it contained into the living grain. So death, to the body and outward show, will liberate the faculties of the fettered soul, and give it joy unspeakable.

"But how utterly useless it is to tell these people that they will come to the spirit-world, naked as they entered the earth! Arouse, ye sleepers! What does the great Creative Power care for your gewgaws and your fame! To that Power, you appear as mites—microscopic specks on the changing page of Time. Learn, while you may, such truths as will be a lamp to your feet, and a light to your eyes, when you enter the spirit-world.

"Ever your true friend, JOSEPHINE."

CHAPTER XXVIII.

TABLE-TESTS REPEATED—DARK SEANCE-GIVING—REMARKABLE STATEMENT OF "OLD SKI," WITH A MORAL—JOSEPHINE HAPPY—EXPERIMENT WITH WATER—SMELLS FROM THE INFERNO—COAL MERCHANT—SPICED MILK—QUEER TASTE—A DARK CIRCLE—THE SPIRITS REFUSE TO MANIFEST—CAUSE, WHISKY—JOSEPHINE ON THE SITUATION—A DOUBTFUL BEVERAGE—QUEER ODORS—A MIRACLE—EXTRAORDINARY BOOK-TEST—DARK CIRCLE—JOSEPHINE AGAIN—BOOK-TEST REPEATED—A CIRCLE OF PROSCRIBED MEN AND WOMEN—JOSEPHINE PLEASED.

THE remarkable character of the phenomena occurring at the table suggested the propriety of having some one besides myself to witness them, as my unsupported statement of the facts might be confronted with a mass of incredulity that would throw discredit upon the entire report. I, therefore, said to Nolan:

"Can't you give these manifestations in the presence of another witness?"

"That depends upon who the witness is," was his reply. "If you can get one who will not disturb the conditions we have established, we can give you still better tests than you have yet received."

"How would Mr. Plimpton do?" I said.

"I would have suggested him, if you had not," said Jim.

"Very well! I'll have him here this evening, if he feels like it."

In my afternoon drive with Mrs. Hollis, we met Mr. Plimpton, and informed him of his selection for the position of analytical inspector of phenomena which I esteemed the most conclusive testimony of spirit-presence it had been my privilege to see. He came early, and the half-hour *seance* before tea was consumed in reproducing the "thread-and-needle test" and "the watch-test," described in the last chapter. Mr. Plimpton will make his report of what he saw at the table, a little farther on.

After tea, we decided to hold a dark circle, and, Mrs. Miller and four members of my family joining us, we went to the dark room. Almost coinstantial with the extinguishment of the light, a spirit-voice requested us to sing. While we were talking about what we should sing, a spirit-voice began to sing or chant alone. At the conclusion of this voluntary, Mrs. Miller's son George addressed her, and spoke of family affairs. Then Mr. Plimpton's mother spoke, asking if he remembered certain persons in the village where they had lived, whom she named, among them the physician who attended in her last illness, and a large number of relatives and friends.

Every member of my family was spoken to by spirits; and Aunt Betsy Lockard did not fail to say a good word to me. Jim Nolan then spoke for half an hour, in a strain of fervid eloquence, on the mission of the "new revealment;" after which, "old Ski" had his "put" on personal tests. He rather surprised me by stating that he "had been out riding with em old chief and mejum, and hear em all em said!"

"Come, come, Ski! I guess you did n't hear every thing we said!"

"So! em did!" he replied.

"Well, tell us the road we went, and what you heard?"

"Went em on Gest Street—up em big hill to toll-gate. Told em old gate chief em go to Warsaw em back; em pay em old gate chief ten cents—five for em go, five for em come. Old chief no stop em Warsaw—stop em Gazlem's! Cheat em gate chief two cents! So!"

It is necessary to rise and make an explanation to this *invisible* charge of fraud upon "em gate chief!" I do this, however, with no view to change the character of the indictment, but to state the circumstances in mitigation of the penalty attached to the guilt confessed. The circumstances which the old Indian has so faithfully presented, were brought about in this way: When paying toll, Mrs. Hollis said, "We'll turn at Warsaw." I paid accordingly, just as "Ski" has represented; but, after getting to Warsaw, we concluded to drive a mile farther to Gazlay's Corners, as the road was good, the evening pleasant, and the topic of conversation entertaining. Rather, it is more truthful to say that the horse took us to the "Corners," from force of habit, and the matter of *two cents* additional toll was entirely overlooked.

The reader will perceive that the interest attached

to this disclosure of "Old Ski's" centers in the fact that we can do nothing, or say nothing, but what is known to our invisible guides, or guardians. Guilt has no protection in the presence of a medium, if the spirit-world determines to bring the offender to justice. Upon the occasion in question, the "old Indian" rendered an almost *verbatim* report of the conversation between Mrs. Hollis and myself. When men get to understand that detection follows crime, as shadow substance, they will cease to do ill, and learn to do well. This is a good place to "stick a pin," in answer to the question which we so frequently hear snivelers ask, "What good can come out of Nazareth?"

On the following morning, April 21st, this letter was received by the spirit post-mistress at the table:

(JOSEPHINE'S LETTERS, No. XXI.)

"MY DEAR FRIEND,—I am grateful that you did not fill your circle last night with skeptical people, to disturb the harmony of the occasion. Mr. Plimpton's mother and sister approached him nearer last night than ever before. After speaking to him, with all the love of a mother's heart, she wept with joy. She stood over him weeping, as if she had just found a long-lost child. Her whole soul was overflowing with love and gratitude to the Power that permitted her to return to her child once more. Again and again can she come to tell the story of her love, which has grown brighter and holier in the spirit-land! Again can she say: 'I'm not dead, but living! My interest in you, my dear child, is just the same! Death cast aside the physical form, but the mother remains in my soul.' Much more could I write this morning; but the subject is exhaustless! Nothing touches my heart so quickly as a mother's devotion to her child.

"And, too, Mrs. Miller, what love she retains for her darlings in the spirit-life! We have a firm friend in her. The whole atmosphere of the woman is an unuttered prayer of thanksgiving that her friends can come back feeling they bring to her love and sympathy.

"Fanny and Tom and Lida, all were remembered by their spirit-friends—the mother's voice blessing her child, whom she left years ago to struggle with a cold world, assuring her of the love and care thrown around her by her spirit-friends.

"All this only adds another link to the chain of evidence which shows the nearness of the spirit-land, and to establish the fact that love never dies, but grows stronger and brighter and purer as we grow wiser and better in the spirit-world.

"I listened to the voices last night, with joy in my heart and peace in my soul; and the prayer arose to my lips in these words: 'Thanks to the creative power for this life! And O, may these truths pervade the souls of all men and women, and teach them there is no death—that they can not die!' and so my soul was wrapped in holy thought. I kneeled by the side of the medium during the entire *seance.* Aunt Betsy first calling you by the name I loved to call my husband, thrilled me through and through, bringing back so much of my life in France, that I could almost hear again the voice of my dear one, as in days long past, when he spoke to me loving words.

"How grateful my soul is, this bright morning, for all your kindness in furnishing us with such good conditions! I fear I have exhausted the medium too much, and must now close; but not before I again assure you, I am ever your devoted friend, JOSEPHINE."

On the 21st of April, having just returned from a drive through Walnut Hills, Mrs. Hollis sat by the table for manifestations, holding the slate in her right-hand. The dissipation of the cake, the wine, and the apple, induced me to ask if they had the power to restore these articles again, promising to believe it a *miracle*, if they did so. They could not do it. I had, at last, found the limit of possibility with them. But Jim Nolan said he would make me a glass of wine, if I furnished him with a glass of water.

"Do you mean to convert the water into wine?" I said.

"Get the water!" was the command.

"Certainly; you shall have it. But I caution you to be careful how you tamper with holy things."

"Get the water!" he said again.

"I 'm a gittin'!" And I got the water—a pitcher full, from the cistern; clear as crystal, and sparkling as diamonds. It may be interesting to the reader to know, in view of what follows, that the water was run in the cistern when the Ohio River was low, so there was no admixture of soil, etc., to vitiate its purity. Well, Jim wanted only a wine-glass full of water, and I gave it to him. He carried it under the table, and, in about ten minutes thereafter, there was the strongest smell of aromatics proceeding from under that little table, that I had sensed for a long time. The odor filled the room, and almost rendered the atmosphere unfit to breathe. There was not the slightest trace of *sulphur* in it, however; and that was a comfort. I can stand any thing but the smell of a coal-merchant. Such, I am always fearful, will burn forever in a blue flame, or expire by spontaneous combustion; so I am always oppressed with a sense of insecurity when in their presence. There were no little jets of "blue blazes" flitting up around the table under which the water was concealed—nothing, only the smell of spices.

In ten minutes, Jim handed out the wine-glass, filled with spiced milk, it seemed. It was a clean, white-looking fluid. I smelt it cautiously, as if it was fortified harsthorn (always be cautious when you smell hartshorn, else you 'll fancy you 've been struck with a slung-shot) ; but it was pleasant ! I rather liked it ; that is, its odor was not obnoxious. "Suppose I taste it," I said, addressing Mrs. Hollis, who was amazed at the milk.

"Do not ; it may be poison !"

"In such a quantity ? Never ! I 'll taste it, if I lose my tongue by it !" So I tasted it, and it tasted very *queer*. It was a *queer* taste. It was *unlike* a kiss ; and yet it reminded you of something of the kind : for you began, at once, to make inverted explosive successions with the lips, something like fanciful kissing. Like a drop of peppermint, it imparted a diffused, pungent warmth to the tongue and faucal appendages. It was a stimulating exhilarant, and caused the salivary glands to secrete copiously. In a few minutes the mouth became comfortable again, and I was prepared to render an opinion.

As a wine, judged by the color and quality of standard wines, this spiritual brew was a failure, and so I informed Jim. He must do better than that, if he desired to compete with Longworth's "Golden Wedding," or the "Muscat" of Werk. But it was no longer water ! It was a transformed fluid, a betweenity of water and wine, which no man would mistake for either, unless he was daft of reason and shorn of sense. Jim felt rather ashamed of this experiment, and promised to renew it on the following evening. As my office is simply to record facts, I offer no comments on the foregoing experiment ; still I am not insensible to the interest which thoughtful minds will attach to it.

As if pleased with the conclusion of this experiment, Jim reached his hand to the little waiter on the chair, and tattooed on it with his fingers for several minutes. He then suddenly took hold of my hand, resting on the top of the table,. and gave it a pretty fair grip. This terminated the table *seance.*

Monday evening was engaged by a man who did not desire to give his name, but who represented himself as doing business on Fourth Street. I declined making this engagement, several times, on the basis that it was an implied reproach upon my integrity to withhold such a civility, when, at the same time, the unknown was seeking admission to my house and the presence of my family. Against my better judgment and an established rule for forming circles, I consented to allow this fellow to interview the spirits on the evening of the 21st of April. I did wrong.

At the time appointed, this man, and four other men, entered my parlors. I knew only him by sight; the remainder were entire strangers to me. It did not require but a few minutes to let him know he had abused the concession I had made in his favor; and I refused, for a time, to allow his party to enter the circle-room. I informed Mrs. Hollis of the state affairs; and she said she was willing to sit, if I consented to admit them. So into the dark room we went, and I very soon ascertained that *two* mistakes had been made. Two spirits attempted to talk, and said enough to be identified as spirits simply, when Nolan said, "I will not speak to men under the influence of whisky."

I lighted that room in a jiffy, and escorted the unknown and his party to the door, with the assurance that they would most probably never enter it again while it was my dwelling-place ; certainly, never to a spirit-circle. I am afraid I was not amiable in taking leave of them. On the following morning, this letter was written at the table:

(JOSEPHINE'S LETTERS, No. XXII.)

"MY DEAR FRIEND,—There are people who come to our circles saturated with whisky and tobacco. These agents generate a bad magnetism, and an odor so unpleasant that the most disagreeable effluvia of earth could scarcely be more obnoxious to our senses. We try to approach them ; but their stench causes us to retire, sick and disgusted. That men should think they must brutalize themselves in this way before they can listen to the voices of those who were dear to them in life, is a dismal pity, and a humiliating infatuation. Such people surely live in the pit of Ashur, where the worm dieth not.

"O men ! will you make devils of yourselves ? We have too many such in the spirit-world ; send us no more. Arouse from this unnatural condition, and aspire to a higher and better life. Do not insult and grieve your friends who have left their pleasant abodes, and come trying to make clear to your understanding the reality of the after-life. You all need the assurance we bring of a higher life Then, for the sake of all concerned, debase yourselves no more. If you could see the hosts of spirits chained to earth by their degrading vices, wandering, year after year, about the haunts of their defilement, you would, in preference to being such, beg for annihilation.

"Your circle, last night, was, to us, unpleasant and hurtful. We will not—can not—approach men who are under the influence of intoxicating drink. We can do them no good, and they do us much harm. When you find such persons in the circle-room, adjourn at once. They outrage our better natures, and stifle inspiration. If such people purposely unfit themselves for our presence, they must take the consequences, and the remorse which comes too late.

"But let them seek us through proper conditions, and we will gladly assure them of an after-life. Their spirit-friends will establish their identity, and impart to them messages of love and encouragement. Beg of those who come, to meet us as pure beings, ready to enfold them lovingly in our arms, if they will permit us to do so. You did well to reject their money; and could you have heard the applause given you by the spirit-hosts about you, when you rebuked these poltroons, you would have realized how much we appreciate your worth.

"JOSEPHINE."

Jim Nolan was not satisfied with his miraculous effort to transform water into wine; so he made request that the experiment should be repeated. Accordingly, in the evening twilight of the 22d of April, another wine-glass, two-thirds filled with the same crystal brew from the cistern, was placed before him, and was soon taken through the aperture, under the table.

In a little time, say five minutes, Mrs. Hollis complained of dizziness of the head, and desired to postpone the experiment for the present. I begged her to remain quiet, the worst was over, and, if she fainted, I promised to throw a pitcher-full of water in her face, indifferent to the sacrifice of so much prospective wine. Again, an odor began to emanate from beneath the table, growing stronger each moment, until the atmosphere became charged, as in a distillery of high wines. Mrs. Hollis grew better under the inhalation of this spirituous vapor; but I began to experience a fullness in the veins and arteries of the head, indicating the approach of asphyxia. I opened the door to admit fresh air, which I could do without moving from my chair or taking my eyes, for an instant, off the medium. In ten minutes, the experiment was completed, and the glass of water—or wine, as you elect—was placed before the aperture, on the chair. The fluid was clear and colorless as when it was taken under the table, but there was a strong vinous smell to it. Jim wrote:

"Let it alone; we are not done with it."

It was again taken through the aperture, and, in four minutes, reproduced; but this time, a clear, transparent, *amber-colored wine!* The transformation was complete! I tasted it; acid and sugar and spirit were pleasantly blended in the beverage; and I believe, if used in equal quantities with intoxicating wines, its effect on the vascular system would be precisely analogous.

I have bottled this wine, and it is in the hands of Professor Wayne, the well-known chemist, for analysis. If his formula of ingredients is received before this chapter is printed, I will insert it here; if not, then the experiment must be considered only as a curious transmutation of water, which

"Looked upon its Maker's face, and blushed."

The plain prose of this experiment is, that Jim Nolan chemicalized the water, and made a wine of it. If I did not know this, I should call it a miracle; information is very bad for the miraculous.

The value of this experiment has not been a leading question in my mind. I have somewhere heard of water being converted into wine, and I only wished to ascertain for myself, while I had the opportunity, whether the thing was practical or not.

The next experiment at the table was with a book. I had purchased, late in the day, a small volume of "Pope's Essay on Man," and had it in my pocket. It had not been opened; so I laid it on the chair, and Nolan carried it under the table. After he did this, I said:

"Can you read that book under the table in the dark?"

The raps indicated an affirmative reply. I said again:

"Please read a passage, and write it on the slate; and indicate the page of the book where the passage may be found."

In a few minutes, not exceeding ten, the book was replaced on the chair, and the slate rapped upon, to have it withdrawn. I took the slate, and read:

"Page 46—

"O Happiness! our being's end and aim."

"Page 48—

"Order is Heaven's first law."

I now opened the book at the pages written above, and found the words as quoted on each page, exactly as it had been represented.

I desire no stronger testimony to prove the presence of an educated mind under the table—a mind that had eyes to see, hands to serve, and brain to comprehend—than is furnished by the experiments with the book and watch. It is not material to the object of my writing that you call such mind *spirit.* But call it something; give it a name of which you will not be ashamed. I have no argument to offer but that which every thoughtful man and woman has already anticipated. The verdict of the reader must rest upon the facts of the case. Rhetoric is dumb in their impressive presence, and all elaborate speech contemptible.

Lay aside prejudice, and look these facts squarely in the face. Let us not turn away from Truth.

> "One vision of her snowy feet
> Is worth the labor of a life."

With all the vigilance I could exercise, I was not able to form good circles for the spirits. One good man would come to arrange for a *seance*, and he would represent his personal friends as being all right; and believed them to be so, too; but when they entered the dark circle, the spirits discovered such people, frequently, to be all wrong. I felicitated myself on having a good circle for the spirits, on the night of the 22d of April,—if I entertained any misgivings during the evening on the subject, the doubt was put to rest by the reception of the following letter, next morning:

(JOSEPHINE'S LETTERS, No. XXIII.)

"My Dear Friend,—My letter will be short this morning, as our medium is very much exhausted. When she gives out her magnetism, she can spare only so much; I will have to write but little until she is quite restored. Monday and Tuesday have been very exhausting days for her, and that is my reason for writing so briefly to day. When she is less worked, I will write more fully my passing thoughts.

"Last night but little good was accomplished in the circle. The people present were simply egotistical and selfish, to an uncommon extent. They are the weeds and brambles we find growing along the highways of life; and objects of pity to the passer-by. And yet they are no worse than two-thirds of the human race.

"O wisdom! how thou art to be coveted! What is wealth without thee? Knowledge is the savior of the world, ignorance its curse and devil! Help me, my friend, to awaken in the souls of these people a realizing sense of their weakness. Tear out the weeds and thistles of ignorance by the roots, that grow rank in their souls; then spiritual light and warmth will quicken their better natures into life.

"You have done much for us, my good friend. We thank you. JOSEPHINE."

The twilight *seance* of the 23d of April was a reproduction of the book-test. This time a large volume of poems, called "The Great Republic," a work published in England only—a copy of which I borrowed for the occasion—was placed on the chair. It was a little cumbersome to handle, and heavy. After going over the same ground we had with the other book, book and slate again appeared in like manner as before stated. It was written on the slate:

"Page 224—

"The ghosts of our dead years, a piteous throng,
Cower on wintry steeps; and, shuddering there,
Mingle their flocks with phantoms borne along—
Powers, splendors, victories, divinely fair,
That might have been, but are not! Fail our fires!
In each, unborn, some heavenly hope expires."

This was a literal extract from the 224th page of a book into which neither Mrs. Hollis nor myself had looked. The quotation was strange, weird, and singularly conceived. Mr. Plimpton came in as the test was concluded.

Recognizing men and women at their par value, I did not discriminate against a class of people whom the wealthy and fashionable butterflies of life call *outcasts*, but granted a *seance* to nine of them, on the night of the 23d of April. If spiritualism can not raise the fallen, and speak comfort to their hearts, it is no better than the Churches, and deserves to have its Christ-like life crushed out of it, as it has been from the stony-hearted creeds of modern paganism.

These people talked intelligently; and it was matter of astonishment to find them so capable of receiving the higher truths of spirit-teachings. Two songs were sung, accompanied by the spirits; after which, the conversations commenced, and continued for two hours and a half. During this time, twelve spirits talked by spells to the different members of the circle, and gave their names, and otherwise identified themselves. The conversations were purely personal and private; but they had the better effect "for a' that." In the morning the table comments were as follows:

(JOSEPHINE'S LETTERS, No. XXIV.)

"MY DEAR FRIEND,—Your circle last night was composed of people who are quite spiritually developed, though not possessing what is fashionably styled a religious education. When their friends came to assure them of their presence, they were received with the happy spirit of confiding love. It was this that opened the avenue to their spheres, and permitted the light to shine upon their hearts.

"All who came last night went away happier and better. They knew that angels were in their midst. I am always happy to assist willing people, no matter what station in life they occupy, or where the world may place them. There was sunshine in their hearts, and joy in their souls; both the spirits and mortals felt this.

"For a large promiscuous circle, it was the best you have had. Those people feel, this morning, that the coffin-lid has been lifted from the face of their friends; and that they are with them, loving with a stronger love and more purified affection. O, I am so glad to bring sunshine to these people, and teach them lessons that will lead them to higher planes of thought, and fit them for happier conditions of life!

"Few are so peculiarly situated as myself. All the love of

my woman's heart must be enlisted while I lead these people out of the wilderness of error and unrest.

"You are assisting us more than any other mortal in making for us good conditions. We are glad when we have a harmonious circle.

"The Monday night circle did us much harm—more than words can tell you. After this, avoid all such people. It has caused me much sorrow, as it has many other spirits. O men! when will you learn that life has a higher purpose than the gratification of your passions? Let us draw near you, and tell you of our homes. We will bring you good news; but do not ruin the work we are trying to accomplish.

"JOSEPHINE."

Josephine speaks of this circle of Pariahs with commendation; and yet, in contrast, she complains of the one I permitted on Monday evening, which was composed of gentlemen (?), two of whom are zealous members of a fashionable Church on Ninth Street. It was one of these Church members who distinguished himself by singing hymns in the circle, when his breath was so poisoned by whisky that neither spirit nor mortal could tolerate his presence. But that women of the pave should be esteemed more spiritually developed than Church members in good standing, is the strangest part of Josephine's communication.

CHAPTER XXIX.

A DARK CIRCLE—A YOUNG MEDIUM—SPIRIT-FLOWER AT THE TABLE—A CIRCLE OF FILTH—JOSEPHINE SPEAKS OF IT—AN ALARMED DUTCHMAN—OSTRACISM—A CONTRAST—SPIRIT-LIGHTS—PREDICTION—COUNTING MONEY—PEARLS, PEARLS—TABLE-LIFTING—FINAL SITTING—VALEDICTORY LETTER.

BEGINNING on the 24th of April, and continuing every evening thereafter to the 1st of May, most of the phenomena recorded in the last two chapters were reproduced in the presence of Mr. Plimpton. Some of these, and others, he will report in a succeeding chapter, to which special reference will be made as I write up my notes.

The book-tests were repeated under more stringent conditions than those I have detailed, as will be seen by Mr. Plimpton's report.

On the 25th of April, a dark circle was formed by Isaac F. Smith and wife, Master Walter Smith, Robert Leslie, George W. Newman, and two other gentlemen.

In the presence of these people, spirit-voices assisted in singing several hymns; after which, they addressed each person in the circle, and gave most indubitable testimony of their identity. Mr. Smith and his family were peculiarly favored by the presence of a number of friends, who spoke freely and intelligently of his family affairs, and the relation they sustained to him. A spirit said that "*Walter*" was a medium, and that if he would sit at a table at home, and hold a slate under it, he would get writing. I have since received messages from the spirits through the mediumship of this lad, and the "watch-test" and "money-counting test" were given as promptly as they were in the presence of Mrs. Hollis. I predict for this boy an extraordinary career as a spirit-medium.

The spirits being interviewed, during the evening, on questions touching their personality, gave remarkable testimony establishing their identity. On the succeeding morning, the *seance* was briefly commented upon as follows:

(JOSEPHINE'S LETTERS, No. XXV.)

"My Dear Friend,—The circle last night was good, although the members of it wanted more personal tests. It would hardly have satisfied them if their friends had given the entire history of their lives. One test of an indisputable character should be sufficient to convince a reasonable mind; but a score will not suffice.

"Our medium is too much exhausted to write more this morning. The poor child has a heavy work to do to-day, and I fear she will hardly have strength to do it. JOSEPHINE."

On the 26th, in the presence of Mr. Plimpton, the drumming experiment was repeated; after which, the following transpired: The cloth at the aperture was agitated and pushed aside, as if by a puff of wind. Under the table could now be seen a spirit-light, which gradually grew more luminous and condensed, until a beautiful flower was perfectly materialized. When this was completed, it was projected into the room far enough to expose to view the entire hand in which the flower was held. It remained, for closest inspection, half a minute, before it was withdrawn; but was soon presented again. In the space of fifteen minutes, the flower was presented nine times, averaging a half a minute at each exposure. Our faces were not more than twelve inches from the flower. By twisting her position a little, Mrs. Hollis was enabled to see this materialization, the first she had ever witnessed. The size, shape, and color of this flower resembled the "hundred-leaf rose." The hand was said to be Mary Plimpton's.

After this, two spirit-hands played with the drum-sticks, knotted a handkerchief, rang a bell in the room—not under the table—and then left two impressions, one of a large hand and the other of a smaller hand, in two dishes of flour.

A dark circle followed the table manifestations, composed of six men, who came begrimed with sweat, coal-smoke, oil, tar, and other abominations, making a combination of odors so offensive that the spirits quickly ordered the relighting of the gas and the dispersion of the "goodlie companie." The moral of this failure is, that people should be undefiled in their habits, before entering a spirit-room. And why not? Such men would be ashamed to enter a fashionable church in their filthy clothes; indeed, they would not be tolerated in "Christ's" (?) Church, or St. Paul's, for a single Sunday, if it were a good day for dress. Speaking of dress, and other matters, the following letter was written at the table, on the morning succeeding the circle of filth.

(JOSEPHINE'S LETTERS, No. XXVI.)

"MY DEAR FRIEND,—Saturday folded its mantle of darkness over a week filled with anxiety and care to spirits and mortals alike. Lights and shades alternated through the week; but the shadows fell heaviest on our path.

"Another bright day has opened its eyes in the morning of a new week. That it may be one of profit and pleasure to all, is my sincere desire. May the light for which we so earnestly pray, come!

"How many there are who do not understand the true relation which the spirit and natural world sustain to each other! nor do they comprehend the conditions which best establish the intercourse of the two worlds. I fear all I can say on the subject will do but little good; for but few realize our actual presence, and fewer still how much we labor to give you evidence of our personality.

"In view of all the circumstances connected with spirit intercourse, I am surprised you get as many spirit communications as you do. There is so much bigotry and prejudice and ignorance in the world, that our task to overcome them is greater than you can imagine.

"If the manifestations we give to Christians were given to pagan savages, their truth would never be questioned. Here, however, our messages are reviled, and our presence denied, because they conflict with your systems of theology, which have no foundation in truth or eternal principles of right and justice. Examine the fruits of this theology. What has been its effects upon the world?—upon society? It is a fearful contemplation. Every-where prevail suspicion, falsehood, and crime. The bonds of brotherhood destroyed, each member of society is made the prey and victim of the other. The soul of a heathen would shrink from doing his neighbor the wrong which these enlightened (?) people are daily inflicting upon their neighbors. Do not send your missionaries abroad to make civilizees of savages. They have as much humanity in their hearts as Christian men and women, and are happier. Every-where there is discontent among your people. False education has developed false relations in living. Examine the principles upon which society is superstructed. Money and Dress are your twin deities; Avarice and Egotism, their hand-maids. What becomes of the universal brotherhood under such teaching?

"But what does all this prelude? MISERY! Soon you will hear of financial crashes that will strike terror to the sordid soul of the nation. Bigotry and religious intolerance is preparing for a terrible conflict with the liberal spirit of the age. War—red-handed war—is imminent! The poor will revolt against the rich, and demand a division of their ill-gotten spoils. The discontent in your midst is an evidence of wrong; and all wrong is righted sooner or later. Light will dawn upon the darkened understandings of men, and then the wrong perishes. The veil will be rent, and light will shine resplendent from the battlements of the spirit-world.

"Be firm! Spiritualism has revealed the rottenness and worthlessness of creeds. They have been a curse instead of a blessing to mankind. The new dispensation will cause an upheaval of the earth, that will shake the foundations of things. Bigotry and superstition will die! Truth, honor, and justice will live forever! JOSEPHINE."

A dark circle was held on the evening of the 27th, Sunday, attended by a number of ladies and gentlemen, whom I had invited as my guests. These people were of different social positions, but met on the plane of spiritual development. The manifestations were excellent, all the members of the circle being spoken to by one or two or three of their spirit-friends. Besides, Jim Nolan was particularly felicitous in his discourse. He reiterated the statements made by "Ski;" namely, that the spirits knew not only every thing we do, but that those who are in deep sympathy with us know our very thoughts.

"Gott in himmel!" said a Teuton present. "I would n't for a tousand dollar, let 'Lizabet' know what I vas tinkin' about last night!"

There was in the circle a son of a presiding elder in the Methodist Church; and a distinguished banker of the city. These two met for the first time, but they were not friends. The sprig of elder held up his chin, and looked down on the banker. Now, the banker never suspended; therefore, he was honorable. He never met his obligations with certified checks. This ought to have secured for him the good opinion of even the presiding elder himself; but it did n't of the son. So, on the morning after the circle, the following letter was given, in which this subject of "I'm holier than thou!" was discussed in

(JOSEPHINE'S LETTERS, No. XXVII.)

"MY DEAR FRIEND,—When we talk about social ostracism, we attack one of the strong props that upholds society, and the very corner-stone of the Church militant. Those who sustain the Church, and who by the Church are upheld, draw their robes about them, and say to their fellow-sinners: 'I'm holier than thou! get thee out of my pathway! It is true you have the same heritage to light and life; but I can not afford to give you the hand of fellowship. My friends would see me do it!'

"But view this subject of social ostracism from a different stand-point, and see how fraught with mischief it is.

"Here is a woman of refinement, of noble and pure impulses, and most sensitive nature. She values her reputation beyond all price; and, for her benevolence and spotless character and blameless life, she is beloved by all who share her friendship and esteem. She could not invite reproach upon herself or friends by an uncomely act or thought.

"To her it was said: 'Your good friend and neighbor is a spirit-medium; if you seek her presence, you will hear the voices again of your loved and lost darlings—those whose eyes you closed when death stole them from your embrace. Will you go to them?'

"Her love is strong, and the temptation is great. Perhaps she is thinking of the face of her mother, of whose voice she dreams, with her eyes half closed, as the maiden dreams of the kisses of her lover. Or, it may be, the memory of a dear child has been awakened, whose soft breathing she almost feels upon her heart. Does she want to hear their accents of love again? O yes! yes! yes! To the world's end would she travel to hear their charming voices, and to be assured that they still live. She yields to the human impulse, and seeks the presence of her darlings. O rapture! she hears them speak again! What inexpressible bliss is this! But now she is informed if she sits in a dark room at home, her loved can and will converse with her there, and bring her messages of joy from the Summer-land.

"Conceiving no guile, she conforms to the instructions, and at last the low whispers of her darlings are heard. O, what pleasure! O, what happiness to untomb the lost, and hear them speak of the beautiful world beyond! She speaks of this marvelous truth to her associates and friends, expecting them to share the rapture of her own joy. But, alas! she finds her friends cooling off, and one by one absenting themselves, until the painful conviction is forced upon her mind that she is avoided. They become reticent, and seal their lips in silence, until their hearts become bitter. She is set aside, the victim of *social ostracism!*

"It is in vain she asks: 'What have I done to offend my friends, that they should treat me thus? Have I been untrue to them in act, word, or deed?' She droops as if smitten with a plague; and after the iron has entered her soul, she rallies to the true dignity of womanly character, and lives a life free from such intolerance.

"In your circle last night you had a preacher's son and a gambler. The first expressed his prejudice against the latter, on account of his profession. Let us look at this matter from a higher stand-point. No man is compelled to gamble; but if he consents to run his chances by obtaining money on the turn of a card, or to lose, it is a fair issue squarely made. If he loses, simply a part or all his money is gone; he must struggle for more, and learn wisdom. He is not disabled. Avarice is his besetting sin, if it is not amusement.

"But how stands it with the preacher? He has planted errors in my soul, which will require ages to uproot; he has trammeled me with dogmas, and blighted me with creeds, which will cling to me for many years, until I finally unlearn them.

"Be governed in all things by reason. Do not allow

prejudice to poison the fountain of pure thought. The profession of one man may do more harm to his fellows than the profession of another; but which is the worst? Be careful how you decide! The teachers of error are not blameless; and as to gambling, who among your conventional saints are entirely exempt from it? 'Taking the chances' is a common maxim in business. Insurance policies on life and property are only shuffles and deals of mercenary gamblers.

"It will not do to condemn hastily. While I do not desire to offer any apology for wrong-doing, still it is only justice to say, that the gambler frequently is no worse than those who condemn him to social ostracism. JOSEPHINE."

On the 28th of April, Mr. Plimpton, after making a careful examination of the table that he might be able to assure the public he had neglected no means to discover fraud, that was proper to be employed upon the occasion, proceeded with the "box-test," the particulars of which he has reported in the next chapter. In referring to this box-test, Jim Nolan said it required the united efforts of "Ski" and himself to make it a success.

The next manifestations at the table were spirit-lights. The light in the room was shaded down a trifle, and the cloth covering the aperture held up, giving an uninterrupted view into the black opening. I thought to improve my facilities for seeing, and proposed to change my position. I was at once told, that to do this would change their batteries, and defeat their purpose.

I remained quiet; and it was only a few minutes after, when the dark hole, into which we were peering, became illuminated by floating dots of light. I should think there were twenty of them visible at one time. Those mos remote from the aperture were the most brilliant, as that part of the chamber was darkest. They were about the size of house-flies; and if you will fancy these pests luminous, flying about in a dark room, you will have a fair conception of these mysterious pyrotechnics. By a close inspection, these lights were seen to rest on the tip-ends of fingers. In some instances, the whole hand could be seen, though very obscurely. As these lights came quite out of the aperture, I placed my hand favorably for having it touched by them. This they did several times, and would instantly expire, as a spark when dropped in water. After several repetitions of this kind, the lights went out; my hand acting, I suppose, as a "wet blanket" on their illuminating power.

After this, the spirits again brushed my hair, that Mr. Plimpton might see the operation, and my "venerable locks" looked the better for it. Jim then grasped me cordially by the hand, in the lighted room, and next patted the back of Mr. Plimpton's hand caressingly; after which, still in the light, he wrote,—

"JAMES."

That concluded the *seance* for the evening.

On the morning following, I asked if there was to be a letter for me; when this was written:

(JOSEPHINE'S LETTERS, No. XXVIII.)

"MY DEAR FRIEND,—I am always glad to write to you, and anticipate the morning lesson (as you are pleased to call it) with pleasure.

"Several days ago, in my letter, I made allusion to the coming conflict. The spirit-world is bringing that about. The truth of spirit-intercourse will soon be generally understood; and as the people obtain a knowledge of the facts of spirit-life, they will cease to be influenced by the romànticisms of priests.

Faith will cease to lead them, when they have positive knowledge to guide. The attempt will then be made to sustain the Churches by invoking legislative action to coerce the people to adopt their spurious system of morality. This will bring on the conflict. The blows of revolt will fall upon every household. The issue will be sanguinary and doubtful for a time; but the spirit-hosts, arrayed upon the side of right, will oppose wrong to the bitter end, and triumph at the last. I contemplate this struggle in sadness; still, when I look at the grand results, I feel that it is right that it should come.

"The experiments last night were quite successful; others will follow, quite as interesting in character, before the medium leaves for home.

"I have been looking over the manuscript of your book. I like your direct method of stating things. Much has been written on the subject of spiritualism; but plain facts tell the best story. The truth should be told with as little adornment of words as possible. Present it to the mind's eye as naked as you can. JOSEPHINE."

Mrs. Hollis sat by the table for manifestations, in the evening twilight of the 29th of April; when, after some desultory conversation, I placed a roll of bank-bills on the chair, and requested the spirits to tell the exact amount it contained. The roll was soon taken under the table, and, after several minutes, was again produced upon the chair. The slate was at the same time rapped upon and withdrawn, on which was written:

Five twenty-dollar bills, ...	$100 00
Fifteen ten-dollar bills, ...	150 00
Twenty-two five-dollar bills, ...	110 00
Four two-dollar bills, ...	8 00
Three one-dollar bills, ...	3 00
	$371 00

This statement was entirely accurate, though I had no knowledge of the amount of money in the roll until it was thus given. The remark was made that the spirits had a favorable opportunity for discounting if they felt like doing a banking business. To which Jim quickly replied on the slate:

"Money is valueless here. The distinctions which wealth creates among men cease at death. They have no existence in the spirit-world."

"Yes," I said; "I suppose the rich and poor meet on a common level."

"Not so," said Jim, "wisdom creates distinctions; but your rich men do not have a monopoly of this spirit-wealth. The reason is, money can not purchase it. The humblest in life may have the greatest abundance of it, and thus become the most exalted in the conclaves of the goodly great and greatly good. It is a rare gem, to be compassed only through trials, suffering, and death. It pays no tribute to wealth, no homage at the shrine of error."

After this writing, no manifestations occurred for a quarter of an hour. There was not even a rap, to announce the presence of a spirit. Finally, the cloth at the aperture began to puff out, as if blown upon by some person under the table. After several spells of this kind, I lifted the cloth, which gave an uninterrupted view of the interior of the dark chamber. I had scarcely fastened the cloth on the top of the table, when a dim, shadowy substance appeared at, and seemed to fill, the entire aperture. I could not distinguish what it was. It retired from the aperture, and in a minute or two reappeared; but this time more clearly defined. I could now see it was a spirit-hand, with the palm surface upturned; and the fingers were festooned with strings of pearls, several inches in length. In the hand lay the medallion likeness of Napoleon. It was the ornament I had seen at the cabinet, a dozen times, on Josephine's neck. The hand moved back and forth several times, giving a corresponding motion to the pendent pearls. I placed the palm of my hand on the chair, when these strands were drawn gently over the back of it, once or twice. I then turned it, and formed a cup of the palm, into which the mass of pearls was laid, for a moment, and then taken under the table. I requested they should be laid in Mr. Plimpton's hand; but the experiment was at an end.

There was an appreciable weight in these spirit-jewels: so at least I thought at the time; but since then I have almost persuaded myself that it was the conscious touch that gave me the impression. If I had not been looking or expecting the touch at the time, would I have recognized it as I did? On the subject of weight and touch, I am not certain; but the sense of seeing accurately is confirmed by the concurrent testimony of Mrs. Hollis and Mr. Plimpton.

The pearls were of varied sizes, and seemed in this particular to be graded—the largest at the bottom of the strands, the smallest at the top. I noticed this more particularly when they were worn on Josephine's neck. In the aggregate, there were enough of them to fill two-thirds of an ordinary-sized tea-cup; the cup of my hand was quite full. After this extraordinary manifestation, Nolan projected his hand and fore-arm through the opening, and picked up a pair of scissors and a sheet of white paper from the chair, and carried them under the table. In a minute, the scissors were replaced, and the paper was handed out. It had been cut in a heart-shape, and, by the folds of the paper, there were four of these formed. No less than two hands could have executed this simple feat.

I now set the heavy music-box on the table, and began winding it. While I was doing this, the table and superadded weight, including the box, being more than twenty pounds, were lifted several times, a foot or more, from the floor. This closed the *seance.*

Mr. Plimpton and myself subsequently placed ourselves in Mrs. Hollis's position at the table, and tried to lift it, as it had been lifted; but neither of us was equal to the task. I strained the tendons of my arm so badly in the effort, that I did not recover its comfortable use again for as much as a week.

On the evening of the 30th of April, Mr. Plimpton and myself had our final sitting for table manifestations with Mrs. Hollis. We had resumed our usual positions but a few minutes, when a spirit-hand was projected, waving a spirit-handkerchief several times, only a few inches from our faces. It stopped, giving us ample time to examine both the hand and delicate texture of the fabric, before it retired. This materialization appeared a second time, when, by request, the *cobwebby* material was drawn over my hand twice, after which it was withdrawn. I had seen this spirit-handkerchief exhibited at the cabinet aperture several times, but never before was I sufficiently near to give it such a close inspection.

The hand and arm were again presented; but this time the arm to the elbow was clad with a sleeve of white tulle. The arm flexed and extended several times, and then disappeared.

A smaller hand and arm were next presented, dressed with a full flowing white illusion sleeve. This was said to belong to Mr. Plimpton's sister Mary. The hand projected toward Mr. Plimpton, who, extending his own, had it caressed for half a minute. He then presented a cluster of apple-blossoms to the spirit, which were received with demonstrations of pleasure, and carried under the table. Here it was written on the slate, that

"The beauty and fragrance of my favorite blossoms give me no less pleasure now than when I enjoyed them in life.

"MARY."

The blossoms were then distributed between Mr. Plimpton, Mrs. Hollis, and myself, each receiving our tiny bouquet from the hand of the spirit. The hand then waved us an adieu; *and, while doing so, the slate was projected by another hand, upon which were written, in Jim Nolan's characters, the words,* "GOOD-BYE!"

This closed the series of table *seances*, whereat had been manifested the most interesting phenomena it has been my privilege to witness. It is not deemed necessary to make special comments upon these manifestations. The reader, no doubt, has scrutinized the record I have made of them, closely. I strung my philosophy and facts together, in the narrative which is now closed.

On the following morning, May 1st, Josephine's valedictory letter was written. Here it is:

(JOSEPHINE'S LETTERS, No. XXIX.)

"MY DEAR FRIEND,—Again our channel of communication with you is to be interrupted. I am sorry for this! It has been a pleasure and a profit to us to be here. We feel grateful for the favorable conditions you have given us, and owe you many thanks.

"This subject of conditions must be better understood by those who desire to have reliable communications with the spirit-world. People of tender minds get 'shaky' when you speak to them of conditions, and become very suspicious that some cunningly contrived machinery lies hidden in its meaning. If not frightened, they become uncivil, and treat us as though we were personal enemies to our fellow-mortals, instead of being the messengers of 'glad tidings' to the race. When a mother comes to speak to her child in loving accents, she is rudely repulsed, or treated with so much discourtesy that she retires in confusion and humiliation. I have listened to people talking, who, by their unwarranted rudeness, insensibly mystified their spirit-friends, until they retired in confusion. Again, I have seen the happy, heart-felt joy of those who were assured that their memories were still cherished by their friends on earth, who listened to their tiniest rap or faintest whisper with love and respect.

"O friends! understand the importance of 'conditions.' Do not sneer at the word; it is the best we can employ to express our meaning. Before you ask us to substitute another word, try to understand and illustrate the signification of this one. Give us better conditions, then we will come nearer to you, and tell you of our lives and homes in the spirit-world. Surely you need information of this character, and should put yourself to some pains to obtain it.

"Last night we were able to give you some pleasant manifestations at the table. These will excite a deep interest in the public mind. Your book would have been incomplete without containing a notice of them. The people are starving for this kind of testimony, which demonstrates to their senses the actuality of the spirit-world.

"And now, my dear friend, I can only say my soul is filled with gratitude for the service you have rendered me. Good-bye.

"JOSEPHINE."

CHAPTER XXX.

MR. PLIMPTON'S SECOND REPORT—THE MEDIUM—OBJECT IN VIEW—THE NEEDLE-TEST—THE WATCH-TEST—THE BOOK-TEST—TWO HANDS IN FLOUR—THE BOX-TEST—THE HAND—MISCELLANEOUS.

WHEN Mr. Plimpton made his first report of his experiences with spirit-phenomena, he had not seen enough to produce solid convictions that the manifestations were really what they purported to be. Since then, he has been a welcome visitor to my house, and has availed himself of the privilege to come and go at pleasure, that he could the better satisfy his mind of the genuine character of these "startling facts in modern spiritualism." After having such facilities for several months, he has deemed it proper to supplement his first report by a second, which was printed in Colonel Donn Piatt's paper, *The Capital*, published at Washington, from which I transfer it to these pages. The article is carefully and ably written, and will command respectful attention from all thinking readers. Colonel Piatt editorially prefaced the article by saying:

"We publish to-day an interesting article from the pen of Mr. F. B. Plimpton, associate editor of the Cincinnati *Commercial*. Mr. Plimpton is one of the ablest journalists in the United States, and we can vouch—as a wide circle of friends among the best people can vouch—for his sincerity and truthfulness. Our readers will find his investigations remarkable, and well worth a study."

HALF-HOURS WITH SPIRITS.

A SERIES OF TEST EXPERIMENTS.

BY F. B. PLIMPTON.

CINCINNATI, *May* 8, 1873.

MY DEAR COLONEL,—In a some-time unanswered letter, you incidentally inquire of me what progress I have made in the investigation of the so-called spiritual manifestations. I am now prepared to reply.

At the conclusion of the *seances* given in the Autumn of 1872, through the mediumship of Mrs. Mary J. Hollis, of Louisville, at the house of Dr. N. B. Wolfe, in this city—several of which I had the pleasure of attending with yourself and the Hon. William M. Corry—I gave over the investigations, determined, however, should opportunity offer, to renew them.

I had seen enough to convince a reasonable mind that the manifestations were not the result of trickery or imposture. They were given under conditions not so satisfactory as one could desire, and yet so good as to take them beyond the possibilities of mere mechanical contrivance and physical adroitness.

No one could accuse the medium of imposture, having seen and heard these things, without impeaching the evidence of his senses, or convicting his own conscience of bearing false witness against his neighbor. The facts were indisputable: there were the slate-writings, the voices in the dark circle, the materializations at the cabinet, heard and seen by every one present, and alike testified to by their faculties. There could have been no fraud, there was no collusion; was there illusion or delusion?

I was not entirely satisfied that the phenomena witnessed might not be explained upon some other hypothesis than that of their spiritual origin; and while I bore cheerful testimony to the things seen and heard, conscious that they had taken place, and were described by myself with more scrupulous faithfulness than any report I had ever made of a public event, I was not prepared to express an opinion that further investigation might make it necessary to modify.

Faith in the occult and mysterious has been with me a plant of slow growth; but I lack the confidence of Mr. Herbert

Spencer, to assume to settle such questions on *a priori* grounds, or to announce a thing to be impossible because it has not come within the range of my own experience. And then the saying, that the impossible is always coming to pass, should qualify our positiveness.

Professor Faraday's theory of involuntary muscular action may have explained satisfactorily to him such so-called spiritual phenomena as he witnessed; but here was a class of facts or manifestations as much beyond those he had seen as his experiments in electricity were beyond the wildest conception of Friar Bacon. Professor Carpenter's theory of unconscious cerebation seemed to offer a better solution of the problems. If to the unconscious working of the brain could be added the power of clear-seeing as a mental faculty developed in peculiarly organized natures, as in the well-attested case of Zschokke, the eminent German writer and historian, it seemed to me a large number of the manifestations might be accounted for without the aid of an unknown quantity.

As you have, in your own happy manner, described the three modes of manifestation through Mrs. Hollis, by writing, speaking, and materialization of forms, I will not weary your readers with repetition of description. Marvelous as they are, they have been so often described and witnessed by thousands of people that I am sure you will pardon me if I pass to other matters.

During the Winter months I was at some pains to inform myself of the character and standing of Mrs. Hollis in the city of her home; and, saving her reputation as a medium, I have yet to hear any thing prejudicial to the lady, or to which even the "unco' gude" could except. The mother of a family, her life has been devoted to domestic duties. Her husband is a gentlemen well known among business men. Both are as sensitive to their own and their family reputations as the most refined people of society elsewhere. I have found Mrs. Hollis at all times a modest, rather retiring lady, possessed of no remarkable intellectual powers, in speech and action candid and sincere, and having absolute confidence in the verity of the manifestations made through her agency.

Here, then, is a woman whose whole life is a protest against the presumption of fraud and trickery, and who is so physically organized as still further to convince one of her inability to perform tricks, if such they were, more marvelous than any recorded of Hermann or Houdin. I have seen many prestidigitators and jugglers, as well in the Old as in the New World, but none of them had her phlegmatic temperament and almost clumsiness of motion. During her sittings she is quiet, and apparently entirely passive to the influence controlling her.

Of Dr. Wolfe himself, it is sufficient to say that he is a very positive and earnest spiritualist. He has given the subject careful investigation during twenty years past, traveling thousands of miles to investigate with mediums of celebrity. He has given up his pleasant home for weeks, during the past two years, to those who have thronged it, seeking evidence of the truth of spiritualism. He has submitted to suspicions and assumptions of fraud on his own part, sure that he was neither deceived nor deceiving, and that he would be ultimately vindicated even in the opinions of those who had entertained doubts of his honesty. He has invited investigation, preferring the skeptic to the believer, and asking only to be credited with the same honesty of purpose that others claimed for themselves.

It seemed to me, in making a series of test experiments, that it was most desirable to reduce the chances of fraud or imposture, and to proceed with them as though convinced that the medium and Dr. Wolfe, in whose presence they were given, were confederated to practice deception. Two objects were then to be sought for,—material evidence of the existence and presence of intelligence apart from our own, and proof of their capacity to act independent of any thoughts or impressions in our own minds. Should conditions be imposed, making the proof inconclusive on these two points, I determined to abandon all further investigations, and, for my own part, remit spiritualism to the limbo in which the ghosts of many delusions wander unregretted.

It is to these tests I now propose to invite your attention. They were given in a chamber-room, over the parlor, in Dr. Wolfe's house. No trap-door could be made available. The floor was covered with elegant tapestry, and showed that it had not been disturbed, the breadths extending across the room being intact. The furniture consisted of a bed, bureau, wash-stand, and chairs, and a small toilet-stand in the center of the room, without drawers in it, and so light that a child could pick it up and carry it with ease. There was no place for the concealment of a confederate, and but one door by which he could pass into or out of the room. Moreover, unless physically as dwarfed as Tom Thumb or Commodore Nutt, he could not have crowded under the stand, supposing him to have got there without detection. During all these experiments the gas was turned on; and this, added to the brightly blazing coal-fire on the grate, made the room bright and cheerful in every corner. Only once were we requested to lower the gas, as will be noticed hereafter.

A strip of black muslin, reaching half-way to the floor, had been fastened round the edge of the stand, the two ends of which met, and could be parted like the curtains of a tent. Over this was thrown a dark plaid shawl, falling to the floor on all sides, and making darkness absolute in the small space under the stand. This was the only condition imposed. A rude diagram may assist, better than any description I can give in words, in showing the location and appointments of the room, the position of the table and the parties seated around it.

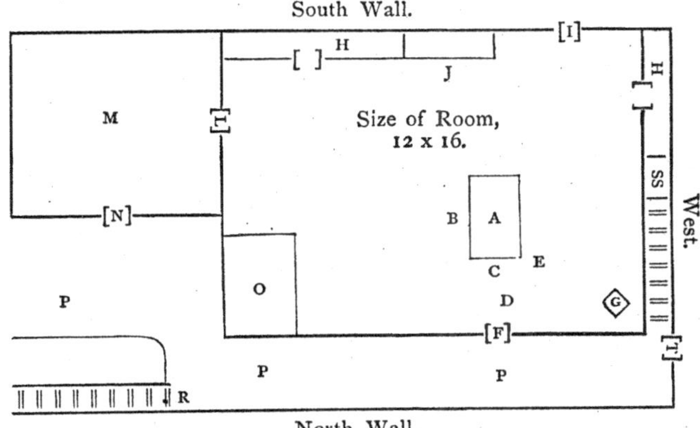

A. The table under which the materializations were formed. B. Mrs. Hollis's position at the table; she facing south. C. The chair under the opening in the valance. D. My chair. E. Dr. Wolfe's position. F. Doorway from the hall to the room. G. A bureau and pivoted mirror. H H. Plastered wardrobes. I. Window opening south. J. Fire-place. L. Window opening to conservatory. M. Conservatory. N. Doorway from hall. O. Bed. P P P. Hall. R. First flight of stairs. SS. Second flight of stairs to third floor. T. Entrance to front chamber.

The door opening into the hall-way was near C, my own chair partly obstructing the passage. Mrs. Hollis sat with her back to the door, and fronting the fire-place. The ends of the black muslin strip, fastened round the top of the stand, met at C, where the materializations took place. The unoccupied chair was used to place articles upon during the experiments, as will be further explained.

It will be observed, from Mrs. Hollis's position, that her right-hand was nearest the table; the left was placed upon it, and, at our request, she *never withdrew it during an experiment.* It was always in sight, and above the stand. She had, therefore, only the right-hand with which to perform the "tricks," if they were of her doing. Of the probability of this, the reader must judge at the conclusion. This, then, was the position of the three parties in the room—certainly, absolutely, the only ones present during the tests. No motion could have been made without being seen.

A full spool of No. 80 Coates's thread, and a paper of needles, No. 5 English make, containing twenty-five needles, was placed on the chair at C. Immediately, a well-defined hand reached out from under the stand, and drew them successively in. After a few moments, the paper of needles was placed outside, followed by the spool of thread. We found four of the needles missing, and a thread taken from the spool. We had scarcely examined these, when the thread reappeared, with the four needles suspended on the thread, the ends of which had been knotted, as a seamstress would do it. We compared the needles with those on the paper; they matched for size. The thread upon which they were strung matched for quality, and filled the place exactly upon the spool. This feat had been performed, it was alleged, under the table, and in total darkness.

Mrs. Hollis could not have done it had both hands been at liberty, and I doubt whether either Dr. Wolfe or myself could have threaded them in daylight, for men are proverbially bunglers at such work. Still, this test was not conclusive. There might have been substitution of thread and needles, though we had ourselves no doubt of the identity of the spool and the paper with those which had been laid on the chair. A more extraordinary test followed.

Taking a stem-winding hunter-case watch, and pressing upon the spring near the stem, the hands were turned backward and forward indifferently. Who could have guessed the time? The watch was placed on the chair, and taken under the stand; the request being that the time indicated on its dial should be written on the slate which Mrs. Hollis held. After a few minutes, the watch was handed out, closed as when it was taken, and the sound of the pencil scratching on the slate was heard. I noted by another watch the time occupied from the handing out of the watch to the announcement on the slate, which was "twenty minutes to one." Opening the watch, and allowing for the time that had elapsed, this was accurate to a second. There could have been no substitution in this case, for the watch had marks of identity not to be mistaken. He would have been a smart confederate who could have read the time from its dial-plate in total darkness. How, then, was it done? By the unconscious cerebration of the medium? Did this mysterious mental emanation or agency take the shape of a hand to touch, to handle, and to write, and, penetrating through the case, read the time which the hands indicated? Or was there some inexplicable illusion by which we were made to see that which had no existence? The reader is welcome to unriddle the riddle.

Could the spirits copy from a book a word or a sentence, writing it on the slate which the medium held under the table? By slight taps on the slate, with the pencil, they indicated their willingness to try. To make sure that the book would be one unknown to the persons present, I took with me a book just received from the publishers, the wrapper of which was unbroken. On the outside of the wrapper it was directed, "To the Editor of the *Commercial*, Cincinnati, Ohio. Care of, and for sale by, George E. Stephens & Co. With the compliments of the publishers. William Wood & Co., Publishers, 27 Great Jones Street, New York." Nothing to indicate the title or character. This book, the wrapper unbroken, and the twine still tied around it, as it had come from the publishing-house, I laid upon the chair at C. Presently a hand reached out through the curtain and took hold of it, and, trying first to draw it under flatwise, but finding the legs of the stand too close together, turned it on its edge. It disappeared. Then the string and the wrapper were handed out, the latter turned inside out, as though peeled off. I watched closely Mrs. Hollis's right-arm, her left-hand being on the table, while the wrapper, the crumpling of which we could distinctly hear, was being taken off. Not a muscle moved. We could hear the turning of the leaves; and, soon after, the scratching of the pencil on the slate was audible. Then the book was put out, and dropped on the chair at C. I took it without opening it. Next came the slate, which was handed to Dr. Wolfe, who, stepping to the gas-light, read: "Page 20. Branches taught." I opened the book to the page indicated. At the third line from the top were the words—the small-capital side-heading of a paragraph. An examination of the title-page of the book showed it to be "The Educational Year-book for 1873." The slate upon which this and all subsequent writing in my presence was done, was one I had purchased on my way to Dr. Wolfe's, and had privately marked.

And here was a test that involved both physical and mental operations. Fraud and collusion were out of the question. I turned the table over, and lifted it from the floor. No mechanism, no concealed confederate, no place on which Mrs. Hollis could have rested the slate which she held, and which she must have dropped in order to take the book, had that been, from her position, a physical possibility. But there was a materialized hand that did take the book. If my eyes saw the book, they also saw the hand that lifted it from the chair. It will not do to say that my senses assured me as to one fact, but were incompetent witnesses to the other. Moreover, even had it been the hand of the medium, how did she see in absolute darkness under the table the words printed on page 20, and copied on the slate? It seems to me, Professor Faraday's theory of involuntary muscular motion is put *hors de combat* by this test; and it fares no better with Professor Carpenter's theory of unconscious cerebration.

I thought this experiment interesting enough to repeat. Calling at the bookstore of Messrs. Robert Clarke & Co., the following day, I requested Mr. A. W. Whelpley to wrap me up two books, one in English, the other in French, without letting me know their titles and character, and to indorse his name on the wrappers. He did so, and in handing me the packages, I understood him to say the smaller contained the English book.

Arriving at Dr. Wolfe's, we resumed our places around the stand as before, the light burning brightly, Mrs. Hollis's left-hand on the table, her right holding the slate under. I remarked that I had with me two books, one in French, the other in English, and that we would try the English first. I then laid it on the chair at C, no one touching it but myself. The hand appeared, drew it under, took off the string and the wrapper, folded the latter neatly, and handed them out. Then, after a few minutes, came the book. When the pencil dropped, rattling along the slate, Mrs. Hollis withdrew it. I handed it to Dr. Wolfe, who read, much to my surprise: "You have made a mistake. This is the wrong book; it is French." I picked up the volume. Sure enough, it was a school edition of the Fables of Æsop in French. I had misunderstood Mr. Whelpley. The other package was then placed on the chair. I need not repeat the description. We could, however, distinctly, hear the operation of unwrapping, the turning of the leaves, etc., and see, as it was carried about, where it disturbed the folds of the covering of the stand. When the slate was handed to Dr. Wolfe, he read: "Page 14. Captain Morris's Songs. Alas! poor Morris—writes one." I opened the book at page 14, and followed the reading. It was copied literally from the print, though not the complete sentence. "Captain Morris's Songs" was the title of the article, the first sentence of which reads, complete: "'Alas! poor Morris!' writes one who knew him well." The book proved to be, "Books and Authors. Curious Facts and Characteristic Sketches. Edinburgh: William P. Nimmo"—a book and publisher of whom I know nothing; and I question whether the volume has been republished in this country.

Does unconscious correct conscious cerebration? If the minds of Dr. Wolfe, the medium, and myself, had any impression with regard to these books, it was that the first one laid in the chair was printed in English, nor was that impression corrected till the announcement of the mistake was made from the slate. Here, then, was an intelligence which had at least elementary education in reading and writing, that acted independent of our own, and corrected the impressions of our minds. What was it?

Many persons who have been present at Mrs. Hollis's cabinet *seances* have seen not only faces, hands, and arms, but flowers of various forms and colors, shown at an aperture in the door. At the conclusion of the book-tests we were informed by slate-writing that a materialized flower could be shown at the end of the stand fronting C. Presently a hand appeared holding a full-blown rose of a deep, rich red, as large and beautiful as could be selected from the congressional conservatory. The flower-stalk and the green leaves were also plainly to be seen. It was put out from four to five inches beyond the curtain, and so close to me I could have touched it. As in the materializations in the cabinet, it seemed to glow and fade, advance and recede, as though sensitive to the light, and unable long to remain in it. This, indeed, is characteristic of all the manifestations I have seen.

Two light sticks were placed in the chair, and were presently picked up, two hands slightly advanced from the curtain taking them, and beating a sort of military rub-a-dub for our edification. It was performed with the precision of a drummer-boy.

Dr. Wolfe procured a platter of flour, and asked if they could leave an impression of the hand in it. They rapped affirmatively. After turning the platter around, but unable to manage it, the request was written that the Doctor would hold it at the corner of the table farthest from Mrs. Hollis; that is, to the right of C. He did so; the hand appeared, and after indescribably fluttering over it with a rapidity of motion that seemed electric, rested in it for a moment, and then shaking off the adhering particles, was withdrawn. Mrs. Hollis was requested to place her own hand in the print. The finger-marks were half an inch longer than her fingers. It was the impression of a man's hand, full-sized, with all the strong, anatomical markings of such a hand. An anatomist would have pronounced it the hand of a full-grown man. Moreover, had Mrs. Hollis undertaken the feat, she must have changed her position, and brought her shoulder even with the top of the stand to have reached so far. But her position was not changed, and the physical impossibility that she could have done it was demonstrated past our doubt. As Dr. Wolfe was employed in holding the platter of flour, and I was looking on, I trust it is not necessary to disclaim any agency on our part. And how could a full-grown man have concealed himself under the table? I turned it over instantly the impression in the flour had been completed. There was nothing to be seen but Mrs. Hollis's right-hand patiently holding the slate. Was it illusion? The impression in the flour was seen by other people afterward. If they saw it, so surely did I see the hand that made it.

On the evening of the 28th of April, when we were seated around the stand as before, I called for a box with a lock and key. The thought of this test had just occurred to me. Miss Fanny, the doctor's niece, brought in a handkerchief-box. It was made of oak-wood, dovetailed at the corners, and finished in walnut. It was about eighteen inches in length, by six wide and deep, and weighed, as we afterward ascertained, two and three-fourths pounds. Opening the box, I put into it a strip of white news-print and a lead-pencil, and locking it (leaving the key in), placed it on the floor close to the corner of the stand nearest my chair. As Dr. Wolfe lifted the covering of the stand, a hand came out, and, taking firm hold of the box, drew it in. I had my doubts, owing to the size of the box, and the narrowness of the space under the stand, whether it could be manipulated. But as we saw it lifted, and evidently held in a horizontal position, the ends pushing out the stand-cloth on both sides, so that we could follow every movement, I concluded they had strength to manage it. Now, mark—for I was at pains to do so myself—that Mrs. Hollis's left-hand was on top of the stand, her right holding the slate under. Dr. Wolfe never approached the stand but once, and then only to receive the box at the opposite end as it was put out, unlocked and empty, the key having been retained under the table. Presently they asked for the box again, and it was put where it had been at first. It was drawn under. We could hear them put the paper in it and turn the key. The box was then handed out at the opposite corner. Dr. Wolfe received it. It was locked. "What have you done with the key?" was asked. The key was thrown into the chair at C, and taken by myself. The doctor gave the box to me, and, unlocking it, I took out the pencil and the paper, on which I found written in a free hand these words:

"Yes, Mr. Plimpton, we can do this.

"JIM NOLAN."

I had privately marked the sheet, and could swear to it in any court as the one I put, blank, into the box.

Jim Nolan, as you have explained to your readers, I believe, is Mrs. Hollis's control. His own account of himself is, that he enlisted in the army from Indiana, was taken sick during Sherman's Georgia campaign, was sent back to Nashville, and died in the Maxwell House when it was used as a hospital. I am told his statement has been verified. In the "dark circle" he speaks with great ease and freedom, in a voice as loud as that of any person, and with an intelligence and native wit and readiness of repartee that make a conversation with him highly entertaining.

Now the reader will please apply to these tests the theories of Faraday or Carpenter, or any other physicists who, in their profound wisdom, have undertaken to account for these phenomena. I must insist that he leave out all twaddle about trickery, sleight-of-hand, collusion, and confederates, and give, if he be able, some rational explanation without admitting spiritual agency.

The tea-bell interrupted the sitting at this point; but Nolan by slate-writing, informed us that, after supper, they would show us "spirit-lights." So, after tea, we resumed our seats. Request was then made that the light in the room should be lowered, the only time during the sittings such a request was made. It was turned down so that the shadow of the stand at C was like a twilight in which the forms but not the colors of things are discernible. These "spirit-lights" have been seen, I am told, floating about the room in the dark circle, by many persons. Here they were to be shown within eighteen inches of my face. Presently a hand, faintly outlined, appeared at the curtains of the stand, and from the tip of each finger successively glowed a low, lambent light of bluish tinge, but without the least illuminating quality, which slowly expired. Sometimes the hand would close, leaving the index-finger straight, with this peculiar phosphorescent gleam at its tip; then it would open and display all the fingers, with the lazy light visible at the front of each. This lasted for about twenty minutes. Once Dr. Wolfe requested the hand to touch his own, and the shock passed from the finger-tip to the back of his hand, producing, as he described it, a slight tingling sensation like a feeble shock from an induction coil. That it was electrical in its nature, I do not doubt.

I had requested the medium to place a ring on one of the fingers of the hand with which she held the slate under the stand. She did so. It was a broad, massive gold ring. When the lights had been shown, this mysterious hand came forward—the light meantime having been turned on—and, advancing the bare arm above the wrist, exhibited its fingers one by one, to show that no ring was upon it.

It repeatedly *touched* the back of my own hand, and the touch was indefinably soft, cool, and moist. The refusal to touch the open palm, which I extended, was afterward explained. "For the reason," said Nolan, "that the palm is the nerve center, and your own magnetic current is too strong for me to overcome."

The hand then picked up the pencil, which lay in the chair at C, and wrote "James," with a natural movement and rapidity that showed him to have been a ready writer. A bell was handed him, which was rung with an amusing imitation of a call to dinner. A hair-brush was also handed him, and the doctor bending down his head, his few scant and rapidly vanishing silver locks were dexterously brushed.

Immediately after, I lifted and turned over the table. There was Mrs. Hollis's hand holding the slate, the massive ring on the finger on which I had seen her place it, and which she had had no opportunity to remove or replace without my having observed it.

The following evening—for these *seances* had been, for my convenience, about seven o'clock, P. M.—we were asked to sing; but as we were doubtful of our vocal ability, a Swiss music-box was substituted, and placed on the stand, Mrs. Hollis putting her left-hand on top of it, so that it should be in sight. Some time elapsed, when a hand appeared at the end of the table, as different in shape to that which we had seen as a delicate woman's is to that of a strong man. It held a handkerchief of a tissue as fine as though made of mist. Indeed I could think of nothing else to which it might be compared. The edge-folds, however, were as of condensed mist, and very white. The ends of this handkerchief were trailed over Dr. Wolfe's hand, and fell upon it in folds as natural as though it were cambric linen.

The next materialization was more beautiful. A hand presented itself, with strings of pearls depending from it. They were in great profusion. The hand presented them in several positions, now hanging in loops or festoons, again falling back over it, and then gathered up and wound about it. To the touch these materializations had an almost impalpable substance, cool, and softer than down.

I had at the time no particular test to make; but, seeing a pair of scissors on the bureau, they were taken, and placed in the chair on top of a block of unglazed paper, letter-size, the edges of which had been sized or glued together, as you find it in any book-store. The hand came out and took the scissors, and, finding the block of paper too large to be admitted under the stand, reached out and tore off one of the sheets. Presently it reappeared with the scissors and the sheet, which had been folded quarto, and a heart-shape piece cut out of it as neatly as though done by an expert. Mrs. Hollis, it must be admitted, is extraordinarily supple-fingered, if with one hand she could hold the slate, take the paper and the scissors, and perform this feat.

I remarked that I had never seen any evidence of great physical power on the part of the spirits, though stories of its manifestation had often been printed. Could they lift the table with the music-box on it? The answer came immediately. It was raised slowly about six inches from the floor, and set down with a jar that was heard in the rooms below. Seated in a chair, in Mrs. Hollis's position, I tried, using both hands, to lift the table, but found it impossible. The music-box weighs a fraction over twenty-one pounds. It was never lifted by Mrs. Hollis.

The last sitting did not occupy more than twenty minutes. The medium had been so much exhausted by sittings during the day, that Nolan said it would not do to draw upon her to any great extent. A hand, purporting to be that of a deceased sister, presented itself at the end of the table, displaying the arm nearly to the elbow. It was dressed in what appeared to be a flowing sleeve of some dark color, lined with what resembled white silk. Again it appeared, with what seemed to be a tulle under-sleeve, and took from my hand a spray of apple-blossoms, afterward presenting them as a bouquet, held at the point of the fingers turned upward. The hand was different in shape from those I had previously seen, the fingers being long and slender.

Now, my dear Colonel, all this while I have been endeavoring to make for you a plain statement of facts, forgetful of the dreadful sentence pronounced by Faraday on such witnesses eight years ago. "They who say they see these things," said he, "are not competent witnesses of facts." Beginning these investigations a skeptic, with a feeling almost of contempt for believers in spiritualism; never having been troubled with a disordered imagination, or by apparitions, warnings, or omens, and accustomed not only to accept the evidences of my own senses, but educated by my profession to a measurably cool observation of events and facts; as ready to set aside the claims of the spiritual origin of these manifestations as to accept them, should the proof be inconclusive; and even then willing to expose fraud or imposture, should any thing lead me to believe they were practiced, but, at the same time, determined to make the investigation honestly, candidly, and testify to the truth, regardless of the consequences to myself,—to what other conclusion can I come, as one after another of my doubts have been vanquished, and my unbelief overcome, than that these manifestations are precisely what they profess to be? The conviction is forced upon me, that intelligences invisible to us, save as they manifest themselves through the medium of persons peculiarly endowed, can and do communicate with the living, and that they have as absolutely a personal existence and identity as we ourselves.

They not only assert this, but assure us that they live in a world as rationally constructed for the development of their finite capacities, and for their progression to still higher conditions of being. In manifesting their presence to our grosser sense, they assure us they employ natural agencies; and as the world becomes more receptive of the truth, they anticipate still greater power to reveal themselves, and convince us that we are indeed compassed about by an innumerable cloud of witnesses, testifying to the immortality of man.

Of the philosophy of materializations, as explained by these intelligences in Mrs. Hollis's *seances*, I forbear to write. My purpose to make a careful statement of facts is accomplished; and I must leave the question of my competency and my disposition to testify to the truth, and nothing but the truth, to those who know me best.

CHAPTER XXXI.

CONCLUSION.

HAVE I been continuously deceived, for a quarter of a century, in regard to the true character of the phenomena I have recorded? Have all the manifestations I have witnessed been delusions? Have I been seeing, hearing, feeling, tasting, smelling frauds half my life-time, and not been able to discover the imposition? Have my friends and enemies, my senses and my better self, all conspired, so long, to maintain an error—a vast system of errors—in the similitude of Truth? Give me some reason to believe my life a lie, and I a dupe. I know all men are liable to be deceived; but to charge me with being continuously deceived while trying the spirits, in season and out of season, in divers forms, ways, means, and places, is simply to charge me with being an imbecile. Can a man testify to what he knows?

But I am not alone in attesting the startling facts recorded in the preceding pages. If it were so, it would make no difference in my statement; but it is not so. Hundreds of reliable citizens, competent to testify on any subject pertaining to the senses, have witnessed the same, or similar facts, on many occasions, and verify my statements in every essential part.

The statements I have made are, therefore, no longer to be held in abeyance as a question of personal veracity; but they must be tried on the broad issue, whether the phenomena are frauds or facts.

I have been at more than ordinary painstaking to gather testimony from every available source to assist me to decide this question. To ascertain the true character of these manifestations, I have spared no expense of time, money, or personal comfort; and have engaged all the scrutinizing powers I possess, to ferret out the great mystery. More: I have engaged others to employ their detective powers in ascertaining whether these startling manifestations of intelligence were of mundane or super-mundane origin—whether they were the product of human agency, or whether a newly discovered law of life was thus giving expression to itself. To one or the other sources, all these phenomena must be attributed. They are either stupendous facts or stupendous falsehoods.

Millions of intelligent men and women *know* the major proposition to be true, and the facts go to sustain it; and millions more are being resistlessly drawn to the same conclusion by the same unassailable array of testimony. If the manifestations are tricks, why not step forward and expose them, and thus save mankind from so humiliating a deception? Tear away the disguises, and let us know the name of the prestidigitator who has been playing such pranks with human credulity, in every part of the globe.

Remember there are millions of men and women

who proclaim a knowledge of the truth of spirit intercourse, who, if not undeceived, will teach the sublime truth to every nation and to every tongue. They will flood the earth as a deluge, and destroy every opposing sect, creed, and tribe that may be found in the way of their conquering march. These people are already a grand power in the world. Without concert of action, without organization, without a paid priesthood, they are waging war upon every form of wrong. They are disturbers of the *rotten* peace which enslaves the life-powers of the soul. They strike at old institutions, and destroy their shells with the reckless daring of the iconoclast. Bound by no creed, belonging to no sect, wearing no livery, bowing at no pagan shrine, they demand freedom as universal as sunlight, *and will have it!* They have no party; neither politicians nor priests can lead them; and enemies they are, not to their fellow-mortals, but to the dogma of infallibility; denouncing, fearlessly, all piracies upon the natural rights of man.

Millions are embraced in this mystic multitude who have accepted common sense and the spirits as their guides. The Czar Alexander, by command of the spirit Czar Nicholas, manumitted his serfs, and transformed millions of slaves into millions of freemen. The politicians of Alabama, in power, enacted a law against the freedom of spirit-speech within the territorial limits of that state; and the spirits declared, in retaliation, that they would cover their land in sackcloth and ashes; and they did it in less than three years. The Queen of the British Empire "is crazy on spiritualism," say the insane multitude. Don

Pedro, Emperor of Brazil, has communications with the spirit-world through the mediumship of one of his children. The late Emperor of France did not disdain to entertain a spirit-medium at the Tuileries. To day, Victor Hugo and Louis Blanc are inverviewing their spirit-friends in the presence of Mrs. Hollis, in France. It is well known that Mr. Lincoln communicated freely with Washington through the mediumship of J. B. Conklin.

A subject embracing so many interests, so far-reaching in its power,, should surely command the attention and respect of the grandest minds of any age or country. Men like Faraday and Agassiz and Carpenter may sneer at it ; but what of that ? Spiritualists sneer at them. What's the difference? This: These educated egotists do not know what they are sneering at. Spiritualists do!

We are not children ; reason with us. We can no longer be frightened in the dark. The incivility of these learned boobies, and the ignorance they display on this subject, make a humiliating exhibit of the poverty of the stuff of which conventional great men are made up. These fellows may sneer at God's eternal verities ; but what then ? Can they change a fact, or a truth, or a principle ? We honor ourselves when we enlist in the service of Truth. It is *a step up* when we join her retinue: her livery ennobles the wearer, be he priest, peasant, or prince. "If God is not on our side," said Mr. Lincoln to the preachers, "I will go to His side."

Science, true science, is invited to explain the phenomena we have recorded. If she has a key by which these mysteries can be explained, let her not stand upon the ceremony of doing, but do it at once. She has a golden opportunity for doing a good and great service to the world, and winning lasting renown.

Let her discover the delusion, and she will rescue millions from the gull-trap, and prevent as many more from falling into it.

> "The simplest peasant who observes a truth,
> And from a fact deduces principle,
> Adds solid treasure to the public wealth."

The mission of science is to exalt the human family by teaching truths whereby its happiness can be increased. To fulfill this purpose, it seeks to discover laws and principles underlying the phenomena of life. Will she now come to the front, and excrcise her legitimate powers in the elucidation of this great mystery? The pulpit and the press have betrayed their incompetency in this direction. They meet the spirit of investigation, on the threshold, with a hostile hand, an unreasoning head, and a savage heart. They let loose the mastiff of defamation to tear to very tatters the reputation of Truth itself, when it comes, Diogenes-like, with a light to discover their blemishes.

Personal opinions are of but little value unless supported by scientific formulæ and demonstration. Here are real, substantial, well-authenticated facts before us. They come to the world, like Christ, in the fullness of time. Not any thing comes before it is needed, nor before it is intended to appear by the Supreme Intelligence. Shall we accept them, or war against the Great Eternal? Who dare defy the Omnipotent to arms?

48

By the advent of these phenomena, it is intended that man shall *know* something more than at present of his future life. It is intended that the mystery and ignorance with which charlatans have invested the subject of death shall be dissipated and denounced, as unbecoming the intelligence of the nineteenth century. It is intended that the systems of theology which find their support through the rudimental condition of the human mind, *Fear*, shall no longer prey upon their insane victims, and harness them to the ponderous, crushing car of sectarianism. It is intended that the human family shall no longer be kept apart in the interests of priests or priestcraft; but that they shall dwell together, animated with one faith, one hope, and one charity. It is intended to take away the fear of death and the terror of the grave, making one the angel of peace, the other the garden of rest.

I do not wish to be misapprehended. Death is not to be spoken of irreverently. O, it is a noble fact, written ineradicably in the constitution of all things. God ordained it when he prepared his laws. Let us revere it, for it is as lovely as Truth. "*Amici mortui, sed magis amica veritas.*" *Every law that finds expression in life is founded in wisdom, and conduces to man's happiness.* When he lives in contravention to these laws, he sins against the holy spirit of justice to himself. O, teach him that principles are the life of laws; ideas are the life of principles; and God is the life of ideas! Let him understand that he represents the cosmos of all created things—infinite in faculties; in apprehension, a god!

These revelations of law are intended for man's happiness, else they would not be proclaimed.

In the construction of an edifice, we first dig in the earth for a foundation. On the rock of facts we lay our granite base. We then cumber the ground about with materials for the superstructure; and these, to the uneducated eye, are but a formless mass, expressing nothing but disorder and confusion. But when the artisan comes, he finds the material ready to his hand. Piece by piece it is put together, each fitting the other, until a shapely form rises from the earth, harmonized in all its parts, and beautiful to the eye for aye.

Thus will the temple of Truth be shaped and fashioned by God's eternal verities. Truth expresses itself in a million of forms,—distinct, as the waves; yet one, as the sea. The materials for her temple are being prepared both by spirits and mortals. Soon the architect will come, when it will rise, from granite base to cloud-crowned dome, "a thing of beauty and a joy forever." In this glorious temple all nations, all tongues, will worship for all time. Upon its ample façade will be inscribed, in dimless blazonry, "THE FATHERHOOD OF GOD; THE MOTHERHOOD OF NATURE; AND THE BROTHERHOOD OF MAN!"

www.ingramcontent.com/pod-product-compliance
Lightning Source LLC
LaVergne TN
LVHW021228110826
845150LV00002B/271